GOOD INTENTIONS
MAKE BAD NEWS

GOOD INTENTIONS MAKE BAD NEWS

Why Americans Hate Campaign Journalism

S. Robert Lichter
and
Richard E. Noyes

Center for Media and Public Affairs

Rowman & Littlefield Publishers, Inc.

ROWMAN & LITTLEFIELD PUBLISHERS, INC.

Published in the United States of America
by Rowman & Littlefield Publishers, Inc.
4720 Boston Way, Lanham, Maryland 20706

3 Henrietta Street
London WC2E 8LU, England

British Cataloging in Publication Information Available

Library of Congress Cataloging-in-Publication Data

Lichter, S. Robert.
Good intentions make bad news : why Americans hate campaign journalism / Robert
Lichter and Richard Noyes.
p. cm.
Includes bibliographical references and index
1. Television broadcasting of news—United States. 2. Presidents—United States—
Election—1992. 3. Press and politics—United States. 4. United States—Politics and
government—1991–
I. Noyes, Richard. II. Title.
PN4888.T4L53   1995   070.1'95—dc20   95-32349 CIP

ISBN 0–8476–8095-9 (cloth : alk. paper)
ISBN 0–8476-8096-7 (pbk. : alk. paper)

Printed in the United States of America

⊖™ The paper used in this publication meets the minimum requirements of
American National Standard for Information Sciences—Permanence of
Paper for Printed Library Materials, ANSI Z39.48–1964.

Contents

Figures

Tables

Preface

This book brings together the key findings from a large body of data on national political news that we accumulated from 1987 through 1995. The bulk of this material consists of content analyses of 1987-88 and 1991-92 election news coverage on the ABC, CBS, and NBC evening newscasts. These data were originally collected for the Campaign Watch project of the Center for Media and Public Affairs (CMPA).

The Campaign Watch conducts rapid response content analysis of election coverage, with updates appearing throughout the course of the campaign. The purpose is to provide an empirical checkpoint for media-related controversies as they occur, rather than after the fact. Throughout the 1988 campaign, we tracked all campaign stories on the ABC, CBS, and NBC evening news, and released this information at critical points — just after the New Hampshire primary, Super Tuesday, the New York primary, the party conventions, and the presidential debates. Results were reported in *Media Monitor*, the Center's bimonthly newsletter; in a post-primary book, *The Video Campaign;* and in articles in *Public Opinion* and other journals.

For the 1992 campaign, we reprised this ongoing monitoring of television news. During the general election, however, we expanded the data collection to include numerous additional sources of political information. This expansion was undertaken in collaboration with the Markle Commission on the Media and the Electorate, under the direction of political scientist Bruce Buchanan. It was intended to provide comparative data for the Commission's 1988 study of political education in presidential election campaigns.

Among the national media, we added CNN's *PrimeNews*, PBS's *MacNeil-Lehrer NewsHour*, and three nationally influential newspapers — the *New York Times, Washington Post*, and *Wall Street Journal*. We also tracked the three major candidates' talk show appearances on nationally televised talk shows such as *Larry King Live, Today, Good Morning America, CBS This Morning*, and *Donahue*. Finally, we collected the candidates' general election speeches and campaign advertisements. After the campaign ended, we added these materials to the content analysis. The findings were presented in a report to the Commission for incorporation into a new volume authored by Dr. Buchanan.

The present work draws on the accumulated data from both campaigns, as well as personal interviews with journalists who covered them, to trace a shift in the national media's approach to election news. We argue that journalists' efforts to intervene more actively in the campaign process, which were intended to improve the quality of information available to voters, instead produced unintended consequences that proved detrimental to both journalism and the electoral system.

A project of this scope would not have been possible without the generous support of several private foundations. Funding for various phases of this research came from the Lynde and Harry Bradley Foundation, Earhart Foundation, J. M. Foundation, John and Mary Markle Foundation, John M. Olin Foundation, Pilot Foundation, RORD Foundation, Robert Stuart Foundation, and the Smith Richardson Foundation.

We benefited less directly, but no less importantly, from the writings of several scholars who have done pioneering work on the media's role in elections. Among them are Thomas Patterson, Michael Robinson, Doris Graber, Christopher Arterton, Bruce Buchanan, and Kathleen Hall Jamieson. Our research was also guided by insights into the broader relationship between the press and politics from Ted Smith, Stanley Rothman, Bill Adams, Larry Sabato, Stephen Hess, Everett Ladd, Austin Ranney, and Nelson Polsby.

Over the years, numerous journalists have given us the benefit of their insights into how the process works from the inside. Special thanks go to four who contributed lengthy formal interviews for this book, and to Luke Britt, who conducted the interviews: Michael Barone of *U.S. News and World Report*, Larry Barrett of *Time*, Peter Brown of *Scripps Howard*, and Joe Klein of *Newsweek*. In addition, we frequently relied on election-related books and/or articles by Howard Kurtz and Paul Taylor of the *Washington Post*, Tom Rosenstiel of *Newsweek*, Fred Barnes of *The New Republic*, Elizabeth Kolbert of the *New York Times,* Ellen Hume, senior fellow at the Annenberg Washington Program, and Marvin Kalb from Harvard's Joan Shorenstein Barone Center.

Our analysis of 1992 general election speeches and ads was assisted by associates of all three candidates. Ross Perot's campaign press secretary,

Sharon Holman, provided a videotape of Mr. Perot's television addresses and major rallies. Dave Lyon of Temerlin McClain sent the Perot campaign's short spot ads. Nancy Ward of the White House Press Office gave us access to Bill Clinton's campaign speeches, while Peter Hutchins of Greer Margolis Mitchell & Associates sent videotapes of the Clinton campaign's short spots. Vivian Ars of Winkler Video Associates provided a copy of the Bush campaign's short spots. Susan Boyd spent the summer of 1993 painstakingly collecting George Bush's campaign speeches from the goverment's *Weekly Compilation of Presidential Documents.*

The CMPA's Director of Research, Dan Amundson, helped develop the initial coding system and provided invaluable counsel and assistance. Julia Zagachin and Salyna Raven assisted in coding the 1988 campaign news stories; in 1992 coding duties fell to Swain Wood, Jennifer Dickemper, and Elizabeth Gross. The skill and dedication of these students was indispensable to the project's outcome. The efforts of Michelle Veloso and Donna Rosenstiel, who labored through much of 1993 coding news stories, the talk shows, and the candidate speeches, are especially appreciated. Special thanks go to Linda Lichter, who contributed her expertise to developing the coding system at the outset and her patience and moral support thereafter.

In preparing this book, Amy Inaba cheerfully offered her (scarce) free time to conduct library research and proofread the text. She also drafted sections of Chapter 8, which focuses on the talk shows. Mary Carroll Gunning and Jeanne Maynard spent long hours working above and beyond the call of duty in preparing the manuscript for publication. John Sheehan and Michelle Fernandez somehow kept the whole operation running, as did their predecessors Toni Mann and Jessica Vaughan in 1988. Without their dedication — and that of the numerous other individuals who also provided support and assistance — this book would not have been possible. We thank them all.

Even as we express our appreciation for the assistance of the foundations that supported this work over the years, the scholars and journalists on whose insights we relied, and the co-workers who contributed their efforts to this project, we recognize that many of these individuals may disagree with the arguments and conclusions that we drew from our research. For all our debts to others, we take full responsibility for the opinions expressed in this book and for any errors or omissions it may contain.

S. Robert Lichter
Richard E. Noyes
Washington, D.C.

Introduction

The Cost of Good Intentions

Can't we just cut this stuff out and get back to grown-up journalism?
— John Leo, *U.S. News & World Report*, 1995

Media bashing has joined the mainstream. Press criticism was once the prerogative of the political right and the academic left; today the catcalls come from all quarters. The profession that prizes its role as the public's tribune is facing a vote of no confidence. Opinion analyst Andrew Kohut puts the case succinctly: "The public is saying the national media is part of the problem."[1]

Even more notable is the rising chorus of mea culpas from journalists themselves: The *Columbia Journalism Review* deplores "a generation of vipers."[2] A National Press Club symposium is plaintively titled, "Why Do They Hate Us?" CBS's Mike Wallace not only confesses to committing journalistic "malpractice," he calls for awarding booby prizes to "censure practices that diminish the public trust in us."[3]

Ironically, the volume of criticism has risen in the wake of a coordinated effort to upgrade the profession's performance by acting more aggressively as the public's surrogate. During the 1992 presidential elections, the national news media's leading lights set out to improve the electoral system by policing the campaign and forcing the candidates to be on their best behavior.

To accomplish this they made virtues out of press practices that were once widely considered to be vices. Journalists were called upon to become participants rather than observers, to take over the campaign agenda from the politicians, and to tell the "truth" rather than just the facts, even if this helped some candidates and hurt others. This book examines the cost of their good intentions to their own profession and to the political system.

There seemed to be good reasons for making these changes. After the 1988 presidential campaign, traditional journalism was widely criticized for triviality and cowardice in its political reporting. The conventional wisdom held that the candidates — especially George Bush — ran superficial and negative campaigns that year. Critics charged that reporters not only failed to challenge such conduct, but that old-style campaign coverage, punctuated by new-style feeding frenzies, just made things worse.

In advance of 1992, leading academics and journalists devised new ways for news organizations to do a better job. Reporters would produce more meaningful coverage by ignoring photo opportunities and cynically crafted sound bites. Instead, they would impose a strict diet of substantive issues on the candidates. They would enforce fair campaign practices by supervising the candidates' speeches and advertisements and calling voters' attention to misleading claims or outright falsehoods.

This high-minded approach was supposed to produce serious, substantive, and even-handed oversight that would redeem both the media and the political system for their past sins against the public interest. But our systematic inquiry into the actual coverage suggests otherwise. In their efforts to cure what ailed the electoral process, they broke the cardinal rule of medicine: First, do no harm.

Not only did the news continue to feature negativism, "horse-racism," and tabloid titillation, but it became less balanced and even more intrusive. In many respects, the candidates and the often-derided talk shows performed better than the mainstream media did during Campaign '92. Moreover, the media have remained in their new campaign mode ever since, creating new impediments to rational public debate and policy making.

Our findings have serious implications for the practice of political journalism, as the media gear up to cover another presidential election. We believe that press cynicism poses less of a threat to public discourse than does misplaced idealism. For journalists have replaced their largely inadvertent influence on political life with a conscious influence that may prove even more detrimental to the political process.

These conclusions are not the product of subjective impressions or anecdotal evidence. They are based on an exhaustive scientific content analysis of how the national media covered the 1988 and 1992 presidential elections. We examined the network evening news coverage of each of those pivotal campaigns, including the 1987 and 1991 "preseasons," the primaries, party conventions, and general election battles.

Trained researchers catalogued every discussion or evaluation of the candidates and issues mentioned in over 7,500 news stories. All told, we analyzed 183 hours of television news coverage, which occupied more airtime than the entire eleven-year run of M*A*S*H. Much of these data were originally collected for the Campaign Watch project of the Center for Media and Public Affairs, which issued regular updates on national election coverage during the course of each campaign.

For the 1992 general election, we expanded the study to include not just the "big three" networks, but also CNN's *PrimeNews*, PBS's *MacNeil-Lehrer NewsHour*, and the triumvirate of newspapers — the *New York Times, Washington Post*, and *Wall Street Journal* — often referred to as the "prestige press." This allowed us to compare the network coverage with that of other nationally influential print and broadcast outlets.

We also supplemented the news media study with a unique reality check: With the cooperation of the Bush, Clinton, and Perot campaigns, we also analyzed the candidates' general election speeches and campaign commercials. This made it possible, for the first time, to determine whether election news mainly reflects the realities of the campaign trail or adds its own "spin" that distorts public perceptions of what the candidates say and do.

Finally, we took a close look at one innovation that caught the national media by surprise in Campaign '92 — the use of talk show formats that allowed candidates to bypass journalists and communicate more directly with voters. We used the same content analysis system to track every comment made by the candidates, hosts, and callers during their appearances on *Larry King Live, Today, Good Morning America, CBS This Morning, Donohue*, and other nationally televised interview shows.

The depth and breadth of these data gave us the ability to chart the shifts in the national media's political coverage, and to make a critical assessment of their performance. Previous long-term studies of election news typically examined briefer time periods within each campaign, a narrower range of media outlets, and fewer characteristics of their messages. By using the same research procedures to investigate every phase of the 1988 and 1992 campaigns, we can measure precisely how they compared in terms of their tone and substance.

For example, to evaluate the debate over media fairness, we noted the source and topic of over 20,000 separate sound bites containing either support or criticism for one or another candidate. These results show how often, by whom, and for what every contender was praised or blamed in the media. This kind of information alone can't tell us whether a politician's bad press is deserved. But it can clarify the subject by showing just how bad it really is, where it comes from, and what it's all about.

Although our argument is rooted in empirical evidence, this book takes the research data as a starting point for an overview of how the media have come to dominate political campaigns and what can (and can't) be done to rein in some of the excesses this has produced. We also draw on additional evidence from our other studies, ranging from changing patterns of economic news to more recent coverage of the Clinton administration, the 1994 congressional elections, and the new Republican Congress.

We begin by tracing how the media's growing power brought journalists into conflict with political leaders and created sentiment to change the rules of political journalism. Then we discuss in detail how this affected the focus, tone, and outcome of Campaign '92. Finally, we assess the public reaction and explore ways in which the media's campaign role might be reshaped to better serve both journalism and the American public.

Chapter 1 explores the historical context of the media's takeover of presidential politics over the past quarter century. We trace the rise of now-familiar distorting factors such as the primacy of journalists' expectations over actual events, the front-loading of primary coverage, and the role of news "spin" in building and breaking a candidate's momentum.

The immediate antecedent of journalism's self-reform movement was a crisis of confidence over being first outflanked by Ronald Reagan throughout the 1980s and then manipulated by George Bush in Campaign '88. Chapter 2 argues that these concerns were largely misplaced. Contrary to the conventional wisdom, the evidence shows that Reagan was neither spared media criticism nor immune to its effects. Nor can Bush's victory in the notorious 1988 campaign be attributed to Willie Horton, Roger Ailes, or televised visits to flag factories.

Armed with the conviction that they could produce a more serious and substantive campaign agenda than the candidates themselves, journalists set out to improve their coverage by focusing on the issues they thought were most important. But the results were mixed at best, as our systematic review of the news content in chapters three and four demonstrates.

The coverage was indeed somewhat more oriented toward policy issues in 1992 than it was in 1988. But not by much — a large majority of news stories still contained little or no substantive information about the candidates' records and proposals. Most references were limited to brief and superficial throw-away lines in discussions of campaign strategy or tactics. Fewer than one in ten mentions of the candidates' policies described their details and implications.

And what of the media's effort to inject more substance into the campaign debate by forcing the candidates to dance to their tune? As it turned out, they struck a sour note. The candidates' own speeches actually discussed policy issues far more frequently and in considerably greater detail than did either print or broadcast reports.

The candidates also ran more positive campaigns than voters might have guessed, since news reports consistently emphasized their most negative rhetoric. In general, the media told people how policy issues were relevant to the horse race; the candidates told people why issues were relevant to their lives.

The negative tone of the coverage extended beyond evaluations of the candidates to the campaign itself. On the major networks alone, nearly 300 on-air sources complained about the quality of the fall campaign, the paid political ads, and the choice of candidates. On-air critics outnumbered defenders of the process by a margin of twenty to one.

By contrast, post-election polls showed that three in five voters were satisfied with the choice of candidates, three in four said they learned enough from the campaign to make an informed choice, and two in five even rated the much-criticized campaign commercials as helpful. You wouldn't know any of that from watching TV news. Such relentless negativism does not simply reflect public alienation, it intensifies it.

We even found instances of network correspondents criticizing the candidates for "not talking about" issues that they had in fact addressed, as texts of the speeches they delivered earlier that same day prove. Their real crime lay in not discussing these issues in a fashion that journalists would have found newsworthy. Unfortunately, the viewers couldn't have known that. Nonetheless, any absence of substance in Campaign '92 was due more to the choices made by journalists than the failure of politicians to address the issues.

The media fared even worse on the fairness issue. After 1988, many journalists felt that a fetish for artificial "balance" had kept them from telling the truth about the men who would be president. In 1992, they resolved to call it the way they saw it. The news went boldly where only editorials had gone before, and news organizations instituted "Ad Watches" and "reality checks" to keep the candidates honest. The result was some of the least balanced, most negative, and most opinionated coverage in the era of mediated elections.

Many journalists regard the "Ad Watches" as their profession's proudest achievement of the campaign. But this innovation seems far more problematic in retrospect. Despite the false sense of certainty they conveyed, these pieces rarely corrected factual misrepresentations. All too frequently, they simply replaced the campaigns' interpretations of ambiguous facts with their own. Further, they had the unintended effect of portraying the candidates' overall advertising campaigns as more negative than they really were.

The most obvious victim of the new rules was the media's old antagonist, George Bush. Bush got by far the worst press of any candidate during both the primary and general elections. Moreover, he was victimized by highly negative and sometimes inaccurate reporting on the economy. Nor could Bush's personal bad press be attributed to any bad behavior during the campaign. Virtually every one of his policies came in for heavier criticism than did those of his opponents.

As we show in chapters 5 through 7, however, other candidates were victimized by the generally hostile and dismissive tone of the coverage. The media's decision to arbitrate the campaign instead of just narrating it encouraged reporters to upstage all the candidates with their own pronouncements. The candidates collectively received far more negative than positive press, just as they did in 1988. All the major contenders, including Clinton, were victimized by the build-'em-up-knock-'em-down syndrome that running the media gauntlet entails.

Even the Bush-bashing was probably less an expression of partisan or ideological bias than most conservatives believe. In recent years, Democratic presidential candidates have suffered as frequently as Republicans from media attacks. Instead, it hints at something far more disquieting, as Bill Clinton's post-election coverage suggests — the routine filtering of journalists' personal feelings into their political coverage, unburdened by old-fashioned concern for objectivity.

Like the character cops of the previous campaign, the media's truth squads may be remembered for opening a Pandora's box of beasties that bedevil political journalism ever after. Commentary has been redefined as news and rationalized as "truth-telling." Mixing news and commentary was hardly an unknown practice in the past, but it was treated as something to be avoided or explained away. The Campaign '92 reforms taught political reporters to regard it as a public service.

Even as journalists were moving aggressively to wrest the campaign agenda from the politicians, voters began moving in the opposite direction, toward more direct and less mediated communication with the candidates. In Chapter 8 we describe how the traditional media's function as the public's principal information broker was challenged by alternative formats, especially "new media" call-in shows.

While mainstream journalists chafed against competition from the likes of Larry King and Phil Donohue, so many citizens voted with their remote controls to endorse the talk show campaign that the networks were forced to join the bandwagon. Our analysis reveals one good reason for the new format's popularity: The talk shows provided more substantive information and a more positive and balanced portrait of the candidates than the "establishment" media did. The most popular campaign news reform in 1992 was not directed by the national media; it was directed against them.

The media's reform agenda for elections was undermined by the very feature that made it so appealing to journalists in the first place — it accelerated the trend toward placing them at center stage and pushing the politicians to the sidelines. Journalists could convince themselves that this was needed because they identified their perspectives and interests with those of the public. Clearly, the public didn't agree. Polls show continued concern over media negativism and intrusiveness, along with rising anger over sensationalism and partisanship.[4]

Why did the skein of good intentions unravel so rapidly? Because the follies of '92 were preordained by the structure and culture of contemporary campaign journalism, which the in-house reformers took for granted. By trying to bring the entire election process into accord with media interests, they undermined the professional norms that had served to check media foibles and excesses. These standards have long been under siege within journalism, but the ramparts were finally breached in 1992.

In our concluding chapter, therefore, we argue that mainstream journalists need to go back to the future. If they are to recover their public mandate, they must rediscover the values and practices that set their trade apart from punditry, propaganda, and melodrama. Above all, they should aim at providing an accurate account of the battle of ideas and values, rather than trying to settle it.[5]

Since the national media are no more likely than anyone else to relish reduced influence (or to interpret the public interest as requiring this), we also suggest some ways the political parties might nudge them along. Areas ranging from nominating convention rules to campaign financing could be reshaped to shift campaign oversight responsibilities from journalists back to party organizations. The rationale for doing so is not that the parties are more public-spirited than the media, but that the public can more easily call them to account for their failures.

This is not to say that journalists will entirely escape the costs of their good intentions. In winning the battle to control the campaign agenda, they are losing the war for the hearts and minds of the public. The sudden popularity of interactive news formats attests to widespread disaffection with the national media as the centerpiece of our political discourse.

Journalists largely ignored the wake-up call they got from voters in 1992. If they do the same thing in 1996, they may find the audience refusing to take *their* calls. Despite their self-image as the public's surrogate, growing perceptions of self-serving and out of touch reporting are creating a popular revolt. The audience has begun to demand information *without* representation from the media insiders whose claim to speak for "the people" looks increasingly shaky. Incumbents beware!

Notes

Opening quote: John Leo, "Staining the Truth While Shading News," *Washington Times*, April 21, 1995.

1.   Andrew Kohut, quoted by Howard Kurtz, "Study Suggests 'Cultural Divide' Separates the Press, the Public," *Washington Post,* May 22, 1995.

2.   Paul Starobia, "A Generation of Vipers," *Columbia Journalism Review,* March/April 1995, pp. 25-32.

3.   Quoted from "Excerpts of Remarks by Mike Wallace at the Goldsmith Awards Ceremony," *Press/Politics,* Spring 1995, p. 13.

4.   Times Mirror Center, *The People, the Press & Their Leaders* (Washington, D.C.: Times Mirror Center 1995).

5.   Ted J. Smith III, "Journalism and the Socrates Syndrome," *The Quill*, April 1988, pp. 14-20.

Chapter One

Power Play

Nothing but a newspaper can drop the same thought into a thousand minds at the same moment.
— Alexis de Tocqueville, *Democracy in America*, 1840

For more than 200 years, journalism has been intertwined with American politics. For all but the past thirty years, however, politicians have enjoyed the upper hand. During the eighteenth and early nineteenth centuries, a newspaper's success or failure often depended on the willingness of powerful politicians to dispense favors and patronage.

Today, new media technologies, the centralization of media power, the fragmentation of American society, and the decline of political parties have combined to create a new environment where journalists have at least as much control over the public images of national leaders as the politicians have themselves.

Early in this century, political parties had their own direct lines of communication with voters. The most efficient method of contacting citizens was through party-owned or -dominated newspapers, but parties supplemented this conduit with more personal forms of contact. Party volunteers would go door-to-door registering voters, handing out information, and engaging voters in political discussion. In most jurisdictions, individual voters were known to the parties' precinct workers, and most citizens re-warded the personal attention with straight-ticket voting. Parties offered rhetorical backing for politicians who embraced controversial positions, and provided insulation to those caught in the throes of scandal.

Perhaps most importantly, party leaders controlled the process of nomi-nating candidates for most public offices (including the presidency) in all but a handful of states. Citizens who wished to participate in the nomina-tion process first needed to become active in their state and local party organizations, where they would gain information through personal exposure to the politicians and the process.

Today, party machines are rusted relics. They face dwindling influence in cities and irrelevance in the suburbs. The prevalence of split-ticket voting and the increase in self-described "independents" are obvious measures of how badly party loyalty has faded. The nomination process — formerly the cornerstone of a political party's influence — is now controlled by voters participating in primaries and caucuses.

Changes in party rules have stripped party activists of much of their clout in deciding nominations. Changes in campaign finance regulations have diverted money from party coffers that individuals and PACs now contribute directly to candidates. Primary voters often have only a casual relationship with their party, or none at all (some states allow independent and cross-over voters to participate in primary elections). As intermediaries between gov-ernment and citizens, political parties are increasingly impotent and irrel-evant.[1]

The intent of these changes was to hand power from political elites to the public, but the effect has been to increase the power of a new political elite: the national news media. No major event takes place in a presidential campaign whose format, substance, or effect is not influenced by whether or not major news organizations decide to cover it.

Two-thirds of American citizens receive most of their information about politics from television news, while only one in twenty receive their news from conversations with other people.[2] Primary voters — often forced to choose among a large number of candidates with similar ideologies and outlooks — are especially dependent on the news media for cues that allow them to differentiate among their party's prospects.

Today's candidates are a self-selected and self-financed group who de-pend heavily on the news media to carry their messages to voters. Candida-cies thrive or die based on decisions made by news persons: on whether a candidate merits coverage, has a likely chance of winning, has committed private indiscretions that require a public airing, etc. Ambitious and intelli-gent politicians court the press in an effort to influence this decision-making, because they know the media is a necessary constituency for a successful campaign.

It is not just parties that have collapsed. Also languishing are other formerly great institutions, which historically served as intermediaries between citizens and their government. In his 1981 essay "The Imperial Media," Joseph Kraft wrote that during the 1960s and '70s "most of the intermediate groupings in society — groups which interpose themselves between government, on the one hand, and the unorganized people, on the other — have lost status." This "decline in competing professions," he noted, "makes the surge in journalistic status look all the more pronounced." Kraft, a newspaperman who began his career before the advent of television, argued that the new journalists were part of a star system — celebrities who "are driven to keep moving forward, and in an adversary way."[3]

By the 1980s, journalism's leading lights were millionaires with household names, whose fame equaled that of movie stars and sports heroes, and whose celebrity outshone the politicians they covered. In 1988, for example, ABC's Sam Donaldson was assigned to cover the Dukakis presidential campaign. "At virtually every stop," according to one report, "crowds react more to Mr. Donaldson than to the candidate, cheering and hounding him for photos and autographs." Dukakis's press secretary, Dayton Duncan, wistfully told an interviewer, "I don't know if people ask [Sam] for more autographs or ask Dukakis for more."[4] After the campaign, Donaldson increased his celebrity as co-anchor of *PrimeTime Live*, while Dukakis returned to Massachusetts and the relative obscurity of his lame-duck governorship.

In the mid-1980s, *The Washington Monthly* noted that "Washington editors, and even reporters, enjoy a status that would shock their counterparts in Cleveland or Chicago; no party today is complete without its representatives from the media." The story quoted a public relations firm representative: "Including a journalist [on the guest list] is just as important as including a diplomat or a Cabinet member."[5]

What was true a decade ago is even more true in today's climate of celebrity journalism. A senior reporter, who refused attribution, described the phenomenon this way: "Journalists traditionally take on the same importance as the people they are covering. When you cover the Senate, you take on a lot of the same importance as a senator. Eventually, you begin to think that you are a senator."[6] It is not too much to say that Washington journalists today serve the same function that old-moneyed families once served in other East Coast cities: their professional and social approval is crucial for any newcomer hoping to "make it," and their active disapproval means sure doom.

Although we have learned to take it for granted, it remains astonishing that yesterday's hack reporters — underpaid, undereducated, held in generally low regard — have within two generations been transformed into "journalists" — the highly paid, sophisticated, party-going descendants of the aboriginal scribblers.

The difference between yesteryear's scribes and today's stars lies in the revolutionary changes that have transformed the news business itself. Eighteenth- and early nineteenth-century newspapers were commercial flops. Most were loss leaders whose true value lay in their ability to disseminate the views of their publishers and financial backers. Newspapers whose specialty was commercial or business information were heavily subsidized (or owned outright) by business interests. Similarly, papers whose focus was political opinion were financially sustained by politicians and political machines.

Beginning in the late nineteenth century, new technologies (including the telegraph and high-speed printing presses) allowed news to reach mass audiences cheaply and profitably. The development of electronic forms of communication in the twentieth century offered new opportunities for profit and, for the first time, made the voice and appearance of the newsman a valuable commodity.

In recent years, media companies have been among the most profitable businesses in the country. National broadcast networks have created a national audience for news. Cable networks supply news to national "niche" markets (relatively small numbers of people who share common interests or perspectives) that would not have been profitable a decade ago. Commercial success has ensured the media's freedom from direct control by politicians, and allowed news organizations to exert their own independent influence on the political system.

Formerly, journalism's power was distributed among dozens of powerful regional newspapers with numerous competitive viewpoints. Two factors — the centralization of government power in Washington that began with FDR's New Deal, and technological advancements such as radio and then television — led to a centralization of news media power.

Reporters descended on Washington to cover the landmark first 100 days of the New Deal. They stayed in town as Franklin Roosevelt increased the size and scope (and news value) of the federal government. Another influx of reporters arrived with World War II, and still another with the inauguration of President Kennedy's "Camelot." By the 1960s, nationwide newscasts provided coverage of news stories with which all Americans could identify. High on the list was Washington politics and the presidency, the office in which all citizens had a stake.

Today, tens of millions of citizens receive news about national affairs directly from Washington, D.C. — from national, not local, media. Television and radio networks, news services, magazines, and most major newspapers cover national politics from inside the Capital Beltway. In 1930, there were only 251 reporters covering the nation's capital.[7] In 1982, the congressional press galleries reported 4,300 members.[8] In 1995, that figure had grown to 6,300 accredited journalists.[9] Thousands of additional Washington journalists do not need accreditation to do their jobs. At the 1992 Democratic convention, for example, more than 15,000 reporters showed up, outnumbering the 5,000 delegates and alternates three-to-one.[10]

By a conservative estimate, the Washington press corps of the 1990s is comprised of more than 10,000 reporters who track the same individuals, institutions, and events. Such a consolidation of reporters in one city, all covering essentially the same stories, has had the effect of enhancing the similarities, and diminishing the differences, of each news organization's coverage of national politics.

Today's national news is more homogenized and contains fewer regional perspectives. The average community is now served by but a single daily newspaper — competition among newspapers is the exception, not the rule. At the national level, "competition" among news organizations such as the networks often resembles that between soft drink giants Coke and Pepsi, whose publicity campaigns use rival celebrities to promote otherwise indistinguishable products.

As mainstream journalism has centralized its focus and its personnel, it has developed a commonality in perspective that reinforces its own dominant beliefs and messages, in sharp contrast to the older system of competition among newspapers of differing ideologies. By and large, those journalists who remain geographically outside Washington look to their on-scene counterparts for raw information and, increasingly, opinion and analysis.

The veteran journalists who occupy the territory at the very center of the political system — whether by virtue of their insight, contacts, or institutional positions — set the tone for what many of their colleagues say and write about politics, and thus much of what the public will hear and read about their leaders. Even though the term encompasses thousands of individuals and scores of news organizations, it is not so very misleading to speak of "the news media" as a singular entity, replete with its own rules, norms, beliefs, leaders, and its own independent ability to shape events.

The attitudes that differentiate the Washington, D.C., political culture — a fascination with power and process, attitudes of paternalism, arrogance, and casual cynicism — permeate both the Washington press corps and their dispatches from the capital. Journalists are less captives of their news sources (as some critics have argued) than co-conspirators with them.

The "usual suspects" to whom reporters turn to for subjective analysis and insight about politics tend to be pillars of the Washington establishment: long-time members of Congress, veteran interest-group leaders, think tank pundits, and the political consultants who remain in town whether their candidates win or lose. For the most part, journalists share the perspectives of this group, who were the source of much of their education about politics. As the media class has emerged as an institution in its own right, reporters now pass along their insights and perspectives to Washington's newcomers, reinforcing the intellectual status quo.[11]

The changes in the national news media that have occurred since the 1960s have altered the mindset that leading journalists bring to their campaign coverage. The country's top reporters — peers with Washington's insiders, and aware of their ability to influence the national agenda — now claim the responsibility to aggressively search through each presidential contender's biography and character, looking for evidence that may reveal a lack of fitness. The broadcast networks refuse to air the parties' nominating conventions without the promise of "news" (typically, some sort of crisis for the prospective nominee).

Above all, news organizations claim a right not to be "used" by candidates as a conduit to inform voters on terms set by the politicians. Indeed, they reject such intrusions as an assault on their journalistic independence. As former CBS correspondent and NBC *Nightly News* anchor Roger Mudd puts it, "Television regards the electoral process as its own. TV sets the rules, the ways of gathering information, the deadlines, the use of exit polls, all to make the process conform to its way of covering the election."[12]

THE RISE OF THE MEDIA AS A POLITICAL FORCE

Journalism's belief in its own importance and social utility has evolved throughout the television age. TV news came into its own in the mid-1960s, concomitant with the climax of the civil rights movement. The dramatic confrontations that occurred in many southern cities and towns were carried via film to national audiences by TV crews and told vividly by print reporters.

The historic 1964 Civil Rights Act revealed television's power to help mold a new national consensus. In one study, almost two-thirds of the network correspondents interviewed credited network news for the passage of civil rights legislation.[13] According to one NBC correspondent, "We showed [the American public] what was happening; the brutality, the police dogs, the miserable conditions [blacks] were forced to live in. We made it impossible for Congress not to act."[14]

Soon after the civil rights drama, the media were thrust into the middle of the Vietnam debate. The tenor of the Vietnam War coverage became the focus of heated debate and acrimony during the Johnson and Nixon administrations. Tensions reached a crescendo during and after the 1968 Tet offensive, when journalistic criticism of Vietnam policy was capped by Walter Cronkite's on-air call for peace negotiations.

Press critics later charged that the media had misrepresented the outcome and the significance of these events.[15] Still, after Tet it was politically impossible to win support for a continuation or expansion of the war. President Lyndon Johnson announced his retirement, and the political prospects of anti-war politicians such as Eugene McCarthy and Robert Kennedy soared.

The debate over Tet and Vietnam inadvertently gave rise to changes in the presidential nominating system that would prove even more momentous. When the 1968 primaries concluded, it was clear that many of those who voted in the Democratic primaries were supporting anti-war candidates such as McCarthy and Kennedy. Yet the rules in place at that time meant that most of the Democrats' convention delegates had already been chosen by state party leaders, some months or even years before the primaries. Anti-war activists rebelled against their disenfranchisement.

Live TV coverage of the raucous and occasionally violent confrontations outside and inside the 1968 Democrats' convention shocked the public and prompted an overhaul of the parties' nominating system. Beginning in 1972, most convention delegates were chosen by voters in either primaries or caucuses, whose principal source of information about the candidates was the news media.[16]

The Nixon campaign's burglary of Democratic party headquarters during the 1972 campaign launched the third major long-running story in a decade to pit the national media against political authority. Although the *Washington Post* took the investigative lead, the *New York Times* and television also played major roles. A national television audience became hooked on the dramatic congressional hearings that probed the scandal and eventually forced President Nixon to resign. For many reporters, Watergate was the final proof of the corruption of politics, and compelling evidence that journalists could, on their own, successfully improve and sanitize the political process.

In the years that followed Watergate, the national media rode a wave of popularity and perceived power. They had prevailed in conflicts with such seemingly entrenched forces as southern segregationists, Vietnam hawks, and two once-popular presidents. To some old-school journalists such as Joseph Kraft, the profession emerged from the early 1970s with an inflated sense of its potency and a smug self-righteousness:

> Since [Watergate] there has been no holding us. The more august the person the hotter the chase. The more secret the agency the more undiscriminating the attack. The general assumption of most of my colleagues, and I do not suppose I am much of an exception, is that behind every story there is a secret,

and behind every secret there is a dirty secret.... The belief that news is what we make happen is now so ingrained that the media often eclipse the event they are reporting.[17]

Even those journalists who had not approached politics with a sense of mission interpreted their profession's "victories" as a validation of journalism's moral superiority. Each episode had revealed that some powerful politicians harbored base and ugly motives. Because of simultaneous changes in the presidential selection process, the major media now had an opportunity to exercise control over the politicians they held in such low regard. Journalists now had the means, motive, and opportunity to exert their own independent influence over the political debate.

Their rise within the political process made the media more responsible than ever for serving the public's information needs. After all, journalism's influence grew largely because of the steady diminution or elimination of competitors in the field of political communication. Political scientists had not generally bothered with the mass media before 1968. But after such pivotal media events as the 1968 conventions, the 1972 primaries, and Watergate, scholars began systematic studies of the political role of the networks and the prestige press. By the late 1980s, studies of the media as a political force were becoming a major part of the social science curriculum.

Much of the academic scrutiny has yielded a negative portrait of the media's influence on electoral politics. Scholars found little evidence that daily news coverage assists the public in learning about the issues or the candidates' records. Only special events (such as conventions and candidate debates), where candidates were allowed uninterrupted access to voters, added substantially to their information base.[18]

Instead, research revealed that voters tend to reflect the language and agenda of journalists who cover politics: their awareness of candidates frequently mentioned by reporters was higher, and their assessments of candidates often reflected opinions about the "insider" campaign issue of the moment (a frequent topic of news coverage) rather than public policy issues (which were less frequently spotlighted).[19] Studies also show that the public's faith in its political leadership has steadily eroded during the television age.[20]

Today's voters display a heightened awareness of each candidate's viability, reflecting news coverage that stresses the "horse race" over substance. Increasing numbers cast their votes not with an eye toward each candidate's relative merits, but with a strategic sense of each candidate's viability.[21] In short, journalists aren't training citizens to become better voters. Instead, they are training them to think about politics as journalists do — cynically and superficially.

TV's TAKEOVER OF PRESIDENTIAL POLITICS

Over the past thirty years, the method by which we choose our presidents has adjusted itself to conform with the values and requirements of journalism. Candidates and their advisers now self-consciously design campaign strategies with an eye toward convincing journalists and other pundits that they are made from presidential timber. Voters subconsciously echo the media's messages, rating candidates on their strategies, tactics, and advertising savvy, as well as on their goofs and gaffes. The existing scholarly research on national elections is organized around two key theories of media influence: *agenda setting* and *spin.*

AGENDA SETTING: CANDIDATES, CONTESTS, AND SUBSTANCE

In 1972, Theodore White wrote, "The power of the press is a primordial one. It sets the agenda of public discussion; and this sweeping political power is unrestrained by any law. It determines what people will talk and think about — an authority in other nations that is reserved for tyrants, priests, parties, and mandarins."[22]

In presidential campaigns, who sets the voters' agenda is more crucial than any other short-term variable. Since television became the battleground for presidential candidacies, the "who," "what," and "where" of campaigns have become increasingly dominated and directed by journalistic values, and less directed by broader civic or societal values.

Candidates: During presidential primaries, nothing is more important than which candidates are treated as serious contenders by the media. News organizations argue that they cannot provide an equal amount of coverage for all candidates because of a scarcity of the necessary resources (such as time, money, or personnel). Further, candidates do not offer equal amounts of news value — one candidate may deliver an important policy address while another takes the day off. But, regardless of *how* such decisions are made — the available evidence indicates that news organizations operate impartially in this regard — media decisions about who deserves coverage carry enormous consequences for the outcome of nomination contests, particularly when the field consists of numerous candidates.

For example, Jimmy Carter was virtually unknown to voters in 1975, but persistently courted journalists covering the campaign in Iowa and New Hampshire. He received heavy (and generally favorable) publicity in the early stages of the 1976 nomination race and parlayed it into the momentum with which he won the presidency.[23] A study of the 1976 race showed that Carter's name recognition among Democratic primary voters — manufactured by his early publicity — was a key ingredient in his primary victories over his more established Democratic rivals.[24]

In 1984, Sen. Gary Hart became the focus of tremendous media fascination when he finished second in the Iowa caucuses with 16% of the vote, far behind caucus winner Walter Mondale's 49%. Political reporters, who for months had been reporting on the invincibility of Mondale's political organization, finally had a fresh angle: the young, practically unknown Hart — not the tired ex-astronaut Sen. John Glenn — had risen from the pack as the main challenger to Mondale.

Prior to the Iowa vote, a majority of Democratic voters were still unfamiliar with Hart.[25] In the week that followed, Hart was the focus of more press coverage than either Mondale or Glenn. Not coincidentally, his support in New Hampshire increased fourfold, according to tracking polls.[26] Eight days after losing the Iowa caucuses to Mondale by a three-to-one margin, Hart beat the former vice president in the New Hampshire primary 37 to 28%. Even Carter's rapid rise paled before Hart's leap from obscurity to frontrunner status. As pollster Claibourne Darden remarked at the time, "It's just the damndest thing I ever saw."[27]

The media attention surrounding Carter and Hart clearly boosted each man's name recognition, helping their candidacies and hurting their rivals. But that is not to say that the media deliberately, or even knowingly, intended to assist those men. Rather, both benefited from the fact that their candidacies became important news stories. That is, journalism's norms and values directed reporters to write and talk about them disproportionately during the crucial early phase of the campaign.

The heavy coverage had important consequences — it vastly enhanced the prospects of Hart and propelled Carter all the way to the White House. Both cases also reveal the artificial nature of such "media momentum." Before 1968, a candidate such as Carter, who lacked a relationship with his own party's leadership, would have dedicated his pre-primary efforts to building such ties. Winning early primaries was important mainly in order to provide proof of voter appeal to party leaders, not to accumulate delegates.

By 1976, winning early primaries was important not for the delegates they yielded, but for the early headlines such victories generated. Winning early ensured a top spot on the media's agenda, and after 1968 that mattered more than winning the hearts and minds of the party elite. So Carter spent the pre-primary season courting reporters, and his lack of a prior national reputation was precisely what made him such a big news story.

Hart's strategy was to obtain his proverbial 15 minutes of fame at precisely the right juncture of the campaign. After Iowa, Hart "grabbed every bit of 'free media' exposure he could get,"[28] in a self-conscious effort to leverage his newfound news value into increased name recognition, and then use this to score further upsets and generate even more news coverage.

The strategy initially proved as successful as Carter's had. Hart parlayed his distant second-place finish in Iowa to a sweep of every contest between New Hampshire and Super Tuesday. Adding fuel to the flames was the fact that journalists and pundits had failed to predict his surge. Hart's instant celebrity was largely based, according to *New York Times* columnist Tom Wicker, on "the publicity that the press gave to the 'upset' of its own erroneous expectations," as pundits scrambled to provide interpretations and analysis of the previously impossible.[29]

Contests: Almost as consequential as the media's agenda in covering candidates is their agenda in covering state primaries and caucuses. The essential equation for news organizations is much the same in both instances: how much immediate news value does each offer? The result has been to increase the front-loading of primary campaign news ever since the early 1970s.[30]

The early contests provide news value because they offer the first chance to ascertain the comparative strength and voter appeal of the entire roster of candidates. In 1976, Carter's Iowa caucus victory received significant attention not because of the number of delegates involved, but because it was the first true "news" to come out of the nomination race that year.

In 1980, Iowa received even more attention, in no small part because the previous victor had gone on to win both his party's nomination and the presidency. As a barometer for predicting presidential success, Iowa — with one "win" under its belt — was perceived as a bigger story than ever. The media's judgment about Iowa's (and New Hampshire's) value as news stories logarithmically increased the political value of these early contests.

George Bush's narrow caucus victory over Ronald Reagan in '80 gave his candidacy a boost similar to what Carter had achieved in 1976. Bush enjoyed neither a delegate advantage, an endorsement advantage, nor a fundraising advantage over Reagan after Iowa; what he did have was a media advantage. As Margaret Robinson and Michael Sheehan documented, "having won Iowa by a pittance, but also by surprise, George Bush had nearly quadrupled his share of the newshole on print and television."[31] Bush's surprise translated into the familiar bandwagon effect: Republican voters flocked to Bush not out of any identification with him on the issues, but because he was portrayed by the media as winning.[32]

The difference in 1980 was that, as the media's attention span dwindled, so too did the half-life of Iowa's momentum. In both 1976 and 1980, the lag between the two early contests was about a month. In '76, Carter was able to sustain enough of his Iowa-generated media momentum to win New Hampshire. In '80, however, Bush's bandwagon didn't roll all the way to New Hampshire.

In 1984, the electoral calender was shifted to place Iowa just eight days ahead of New Hampshire. The change was intended to erode the ability of a challenger to capitalize on a strong Iowa showing. But this calculation was built on a flawed understanding of momentum. As Hart showed in 1984, by compressing the calender, a candidate could more effectively translate a strong showing one week into victory the next, before the media lost interest in the story. After 1984, candidates hoping for momentum increased the time and attention they paid to the caucuses. As candidates increased their commitment, the news value of Iowa grew once again, and the media presence — and the political stakes — grew along with it.

Four years later, the front-loading had reached the point where one candidate — Missouri Congressman Richard Gephardt — relocated his elderly mother from Missouri to Des Moines in an effort to win local support. According to our own review of 1988 election news, more than one-third (34%) of all primary contest coverage on the evening newscasts pertained to either Iowa or New Hampshire. (These two contests accounted for barely 2% of the convention delegates to be selected that year, and only 3% of the nation's population.)

This was also the year that Iowa finally surpassed New Hampshire in the early-bird news derby. In 1980 and 1984, the two states had attracted about an equal amount of network coverage, but during Campaign '88, TV offered up 285 stories about the Iowa caucuses that spring, a third more than New Hampshire (210), and more than the three most populous states (California, New York, and Texas) combined.

One effect of the media's front-loading in Campaign '88 was to end the possibility that any major party candidate could successfully bypass Iowa and New Hampshire in their quest for the nomination. That was the strategy of then-Tennessee Sen. Albert Gore, Jr. He hoped to fare well on "Super Tuesday," a date when nearly all the states in Gore's native South would select their candidates.

Super Tuesday followed New Hampshire by just three weeks, placing it ahead of most other contests. Its delegate yield, however, was huge: more than 1,000 Democratic delegates were at stake that day, compared to a few dozen in Iowa and New Hampshire. Gore expected that his capture of hundreds of convention delegates on Super Tuesday would more than make up for the early publicity he sacrificed by skipping the first two contests.

Unfortunately for Gore, the Super Tuesday campaign coverage did not reflect his purported regional strength as much as the publicity that Richard Gephardt, Michael Dukakis, and Jesse Jackson had generated with their strong showings in the earlier northern contests. Gore — little-known going into the Super Tuesday campaigns — had to settle for a mere one-fifth of the TV coverage. His five victories that day (in the Kentucky, North Carolina,

Oklahoma, and Tennessee primaries, and the Nevada caucuses) were over-shadowed by more numerous Jackson (6) and Dukakis (9) victories else-where.

Further, while Gore's overall performance rivaled those of his chief com-petitors (he won 30% of southern voters, compared with 28% for Jackson and 23% for Dukakis), TV's Wednesday-morning quarterbacks immediately questioned where else the Tennessee senator would win with the southern primaries over. Gore's coverage reflected prognostications that he would finish no better than third in the nomination sweepstakes. True to the prophecies, he did not win any additional primaries or caucuses.

Would Gore have fared better had the media not offered such intensive coverage of the preliminary contests, and not based their pre- and post-Super Tuesday coverage so much on "expectations"? Possibly, but it is impossible to separate the impact of front-loaded coverage from the candidates' antici-pation of this factor in their own strategies.

Paramount among the factors that hurt Gore's campaign was his failure to appreciate the enormity of the publicity benefits that accrue to the earliest contest winners. Gore's case also illuminates the degree to which the importance of a state contest depends far more on the media's anticipation of it and subsequent coverage than on its other attributes — including its portion of convention delegates. Journalistic judgment about the relative news value of the early contests has transformed the political value of these contests, and candidates who fail to recognize that fact at the outset will learn it through painful experience.[33]

Issues: The media's influence on the issue agenda is similar to their impact on the candidate and contest agendas. Their major effect is to diminish all policy issues in favor of the "horse race" — news about whether the candidates are winning or losing. In 1980, Michael Robinson and Margaret Sheehan observed that "no systematic study of any national medium has ever uncovered a campaign in which the modern press, during the course of an election year, emphasized anything more heavily than it emphasized the 'horse race.' "[34] It can be added that no study since 1980 has found the horse race to be neglected, either. The horse race, as Kathleen Hall Jamieson describes it, permeates practically all campaign news:

> The language through which the press reports on politics assumes that the American electorate selects a president through a process called a "campaign" seen as a "game" or "war" between a "frontrunner" and an "underdog" in which each "candidate's" goal is "winning." Candidates' words and actions are seen as their choice of what they presumably envision as a means to

victory. So enmeshed is the vocabulary of horse race and war in our thoughts about politics that we are not conscious that the "race" is a metaphor and "spectatorship" an inappropriate role for the electorate.[35]

Disentangling the issues from the horse race is a hopeless exercise. News reporters' agendas are topped by a constant curiosity about which candidate is winning, what events might change the dynamic of the race, and what the various contenders plan to do next to improve their chances. The issues, when they are covered, are mostly presented as tools to understand the candidates' strategies, and seldom as a means to uncover what each offers as a prospective president.[36]

For the most part, those "issues" that end up on the media's agenda consist of controversies that arise during the course of campaigning, or aspects of the candidates' personal lives. A candidate's general ideology, specific policy proposals, and governing record all tend to be ignored from day to day, receiving attention mainly as part of an occasional biographical feature or in-depth issue discussion.

Substantive aspects of the campaign will also generate news coverage if they become entangled in campaign trail controversies. For example, among the stories receiving the most television news play during the 1984 general election were Democratic vice presidential nominee Geraldine Ferraro's differences with the Catholic Church and President Reagan's inaccessibility to reporters, his age, and his remark comparing the U.S. embassy in Beirut's unpreparedness for a truck bomb (plans for beefing up security were in the works when the terrorists struck) with a home repair job gone awry: "Anybody that's ever had their kitchen done over knows that it never gets done as soon as you wish it would."[37]

Reagan's comment, portrayed as a gaffe by campaign reporters, was the focus of 17 campaign stories — more than any other campaign issue.[38] While it might have included some substance (such as a debate about U.S. anti-terrorism policy, or America's general approach to the Middle East, for example), it was not treated as a policy issue, but as a campaign issue: a misstatement by a candidate on the campaign trail that might affect the conduct or outcome of the race.

While Reagan's kitchen remark topped TV's campaign news agenda, polls of voters found their top concerns were unemployment and the state of the economy. Neither of these major issues, it turns out, were among the networks' heavily covered topics during Campaign '84.[39]

This trend continued in 1988, as the major candidates were judged by the content of their characters more than their programs and policies. The most exhaustively covered campaign story of the Campaign '88 pre-season was Gary Hart's sex life, followed by Sen. Joseph Biden's alleged plagiarism. Both these stories were at least partially initiated by news organizations.

Then, just before the Iowa caucuses, CBS News took aim at Vice President George Bush. CBS had asked for an extended interview with Bush, which they proposed to edit down to about five minutes and broadcast on the *Evening News*. Bush's aides insisted that the interview be conducted live, without editing. When told of his aides' concerns that the interview might be a setup, Bush himself reportedly laughed and said, "No, no. Dan Rather is a good newsman. He won't do that."[40]

Bush's aides, however, were right. Each of the other eleven candidates had been the subject of a two-to-three-minute story that summarized his biography, campaign platform, and prospects. CBS's "profile" of Bush was over five minutes long and devoted to a single issue: the Iran/contra scandal. According to some reports, CBS employees were boasting that their report would "take Bush out of the race."[41] But one CBS insider tipped off the Republicans: "They've cut a five-minute piece which basically indicts him, and Dan's job is to execute him on the air."[42] When Rather, began peppering Bush with questions about his role in the scandal, the campaign's fears of a CBS ambush were realized.

The forewarned Bush was prepared to joust. "It's not fair to judge my whole career by a rehash on Iran," the vice president told Rather. "How would you like it if I judged your career by those seven minutes when you walked off the set in New York?" Rather was momentarily speechless.[43] It did not matter that he had actually walked off the CBS set for six minutes, not seven, and in Miami, not New York. By criticizing Rather's own behavior, Bush undermined the newsman's Olympian persona of public arbiter devoid of personal interests or prejudices. By turning Rather the public tribune into Rather the controversial public figure, Bush gained an equal footing with his antagonist. After the interview, Bush's approval ratings rose. Rather's dropped.

Politically, Bush's tactic was to use Rather's own intensity as leverage with which to score political points among his own constituents. Substantively, the issue was Iran/contra, and the question was: why did CBS News care? From a policy perspective, the scandal was a buried corpse. The revelations that the Reagan administration had traded arms for hostages had been made 14 months earlier, and media interest had faded after congressional hearings during the summer of 1987. There was also no real possibility, especially given the outcry over Reagan's deal-making, that a prospective Bush administration would resurrect the arms trade with Iran.

For CBS and the other networks, Iran/contra was a character story, like the reports of Hart's hanky-panky and Biden's plagiarism, and it topped all three networks' campaign agendas prior to Iowa. Farm issues, a leading concern among Iowa voters, finished a distant second with 20 evening news stories, compared with Iran/contra's 46.[44]

The on-air confrontation between Rather and Bush, much ballyhooed at the time, also showed how far the media's self-perceptions had changed during the previous twenty years. When one tries to contemplate the spectacle of Rather's predecessor, the avuncular Walter Cronkite, similarly badgering Vice President Hubert Humphrey about Vietnam policy in 1968, it becomes clear just how much had changed. (Imagine, for example, Cronkite charging, "You've made us hypocrites in the face of the world," as Rather did in 1988.)[45]

In 1968, the role of the television networks and other major media was still largely to observe and report upon the process by which politicians and voters selected a president. By 1988, the media had enveloped the process and made it their own. Dan Rather didn't break the rules; he acted as the new rules allowed and even encouraged. By 1988, some journalists — tired of acting as transmission belts for evasive or manipulative candidates — envisioned their role as enforcing their own agenda as a means to keep candidates "honest." By 1988, the process had evolved to a point where the media had the power to make their agenda and their rules stick.

NEWS MEDIA "SPIN": FAVORABILITY AND VIABILITY

As many candidates will attest, the "spin" of news coverage matters as much as the agenda. Particularly in the general election, when both candidates enjoy high levels of name recognition and the media's geographic focus is established by the candidates' strategies, the tone of news coverage accounts for much of the media's influence.

There are two main types of judgments that the media convey about the party nominees: what kind of people they are, and how likely they are to win. If a candidate can receive positive reviews on at least one (although preferably both) of these criteria, his or her campaign stands an increased chance of winning on Election Day.

Favorability: Many of the subjective statements uttered about a candidate on the evening news (or reprinted in the morning papers) originate with the candidates and their campaigns. Because even the tone of campaign debate is revealed to citizens through the filter of news judgment, however, distortions invariably occur. If a candidate is seen as winning, journalists will attempt to illustrate that by presenting favorable comments about that candidate's chances from voters or political experts. If a candidate commits a gaffe, subsequent news stories will probably not convey any hint that the candidate enjoys strong support on a variety of other issues.

There is little evidence to support the contention that reporters intentionally and systematically provide favorable coverage to candidates with whom they agree on most issues, or manufacture criticism of candidates with whom they disagree. In 1980, a major study found that the Republican and Democratic nominees each received about the same share of good and bad press, with slightly better press going to the Republican.[46]

A similar study of the 1984 race found that the tone of the Democrats' coverage was more favorable, but that the Republicans were consistently portrayed as the likely winners.[47] In 1988, there was little difference between the cumulative proportions of good and bad press directed at Republican and Democratic candidates during the primaries.[48] The Republican and Democratic tickets received similar proportions of good and bad press during the general election (although the Bush-Quayle ticket was portrayed as probable victors).[49]

Even if partisanship is not a consistent factor, there is considerable evidence that good press has aided some candidates and bad press has hurt others.   During the 1984 primaries, political scientist William C. Adams documented how public support for Hart rose and fell as a consequence of his media coverage.

Just after the Iowa caucuses, Adams noted, "Hart's coverage was virtually free of any harsh criticism, unflattering issues, or cynical commentary." That corresponded with heavy coverage of the Colorado Senator, and Hart's meteoric rise in both New Hampshire and national polls. But after Hart's New Hampshire victory, reporters began scrutinizing his past, and the new frontrunner became the focus of unflattering TV stories about his campaign style and his personal character. The criticism reached a crescendo on Monday, March 12, the night before the important Super Tuesday primaries, when all three network newscasts broadcast what Adams terms "biting and one-sided critiques of Hart."[50]

The harshness of the coverage took its toll. Democratic voters who made up their minds on that Monday night "were far less likely to favor Hart than were those who had decided soon after New Hampshire." Adams concludes: "All of the available evidence indicates that the [1984 Democratic nomination] race was fundamentally influenced... by news media choices."[51]

Media scholar Michael Robinson agrees. While he believes "the national press played a fairly inadvertent role in making Hart..., it played a very conscious role in bringing him down [in 1984]."[52] Hart's support grew mainly as a product of his increased name recognition, and his name recognition grew as an artifact of the intense coverage given his candidacy after Iowa.

Almost as soon as his name became a household word, though, media criticism caused Hart's bubble to burst. The old adage is wrong: not all publicity is good publicity, particularly once a candidate becomes well-known. Bad press, especially in concentrated doses, can be poisonous to a politician's political health.

If Hart hadn't already learned that lesson in 1984, he became an object lesson in 1988. Hart abandoned his campaign for the nomination in May 1987, amid devastating publicity about an alleged extramarital affair. When he re-entered the Democratic race in December 1987, however, he began with high levels of name recognition, which translated into a decent lead in national Democratic preference polls. More than 90% of voters recognized Hart and his rival Rev. Jesse Jackson; none of the other contenders for the Democratic nomination were known by more than half of those surveyed in January 1988.[53]

But Hart's re-entry was derided by reporters: Most of the media coverage focused on his lesser-known rivals, and when Hart was covered, the spin was brutally negative. "Gary Hart yesterday, [campaigning in] a mall in Davenport [Iowa] — looking for hands to shake, and finding few," reported NBC's Dennis Murphy. The picture showed a slightly lost-looking Hart wandering the shopping center. Murphy then quoted an Iowa voter: "I think he's an embarrassment to the Democratic Party. He never should have re-entered the race." NBC then reported that the *Des Moines Register* had editorialized against Hart, saying "Name recognition is about all he has going for him... the others didn't betray their supporters through acts of self-indulgence."

Murphy then followed Hart to another campaign stop, a Davenport bar. The event, the reporter pronounced, was "a dud. The guy playing the arcade game doesn't even look up. Hart plays some pool with the owner, killing time." The visual again showed Hart looking lonely. Murphy's closer drove the point home: "This election year he started as the frontrunner. Now, once again he's the underdog, in a campaign that seems adrift."[54] Hart's public support in preference polls quickly evaporated from a healthy 29% in December, when he led the field, to 17% in mid-January, to a mere 9% in mid-February.[55]

The only other candidate to receive as much bad press as Hart that year was *700 Club* founder Rev. Pat Robertson, who ran as a Republican. His campaign viewed the national media as a hostile and potentially dangerous force. Shortly before announcing his candidacy, Robertson told supporters, "Somebody says they wrap fish in yesterday's newspapers. But, thank the Lord, most of the Christians neither read the *New York Times* or the *Washington Post*. If they do read them they don't believe them, thank goodness."[56]

It didn't help relations when journalists discovered (and reported) that Robertson's wife was already pregnant when they got married many years earlier. The angry candidate fired back, "It is outrageous to intrude into a man's family, and to do damage to a man's wife and children, under the guise of journalism."[57] Such periodic flare-ups over the candidate's personal and professional background culminated in Robertson's charge of "religious bigotry" against Tom Brokaw during a live national broadcast. Brokaw had called him a former "television evangelist." Robertson preferred the more neutral tag, "religious broadcaster."[58]

Early in his candidacy, assessments of Robertson seemed to belie the ill feelings. Until the New Hampshire primary, in fact, he received better press than any of his Republican opponents. Much of the good press, however, came not from sympathy with either the man or his views, but from reporters surprised at the professional skill with which Robertson, a political novice, was managing his candidacy. He also benefited from the fact that his opponents chose to ignore his candidacy and snipe at each other.

After New Hampshire, however, Robertson was discovered by both his Republican rivals and the media. He was hurt badly by harsh media coverage of his misstatements regarding such diverse topics as Soviet missiles in Cuba, hostages in Beirut, and alleged political motives behind the Jimmy Swaggart scandal. After New Hampshire, Robertson's bad press outnumbered his good press by a margin of four to one.

The flavor of Robertson's coverage was captured in an ABC story that took him to task for a series of "remarkable statements," going back to his 1982 assertion that only Christian and Jews are qualified to serve in government. After ABC's John Martin criticized Robertson for a "remarkably undisciplined tongue," he quoted political analyst Kevin Phillips, who pronounced Robertson "a little bit of a wacko."[59]

While Robertson stayed in the race and competed for delegates through the California primary, any hopes he might have entertained were dashed early on. He had begun his candidacy in September 1987, by unveiling three million signatures on a petition urging him to run. By the time the primaries had ended, he had converted barely a third of those names into votes.

Viability: It is easy to see how good and bad press can affect candidacies. Constructing a model showing how voters are affected by media assessments of a candidate's viability or electability is more difficult. Further, such "horse race" assessments tend to be based on concrete indicators, such as polls, contest results, amount of money raised, etc. Because of the availability of such real-world indicators, journalists themselves have little difficulty offering their own "objective" assessments of how well (or poorly) candidates are faring in the horse race.

Viability, however, is as ripe an area for "spin" as is favorability. Candidates and their managers frequently offer reporters their own analysis of how the race is progressing, in hopes of affecting reportage of their prospects. And the media's tendencies to seize on the significance of immediate events, while ignoring long-term trends, means that voters are sometimes presented with a distorted picture of how the race stands.

Horse race news does not offer voters a steady gauge of who is ahead and who is behind, but rather an erratic spotlight on changes in the conventional wisdom about a candidate's prospects. In 1984, for example, Mondale trounced Hart by a margin of three to one in the Iowa caucuses. Yet reporters stressed Hart's improved viability rather than Mondale's impressive victory.

Some recent research suggests that a significant portion of the electorate incorporates news about a candidate's viability when settling on a vote choice.[60] Those individuals do not (generally) cast merely reflexive votes for a winner but rather use viability as a method of narrowing their range of choices down to a manageable few.

In a multi-candidate race, voters may be reluctant to "waste" a vote on a candidate portrayed as weak. Instead, some prefer to boost their second choice in an effort to block the election of less desirable candidates. Alternatively, voters may rate two candidates approximately evenly in terms of issue identification or general favorability, but cast their vote for the candidate who appears more viable.

Most often, such situations exist in primary elections. However, there have been strong third candidates in several recent general elections. In 1980, Independent John Anderson was running five percentage points behind President Carter at the Labor Day general election kickoff. As election day drew closer, however, a spate of news stories questioned his ability to win. In September, for example, Jack Germond and Jules Witcover averred that Anderson's leading supporters had "abandoned their dream of winning... against essentially hopeless odds."[61] Consecutive polls showed Anderson dropping from 24% of likely voters in late August to 19% in late September and 12% in mid-October.[62] On Election Day, Anderson drew just 7% of the vote, barely a quarter of the number of supporters he might have claimed on Labor Day.

Further evidence comes from the 1988 primaries. In the Iowa caucuses, Bush was unexpectedly surpassed by Pat Robertson, who finished second behind Kansas Sen. Robert Dole. Bush's 18.6% of the caucus vote (just 6,000 votes fewer than Robertson) seriously damaged the credibility of his candidacy in the eyes of the media's "experts." That night, Dan Rather called Bush's third-place showing "close to a nightmare scenario."

Bob Schieffer picked up this theme during CBS's live coverage: "For George Bush, this is the nightmare of nightmares that his people have been hoping against hope would not come about.... This has been a severe blow to George Bush, and it cannot be read any other way."[63] ABC's Barry Serafin followed the vice president to the Granite State, where, campaigning on a street corner, he looked "a little lonely. Before last night's beating in the caucuses, Bush was the clear favorite in New Hampshire. Now, this is a must-win state for the vice president."[64]

How could one caucus so scramble the odds? Partly because the odds makers had already considered this contingency. The cadre of professional pollsters, consultants, and experts — who serve modern presidential campaigns in much the way the Chorus added their commentary to ancient Greek plays — had not only designated Bush as the Republican frontrunner, but also named Dole as the candidate most likely to upset him. Finally, they fingered Iowa as the state most likely to provide the setting for such an upset.

Dole was, in super-pundit William Schneider's apt phrase, "the understudy" of the campaign, waiting for leading man Bush to catch a cold or break a leg. After Iowa, Bush was universally portrayed as being on the ropes, while the sometimes dour Dole was shown smiling and licking an ice cream cone on NBC.[65]

The media's response to the Iowa caucuses in 1988 added another installment to the ongoing saga of the legendary "Iowa bounce" that had helped Hart in 1984, Bush in 1980, and Carter in 1976. Just before the caucuses, a CBS News tracking poll of New Hampshire voters and found that Dole trailed Bush there by 22 percentage points. After the caucuses, the gap narrowed to single digits.[66] While the percentages varied from day to day over the next week, Dole kept most of his converts when the votes were cast.

For many pundits, the fact that Bush had ultimately won New Hampshire's primary by 38% to 29% was misinterpreted as the "end" of the Iowa bounce. In fact, Dole had substantially cut into Bush's lead in the 24 hours that followed the caucuses, and he nearly beat the vice president in a state where he had been trailing by over 20 points just a fortnight earlier.

The story was similar on the Democratic side. Massachusetts Governor Michael Dukakis was the overwhelming frontrunner in New Hampshire in CBS's late January poll, holding a 40% to 7% lead over Missouri congressman Richard Gephardt. After Gephardt won the Iowa caucuses, he surged to 19%, while Dukakis's support dropped slightly to 38%. Democrat Gephardt had bounced after Iowa just as Republican Dole had, but he didn't bounce high enough to wrest the primary victory from regional heavyweight Dukakis.

The 1988 "bounce" was no surprise to the political scientists who track such things, but research conducted after the campaign shed some new light on *why* the Iowa winners got a boost. Political scientist Paul Abramson and his colleagues found that Republicans switched from Bush to Dole after Iowa not because their image of Dole had improved (or their image of Bush worsened), but because they perceived that Dole had a better chance of winning the nomination.

Abramson and his colleagues also found a similar, although less pronounced, effect among Democrats who switched from Dukakis to Gephardt.[67] As one might expect, most of the news reports voters saw or read in the eight days between Iowa and New Hampshire had little to do with the candidates' stands on issues, or biographies, or anything else except their chances of winning.

Our own analysis of the '88 coverage reinforces this point. News about the strength or prospects of each candidacy was the focus of nearly 70% of all campaign stories between Iowa and New Hampshire (from February 9 through February 16). Thus, practically speaking, nearly all of the new information that voters received about the candidates during this period reflected estimations of their chances for winning.

The Abramson study shows that a measurable percentage of voters do, in fact, incorporate such news about a candidate's prospects into their decision-making process. Thus, the media's "spin" about each candidate's viability affects not only the activists and donors who closely follow such matters, but also the calculus by which ordinary voters cast their ballots.

POWER OR PERCEPTION?

Few reporters have thought more about the media's role in covering political campaigns than ABC's Jeff Greenfield. In his book on the media and the 1980 campaign, he argued that there are many factors more important than the press in deciding the outcome of presidential elections, and that the media are not as powerful as its critics believe.[68] Greenfield repeated this view in a speech prior to the start of the 1988 race, arguing that political campaigns and their outcomes have "much more to do with real events, real life, than has been assumed."[69]

A report published by the Gannett Center for Media Studies recounted the following exchange:

> Jeff Greenfield, the gifted political and media analyst at ABC News, spoke earlier this year about the presumed power of television on campaign decision-making. "The mass media, television in particular, have changed American politics much less than most smart people think," Greenfield said.... "The mass media, television in particular, have much less to do with the outcome of an election." The eminent political scientist James David Barber, who was in the audience listening to Greenfield, asked aloud, "How can someone so smart be so wrong?"[70]

Greenfield's remarks represent the views of many political reporters, who still envision their role as that of observer, chronicler, and interpreter of campaign events. Real power, in their view, remains where it always has: in the hands of the candidates and the voters. Barber, for his part, was reflecting the views of many other campaign observers — politicians, consultants, and academics — who believe that the media are indeed a powerful influence on presidential elections.

The disparity between journalists and other observers has much to do with their respective definitions of "power." Greenfield and others who disagree with the idea of "media power" do so because they restrict the definition of power to require *intent* as an antecedent. According to this logic, power is like money — worthless unless it is used. Whatever power the media might have is unmanageable and diffuse, shared by hundreds of organizations and thousands of individuals.

"The media" do not select candidates, nor do they deliberately assist candidates, and the media's component parts often work at cross-purposes. Without the singularity and intent that denotes the conscious and deliberate use of power, the media's influence is, at most, inadvertent. The problem, as Greenfield stated it in January 1988, is that "the assumption of massive media power is simply no longer challenged: it is built into campaign coverage and campaign strategy, and it is an assumption which needs examining."[71]

We would argue for a more expansive definition of power: the media's actions, and sometimes mere presence, cause significant changes in the electoral process, as well as in candidate and voter behavior. This kind of "power" is not like money, but rather like gravity — its existence exerts a powerful tug on everything within its range.

The proof lies in the trends we have already noted: candidates invest huge amounts of effort to place themselves on the media's agenda; the political clout of the early contests in Iowa and New Hampshire springs entirely from the tremendous publicity they receive; and the discourse of election campaigns is heavily weighted toward the media's preferences for conflict, strategy, and process.

Imagine a world without television, and presidential campaigns — especially nomination races — become entirely different events. In this sense, to state that the media exert an influence on presidential campaigns is merely to state a fact, much like stating that gravity exerts an influence on the solar system.

This distinction implies an important corollary. Under Greenfield's definition, journalists can, by the simple exercise of good judgment and objective standards, eliminate any hypothetical problems the media may cause. Under our definition no one, including journalists themselves, can eliminate the consequences of the media's influence.

Journalists can follow all of their rules, arrange their coverage as objectively as possible, and still cause a tremendous distortion of the electoral process. This occurs not because journalists wish to create such distortions or exert their own influence. It is simply because journalists will always be guided primarily by the values and norms of their own profession, and news judgment and news values are inherently at odds with rational presidential campaigns.

In his exhaustive study of presidential campaigns, Thomas Patterson similarly concluded that: "the United States cannot have a sensible campaign as long as it is built around the news media."[72] The electoral structure is designed to create leaders accountable to the people, and it must be arranged around political values in order for it to succeed.

Citizens require information that does not meet any standard definition of "news," and some sort of intermediary is needed to ensure its availability to voters. Politicians must occasionally compromise and even reverse their positions on issues in order to build majority coalitions. Today's journalism rewards rhetoric that serves the opposite goals.

The media have power because they establish so much of the context of campaigns in their own image, leading voters and candidates to adjust their actions accordingly. The procedural arrangements of power are tremendously important, because they provide the framework that governs the competition for political authority among competing societal interests. While such guidelines are generally impartial, they are not neutral in their effect. The media have such an effect on campaigns — their structures and norms offer powerful, albeit unintended, assistance to some candidates and interest groups, and create obstacles for others.

In this sense, the media have enormous power over national elections. As we have shown, those candidates who are placed on the media's agenda have a chance to win; those that are ignored languish. Those issues — either policy or personal — which the media spotlight become the yardsticks for measuring candidates. When candidates receive heavy (and favorable) publicity, their campaigns flourish. If candidates are doused with heavy doses of bad press, their chances of success are measurably reduced. Media spin can create a bandwagon effect for some candidates, or it can convince large numbers of voters not to "waste" their vote on an unlikely winner.

Further, many of the reporters and political editors who cover campaigns fully understand the media's effect on the process. Over time, such awareness has led to disorganized efforts to compensate for the media's effects. Prior to 1992, the best example was the semi-organized backlash against Gary Hart during the 1984 campaign. As Michael Robinson writes:

> If power is best defined as effect plus premeditation, what the free media did with and to Hart during the middle of March was press power, pure and palpable — much more so than in the week after the Iowa vote.
>
> The press knew what it was doing. It was getting the bad news out about the year's media-based "phenomenon" just in time for the big vote on super

Tuesday and beyond.... The odyssey of Hart after New Hampshire proves that press people believe they have the right to change the standards once anybody starts to ride the New Hampshire bandwagon. The press does this deliberately and, for the most part, unashamedly. Their decision to resurrect and to emphasize the dark-side information about Hart, information known years before, was both premeditated and effective — in a word, powerful.[73]

The incentive to "go negative" against Hart in 1984 was the sense among reporters that he was a candidate of their own creation. But as Hart's news (and his candidacy) began to go south, a new line had been crossed. Reporters' actions indicated a *prima facie* acceptance of the notion that media power can be deliberately and effectively employed to remedy electoral problems traceable to the media's own inadvertent effects on the process.

Robinson cautioned that "to argue that the free media exerted real influence — power — is not necessarily to disparage them."[74] Journalists' norms may eschew the exertion of power, particularly in political battles. But it does no good to turn a blind eye towards such situations, nor to develop convoluted rationales for them.

By 1988, it was common for politicians, voters, and academics to regard the media as a central player in American politics. As a consequence of the 1988 presidential campaign, a significant portion of the journalistic community began to realize the same thing. As they contemplated the consequences of their role, however, journalists began to consider taking steps to remedy those problems within the electoral structure that many academics traced to the news media's own influences. The result was an ill-fated attempt to consolidate and amplify their role as political power brokers.

Notes

Opening quote: Alexis de Tocqueville; *Democracy in America*, the Henry Reeve text, as revised by Francis Bowen, now further corrected and edited with a historical essay, editorial notes, and bibliographies by Phillips Bradley, vol. 2 (New York: Vintage Books, 1945) p. 119.

1. The diminished power of political parties has been well-documented in recent years. Among others, see Everett Carll Ladd with Charles D. Hadley,

Transformations of the American Party System: Political Coalitions from the New Deal to the 1970s, 2nd ed. (New York: W. W. Norton & Company, 1978); Martin P. Wattenberg, *The Decline of American Political Parties*, 1952-1984 (Cambridge, MA: Harvard University Press, 1986); and Nelson W. Polsby, *Consequences of Party Reform* (New York: Oxford University Press, 1983).

2.   Harold W. Stanley and Richard G. Niemi, eds., *Vital Statistics on American Politics*, 4th ed. (Washington, DC: CQ Press, 1994), p. 74.

3.   Joseph Kraft, "The Imperial Media," *Commentary*, May 1981, pp. 36-47.

4.   Frank J. Murray, "Sam: A Press Corps 'Ayatollah' and How He Got That Way," *Washington Times*, November 7, 1988.

5.   Charlotte Hays and Jonathan Rows, "Reporters: The New Washington Elite," *The Washington Monthly*, July/August 1985, pp. 21-27.

6.   Quoted by Howard Means, "Next, Kill All the Journalists," *The Washingtonian*, May, 1991, pp. 72-76, 145-151.

7.   Leo C. Rosten, *The Washington Correspondents* (New York: Harcourt, Brace, 1937).

8.   James Deakin, *Straight Stuff: The Reporters, the White House and the Truth* (New York: William Marrow and Co., 1984), p. 330.

9.   In May 1995, the congressional press galleries reported 2,200 accredited radio and television journalists, 2,000 periodical reporters, and 2,100 members from the daily press.

10.   Roxanne Roberts, "Un-Conventional Activities for Ordering Dems," *Washington Post*, July 11, 1992.

11.   For more about the Washington culture, see Kevin Phillips, *Arrogant Capital: Washington, Wall Street, and the Frustration of American Politics* (Boston: Little, Brown and Company, 1994).

12.   Quoted by Tom Hopkins, "Television Makes News as it Covers Campaign," *Dayton Daily News*, April 24, 1988.

13.   Edward Jay Epstein, *News From Nowhere* (New York: Vintage Books, 1973), p. 219.

14.   Quoted by Epstein, *News From Nowhere*, pp. 219-220.

15.   See Peter Braestrup, *Big Story: How the American Press and Television Reported and Interpreted the Crisis of Tet 1968 in Vietnam and Washington* (New Haven: Yale University Press, 1977).

16.   Since Democrats controlled most of the state legislatures that make electoral law, the Democrats' new rules were, with minor exceptions, applied to nominating contests in both the Republican and Democratic parties. For a more complete discussion of how the 1968 reforms affected national politics, see Polsby, *Consequences of Party Reform*.

17.   Kraft, "The Imperial Media."

18.   See Dan Drew and David Weaver, "Voter Learning in the 1988 Presidential Election: Did the Debates and the Media Matter?" *Journalism Quarterly* 68, nos. 1, 2 (Spring/Summer 1991), 27-37. See also Thomas E. Patterson, *The Mass Media Election: How Americans Choose Their President* (New York: Praeger Publishers, 1980).

19.   See Joseph N. Cappella and Kathleen Hall Jamieson, "Public Cynicism and News Coverage in Campaigns and Policy Debates: Three Field Experiments," paper

presented to the American Political Science Association Conference in New York, September 1994. Also, Doris Graber, *Processing the News: How People Tame the Information Tide* (New York: Longman, 1984).

20. See, among others, Thomas E. Patterson, *Out of Order* (New York: Alfred A. Knopf, 1993), pp. 21-27.

21. Paul R. Abramson et al. "'Sophisticated' Voting in the 1988 Presidential Primaries" *American Political Science Review* 86, no. 1 (March 1992): 55-69.

22. Theodore H. White, *The Making of the President, 1972* (New York: Bantam, 1973)

23. Martin Schram, *Running for President 1976: The Carter Campaign* (New York: Stein and Day, 1977). See also James Wooten, *Dasher: The Roots and the Rising of Jimmy Carter* (New York: Summit Books, 1978); Arthur T. Hadley, *The Invisible Primary* (Englewood Cliffs, NJ: Prentice Hall, 1976); and Kandy Stroud, *How Jimmy Won: The Victor's Campaign From Plains to the White House* (New York: William Morrow, 1971).

24. Thomas E. Patterson, *The Mass Media Election: How Americans Choose Their President* (New York: Praeger Publishers, 1980).

25. Poll conducted by Yankelovich, Skelly & White, Jan. 31 to Feb 2, 1984, and reported in *Time*, February 20, 1984, p. 55.

26. William C. Adams, "Media Coverage of Campaign '84: A Preliminary Report," *Public Opinion* 7, no. 2 (April/May 1984): 9-13.

27. George J. Church, "Now It's Really a Race," *Time*, March 12, 1984, p. 16.

28. David Broder, "Hart Defeats Mondale in Maine Party Caucuses; Own Strategy Tripped Candidate," *Washington Post*, March 5, 1984.

29. Quoted by Kurt Andersen, "Charting the Big Shift," *Time*, March 19, 1984, p. 17.

30. One unusual by-product of the media's gravitation toward the earliest primaries and caucuses has been a corresponding move by various state legislatures to move up the dates of their own presidential selection contests, as the states themselves vie for attention on the evening news.

31. Michael J. Robinson and Margaret A. Sheehan, *Over the Wire & On TV: CBS and UPI in Campaign '88,* (New York: Russell Sage Foundation, 1983), p. 80.

32. Larry M. Bartels, "Expectations and Preferences in Presidential Nominating Campaigns," *American Political Science Review* 79 (September/October 1985): 804-815.

33. Despite the tremendous coverage the caucuses received in 1988, the perceived importance of Iowa faded in retrospect. After Super Tuesday, analysts noted with some irony that Sen. Robert Dole and Rep. Richard Gephardt had been knocked out of the race barely a month after their Iowa victories. NBC's Tom Pettit returned to Iowa in mid-May to report on a dispute about which Democratic candidate had actually received the most votes (Gephardt and Sen. Paul Simon were practically even when the counting inexplicably stopped with just under 70% of the votes counted). His story included a quote from the *Des Moines Register*'s James Gannon, who laughed about Pettit's doggedness at trying to pinpoint a winner: "It's all irrelevant now. Gephardt's irrelevant. Iowa is irrelevant. What difference does it make?" *NBC Nightly News*, May 15, 1988.

34. Robinson and Sheehan, *Over the Wire and On TV*, p. 24.

35.	Kathleen Hall Jamieson, *Dirty Politics: Deception, Distraction, and Democracy* (New York: Oxford University Press, 1992), p. 165.

36.	See, among others, Bruce Buchanan, *Electing a President: The Markle Commission Research on Campaign '88* (Austin: University of Texas Press, 1991).

37.	Bernard Gwertzman, "Reagan Concedes Embassy Security Was Not Complete," *New York Times*, September 24, 1984.

38.	Maura Clancey and Michael J. Robinson, "General Election Coverage: Part I," *Public Opinion* (December/January 1985).

39.	Michael J. Robinson, "Where's the Beef?: Media and Media Elites in 1984," in *The American Elections of 1984*, ed. Austin Ranney (Washington, D.C.: American Enterprise Institute, 1985), pp. 185-187. Unemployment and the economy were not among the twelve top policy and campaign issues receiving the most media coverage in the general election.

40.	Recounted in Jack W. Germond and Jules Witcover, *Whose Broad Stripes and Bright Stars? The Trivial Pursuit of the Presidency 1988* (New York: Warner Books, 1989), pp. 118-130, and Peter Goldman and Tom Mathews, *The Quest for the Presidency, 1988* (New York: Simon & Schuster, 1989), pp. 198-201.

41.	Germond and Witcover, p. 118, and Goldman and Mathews, p. 198.

42.	Germond and Witcover, p. 118.

43.	*CBS Evening News*, January 26, 1988

44.	S. Robert Lichter, Daniel Amundson, and Richard E. Noyes, *The Video Campaign: Network Coverage of the 1988 Primaries* (Washington, D.C.: American Enterprise Institute, 1988), pp. 21-24.

45.	*CBS Evening News*, January 26, 1988.

46.	Robinson and Sheehan, *Over the Wire and On TV*.

47.	Michael J. Robinson, "The Media in Campaign '84 Part II: Wingless, Toothless, and Hopeless," *Public Opinion* 8, no. 1 (February/March 1985).

48.	Lichter et al., *The Video Campaign*.

49.	S. Robert Lichter et al., "Election '88: Media Coverage," *Public Opinion* 11, no. 5 (January/February 1989).

50.	William C. Adams, "Media Coverage of Campaign '84: A Preliminary Report," *Public Opinion* 7, no. 2 (April/May 1984): 9-13.

51.	Ibid.

52.	Robinson, "Where's the Beef?", p. 201.

53.	Survey by the Gallup Organization for the Times Mirror Company, January 4-11, 1988.

54.	*NBC Nightly News*, February 2, 1988.

55.	Surveys by Gordon S. Black Corporation for *USA Today*, December 15, 1987, January 22-27, 1988, and February 10-13, 1988.

56.	Lloyd Grove, "Robertson, Taking Aim at the Critics," *Washington Post*, February 22, 1988.

57.	Larry Eichel, "Robertson Rips Reports on Son's Birth," *Chicago Tribune*, October 9, 1987.

58.	NBC News live coverage of the Iowa Caucus returns, February 8, 1988.

59.	ABC's *World News Tonight*, February 26, 1988.

60.	Abramson et al., "'Sophisticated' Voting..."

61. Jack W. Germond and Jules Witcover, "Anderson's Aides Doubt His Viability," *Washington Star*, September 26, 1980.

62. Data from Harris polls, cited in *Public Opinion*, December/January 1981, p. 30.

63. CBS News live coverage of the Iowa Caucus returns, February 8, 1988.

64. ABC's *World News Tonight*, February 9, 1988.

65. *NBC Nightly News*, February 8, 1988.

66. According to the CBS tracking polls, Dole had bounced from 20% on January 30, 1988 to 27% on February 9-10 (a day after the Iowa caucuses) among likely New Hampshire primary voters, while Bush fell from 42% to 35%.

67. Abramson et al., "'Sophisticated' Voting..." The study surveyed 672 Republicans and 394 Democrats from January 17 to March 8, 1988. Respondents were asked to evaluate their own party's candidates on both a 100-point feeling thermometer and then rate the candidates' prospects on a similar 100-point scale.

68. Jeff Greenfield, *The Real Campaign* (New York: Summit Books, 1982).

69. Jeff Greenfield's comments are found in his essay "Presidential Politics and Myths of Media Power," adopted from his keynote address to a Gannett conference on "Campaign '88: The Politics of Character and the Character of Politics," January 26, 1988. Greenfield's essay was included in a Gannett report on the conference published in 1988.

70. Recounted in "The New Elector," *Gannett Center Journal* 2, no. 4 (Fall 1988), pp. vii-x.

71. Greenfield, "Presidential Politics and Myths of Media Power."

72. Patterson, *Out of Order*, p. 25.

73. Robinson, "Where's the Beef?"

74. Ibid., p. 192.

Chapter Two

The Reagan Reaction

When it comes to the way in which presidential campaigns are conducted in the media age, the public again is the loser.... For shame, indeed. The shame is exclusively the media's.
— Haynes Johnson, *The Washington Post*, 1988

The powerful, centralized "media elite" that emerged during the mid-1960s were criticized from the start by some conservatives and Republicans, largely for their perceived animosity in such national controversies as the civil rights movement, the Vietnam anti-war movement, and Watergate. In addition, critics from the academic left charged that the Big Media, owned and dominated by large corporations, were an obstacle to radical social change. But during the '60s and '70s the press faced relatively little criticism from mainstream liberals, perhaps because they sensed that the media shared their goal of gradual but progressive social reform.

As long as the leading critics were either academic leftists or social conservatives — both of whom had been on the losing side of many recent battles — their criticism could be dismissed as sour grapes. In any event, few journalists felt much need for soul-searching. In the wake of Watergate, self-congratulation seemed more appropriate than self-criticism. Thus, the media's role in shaping the parameters of political debate continued to grow, as journalists cheerfully expanded their influence at the expense of politicians.

RONALD REAGAN AND THE MEDIA'S CRISIS OF CONFIDENCE

This tide crested with the election of a conservative Republican president in 1980. Ronald Reagan's core conservative constituency possessed a basic mistrust of the media traceable to the late 1960s and early 1970s. His people, for the most part, had been the losers in those very battles that enhanced the news media's self-image.

The memory of those earlier skirmishes did not subside when conservatives won the White House, but rather aggravated the traditionally ambivalent relationship between the press and presidents. As the *Washington Post's* editorial page editor Meg Greenfield put it during the 1980 campaign, "Most of the journalists I know... find Reagan's candidacy preposterous. He is to them what Margaret Thatcher was to many in the British electorate for years — the ultimate menace, what would get you in the night if you didn't eat your carrots."[1]

The feeling was mutual. Former White House Chief of Staff Donald Regan wrote in his memoirs that, "The Reagan White House had understood from the beginning that the press was not its natural ally.... Few journalists sympathized with Reagan's policies or were attracted by his personality."[2]

Not expecting to find adoration in the media's persistent gaze, the Reagan White House did not bother to seek it. This president possessed unusually strong communications skills, which enhanced his ability to bypass the media and win over many voters with direct appeals. In the eyes of many citizens, Reagan often "won" disputes with journalists over his policies, statements, and his facts.

Reporters themselves were frequently dumbfounded by the public's affection for Reagan in the face of critical coverage. Reported *Time* magazine in 1984: "Even Reagan's enemies marvel at his dirt-doesn't-stick 'Teflon' presidency. Voters forgive Reagan his verbal gaffes, and even his policy blunders."[3] In 1989, Reagan became the only president since the advent of modern television news to leave office with high levels of public support and approval, despite fallout from the Iran/contra scandal.

The fact that Reagan's popularity thrived in a supposedly hostile media environment prompted liberals to excoriate the press with a ferocity formerly mustered only by conservative critics. Once journalists' most dependable allies, many liberals now argued that the press had pulled its punches in covering Reagan and his administration.

Attempting to revive the sense of moral mission that reporters had developed in the 1960s, these critics charged the press with abandoning its role as public tribune. It had "abdicated its responsibility," according to Mark Hertsgaard, whose critique of media treatment of Reagan is evident from the title of his book, *On Bended Knee.*[4]

According to these critics, journalists — aware of the conservatives' animosity and distrust of the press — had failed to conduct a critical examination of the Reagan administration out of a fear of *seeming* partisan. "The press was struggling to overcome its parricidal guilt over Vietnam and Watergate," argued Berkeley sociologist Todd Gitlin. Reporters felt that "the temper of the country had shifted radically as a result of the 1980 election and they didn't want to be out of step."[5] In other words, liberals now argued that repeated attacks by conservative critics had rendered the press passive and ineffectual, content to be spoon-fed their "scoops" by a reactionary Republican administration.

For the most part, the mainstream media rejected the charge of a conservative bias. Journalists argued that liberals, like conservatives before them, were simply blaming the messenger. "There has not been a president in modern times," said the *New York Times'* Howell Raines, "whose intelligence was more thoroughly ridiculed and whose factual information was more routinely questioned" by the media.[6]

Steven Weisman, the *Times'* chief White House correspondent, also argued that reporters had been quite critical of Reagan. But, Weisman added, the president's ability to shape the content of his own message rendered him so powerful that media criticism had no effect:

The phenomenon of Ronald Reagan raises new questions about the appropriate role of the press. In the last three years, for example, some of the President's critics have said that reporters should more forcefully "take on" Mr. Reagan. Their assumption seems to have been that if the press would only expose the President and his techniques, or challenge him to his face, the public would rise up and repudiate him. In fact, reporters have been doing that quite diligently, but the President has successfully ignored them. On television, the President's rebuffs have reduced the role of reporters to the level of actors or even props in a presentation over which he has wielded nearly total control....

Mr. Reagan's success raises important concerns. The future application of his techniques may add to the already formidable powers of a President, both as Chief Executive and as candidate for re-election. Moreover, it could lead to a decline in the press's effectiveness as the stubborn, sometimes cantankerous monitor of the Presidency. Such a development could blunt one of the traditional checks and balances that have given flexibility and strength to the American political system.[7]

We shall return later to Weisman's contention — one shared by many of his colleagues — that by circumventing the daily press, the president developed an immunity against criticism. But the argument that the press had indeed challenged both Reagan and his policies is supported by systematic research. The scholarly evidence consistently indicates that Reagan's administration received more than its share of bad press — the watchdogs still had teeth. For example, based on an exhaustive content analysis of sixteen years' worth of presidential news, political scientist Fred Smoller concluded that, "Contrary to his popular image as a 'great communicator,' his acting skills, his landslide defeat of Carter, Ronald Reagan received more negative coverage than any of the [other] presidents" in his study.[8]

That would appear to be a difficult feat in itself, considering the other presidents were Richard Nixon, Gerald Ford, and Jimmy Carter, each of whom had his own problems with the national press corps. (Of course, Nixon fared worst of all during his second, Watergate-shortened term.) According to Smoller, Reagan was able to combat the media hostility and maintain his public support through a strategy of direct communication with voters, including weekly radio broadcasts, TV speeches, and political ads.

For a more limited time period, Michael Robinson and his colleagues analyzed all coverage of Reagan's policies from a wide range of news outlets — including the news magazines and major newspapers, as well as the networks — during 1983. They found *thirteen times* as many negative stories as positive ones. On a line-by-line basis, they counted 133 *more* critical statements than supportive ones. The authors call their findings "a stunning rebuke to those who believe that the media have somehow let Ronald Reagan get away with his presidency."[9]

In his study of the 1984 presidential campaign, Robinson found network news "painted Reagan as unavailable, uninvolved, uninformed, unengaged, and, above all, unrelenting in his manipulation of the media." "Nobody disputes that Reagan and Bush won the election," Robinson wrote, "but our measure of candidate spin shows that they lost the battle for the network news and lost it badly."[10]

Excluding references to polls, Robinson's study assigned Mondale an average media spin score of +1, which translates into a slight preponderance of positive over negative stories about the Democratic nominee. Reagan's spin was -33, which, according to Robinson's content analysis system, represents very bad press indeed: "All the networks reached an implicit consensus about Reagan," he reported: "He was winning but, given his politics and his behavior, [he] probably did not deserve to be."[11]

Robinson correlated his data on press spin with public opinion polls, and found a match: during periods when Reagan received better press, his favorability rating among voters went up; increased negative press cost him public support.[12] To be sure, the drop in Reagan's popularity was slight — negative news coverage obviously didn't cost Reagan the election — but it seems to have cost him at least some votes.

Smoller, too, found that shifts in the tone of Reagan's TV coverage matched, to a significant degree, shifts in his public approval rating.[13] Although both studies found that the price Reagan paid for his bad press was relatively small, both Smoller and Robinson convincingly refute the notion that Reagan enjoyed mild or positive treatment by the media. The data show that Reagan wasn't coasting during the 1980s. He faced at least his share of tough press (maybe more), but he and his advisors had developed tactics to blunt its consequences.

Those tactics — engaging in direct communication with voters, keeping his rhetoric and his message consistent, and avoiding exchanges with reporters when there was no benefit attached — became the stuff of legend among frustrated reporters trying to explain Reagan's approval ratings. But the scholarly studies suggest that, while the White House's scripted "media events" produced mild positive effects for Reagan throughout his presidency, these were easily overwhelmed by dramatic real-world events.

An examination of the ebb and flow of Reagan's public approval by political scientists Charles Ostrom and Dennis Simon showed that the president's speeches (mostly delivered in prime time) exerted a slight upward tug on his approval rating, while his foreign trips accounted for modest upticks. The state of the economy and other "uncontrollable political drama" exerted far more powerful effects on public opinion, pulling it either in a positive direction (such as the 1981 assassination attempt or the Soviet shootdown of KAL Flight 007 in 1983) or in a negative direction (such as the stock market crash in 1987 or the Iran/contra scandal). The authors concluded that their "analysis casts doubt on the claim that political drama is an effective general strategy for influencing public support." Reagan's speeches, while helpful to his cause, "[were not] sizable enough to neutralize the adverse effect of negative effects."[14]

If the Reagan team's stagecraft accounted for only a small portion of his overall popularity, it apparently accounted for much of the White House press corps' frustration. "A day-to-day fact of life in covering Reagan is that contact with him can be scarce," complained David Hoffman, a *Washington Post* reporter who covered the White House in 1984.

Days pass with only distant glimpses of Reagan at ceremonial events, and the White House is on constant vigil to protect him from reporters' questions. Apparently the loud engines of presidential helicopter Marine One are revved up deliberately on Friday afternoons so Reagan cannot hear — and thus cannot answer — the shouted questions as he leaves for Camp David.[15]

The helicopter complaint was routinely cited by reporters demanding more access to both Reagan and his administration.

CBS's Lesley Stahl grew so frustrated during the 1984 campaign that she crafted a four-minute story for the *Evening News* that, she hoped, would expose the White House's media strategy to the public. "The orchestration of television coverage absorbs the White House," she told her audience. Her story included harsh rhetoric about Reagan's policies, coupled with pictures of him at ceremonial events. The videotape, Stahl charged, was designed to mask the reality of the president's record:

> Mr. Reagan tries to counter the memory of an unpopular issue with a carefully chosen backdrop that actually contradicts the President's policy. Look at the handicapped Olympics, or the opening ceremony of an old-age home. No hint that he tried to cut the budgets for the disabled and for federally subsidized housing for the elderly.[16]

What happened after CBS broadcast Stahl's piece transformed it from just another negative story into the anecdote that crystallized journalists' frustration with Ronald Reagan. As she recounted soon after the 1984 election,

> No sooner was this fairly tough piece off the air than the White House called me to tell me how much they *liked* the piece. And I said, "Why?" And they said, "Because people don't hear what you say, they only see those great pictures of Ronald Reagan, and that's all they're seeing." So I think the press is reporting the issues and is pointing out when the president misspeaks, but the public isn't hearing it; they're just seeing the great pictures. And, you know, I don't know if therefore you could turn around and fault the press.[17]

Reporters already frustrated by Reagan's ability to communicate directly with voters must have despaired when told that their attempts to thwart the White House only rebounded in the president's favor. But that reaction may have been just the point of the phone call. This interpretation of Reagan's success, as founded on imagery rather than substance, promoted the impression that reporters were impotent against the Republican spinmeisters, who were the nation's real agenda setters.

It might have been instructive for Stahl to contemplate whether she herself was a victim of self-serving "spin" from a White House staffer seeking to aggrandize his own role in his boss's success. (Such activities are not unknown among political consultants.) The Reagan aide who applauded Stahl's story may well have been responsible for arranging the photogenic backdrops and contexts, which, the aide informed her, were so impressive that they overshadowed her text.

There is simply no empirical evidence for the alleged primacy of visual over verbal cues in explaining television's impact on presidential approval.[18] Indeed, the strong correlations various studies have reported between verbal TV news content and subsequent opinion change argue against the existence of strongly countervailing visual messages.[19] Sociologist Michael Schudson, who is no friend of the "Reagan revolution," calls the Stahl episode an instance of "telemythology" — an unfounded belief in the mystical power of video images to cloud the minds of TV viewers.[20]

Nonetheless, this often-repeated incident crystallized an argument that journalists came to embrace, despite its purely anecdotal status. Among those who accepted (and repeated) it at face value were such media heavy-weights as David Broder, Martin Schram, and Hedrick Smith. The notion that pictures of Reagan had more persuasive ability than reporters' tough words gained widespread credence because it served an important function: it explained his persistent popularity, while absolving journalism of the charge of going soft.

Not surprisingly, therefore, the notion of shadowy White House "spin doctors" became a mantra for reporters trying to explain Reagan's political success. "One poll reports many people are going to vote for Mr. Reagan despite their belief that [Democratic nominee Walter Mondale] is right on the fairness issue," opined Bill Moyers in his *CBS Evening News* commentary. "[Voters] like the President's personality. He projects the public persona, *helped by a vast propaganda machine.* Walter Mondale doesn't."[21] (Emphasis added.) The subtext of such arguments was that the news media, for all their vaunted success during the '60s and '70s, were losing influence to politicians and their public relations wizards.

Others wondered whether Reagan's popularity demonstrated a failing of the entire media system, or perhaps the citizenry itself. Social critic Neil Postman voiced his concern that television was destroying people's ability to understand civic discourse. Among the troubles he diagnosed was that citizens continued their support of a president who, the *New York Times* reported, made misleading statements.

Postman rhetorically wondered why the *Times'* report, along with similar stories, was not sufficient to sway the public against Reagan. To him, it was evidence that television had turned the public into ignoramuses:

> We [Americans] are losing our sense of what it means to be well informed. Ignorance is always correctable. But what shall we do if we take ignorance to be knowledge?.... The reporters who cover the White House are ready and able to expose lies, and thus create the grounds for informed and indignant opinion. But apparently the public declines to take an interest.[22]

By 1988, it had became conventional wisdom that President Reagan's political fortunes had been a function of blue smoke and mirrors, produced by the skillful practitioners of video politics. Even as it troubled those reporters like Hoffman, Weisman, and Stahl, who felt a loss of control over the political agenda, analyses like this offered assurances to those who resisted Reagan's allure during the '80s. Journalism professor Jay Rosen argued that for the "Reagan doubters and critics," the assumption that Reagan's strengths were purely a function of image served to confirm, the savvy and cynical tone that separates the political sophisticate from the aging hippie, the youthful idealist, the ignorant masses. In many conversations about politics during the 1980s I would hear someone say of Reagan (in that savvy and cynical way), "What do you expect? He's an actor for chrissakes." All would agree that this was the really important fact, not only about Reagan, but about America under Reagan: it had elected an actor because, through TV, its politics had become the management of illusions.[23]

By the end of his term, the journalistic consensus on Reagan was that he was a media manipulator, surrounded by skilled public relations experts who "controlled" the content of TV news. The word "control" appeared repeatedly in journalistic accounts of the Reagan media strategy. Weisman, for example, wrote that on television Reagan "wielded nearly total control."[24] The implication is that reporters and/or news organizations were somehow *compelled* to broadcast favorable pictures, soften their commentary, or otherwise aid in the care and feeding of Reagan's image.

In truth, what most "controlled" news organizations' political coverage during the '80s, as before and since, were journalists' professional norms regarding what is newsworthy and how it should be covered. What might have been unusual about the Reagan White House is that the staff understood how to anticipate the decisions news departments would make, and arranged their own schedules in order to maximize the political benefit for themselves. "Night after night, Reagan had his way with television news. He had succeeded in setting their agenda and framing their stories," Martin Schram wrote in 1987, "by posing for the cameras in one beautiful and compelling setting after another."[25]

Yet, "posing for the cameras" is hardly tantamount to compulsion. Such "wizardry" did not mean favorable press coverage for the president, as scholarly studies demonstrate. Nor did it protect him from severe losses in public support both during the 1981-82 recession and again after the initial Iran/contra disclosures.[26]

Ronald Reagan's White House had no special magic when it came to "news management," although his staff may have been more skilled than most. Reporters imputed such "magic" out of their own frustration and as a defense against charges from liberals who could not reconcile public support for Reagan with notions of an aggressive press corps or a well-informed public.

One other factor added to journalists' sense of being on the losing side of a public relations battle. It rankled reporters that the Reaganauts, in spite of their seeming wealth of media riches, missed no opportunity to express disdain and hostility toward the news media. Even while liberals were arguing that the media had gone *soft* on Reagan, conservatives were angry that the media were being too *tough* on him. The hostile coverage of

Reagan's agenda that journalists brandished in their defense against liberals was interpreted by conservatives as proof of liberal media bias.

In the early 1980s, a conservative group led by Jesse Helms attempted a hostile takeover of the CBS network, with the stated objective of dethroning news anchor Dan Rather and altering the news division's editorial policies. Conservative media-bashing resonated with citizens sympathetic to the Reagan regime; the faithful vented their ire in a barrage of postcards and letters. "The American people like Ronald Reagan, and they think the press are vultures, piranhas," UPI's Helen Thomas told a television interviewer. "Read my mail."[27] It was hardly a morale-builder.

Despite the absence of titanic political struggles such as those of the 1960s, the news media were again in the eye of the storm, surrounded by angry denunciations from liberals and conservatives alike. Both sides were angry with a media that they portrayed respectively as lapdogs or attack dogs. But both sides shared the assumptions that the media had power and that their messages mattered a great deal. Thus, the criticism also had the ironic effect of adding to the media's sense of self-importance as a social institution.

Journalists responded to these volleys of criticism by blaming the messengers. They dismissed liberals as too blinded by their own rage against Reagan to appreciate the fact that the media had consistently confronted the hard edges of the Reagan Revolution. They saw conservatives, who were winning elections and reducing reporters to TV props, as so power-hungry that they begrudged the media their constitutional right to check that power. Reporters knew very well that their conservative critics were often the same people who had fought them over civil rights, Vietnam, and Watergate.

Thus, media-bashing by Republicans was perceived as little more than a diversionary tactic to facilitate the conservative agenda by bypassing media scrutiny. Eminent journalists argued that conservatives were conspiring to create public disaffection with their profession. Haynes Johnson of the *Washington Post* wrote that "there has been a deliberate attempt to portray the press as the agent of America's problems, the enemy within... the political zealots, the hard-eyed haters and the lunatic conspiracy theorists have combined with public figures to poison the well about the press."[28]

Veteran Washington reporter James Deakin, who covered Presidents Eisenhower through Carter for the *St. Louis Post-Dispatch*, went even further. In his memoirs, he warned that, "There are people in the United States who very much want the public to believe the worst about the nation's journalists." These people were the "far right," and their goal was to create "the gravest possible distrust of the news media." Why? Because "the extreme right hopes to take the American nation as deeply as it can into authoritarian regions and absolutist doctrines.... *But the news media are standing in its way.*"[29] [Emphasis in the original.]

CAMPAIGN '88: THE CRISIS DEEPENS

After decades of steadily increasing political influence, many journalists came to believe that society needed them to assess the judgment, character, and policy proposals of politicians. Hence their frustration at Ronald Reagan's perceived success in diminishing their ability to challenge Republican policies. But many assumed that the problems Reagan and his media strategists had caused for their profession would depart Washington with him in 1988.

Among the candidates most likely to use Reagan's media tactics, attention centered on George Bush. Reagan's vice president had hired many of the same image-makers and consultants involved in the successful 1980 and 1984 campaigns. But Bush struck many as a weak candidate, whose jerky and uneven performances stood in stark contrast to Reagan's professional smoothness. "The widespread view in Washington and beyond was that there was something damp about Bush.... It had become nearly a mantra about Bush at the eve of battle; no one seemed to believe in him as a presidential politician, not even his friends."[30]

Bush only reinforced this view with his poor third-place showing in the Iowa caucuses (a state where he had beaten Reagan in 1980). His candidacy appeared to survive only because his organization had the muscle and money to capitalize on the calender's front-loading of contests. But even after he overshadowed his Republican opponents on Super Tuesday, clearing his path toward the nomination, Bush still struck many reporters as a weak nominee, particularly in comparison with the Great Communicator.

The general public was also hesitant about Bush. In mid-May, according to a Gallup poll, four out of ten Americans viewed him unfavorably, compared with 15% who viewed Democratic nominee-presumptive Michael Dukakis with disfavor. Bush trailed Dukakis by 16 percentage points (54% to 38%) in a trial heat conducted by Gallup.[31]

According to the *Newsweek* staff's collective account of the campaign, at that time Bush's own "strategists were quoting odds as high as 60-40 that a rank unknown named Dukakis was going to beat the vice president, decisively, in the fall."[32] The conventional wisdom among reporters during the spring and early summer was that the Republican lease on the White House was about to expire.

The Democrats, for their part, were giving more support than ever before to the Rev. Jesse Jackson. A protest candidate in 1984, this time around he was building a credible coalition of minorities and white progressives. Campaign reporters, normally a jaded lot, became swept up in his campaign's enthusiasm, and it showed in their reports. While his opponents fizzled on TV, Jackson sizzled.

Even as his delegate count climbed and his Democratic rivals dropped from the race, Jackson was largely exempted from the tough scrutiny that marked the other major candidates' coverage. Correspondent Judy Muller, then with CBS Radio News, described her response to one of Jackson's exhortative, motivational, and inspirational rallies:

> When Geraldine Ferraro became the Democratic candidate for vice president, I stood on the convention floor and fought back tears. Forget objectivity: the moment transcended politics. As I followed the Jesse Jackson campaign in Philadelphia yesterday [April 25], I fell on the same phenomenon: a transcendent pride in this person's breakthrough. You could see it on the faces of people on Locust Street... you could hear it in the voice of the gospel singer at a Jackson rally.[33]

But the race factor cut both ways in defining Jackson's coverage. Despite the praise, Jackson's supporters charged that both his 1984 and 1988 campaigns were hobbled by reporters' unwillingness to treat him as a serious presidential candidate. Political scientist Anthony Broh documented the media's skepticism toward Jackson's electability in 1984. Our examination of network news confirmed that, despite heavy praise for the man, reporters did not treat Jackson's candidacy as viable either in 1984 or during the early primaries in 1988.[34]

Reporters' perceptions changed after Jackson soundly defeated Michael Dukakis in the March 26 caucuses in Michigan. The media's newfound appreciation for Jackson's viability led them to change their approach to covering his candidacy. As the first black to mount a "serious" presidential candidacy, his campaign acquired a historic significance that endowed his coverage with a positive cast unavailable to his opponents.

Even as Michael Dukakis systematically accumulated delegates, Jackson remained the campaign's media superstar, getting by far the best press of any candidate.[35] Reporters were largely reluctant to tarnish his historic candidacy by treating Jackson as just another politician. The "transcendent pride" that radiated from his audiences to journalists like Judy Muller left no room for the usual sniping about strategy and tactics.

Despite the media groundswell for Jackson, the emerging nominee was Michael Dukakis, the previously obscure liberal governor of Massachusetts. Dukakis was helped by his newness to the national scene and the sense that his stewardship in Massachusetts was a solid success, even if it lacked glamour and glitz.

Dukakis was a candidate whom most Democrats initially felt comfortable with at the top of their '88 ticket. Prior to the Iowa caucuses, a *Newsweek* poll of party insiders — including governors, senators, state, local, and county officials — showed 60% believed Democratic chances of victory were "good" or "excellent" in 1988 and that Dukakis was "the nominee most likely to beat a G.O.P. opponent."[36]

By the time of his nomination in July, the governor led Bush in the polls, and the Democratic party was growing increasingly comfortable with the campaign abilities and prospects of its frontrunning nominee: "To the surprise of many in the party," the *New York Times'* E. J. Dionne wrote on the eve of the nominating convention, "their prospective Presidential nominee, Michael S. Dukakis, is in an unusually strong position to win the election."[37]

Similarly, David Gergen told a national television audience that "Republicans are in for a tough race... the country is ready for change and they've got a candidate who is willing to rise to the occasion."[38] The early polls seemed to affirm the instant analysis: Dukakis emerged from Atlanta with a 17-point lead over Bush, and the vice president arrived at his Republican convention as the widely perceived underdog in the general election match-up.[39]

The apparent weakness of Bush's campaign, and the perceived strength of the Democrats, radically altered the perceptual relationship between the media and the Republicans. While the G.O.P. continued to complain about the "liberal media elite," their grumblings once again resembled sour grapes. Reporters still believed Bush was doing his best to pull off a Reaganesque campaign — replete with staged events, a shallow agenda, and the avoidance of all contact with reporters — but it did not appear to be paying off. Perhaps the Republicans weren't so tough, after all.

The toughness would reappear in unexpected circumstances. Setting the stage was Vice President Bush's surprise pick of Indiana Senator Dan Quayle as his running mate, a selection revealed on the second day of the Republican nominating convention. It took only hours for Quayle to become, in the words of CBS's Lesley Stahl, "the vice presidential pick that ate the Republican convention."[40]

Bush's campaign had meant to showcase their new co-star by making him available for live interviews with each of the three network anchors at the start of Wednesday night's prime time coverage. Instead, the interviews highlighted new details and possible inconsistencies in Quayle's discussion of his military service record. Perhaps, he offered to Tom Brokaw, some telephone calls were made on his behalf to arrange his admittance to the Indiana National Guard. Some began to wonder whether or not a young Dan Quayle had used his Guard duty as a means to avoid active military service in the Vietnam War. A "feeding frenzy" began.

It can hardly be considered a surprise that the press would pounce on a story like Quayle's military service. After all, political conventions are scripted by political consultants rather than network producers. A well-managed convention that follows its script normally produces no surprises and certainly generates no unexpected headlines. In such an environment, a genuine news story can act as a trumpet blast, startling a somnolent press corps into frantic activity. The "feeding flurry," as Bush originally termed it, was due in no small part to the starvation diet that preceded it.

Nor can it be overlooked that the Quayle story was partially fueled by some of the Republicans who considered his selection a mistake. NBC correspondent Ken Bode offered his audience a series of stinging critiques of Quayle, all of which bore the fingerprints of G.O.P. insiders:

> The selection of Dan Quayle was a big surprise to the folks on this [convention] floor tonight, and that's why many of the Republican sources that we usually talk to are speaking to us only, honestly, only off-the-record. Let me share with you some of the remarks without identifying these sources any more than I'm about to — what they really think of this selection of Quayle. A seasoned politician from California told me that he thought Quayle had only been on the list to give him some publicity. A former Republican National Committee official said, "Last night at dinner we were joking about Quayle. We trashed him!" A very famous conservative said, "It makes Bush look like he wasn't strong enough to pick Dole or Kemp." And from Indiana today, one of Dan Quayle's home-state politicians said, "It can't be Quayle. Can it really?"[41]

Of course, reporters aren't lemmings. The coverage reflected their own judgments as well as "reality." In Quayle's case, for example, ABC chose to give the story only about half as much prime time coverage as its competitors at CBS and NBC.[42] Thus, journalists had powerful incentives — based on their own definition of news — to cover the Quayle story, but some news organizations displayed enough restraint to prevent the story from "eating" the Republican convention. What made the Quayle story seem unusual was the incredible number of reporters on-site (one estimate put the total at more than 15,000), and the fact that the entire news-gathering process was broadcast on live national television.

Regardless of what fueled it, the Quayle case stands as a classic example of media overkill. Our analysis of the convention coverage that year showed that Quayle received more than twice as much coverage during the four-day convention as Bush himself. In the 12 days that followed his selection, Quayle was the focus of 93 stories on the evening news. That amounted to more coverage in two weeks than Jackson, Dukakis, or any other Democrat received during the first six months of 1988.

During that brief period, 50 news stories — over four a night — targeted Quayle's military service record; another 19 talked about his privileged background, and 13 focused on his alleged relationship with lobbyist (and one-time *Playboy* pin-up) Paula Parkinson. By contrast, Quayle's career in Congress was noted in only 15 stories.

While Republicans gamely continued to praise Quayle, and Democrats began to find their voice in opposition, reporters — freed from the confines of the Superdome — sought out quotes from "non-partisan" sources, or individuals not directly affiliated with either campaign or party. The opinions of non-partisan sources are the most important for imparting an overall tone to a news story, and studies have found that they have the most impact on public opinion.[43] On-air judgments of Quayle from these sources were 67% negative (i.e. only 33% positive).[44] In 1988, only Gary Hart fared worse.

The disdain felt by reporters also began to show up in their own comments. For example, CBS's Jacqueline Adams zapped Quayle as "a not-ready-for-prime-time player" whose "pro-defense rhetoric was almost comical."[45] Dan Quayle's introduction to the American public failed because the Bush campaign had not impressed those who truly mattered: the political press corps who would transmit Quayle's story to the public. Their assessment that Quayle was "comical" set the stage for a confrontation that would aggrieve reporters as much as any act of stage-management during the Reagan years.

The campaign journeyed to Quayle's boyhood home in Huntington, Indiana, on the Friday after the convention. According to press reports, the rally was studded with anti-media signs ("Media Poachers Beware," "Sam Donaldson, Rip Out Your Tongue," and "Save the Quayles from Media Bull"), an indication that the campaign intended to use the rally to protest the media's ongoing scrutiny of Quayle.

After speeches by both nominees, Quayle agreed to take reporters' questions about the controversies that had been swirling for three days. Ostensibly to help reporters hear the give-and-take, Quayle used a public address system to broadcast the questions and answers to the reporters and the crowd that was still assembled.

According to several reports, the press's questions were "combative" (Sample: "[How did you feel] when people were dying in Vietnam while you were writing press releases?"), and the crowd grew surly: "The crowd, visibly angry, booed question after question," and "cursed and catcalled as Quayle was asked if he used [his family's influence] to enter the Guard in 1969."[46]

News stories quoted Huntington residents expressing their displeasure with the media. David Summers, also a former National Guardsman, appeared in several newspaper articles saying, "Dan Quayle is a clean, decent family man and it's time the national press understood that."[47]

At the time, some reporters expressed the belief that the entire confrontation had been arranged by Republican operatives hoping to intimidate them into dropping the story. Campaign chairman James Baker went out of his way to assure reporters (who were described as "furious" in one story) that the incident was not a "setup." In spite of the denials, some reporters continued to believe that the set-to was "a deliberate G.O.P. setup designed to make the press do (and look) its worst."[48]

If the Republicans did stage the event in order to soften the tone of Quayle's coverage, it had the opposite effect. After the Huntington confrontation, the tone of his on-air evaluations dropped to a remarkable four-to-one negative margin (79% negative, 21% positive). The Huntington incident put reporters on their guard that the Bush campaign had no qualms about using (or abusing) them, and that media manipulation in Campaign '88 might not be as smooth and painless as it was during Reagan's campaigns.

The conventional wisdom that Bush was a weak or inept candidate was also collapsing, as the vice president seemingly re-invented himself after the convention. In his speeches and his paid TV commercials, he aggressively painted Dukakis as a liberal failure, ridiculed him as both weak on defense and short on foreign policy expertise, and tweaked him for deficits in Boston and refuse in Boston Harbor. Despite the media's Quayle hunt, Bush's convention "bounce" took him from seven percentage points behind Dukakis in the polls to four points in front.[49]

As the fall campaign progressed, Bush's lead did not prove transitory, as often happens to post-convention increases. Instead, it continued to swell. By the first presidential debate, in Winston-Salem on September 25, Dukakis trailed by nearly 10 points.[50] Bush's "favorability" rating among the public had remained steady at about 50%, while Dukakis's favorability had deteriorated from about 50% to 40%.

The debates marked the decisive turning point in the conventional wisdom on Bush's campaign skills. Long derided for his occasionally antic style, Bush was roundly criticized for exclaiming after his 1984 debate with Geraldine Ferraro that he had "kicked a little ass." Many pundits looked for Bush to blow the election in a fit of wild gesticulation or verbal malapropism during the Winston-Salem debate or the rematch in Los Angeles on October 13. According to the pundits' post-debate analysis, however, he did not.

It was also considered possible that Quayle's defeat by Lloyd Bentsen in the vice presidential debate on October 5 might prompt significant numbers of Bush voters to bolt to Dukakis and Bentsen. According to post-debate polls, they did not. For the first time during the long campaign, campaign trail insiders began to view a Bush victory as a *fait accompli.*

The remainder of the campaign coverage was heavily salted with an incongruous series of pre-election post-mortems, which attempted to put Bush's victory into context before it even occurred. Three weeks before the election, *Newsweek's* Howard Fineman answered the question "Why Bush is

Winning." His take: "He benefits from the Republicans' well-honed marketing skills, hardball tactics and skillful manipulation of 'hot-button' issues."[51]

The story reflected perfectly the emerging consensus among campaign reporters. Having reported mainly on the candidates' strategies and tactics for the past ten months, they now gave these same factors the lion's share of credit for the prospective outcome. What this emphasis on the "inside story" neglects is the degree to which voters' perceptions (and ultimate choices) are structured by conditions external to (and even prior to) the campaign.

This insight forms the rationale for econometric models that have accurately predicted the popular and electoral voting distributions in presidential elections prior to the party conventions, on the basis of variables such as the inflation rate, G.D.P., and presidential approval ratings (even for retiring incumbents).[52] For example, one such model came within one percentage point of predicting the Democratic popular vote in 1988, *before* Michael Dukakis became the nominee, Willie Horton became a household name, or George Bush became a master media manipulator.[53]

These models are the subject of a rather esoteric scholarly debate, and they do not necessarily demonstrate that campaigns don't count.[54] At minimum, though, they serve as a reminder that journalists can be too quick to lend a "halo effect" to victorious campaigns, attributing success to campaign skills and failure to ineptitude almost by reflex.

As journalists sifted through the entrails of the still-ongoing campaign, Bush and the Republicans also came in for criticism of the propriety of their winning ways. "Almost from the beginning" of the campaign, according to *U.S. News & World Report*, "the print press (sic), while faithfully reporting the boost Bush got from his clever, media-genic stunts, also remarked on their essential emptiness."[55] While television may have joined the game late, network correspondents disparaged Bush's tactics with a gusto that matched their print counterparts.

A case in point was Bush's visit to a New Jersey flag factory on September 20. The candidates' ongoing game of capture-the-flag prompted NBC's Lisa Myers to remind her audience of "Samuel Johnson's observation that 'patriotism is the last refuge of a scoundrel.'" She also noted sarcastically that the American flags handed out at campaign rallies were made in Taiwan. That same day, after Gov. Dukakis unveiled his proposals on national health care, NBC resurrected an archival clip of Bush saying he didn't know how many Americans lacked coverage.[56]

The juxtaposition of old quotes, new quotes, and commentary left no doubt that reporters agreed with the Dukakis aides who, according to NBC's Chris Wallace, "hope the vice president's highly packaged events are beginning to wear thin, especially in contrast to their man's detailed new programs."[57]

Over on CBS that same night, correspondents Bob Schieffer and Bruce Morton commiserated about the candidates' media strategies with anchor Dan Rather. After spending nearly six minutes reporting on how candidates seek to "control the pictures and content of day-to-day press coverage," Morton asked, "When was the last time you heard [about] the deficit in one of those little sound bites?" Rather, chuckling: "Can't remember."[58]

Democrats, hoping to spark a backlash, echoed the media's criticism of Bush's campaign tactics in their own paid advertising. One series of ads featured actors who portrayed Bush's "handlers," a cynical gang scheming ways to evade the issues and promote their candidate. Its tag line: "They'd like to sell you a package. Wouldn't you rather choose a President?" Dukakis also aired a TV commercial in which he angrily turned off his television set when it aired a Bush attack ad. On the stump, he accused Bush of lying and "dragging the truth into the gutter."[59]

In late October, Lloyd Bentsen and Jesse Jackson raised this line of criticism to a new level when they characterized Bush's campaign tactics as "racist." The reason: a Bush ad that criticized a Massachusetts prison furlough program from which 268 convicted criminals had escaped.[60] The Bush campaign's ad made the same points as one sponsored by an independent conservative group that spotlighted the case of one escapee, an African-American murderer named Willie Horton. While at large, Horton had kidnapped and terrorized a married couple. Bush had spoken about the case in his speeches, without mentioning Horton's race.

The implied message, charged Texas Democratic Rep. Mickey Leland, was that "if Dukakis gets into the White House, they're going to let a bunch of black people loose and they're going to rape and kill and pillage."[61] *Time* accused the ad of "stirring racial fears," and questioned the "relish," "glee," and "ardor" with which Bush's staff promoted the Horton story. The magazine called the convicted murderer the "most valuable player in George Bush's no-holds-barred bid for the White House."[62]

Notwithstanding the critics' outrage, empirical evidence of Horton's impact on the campaign is minimal. The independent ad, produced by a group called the National Security Political Action Committee (and the only one to reveal Horton's race) began airing in September. The ad was seen only on cable stations that reached about 5% of the population. Bush's own ad, called "Revolving Door," did not begin airing until October 3. It featured mostly white "prisoners" walking through a turnstile.

Thus, both the Horton ad and "Revolving Door" debuted *after* the opinion turnaround that had propelled Bush to a solid lead in the polls. In spite of the news media attention paid to both ads, neither appears to have moved significant numbers of voters away from Dukakis and toward Bush (although it may be that the charges against Dukakis helped to solidify Bush's support among voters who had switched earlier).

In the wake of the Willie Horton controversy, critics developed a new charge against television news: In the process of reporting the use of campaign commercials, journalists were inadvertently providing free publicity to ads the networks would have otherwise refused to broadcast.[63] Although the networks took a tough tone, the news stories also included the essentials of both ads — that Dukakis was signing furloughs for hardened criminals, some of whom juries had sentenced to life in prison, and some of whom escaped while on furlough.

While the ads themselves appear to have provided, at best, a minor boost for Bush, journalists' criticisms served to further publicize their basic message. Notably, the critics did not argue against the ads' factual correctness, only that they were negative, unfair, or needed to be understood in a broader context — the sort of qualified criticism that carries less weight than a charge of outright lying.

More consequential may have been the damage to Bush's reputation and the backlash among news organizations. Even after the start of his "kinder, gentler" presidency, journalists such as the *Boston Globe's* Tom Oliphant scorned his attempt to cover "his Dr. Faustus pact with his media meisters with a protective blanket of puppies, horseshoes and affability."[64]

Bush's alleged culpability was not the only problem. Reporters also believed that, if a wrong had been done, they had been unwitting accomplices. They perceived the Horton ad as negative and extreme, and their response (appropriate, they thought) was to single it out for condemnation in their news stories. However harsh the glare, though, their coverage had the effect of moving the Horton story from the shadows to the spotlight. Thus, journalists faced condemnation from Democrats and from each other for disseminating its odious message freely in their news stories.

News organizations were troubled by more than the expert use of negative advertising to engineer another Republican presidency. They were beset by charges, which grew in frequency after Election Day, that the news media was an obliging partner in Bush's victory. This echoed similar complaints heard during Reagan's presidency. But the charges in 1988 seemed much more telling, since George Bush the candidate lacked most of Ronald Reagan's skills as a communicator. To wit:

> [Bush's] public appearances were choreographed as carefully as Ronald Reagan's, by some of the same dance masters. His settings were chosen to flatter him on television, usually in sunshine, sometimes in shirtsleeves. His performances were stage-managed down to the last spontaneous gesture; an advance man down front would signal him when to flash a thumbs-up sign, when to fling his

arms aloft and when to start speaking. His texts were reduced to five-by-seven index cards, periodically modified in form to break his habit of tromping on his own material.

Whatever Bush was, an aide said, he was not Reagan; he could actually correct lines to ensure that they *wouldn't* get applause. His card-makers first tried putting his best shots at the ends of paragraphs, hoping he would get the hint and pause a moment before plunging on. He didn't, not till his people, in desperation, redid his cards with the punch lines at the bottom; he *had* to stop at least long enough to flip the next card.[65]

Bush's success could not be explained by his skills as a speechmaker, television presence, or communicator. Reporters ascribed to him none of Reagan's magic "Teflon" that allegedly enabled him to survive damning criticism with his popularity intact. Bush's electoral success was, for many journalists, the "smoking gun" that proved their liberal critics were right: the press was indeed too passive in its approach to politics. As that conclusion rippled through the media in a stream of angry op-ed articles, many reporters began to reconsider whether liberals had been correct all along in condemning a passive press.

For their part, many Democrats — eager to find excuses for the painful and unexpected loss of their third presidential campaign in a row — sought to exploit the media's fears that it had been used by the Republicans. "I said in my acceptance speech at Atlanta that the 1988 election was not about ideology, but about competence," Dukakis said in 1990 "I was wrong. It was about phraseology. It was about 10-second soundbites. And made-for-TV backdrops. And going negative."[66]

Dukakis, perhaps unconsciously, echoed the remarks made by Walter Mondale after his loss in 1984: "Modern politics requires mastery of television," he told a gathering of reporters on the morning after his landslide defeat. "I've never warmed up to television, and it's never warmed up to me."[67]

Four Democratic members of Congress (including future White House Chief of Staff Leon Panetta) issued a public letter to ABC, CBS, CNN, and NBC asking them, in effect, to withhold the carrot of TV coverage from those candidates who used the stick of negative campaigning. "It is only the assurance that the networks will provide daily coverage of campaign events, no matter how superficial or lacking in news content, that allows current campaign practices to continue," the congressmen wrote.[68]

The victors in '88 had their own reasons for accepting this criticism of the campaign. The professional political operatives — chiefly Lee Atwater, James Baker, and Roger Ailes — wanted to apply some polish to their own tarnished images. First, they did not offer much resistance to the charge that an unusually negative and trivial campaign had been run (note the passive voice). That implied concession carried no particular costs after the election, and the act of contrition made for good public relations. In any case, the charge was so widely held that the labor of debunking it required expense far more than an apology.

They also offered their own critique of Campaign '88. The Republicans argued that the underlying problem was the news media's approach to campaign coverage: Campaign tactics had been transformed by television and its short attention span. Sound bites were a campaign response to television's time constraints. Blistering negative comments from the candidates were a response to the observation that TV is most likely to cover a story about conflict. Staging a campaign event in a photogenic manner is more likely to attract coverage.

They also brought back the argument that had worked so well with Lesley Stahl in 1984: If the visual image conveyed the point of the event, it would "speak" to viewers even if newscasts omitted the candidate's own words in favor of a reporter's voice-over. "Unless there were radical changes in press coverage and expectations, [Roger Ailes] warned, the politicians were not going to change the rules of the game and '92 would very likely be worse than '88."[69]

Each for their own reasons, then, Republicans and Democrats offered news reporters a bipartisan critique of the problems caused by their coverage. They argued that the effect of two of the media's most well-documented traits — the penchant for horse race news and lack of interest in policy issues — gave network news a predictive quality that campaigns could exploit. The norms of television news production could be anticipated by savvy campaign strategists who manufacture sound bites and sound bombs, telegenic backdrops and enthusiastic crowds, in order to ensure that the finished news story is helpful to their candidates.

Those aspects of modern campaigns that academics, journalists, and voters thought most objectionable, the politicians argued, were the result of the peculiar incentives campaigns were given by the news media. It followed that, if this incentive structure (free TV coverage for candidates who used snappy sound bites and engaged in negative campaigns, and no coverage for those who favored boring policy discussions and lacked vivid pictures) were changed, then campaigns would react by ending the offensive practices and instituting those rewarded by the new system.

Academic critics offered a third critique that was not shared by the conservatives: namely, that a professional commitment to objectivity prevented journalists from condemning egregious campaign tactics without skewing coverage toward an artificial (and unfair) balance. In 1988, that tendency played into the hands of the Bush operatives, who, it was charged, played fast and loose with the truth, knowing that the news would not single out his candidacy for blame.

Writing soon after the election, Marvin Kalb called the coverage "shallow and distinctly timid." Kalb, a former network correspondent who now heads Harvard University's Joan Shorenstein Barone Center on the Press, Politics, and Public Policy, faulted television for not challenging the candidates, particularly Bush.[70] "It was very difficult, given that visual structure," added Annenberg School of Communications Dean Kathleen Hall Jamieson, "to make the point that Bush's ads were, one, effective and, two, lies, and that Dukakis's ads were, one, ineffective and, two, truthful."[71]

As the critics saw it, Bush had run by far the dirtier campaign, but the media balanced the blame between both candidates. For campaigns to improve, journalists had to move beyond "balance" toward truth-telling. They must single out those candidates whose speeches or ads contained verifiable falsehoods or were otherwise misleading. Otherwise, candidates would continue to engage in disreputable campaign practices, knowing that the blame would be spread evenly.

For years, academics had criticized campaign journalism for its games-manship and superficiality. Now, Democrats and journalists themselves added their conviction that these tendencies had adversely affected the outcome of the '88 presidential race. If the media had cared more about substance and issues, and less about strategies and tactics, they agreed, then Bush would not have enjoyed an unfair advantage over his all-substance and no-tactics opponent.

The Republicans offered no rebuttal, except to argue that their choice of tactics was a product of the media environment they confronted in 1988. Journalists were especially troubled at the politicians' apparent consensus that they had been used, to great effect, by one campaign against the other. If a candidate as weak as George Bush could use them as a weapon to gain a partisan advantage, then the rules and norms of political journalism needed to be changed.

CORRECTING THE RECORD

The normative standard for judging campaign news differs somewhat from one critic to another and is not readily measurable. But a preferred version of media coverage is at least an implicit component of most criti-cisms of actual coverage. To varying degrees, the critics faulted the media (especially television) for failing to provide coverage that was substantive and tough-minded while being in some sense "fair" to both candidates.

Were the critics right? The actual content of the Campaign '88 news, happily, is more easily measured than the normative ideal. Indeed, political scientists have used content analysis to put the media under the microscope during campaigns as far back as 1968. Measuring the content of the news coverage is useful in two ways: it allows for a contextual understanding of those traits (both admirable and objectionable) which become the targets of media criticism; and it provides an empirical test of the specific criticisms that are raised.

Content analysis has been used frequently by social science researchers to quantitatively describe and analyze news media content. This technique allows researchers to classify the news rigorously and systematically according to explicit rules and clear criteria. It occupies the same status in communications research that scientific polling does in public opinion research.

The goal is to produce valid measures of news content, and the hallmark of success lies in reliability. Other investigators who apply the same procedures to the same material should obtain the same results (although their interpretations of those results may differ). Put differently, content analysis is an excellent tool for settling disputes over the "who," "what," "when," and "where" of media coverage. As in journalism, the "how" and "why" are more difficult to establish.

Our content analysis of television news during the 1988 campaign reveals a quite different picture from that painted by many critics. Most importantly, the networks' coverage was notable for both its balance and its toughness. The networks offered viewers more than incidental discussion of the issues — there was substance in the networks' Campaign '88 coverage. The campaign "horse race" was the focal point for much of the coverage, but no more so than in previous campaigns. In fact, the crucial final weeks of the campaign saw declining coverage of the race itself, and increased media attention to the voters and the issues.

We found that Bush and Dukakis received similar proportions of good and bad press (each was the subject of twice as much criticism as praise), a datum that may not alleviate the suspicions of those who saw an "artificial" balance in the coverage. Yet this goes back to our earlier point — different individuals and groups preferred a different type of coverage. For many reporters, balance remains an appropriate and desirable goal. Our measure of good and bad press is not a measure of good and bad journalism, but it does provide a solid foundation for understanding the real story of Campaign '88.

Focus on the Issues: Critics charged that news coverage of the 1988 general election campaign failed to focus on the issues. Our monitoring of every

Figure 2-1

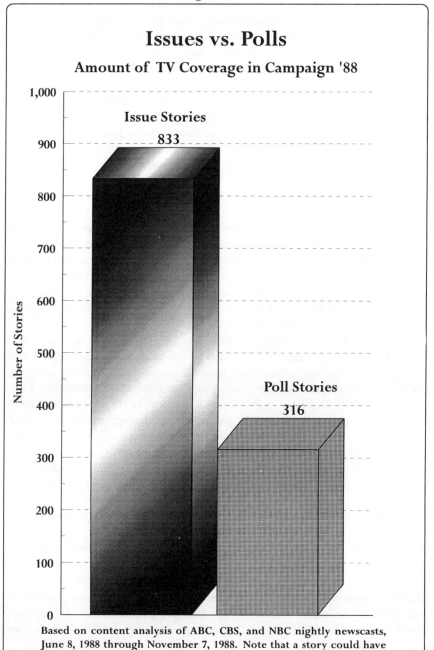

Issues vs. Polls

Amount of TV Coverage in Campaign '88

Issue Stories
833

Poll Stories
316

Number of Stories

Based on content analysis of ABC, CBS, and NBC nightly newscasts,
June 8, 1988 through November 7, 1988. Note that a story could have
featured both issues and polls.

election story on the ABC, CBS, and NBC evening newscasts tells a different story. From the end of the primaries until election day, more than 200
network evening news stories discussed the state of the national economy.
Major policy areas such as defense, crime, taxes, unemployment, illegal
drugs, and foreign policy were each discussed in over 100 stories. (Many
stories discussed more than one issue.)

Overall, two out of three post-primary campaign news stories (65%, or
833 in all) dealt with at least one policy issue, while fewer than half as many
(316, or 25% of all stories) reported on the results of public opinion polls.
(See Figure 2-1.) While the critics may be right to argue that this is an
excessive number of polling stories, they are wrong in assuming that the
horse race drove the issues from the airwaves.

Why, then, did the impression exist that the TV coverage gave short shrift
to the issues in '88? In his speech to the National Press Club, Bush
campaign chairman James Baker recounted how a network newscast refused
to cover the vice president when he gave a policy address because, the
producer told him, "You didn't have any sound bites, and you didn't attack
Dukakis." Baker said that "the frustration that the press and the public have
expressed with respect to the candidates not talking about substance is
matched... by the frustration of the candidates that the substance that they
do put forward is too often lost in the noise."[72]

We suggest that the substance that journalists put forward is also "often
lost in the noise" of a campaign. Issue stories tend to be less dramatic and
therefore less memorable than other kinds of stories (such as those featuring
the latest poll results, candidate contretemps, or interesting "visuals"). Even
when journalists dutifully report on the "issues," they do not consider them
as interesting or "newsworthy" as the more exciting personality aspects of
campaigns. Both the issues and the coverage they receive are easily forgot-
ten, and hence underestimated in retrospective appraisals.

We already noted, for example, that on September 20 Vice President Bush
visited a flag factory and Gov. Dukakis unveiled his health care plan. Both
received network coverage that day. In the weeks that followed, however, it
was the notorious flag factory visit that inspired the pens of pundits and
columnists, while the Dukakis health care plan was all but ignored.

Even as the day-to-day coverage moved on to other issues and events, the
more general media "buzz" continued to dwell on the Bush campaign's use
of the flag issue (and its connection to other symbolic issues, such as
patriotism and fair campaigning) because such things were of interest to
journalists. The health insurance issue was not of much interest that year.
While it received a dutiful news account, its half-life was far shorter than
that of the flag "issue."

Similarly, on October 12, ABC's *World News Tonight* spent more than half
of the newscast reporting on a poll, conducted jointly with the *Washington*

Table 2-1

Rank of Partisan Issues
in Overall News Agenda

Rank	Issue	Stories	Whose Issue
1.	Economy	213	—
2.	Defense	191	**Republican**
3.	Crime	175	**Republican**
4.	Taxes	143	**Republican**
5.	Unemployment	127	—
6.	Drugs	114	*Democrat*
7.	Foreign Policy	109	**Republican**
8.	Civil Rights	85	*Democrat*
9.	Education	70	*Democrat*
10.	Budget Deficit	70	*Democrat*

Note -- Based on content analysis of ABC, CBS, and NBC evening newscasts, June 8, 1988 through November 7, 1988. Stories may have included more than one issue mention.

Post, which showed Bush with a significant lead in likely electoral college votes. The story aired the night before the final debate between the two presidential candidates. It quickly became a source of controversy, with the Dukakis camp and some journalists that charging ABC was attempting to declare Bush the de facto winner.[73] The policy issues addressed in the final debate — taxes, deficits, the death penalty, military spending, arms control, and abortion, among others — faded from memory as the ABC poll was challenged or reinforced by dozens of new surveys in the campaign's final days.

Voters interested in substantive issues had plenty of chances to hear about the candidates' policy views in those final weeks of Campaign '88, even though none of the issue stories had as much effect among journalists and the political community as the ABC poll. While the voters' opportunity for learning was certainly no worse than that of previous campaigns, the recollections of the coverage were more heavily influenced by the bumps, bounces, and spikes of the horse race.

What, then, accounts for the strenuous objections raised against issue coverage during Campaign '88? One factor may have been the G.O.P.'s success in shaping the policy debate. Of the ten most frequently discussed issues of the campaign, four could be reliably classified as "Republican" issues, and four others categorized as "Democratic" issues.[74] As Table 2-1 shows, the Republican-favored issues received the most news coverage, with three of the four (defense, crime, and taxes) receiving more TV time than any Democratic issue.

The higher profile given to the Republicans' issue agenda may have fueled the criticism that the networks were acting as little more than mouthpieces of the Bush campaign, despite the fact that the G.O.P. was mostly dishing out standard campaign fare.

While the data offer some support to those who argued that the news agenda favored Bush in '88, they contradict those who claimed the Republicans were aided by the superficiality of the coverage. Bush's (and the G.O.P.'s) "advantage" was that the campaign debate was dominated by talk of taxes, crime, and national defense. But that is quite different from the assertions that the coverage was lacking in issue content, or that the networks gave Bush a free ride in the way they covered those issues.

Hyping the Horse Race? The horse race has been documented as a dominant feature of campaign news as long as systematic studies have been conducted. Over the entire ten months of the 1988 campaign, more than one-third of the network stories (777 stories, or 35%) featured lengthy discussions of the viability and prospects of the various candidates. Yet, as Figure 2-2 shows, horse race news peaked during primary season rather than

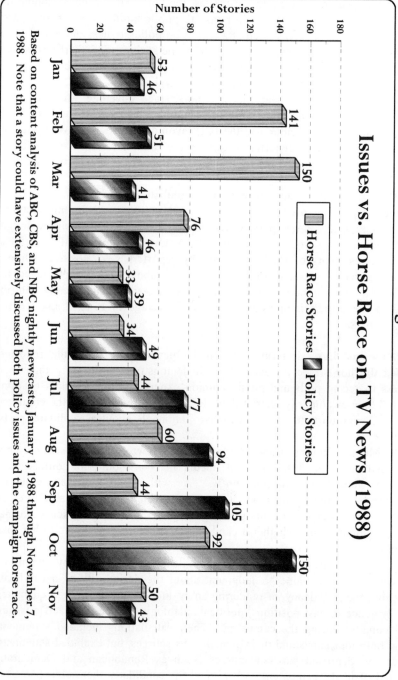

Figure 2-2

Issues vs. Horse Race on TV News (1988)

Number of Stories

Horse Race Stories
Policy Stories

	Horse Race	Policy
Jan	53	46
Feb	141	51
Mar	150	41
Apr	76	46
May	33	39
Jun	34	49
Jul	44	77
Aug	60	94
Sep	44	105
Oct	92	150
Nov	50	43

Based on content analysis of ABC, CBS, and NBC nightly newscasts, January 1, 1988 through November 7, 1988. Note that a story could have extensively discussed both policy issues and the campaign horse race.

the fall campaign. During the primaries, the horse race received double the TV coverage devoted to discussions of public policy. After the party conventions, the networks aired 282 stories on policy issues, and only 168 on the horse race — a complete reversal from the spring. The chart also shows that policy issues, neglected during the spring and summer, received extensive air time during the much-maligned general election period.

Although it is not clear that the horse race coverage was any more excessive in 1988 than in previous presidential campaigns, the tone of horse race predictions (particularly in the fall) favored Republicans. We tallied all statements from news reporters regarding the candidates' chances, including poll results, analysis, and reporter speculation about the impact of each day's events.

After the Republican convention, journalists judged Bush as a likely winner, especially after the ABC electoral college poll in mid-October. Conversely, Dukakis was portrayed as a likely loser, whose odds grew longer with each passing week. (See Figure 2-3.) Overall, four out of five (80%) on-air assessments of Bush's viability by reporters were positive, while a similar percentage (82%) of their comments about Dukakis portrayed his chances as poor. The tone of the horse race coverage undoubtedly contributed to the critic's impressions that TV's coverage *in general* favored the G.O.P. in '88.

Balance and Bias   In terms of the media bias debate, the fact that reporters called the horse race in favor of Bush demonstrates little more than their access to recent polls and public opinion experts. When scholars examine "bias," they customarily restrict their definition to include only the commentary and opinion that reflect normative judgments about a candidate, party, or policy.

As Michael Robinson and Margaret Sheehan wrote in their seminal content analysis of the 1980 elections, media analysis should not confuse good news or good luck with *good press.* "As with events, polls and electoral success do not tell us much about the way in which the media treat a person running for office."[75]   In this sense, good press measures explicitly normative judgments about whether a candidate is suitable or desirable rather than viable.

Specifically, Robinson and Sheehan calculated good press by examining statements that contained a judgment about the desirability of a candidate reaching the presidency, or rendering an evaluation of his personal character, performance in past positions, political ideology, stance on specific issues, and conduct during the campaign. Their calculations included statements from both journalists and their quoted news sources, but excluded statements made by identified partisan sources (such as Republican and Democratic elected officials, campaign workers, and the candidates themselves).

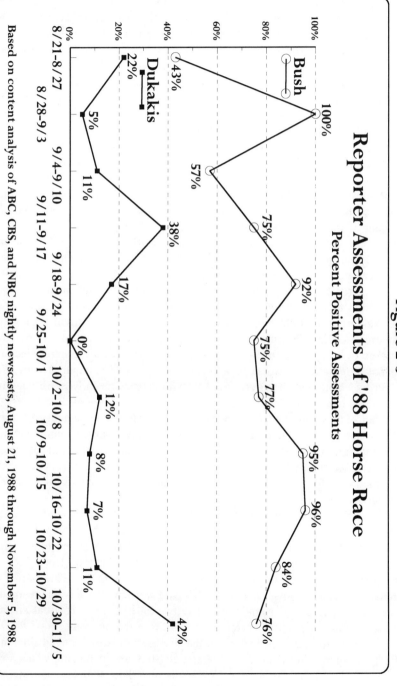

Figure 2-3

Reporter Assessments of '88 Horse Race

Percent Positive Assessments

Based on content analysis of ABC, CBS, and NBC nightly newscasts, August 21, 1988 through November 5, 1988.

We adopted the basic methodology created by Robinson and Sheehan with some additional refinements. We accepted the distinction between judgments about the suitability and viability of presidential candidates, as well as the notion that statements by partisan sources don't reflect journalistic judgments as much as the largely pre-scripted events along the campaign trail. Therefore, we did not include horse race judgments or statements by partisan sources in calculating good and bad press. Rather than discarding such statements completely, however, they were catalogued and analyzed separately. We will refer to them when appropriate.

The remaining statements by reporters, pundits, experts, and voters most clearly represent the "value-added" component that each news organization's collective news judgments bring to the viewer's understanding. By the same token, they represent the area in which journalists have the greatest latitude to shape the coverage by exercising their subjective judgments about the meaning of the events they are describing.

Over the course of the entire year, the networks' treatment of Bush and Dukakis was precisely balanced: 57% of all stated judgments about each man were negative, and 43% of the judgments were positive. (Percentages are calculated based on the total of positive and negative statements and thus always sum to 100%.)

Dukakis had a slight edge over Bush (57% to 52% positive) during the primaries. During the summer months, each received somewhat less positive coverage (47% positive for Dukakis, 46% for Bush). In the general election, Dukakis fared slightly worse than Bush (32% positive, compared with 37% for Bush). Note that the coverage of both men grew steadily more negative over the course of the year.

Because these percentages are based only on the statements of non-partisan news sources, they do not include the many negative soundbites that the campaigns flung at each other. They represent the opinions of voters who were interviewed, political experts asked to make assessments about each man's performance in the campaign, and the judgments of reporters themselves.

The partisan soundbites, however, were about as balanced and no more negative. Republicans, of course, praised Bush and castigated Dukakis. Democrats did the reverse. Adding both parties' sound bites to the mix *improves* Dukakis's good press during the general election (from 32% to 35% positive), and diminishes Bush's (from 37% to 32%). This parity of partisan comments shows that the G.O.P. did *not* have an advantage in the battle of campaign trail soundbites. The two sides got about equal airtime for their efforts to praise themselves and criticize the opposition.

The steady increases in bad press that both candidates received does not reflect an increasingly negative campaign, but an increasingly negative reaction to the campaign among journalists and their sources. During the

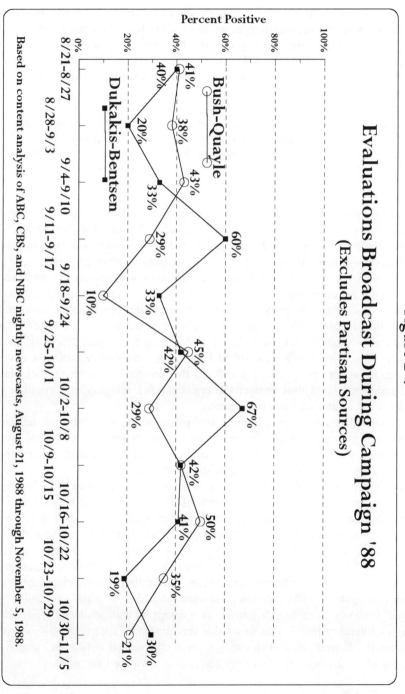

Figure 2–4

Evaluations Broadcast During Campaign '88
(Excludes Partisan Sources)

Based on content analysis of ABC, CBS, and NBC nightly newscasts, August 21, 1988 through November 5, 1988.

general election, Bush received better press just after the conventions ended and again after the second debate, while Dukakis fared best from Labor Day to Columbus Day. But, as Figure 2-4 illustrates, there was no consistent pattern favoring Bush (or Dukakis) in the good press category.

Was that unfair? Writing in *Newsweek* shortly after the election, Jonathan Alter asserted,

> By almost any standard, Bush slung several tons more mud than Dukakis, who for weeks was criticized for not fighting back. But misguided ideas of fairness required that reporters implicate both equally, lest they be seen as taking sides.... Fear of seeming slanted overcame any interest in reporting a larger truth.[76]

As noted, others shared this view of a press corps that "bent over backwards not to seem at all critical of the Republicans."[77] By this standard, it would have been more "fair" to subject Bush to greater criticism, and thus to give Dukakis more favorable coverage, in light of Bush's campaign conduct.

Our data cannot address whether the "balance" we measured is evidence of fairness or unfairness, truth or timidity. But it is worth pointing out that balance has long been prominent among journalists' professional standards for political coverage, and for not insignificant reasons. "Balance" is a measurable attribute and, as such, far easier to sort out than "fairness" and "truth." By hewing to a standard of balance in campaign reporting, a news organization can easily defend itself and its personnel from charges of bias and unfairness, and thus protect the organization's integrity and credibility as a source of non-partisan information.

"Balance" is surely not the most sophisticated way of arbitrating among competing philosophies and personalities, but for generations of journalists, it provided a safe middle ground that could be occupied without (too much) fear of alienating either the public or the politicians.

To be sure, this was no mere public relations strategy aimed at deflecting criticism and improving public perceptions of journalism. It was a way of protecting news organizations against the danger that their product would be colored by either conscious or unconscious partisanship in the newsroom. In a real sense, it ensured the political integrity of campaign reportage.

By 1988, however, journalism had acquired a level of intellectual sophistication and political influence that made its tradition of partisan neutrality seem constricting. The balanced treatment accorded to Bush and Dukakis would formerly have been regarded as a badge of independence. For the media's liberal critics, it was proof that this timeworn approach was passive and timid. Conservative critics of the press complained not about objectivity, but about a liberal tilt that they claimed to have seen for years.

The public's displeasure increased apace — the proportion of voters who rated the press's campaign performance as only "fair" or "poor" nearly doubled from May to October, rising from 22% to 39%. Even more ominously, after 1988 a majority of voters (57%) believed that news organizations tended to favor one side when reporting political issues, and half believed that news reports were "often inaccurate."[78]

Amid the blur of charges and countercharges, a consensus developed among the journalism establishment that their role as campaign mediators needed to change. The *Washington Post's* David Broder was perhaps the most influential reporter to make this argument. He called upon his journalistic brethren to take a more active stance in ensuring that the substantive policy issues of a campaign were fully presented to voters. Reporters, he wrote in 1990, "need to become partisan — not on behalf of a candidate or a party — but on behalf of the process."[79] Early in 1992, he expanded his indictment of journalism-as-usual:

> We've become so accustomed to taking our cues from the officials, the insiders, and the activists we find on our beats that we have, I'm afraid, ignored the basic idea that in a republic like ours, the people are supposed to have some say in their government. We need to become once again "the voice of the people" by letting their voice be heard in the news columns of our paper.[80]

Broder's view was shared by many academic critics of the media. Among the most influential was Harvard's Barone Center, which brings together leading scholars and journalists engaged in communications studies. In a report titled "Campaign Lessons for '92," Barone Center scholars argued that the excessive coverage of strategy and inside dope amounted to misguided efforts to reveal the "truth" about campaigns: "Journalists' attempts to pierce the candidates' 'manufactured news' armor consisted too often of elevating the gaffe, the unguarded moment, the unexpected 'tough' question beyond its real importance...."[81]

Their study recommended that reporters stick to a baseline agenda to ensure adequate coverage of the issues and the candidates' biographies, and that news organizations reduce the attention paid to the campaign trail in favor of increased research and analysis, reduce the role of sound bites and polling, increase the use of "outsider voices," decode campaign ads for voters, and stress "fairness" (rather than balance) in covering the candidates.[82]

The networks signaled that they agreed with not only the general indictment, but many of the specific prescriptions for change. NBC's Washington bureau chief, Tim Russert, published his own roadmap to improved election coverage. It included reduced coverage of photo-ops, more coverage of the stump speech, increased scrutiny of the candidates' ads, and a commitment by the networks to host prime-time debates.[83] ABC and CBS made similar, although less formal, pledges for improvement in the coverage.

With the 1992 campaign still months away, it was clear that something had changed in the way campaign journalists saw their job. Reporters were being encouraged to go far beyond either transmitting or translating the candidates' campaign trail messages, speeches, and other activities to their audience. Instead, they were urged to resist the candidates' messages and substitute their own. News organizations were urged to assert some measure of control over the campaign agenda.

Journalists were preparing themselves to take a more active role in covering campaigns. While not everyone agreed, and not every proposed reform was pursued with equal vigor, the debate within the journalistic community was a landmark event: For the first time, many leading journalists were exhorting their peers to consciously change their rules regarding election coverage, in an effort to improve the conduct of campaigns. Their response to the complaints about Campaign '88 laid the intellectual framework for systematic changes in the coverage that would be implemented in Campaign '92.

Notes

Opening quote: Haynes Johnson, "The Media as Campaign Pawns," *Washington Post*, September 23, 1988.

1. Meg Greenfield, "Politics and Play-Acting," *Washington Post*, March 5, 1980.

2. Donald T. Regan, *For the Record: From Wall Street to Washington* (San Diego: Harcourt Brace Jovanovich, 1988), p. 251.

3. Evan Thomas, "Tackling the Teflon President," *Time*, June 14, 1984.

4. Mark Hertsgaard, *On Bended Knee* (New York: Pantheon, 1988).

5. Quoted by David Shaw, "Did the Press Apply the Teflon to Reagan's Presidency?" *Los Angeles Times*, October 27, 1992.

6. Quoted by Shaw, "Did the Press Apply the Teflon..."

7. Steven R. Weisman, "The President and the Press," *New York Times Magazine*, October 14, 1984.

8. Fred Smoller, "The Six O'Clock Presidency: Patterns of Network News

Coverage of the President," *Presidential Studies Quarterly* 16, no. 1 (Winter 1986): 31-49.

9. Michael J. Robinson, "With Friends Like These... " *Public Opinion*, June/July 1983, p. 2-3, 52-54.

10. Michael J. Robinson, "Where's the Beef? Media and Media Elites in 1984," in *The American Elections of 1984*, ed. Austin Ranney (Washington, D.C.: American Enterprise Institute, 1985).

11. Ibid.

12. Ibid.

13. Smoller, p. 43. The correlation coefficient for net tone score with Gallup approval ratings was 0.72 for Reagan. Nixon (0.89) and Carter (0.83) posted similarly high coefficients, but the connection between Ford's coverage and poll ratings was weaker (0.54), possibly due to the truncated nature of his term.

14. Charles W. Ostrom, Jr. and Dennis M. Simon, "The Man in the Teflon Suit? The Environmental Connection, Political Drama, and Popular Support in the Reagan Presidency," *Public Opinion Quarterly* 53 (1989) 353-387. William C. Adams, "Recent Fables About Ronald Reagan," *Public Opinion* 7, no. 5 (October/November 1984): 6-9.

15. David Hoffman, "The Candidate, Packaged and Protected," *Washington Journalism Review*, September 1984.

16. *CBS Evening News*, October 4, 1984.

17. *CBS Morning News*, November 5, 1984

18. There is far less systematic evidence on visual than on verbal content in television campaign news. Following the pathbreaking research of political scientist Doris Graber, scholars have only recently begun to determine the relationships between these two elements in news stories, much less their differential audience impact.

In her pioneering study of the 1984 campaign, Graber found that TV news pictures were indeed more favorable toward Reagan than was the accompanying text, but the same was true for Mondale. While taking note of Reagan's "exceptionally photogenic and personable" qualities, she concluded, "On balance in both words and pictures, the Democrats were favored." See Doris Graber, "Kind Pictures and Harsh Words," in *Elections in America*, ed. Kay Lehman-Schlozman (Boston: Allen & Unwin, 1987), pp. 137-138.

In any event, as Graber noted in a recent survey of the literature, "Studies that try to determine the interaction affects of such complex stimuli [as visual and verbal images] are still in their infancy." Doris Graber, "Political Communication," in *Political Science: The State of the Discipline II*, ed. Ada Finifter (Washington, D.C.: American Political Science Association, 1993), p. 319.

19. In addition to Smoller, see, e.g., Benjamin Page, Robert Y. Shapiro, and Glenn R. Dempsey, "What Moves Public Opinion?" *American Political Science Review* 81 (March 1987): 23-43.

20. Michael Schudson, "Trout or Hamburger: Politics and Telemythology," *Tikkun* 6, no. 2 (February 1991): 47-51, 86-87.

21. *CBS Evening News*, September 14, 1984.

22. Neil Postman, *Amusing Ourselves to Death: Public Discourse in the Age of*

Show Business (New York: Penguin Books, 1985).

23. Jay Rosen, "TV as Alibi: A Response to Michael Schudson," *Tikkun* 6, no. 2 (February 1991): 52-54, 87.

24. Weisman, "The President and the Press."

25. Martin Schram, *The Great American Video Game* (New York: William Morrow and Co., 1987), p. 26.

26. William C. Adams, "Recent Fables About Ronald Reagan," *Public Opinion* 7, no. 5 (October/November 1984).

27. Quoted on *Inside Washington*, January 17, 1989.

28. Haynes Johnson, "Unfettered Press, Despite Its Sins, Needed Most During Crisis," *Washington Post*, October 30, 1983.

29. James Deakin, *Straight Stuff: The Reporters, the White House, and the Truth* (New York: William Morrow and Co., 1984), pp. 352-53.

30. Goldman and Mathews, *The Quest for the Presidency, 1988* (New York: Simon and Schuster, 1989), pp. 26-29.

31. A Gallup poll of registered voters taken May 13-15, 1988.

32. Goldman and Mathews, *The Quest for the Presidency, 1988*, p. 292.

33. *Correspondent's Notebook*, CBS Radio, April 26, 1988.

34. C. Anthony Broh, *A Horse of a Different Color: Television's Treatment of Jesse Jackson's 1984 Presidential Campaign* (Washington, D.C.: Joint Center for Political Studies, 1987); and S. Robert Lichter, Daniel Amundson, and Richard Noyes, *The Video Campaign* (Washington, D.C.: American Enterprise Institute, 1988).

35. As the following chart illustrates, Jackson received far more positive press than any of the other major 1988 candidates. See Richard E. Noyes, S. Robert Lichter, and Daniel Amundson, "Was TV Election News Better This Time? A Content Analysis of 1988 and 1992 Campaign Coverage," *Journal of Political Science* 21 (Summer 1993): 3-25.

Candidate	Percent Positive Press
Jesse Jackson	73%
Sen. Paul Simon	63
Sen. Robert Dole	62
Rep. Richard Gephardt	62
Gov. Michael Dukakis	57
Rep. Jack Kemp	56
V. P. George Bush	52
Sen. Albert Gore, Jr.	48
Pat Robertson	37
Sen. Gary Hart	10

36. "Newsweek VIP Poll: Democrats '88," *Newsweek*, February 1, 1988.

37. E. J. Dionne, "The Democrats in Atlanta," *New York Times*, July 17, 1988.

38. *MacNeil-Lehrer NewsHour*, July 22, 1988.

39. Three polls showed Dukakis with a 17-point lead during this period: A Gallup poll taken for *Newsweek*, July 21-22, 1988 (Dukakis 55%, Bush 38%); a Gallup poll taken July 22-24, 1988 (Dukakis 54%, Bush 37%); and a CBS/*New York*

Times poll taken July 31-August 3, 1988 (Dukakis 50%, Bush 33%).

40. *CBS Evening News*, August 17, 1988.

41. NBC's *Decision '88: The Republican Convention*, August 16, 1988.

42. S. Robert Lichter and Linda S. Lichter, "Covering the Convention Coverage," *Public Opinion* (September/October 1988): 41-44.

43. Benjamin I. Page et al., "What Moves Public Opinion," 23-43.

44. "Quayle Hunt," *Media Monitor* 2, no. 7 (September 1988).

45. Jacqueline Adams, *CBS Evening News*, August 20, 1988.

46. Catherine Woodard, "Town Rallies Behind a Local Hero," *Newsday,* August 20, 1988; Saul Friedman, "A Hero's Welcome; Crowds Cheer Quayle and Boo the Media," *Newsday,* August 20, 1988; Maureen Dowd, "Hometown Crowd Turns Tables on Press for Questioning Quayle," *New York Times*, August 20, 1988; and Thomas B. Edsall and Bill Peterson, "Quayle Defends Using Connections to Enter Guard; Republican Nominee Says 'No Rules Were Broken' As Home Town Supporters Boo Reporters," *Washington Post*, August 20, 1988.

47. Ibid.

48. Ellen Hume, "The Follies of '88," *Columbia Journalism Review,* September/October 1990, pp. 54-55. See also "Ellen Hume's Legacy," *St. Louis Post-Dispatch*, March 22, 1989.

49. The Gallup poll taken August 5-7, 1988 placed Bush with 42% support, Dukakis with 49%. The Gallup survey of August 19-21 (immediately following the convention) showed Bush rising to 48% and Dukakis dropping to 44%.

50. Gallup tracking poll from September 24 showed Bush 48%, Dukakis 39%; for September 25 (the day of the debate), it stood at Bush 50%, Dukakis 38%

51. Howard Fineman, "Why Bush is Winning," *Newsweek*, October 24, 1988.

52. Michael Lewis-Beck and Tom Rice, *Forcasting Elections* (Washington, D.C.: CQ Press, 1992); Ray Fair, "The Effect of Economic Events on Votes for President," *Review of Economics and Statistics* 60 (1978): 159-173.

53. Jonathon Rauch, "Election Day Economy," *National Journal,* October 24, 1987.

54. For a critical review, see Jay Greene, "Forwarned Before Forecast," *PS: Political Science and Politics* (March 1993): 17-21.

55. Jeff Greenfield and Michael Kramer, "The Week the Sound Bites Bit Bush," *U.S. News & World Report*, October 3, 1988, p. 20.

56. On NBC's *Meet the Press*, December 13, 1987, Bush was asked by panelist David Broder if he knew how many Americans lacked health insurance coverage. He responded, "Well, I think some people have health insurance that can take care of their own needs, so I don't know the answer to it, no." Clip shown on *NBC Nightly News*, September 20, 1988.

57. *NBC Nightly News*, September 20, 1988.

58. *CBS Evening News*, September 20, 1988.

59. "The Smear Campaign," *Newsweek*, October 31, 1988.

60. The true number of escapees, according to Kathleen Hall Jamieson, is 275; only four of those who escaped were "first-degree murderers not eligible for parole" such as Horton. See Jamieson, *Dirty Politics: Deception, Distraction, and Democracy* (New York: Oxford University Press, 1992), pp. 15-42.

61. "The Smear Campaign," *Newsweek*, October 31, 1988.

62. "Bush's Most Valuable Player," *Time*, November 14, 1988.

63. Martin Schram, "The Making of Willie Horton: The Mug Shot Roger Ailes Couldn't Touch," *The New Republic*, May 28, 1990. Schram reports that the ad's producer, Harry McCarthy, presented the cable networks with a benign ad for preview, and then substituted the ad with Horton's face a few days later. Then, according to Schram and others, McCarthy showed the ad to producers of *The McLaughlin Group*, which showed the ad and then discussed it as part of a regular political roundtable. *Regardie's Magazine* reported that to place a one-minute ad on all three evening newscasts costs more than $250,000, and that McCarthy's tactics earned him the same amount of airtime, without cost. See Roger Simon, "The Killer and the Candidate: How Willie Horton and George Bush rewrote the rules of political advertising," *Regardie's Magazine*, October 1990.

64. Thomas Oliphant, "For Two Bush Campaign Aides, a Turning of the Tide," *Boston Globe*, May 19, 1989.

65. Goldman and Mathews, *Quest... 1988*, p. 367.

66. Quoted by Fox Butterfield, "Dukakis Says Race Was Harmed By TV" *New York Times*, April 22, 1990.

67. Quoted by Robert E. Denton, Jr., *The Primetime Presidency of Ronald Reagan* (New York: Praeger, 1988).

68. Quoted by Michael Oreskes, "TV and the Election: Debating an Ugly War," *New York Times*, November 14, 1988.

69. Ailes, quoted by Marvin Kalb, in his introduction to Ellen Hume, *Restoring the Bond: Connecting Campaign Coverage to Voters*, published by the Joan Shorenstein Barone Center on the Press, Politics and Public Policy, John F. Kennedy School of Government, Harvard University, 1991. See also Larry McCarthy, "The Selling of the President: An Interview with Roger Ailes," *Gannett Center Journal* (Fall 1988); James A. Baker III speech to the National Press Club, November 3, 1988, and Michael Deaver, "Sound Bite Campaigning: TV Made Us Do It," *Washington Post*, October 30, 1988.

70. Marvin Kalb, "TV, Election Spoiler," *New York Times*, November 28, 1988.

71. Quoted by William Boot, "Campaign '88: TV Overdoses on the Inside Dope," *Columbia Journalism Review*, January/February 1989.

72. James A. Baker III, speech to the National Press Club, November 3, 1988.

73. See Jack W. Germond and Jules Witcover, *Whose Broad Stripes and Bright Stars? The Trivial Pursuit of the Presidency 1988* (New York: Warner Books, 1989), pp. 411-413. They write that "the ABC poll was so far out of bounds that even [Bush campaign manager] Lee Atwater was taken aback. As he put it later, "I thought the most devastating thing of the whole campaign — I found myself for the first and only time ever feeling sorry for Dukakis — was the ABC coverage of the poll results announced the night [before] the debate. It had to be unnerving."

74. Our methodology for designating issues as part of the Republican or Democratic agendas was based on an examination of which sources tended to discuss issues on evening newscasts. Issues were assigned to the Republicans when G.O.P. sources were 10% more likely to discuss them than Democratic sources (and vice versa for assigning Democratic issues). Among the top issues, this methodology yielded agendas that were easily validated by anecdotal representations in the press of each campaign's agenda and strategy. Issues (such as the economy and unemploy-

ment) that were dealt with equally by both parties were not assigned to either campaign's agenda.

75. Robinson and Sheehan, *Over the Wire and On TV: CBS and UPI in Campaign '80* (New York: Russell Sage Foundation, 1983), pp. 94-96.

76. Jonathon Alter, "How the Media Blew It," *Newsweek*, November 21, 1988

77. Mark Crispin Miller, "TV's Anti-Liberal Bias," *New York Times,* November 16, 1988.

78. Polls taken by the Times Mirror Center for the People and the Press, 1989.

79. David Broder, "Five Ways to Put Some Sanity Back in Elections," *Washington Post*, January 14, 1990.

80. David Broder, "It's Time to Replace Sloganeering with Simple Shoe-leather Reporting," *The Quill*, March 1992, pp. 8-9.

81. Ibid., p. 127

82. Ellen Hume, *Restoring the Bond,* pp. 126-147.

83. Timothy J. Russert, "For '92, the Networks Have to Do Better," *New York Times*, March 4, 1990.

Chapter Three

The Search for Substance

*We intend to do the best job of covering a political campaign that any
network news broadcast has ever done.*
—Paul Friedman, Executive Producer, ABC *World News Tonight,* 1992

After every presidential campaign, it seems, the news media are
criticized for the shallowness and superficiality of their coverage.
The charge is a potent one because, in national elections, citizens
have no direct opportunity to choose among competing proposals and priorities. Instead, voters exercise indirect authority over government policies by
choosing those individuals whom they believe best represent their views and
interests. For voters to participate meaningfully within such a system, they
need to understand both the priorities and the policy positions of the various
candidates.

Of course, there is no law compelling citizens to educate themselves
before they exercise their franchise. But a well-informed electorate is
possible only if the basic facts about a candidate's biography, prior government service, statements about various issues, and proposals put forward
about contemporary problems are made available and accessible prior to an
election.

Over the past thirty years, our system of informing voters has broken
down. The information that does reach voters is frequently overshadowed by
its context. News reports stress those aspects of campaigns that most
interest news organizations, and that journalists (often incorrectly) presume

are of greatest interest to their audiences. Thus, candidates' private lives are investigated; their spouses, parents, children, and even their pets are profiled; top campaign staffers are treated as celebrities; any verbal conflict among the candidates is headlined, while reporters tally the number of direct hits, near-misses, and low blows. The media treat the campaign as a sporting event — a daily scorecard tells "fans" which "team" is gaining or losing ground in the race for the White House.

Rather than exploring the probable consequences of each candidate's election, reporters delve into the nuts-and-bolts of campaigning — how the process works, what to expect next, *why* candidates say what they say (the assumption being, of course, that no candidate says what he or she truly believes).

When substantive information pokes through this haze of insider gossip and speculation, it is often ignored or overlooked by an audience numbed by a surfeit of reportage and a dearth of information. Numerous studies have demonstrated that voters learn little about the fundamentals of key policy problems, or the candidates' competing proposals to deal with them, from daily news coverage.[1]

Traditionally, reporters presented their audiences with each campaign's latest developments, featuring interesting stories or colorful anecdotes from the campaign trail. The broader task of educating voters fell to the candidates and the political parties, who paid for their own leaflets, newsletters, or advertising to reach their constituents.

As parties lost the ability to effectively organize and communicate at the grass roots level, and campaigns increasingly focused their advertising efforts on brief television commercials, voters lost the conduit through which they received their election-year educations. What vanished was that assortment of facts and data that, while lacking the qualities of "news," are necessary and relevant for citizens seeking to cast an informed vote.

Over the past several presidential campaign cycles, reporters and news organizations have been expected to fill this vacuum. When they fail, the media are blamed for voters' lack of knowledge about key issues. After 1988, media critics were exceptionally vigorous in their judgment that journalism (particularly television) had failed in its obligation to inform the American public.[2] As Marvin Kalb wrote in the *New York Times*,

> Once upon a time, TV news was no more important than newspapers or magazines. But as primaries proliferated and parties atrophied, TV became the key to the kingdom. Along the way, television acquired new responsibilities it did not seek and is poorly equipped to handle. Indeed, judging by its performance during the [1988] campaign, it is incapable even of defining its new role.[3]

Kalb criticized television for allowing itself to be "seduced" by candidate "photo-ops," for sponsoring and then over-reporting public opinion polls, and for making no sustained effort to challenge the candidates. "If the campaign was, to use Richard Nixon's description, 'trivial, superficial and inane,' then TV news must shoulder a large measure of the blame."[4]

Such criticisms had been heard before, but this time the tone was more urgent. "This is unassailable stuff," wrote the *Washington Post*'s Richard Harwood, "but the press has been hearing it for years and hasn't changed its ways." After 1988, however, Harwood ventured, "It's time to think anew."[5]

Others agreed. "I don't think anyone in the media was much pleased with the coverage in 1988," said Bill Wheatley, director of political coverage for NBC News. He indicated that NBC intended to change its approach in 1992.[6] Wheatley's NBC colleague, Washington bureau chief Tim Russert, told the *Wall Street Journal* that, "after the 1988 election, there were endless post-mortem conferences at all the networks. And the sense of them all was, 'Never again.'"[7] As the 1992 campaign began, all of the major broadcasters publicly agreed on the need for television to provide voters with more in-depth, issue-oriented material.[8]

The problem was that traditional news coverage was failing to inform voters about the serious issues of the day. As many influential journalists saw it, however, the chief culprits were not reporters but candidates who cynically and deliberately avoided serious debate about issues. According to this school of thought, journalists' guilt lay in their failure to use their clout to force candidates to focus on substantive matters. As CNN's Ken Bode wrote,

There are two points of view on this matter. The first says that the presidential candidates have a right to set their own agenda, and whatever they do on a given day is the news and must be covered. The other view holds that providing coverage for the carefully contrived theme-of-the-day photo-op amounts to nothing more than conveyer belt journalism. From the campaign's point of view, the objective is to prevent reporters and broadcasters from having any choice about what they cover; the campaign provides the message, we provide the airwaves....

The conclusion is obvious. *We [reporters] know what the issues are and we owe it to the public to go beyond the daily photo-op handout and provide serious analysis of the positions and the candidates.* The question is not "Did the candidate do something today?"; of course he did. The standard must be, "Is what the candidate did today newsworthy? Or was it a video contrivance designed to be irresistible television?" [Emphasis added.]

On those occasions when presidential candidates failed to provide "news-worthy" statements in their stump speeches, Bode offered colleagues this solution: "Pull the plug."[9] That is, don't put the candidate on TV that night. By depriving politicians of media coverage when they failed to make substantive comments in their speeches and rallies, journalists would provide campaigns with incentives to adjust their behavior. If the candidates responded to the pressure, the political process would improve. According to NBC's Russert, if the networks ended coverage of photo-ops, "Believe me, the staging would stop. The campaigns would instead spend their time developing and distinguishing their positions on the issues."[10]

A momentous debate was developing, with reformers pressing for radical shifts in journalism's standards and operating procedures. "The first step — and the most important — is to challenge the operating assumption of the candidates and consultants that the campaign agenda is theirs to determine," argued David Broder in an influential article written for the *Washington Post's* Sunday "Outlook" section. "That assumption is a lot of malarkey. The campaign really belongs to the voters.... It's the voters who deserve to be in the driver's seat."

Broder suggested that reporters use polling data and interviews with voters to discern their concerns, and then hold the candidates accountable to the "voters' agenda." He continued,

> The candidates are, of course, free to talk and advertise about any subject in the world. But we in the press are free — and obligated — to keep calling them back to the voters' agenda in every news conference and in every public forum. Being persistent — to the point of being obnoxious — is fully justified when we know we are asking the questions the voters want answered.[11]

Note that Broder's proposals were not aimed primarily at improving the quality of campaign journalism, but at refining journalism as a tool to improve the political process itself. (His *Post* article was titled, "Five Ways to Put Some Sanity Back in Elections.") Broder was a leading crusader for change, arguing that journalists' coziness with political professionals left voters excluded. "We're all drawn to our work, in part, because of our love of the kind of gossip, maneuver and individual idiosyncrasies that make politics such a fascinating game for the insider," he said in a 1991 speech at the University of California.[12]

The public believed the press's insider approach to campaigns was out of step with their own concerns, Broder argued. As a result, "it's not only the politicians from whom the people are turning away," but from the media as well.[13] For the sake of its own credibility, as well as the cause of sane elections, journalism had to change its rules.

Broder's vigorous advocacy of a "voters' agenda" was echoed in a Harvard University white paper offering "Campaign Lessons for '92." Harvard's

Barone Center, whose ranks include prominent former journalists as well as traditional academics, adopted a leadership role in many of the media reform efforts. Gov. Clinton's campaign manager, James Carville, even joked that top reporters had flocked like alcoholics to the Barone Center to "dry out after the '88 campaign."[14]

The Harvard group offered their colleagues their own version of a 12-step recovery program. Their first recommendation: "Establish a baseline agenda and coverage plan to monitor relevance and keep a balance in news coverage." It offered detailed advice to news organizations:

> A proportion of campaign "manufactured" images, insider and horse race news is essential to good coverage, but in 1988 the amount was out of balance. To establish a better balance, each news organization might start out with a "relevant issues" baseline agenda reflecting ideas and concerns from diverse sources. It should include the issues, values and concerns expressed by voters through polls and interviews. Also part of this baseline agenda are matters that political experts and "insiders" acknowledge will be on the candidate's desk once he or she is elected, such as the savings and loan crisis in 1988 and the looming Gulf War in 1990. Another critical source of such agenda items is, of course, the candidates themselves, including their own priorities and initial substantive campaign presentations.
>
> This list of issues can be summarized in an initial story, identifying what the race is likely to be all about, and then used throughout the campaign as a "relevance" test for campaign discourse. The point of establishing this initial issues agenda is not to denigrate "values" or "character" as legitimate political subjects, nor is it to dismiss the new issues or themes that emerge during the campaign season. Instead, this baseline is a tool that can be used as needed by journalists, politicians and voters alike to *hold candidates accountable for addressing serious, relevant matters* affected by the election.[15] [Emphasis added.]

The baseline agenda advocated by the Barone Center would be the "backbone" of a news organization's "coverage plan." It would serve as a "voters' and journalists' guide both to the quality of the candidates' campaigns and to the accountability of the winner afterwards."[16]

The thread running through these suggestions was the belief that the press was guilty of *passivity* during the 1988 campaign. Its sin was one not of commission, but of omission — they allowed the candidates' worst tendencies to go unchecked. As we have seen, the conventional critique of the 1988 campaign coverage was partly wrong and partly exaggerated. While 1988 saw no *more* issue content than previous years, it certainly saw no less. The balanced portrayal of the candidates was a perfect illustration of journalism's prevailing norms.

But the reformers' grievance with 1988 was not that the coverage failed by the standards of existing norms. Instead, the criticism was designed to illustrate the need for journalism to adopt *new norms* in its campaign reporting. "Balance" was equated with "mindlessness." The candidates' agendas were considered trivial. Reformers desired news agenda that conformed to their sense of what they thought the *real* issues were, and what voters *really* cared about.

In other words, the journalists in the vanguard of the reform movement saw themselves as better interpreters of the public interest than the politicians who have traditionally fulfilled that function. Implicit in these critiques, and the reform proposals, was the notion that journalists would succeed where the politicians had failed in offering voters an appropriate campaign agenda. In essence, the reformers urged news organizations to assume a more aggressive role in setting their own agendas, bypassing candidates who deviated from the script.

From the outset, this was a problematic formula for reform. Shouldering aside the candidates' agendas, however flawed they might appear, in favor of one divined by the media, would further weaken the connection voters made between their policy preferences and their choice of candidates. Forcing the campaigns to conform to the media's template could actually diminish the available information citizens had about the candidates' own agendas, particularly those who dissented from the media's agenda.

In one sense, the point was not so much to improve voters' understanding of the candidates' platforms as to "improve" those platforms themselves. The Barone Center's recommendations are anchored in a concept credited by other participants to philosopher Sissela Bok: "There are three 'vicious circles' at play in any political campaign: the people, the politicians, and the press.... If any of these three systems could be changed for the better, the other two would be similarly affected."[17]

Changing journalism's rules would change the publicity incentives guiding candidates; if reporters would shed their passivity and use their clout to reward or punish politicians, they could encourage an improved political order. Candidates, whose prospects would dwindle without publicity, would be forced to beef up the substantive aspects of their campaigns. Exhorted the *Post's* Broder: "We have been inhibited by thinking that if we did any more [than merely report], we would be thought partisan. But we need to become partisan — not on behalf of a candidate or party — but on behalf of the process."[18]

Such prescriptions were based on two crucial assumptions about modern presidential campaigns: they are devoid of serious issue content, and the responsibility for penalizing candidates and informing voters properly rests with journalists. If these premises are true, the baseline agenda could correct campaigns in two ways: it would add to voters' information about the issues, and it would offer an incentive to candidates to begin addressing the media's issue agenda, stimulating real substantive debate. Candidates who failed to offer "substance" could be singled out and held "accountable for addressing serious, relevant matters."[19]

But what if the reformers' premise isn't true? In Chapter 2, we argued that the journalistic critique of the 1988 campaign coverage does not withstand close scrutiny. Might journalists prove equally fallible in their attempts to improve presidential campaigns? Our study of the 1992 campaign was designed to find out exactly how much substance was made available to citizens by the new and improved campaign journalism that resulted from the post-1988 reforms.

We examined the issue content of the major network evening news coverage of the presidential campaign from January 1 through November 2, 1992. This involved a sound bite-by-sound bite content analysis of 2,386 news stories broadcast on ABC, CBS, and NBC. For the general election (September 7 through November 2), we broadened the study to include five additional national media outlets that might be expected to provide more substance than the "big three" networks: CNN's *PrimeNews*, PBS's *MacNeil-Lehrer NewsHour*, and the "prestige press"— the *New York Times*, the *Washington Post*, and the *Wall Street Journal*. These outlets collectively contributed an additional 2,903 stories to the study.

The benefits of a systematic analysis of the media coverage are several. First, because it is comprehensive, our analysis ensures that all election coverage is considered — not just the most interesting or controversial stories, or a sample week that may or may not be representative. Second, by quantifying the amount of news space devoted to substance and seriousness, we can compare the efforts of various news organizations, to see if one network or one newspaper offered a better mix than its rivals.

Further, as we saw in Chapter 2, the impressions that remain when a campaign is over can be misleading. The most dramatic or most reprehensible aspects of the news coverage are often all that are remembered by critics. With the passage of time, they became a flawed stand-in for the coverage as a whole. Only by scrutinizing each story and each statement, and aggregating the results, can one make accurate conclusions about the coverage as a whole.

In addition to systematically examining the news content, we applied the same content analysis system to the presidential candidates' general election speeches. The 124 speeches that we analyzed provide a unique benchmark against with which to judge the quantity and the quality of the media's issue coverage. The results undermine the reformers' claim that journalists are better able than candidates to offer voters detailed, substantive and relevant information during election campaigns. In fact, the results call into question whether contemporary mainstream journalism is competent to assume any serious role in voter education.

THE 1992 CAMPAIGN AGENDA

The "campaign agenda" and the "news agenda" are terms that, although they reflect different concepts, are practically interchangeable during an election year. Voters seldom hear from the candidates without the interposition of news reporters, producers, or editors. The few exceptions — campaign visits to their locality, live TV coverage of the nominating conventions or debates — are episodic and infrequent, and are not conducive to engaging voters' long-term attention. Similarly, for most people, most issues — even those as encompassing as the economy or crime — are experienced vicariously through news coverage rather than a direct intrusion into day-to-day life.[20] While candidate advertising provides a steadier and more repetitive source of information, the brevity of most spot ads precludes much educational value.

Thus, while the campaign agenda is necessarily a hybrid composed of both the candidates' and the media's issues, the news media play a significant role. According to media scholar David Weaver,

> By making certain issues, candidates, and characteristics of candidates more prominent than others, the news media contribute greatly to the construction of a secondhand reality that is relied upon [by voters] in making decisions about whether and for whom to vote.... Political messages and agendas emerge as the joint process involving political figures and journalists.[21]

COMPONENTS OF THE NEWS AGENDA

Horse Race News: Recent developments in polling have actually increased the prominence of the horse race in the media's campaign agenda. National news organizations now routinely pay polling firms to conduct regular surveys of public opinion. The results automatically become "news," albeit news manufactured by the news outlet itself. In covering the earliest contests such as Iowa and New Hampshire, media-sponsored tracking polls are used to provide a daily update on the most minute shifts in the race. Tracking polls have also become a feature of the final month of a general election campaign.

One measure of the importance journalists place on election polls is that newspapers and television networks regularly publicize poll results generated by their direct competitors (NBC will report on a CBS poll, for example, or the *New York Times* will print the results of a *Washington Post* poll), while many other types of "exclusive" stories are regularly downplayed or ignored.

Essentially, news organizations spend a great deal of their time and money during campaign years telling voters what the voters have already told them. Polls have become the centerpiece of the campaign puzzle, the self-constructed prism through which campaign journalists view the candidates, the issues, the voters, and even their own role.

Candidate Issues: Coverage of recent elections has seen a surge of what Michael Robinson termed "candidate issues." These involve controversies surrounding the questionable campaign conduct or past behavior of the various aspirants, which are not otherwise connected to their public records or policy preferences.[22] After the horse race, candidate issues are the second principal focus of the media's campaign news agenda. They are an outgrowth of the trend toward the "insider" agenda that Broder deplored for its focus on "gossip, maneuver and individual idiosyncrasies."

Among the typical instances of such controversies in recent elections are the numerous stories in 1984 about how Sen. Gary Hart purportedly changed his name, age, and signature; stories in 1987 that calculated the number of months that transpired between Pat Robertson's marriage and the birth of his first child; and stories from 1988 about allegations that Gov. Dukakis was once treated by a psychiatrist.

While the content of such candidate news occasionally yields useful insights into an aspirant's character and personality, the preoccupation with personal questions often leaves viewers and readers ill-informed about the candidate's qualifications and policies. A major problem with candidate issues is that the focus is usually not biographical or contextual. Rather, the media provide breathless updates on immediate controversies that are played out along the campaign trail. Too often, the hastily assembled reports offer voters little more than titillating glimpses into private foibles whose political import is magnified by the glare of the campaign spotlight.

Policy Issues: The third main component of the media's campaign agenda are policy issues — information about the various problems facing the country, and the debate over competing solutions. Historically, the percentage of campaign news devoted to "the issues" has ranged between one-fifth and one-third of the total amount of news coverage, far below the proportion involving candidate issues and the horse race.[23] This accounts for the rising scholarly criticism of campaign coverage since the 1970s, as studies repeatedly documented that the media fail to provide coherent presentations about the policy preferences of presidential candidates.

Part of the reason issues are shortchanged by reporters is that their definition of "news" stresses that which is new and interesting, rather than information that is merely relevant and educational. In a political campaign, the issues are "newsworthy" when they are the vehicles for conflict among the candidates or otherwise carry horse race implications for the contenders.

A successful campaign will try to avoid public discussion of issues that make the candidate a target for attacks by rivals or bad reviews from pundits. Rather, candidates approach the issues from a consensual perspective, seeking to present their solutions in a non-controversial and non-conflictual manner. As such, their policy proposals fail to stimulate news interest. As one reporter described his frustration: "[The] candidates give bland speeches over and over again, hoping not to offend anyone. Reporters covering candidates get irritated about this. It's boring to listen to deliberate nothingness for days on end. The only way to cope is by eating."[24]

For 1992, news organizations vowed to offer voters increased information about the substance of the campaign. In at least one respect, such a pledge would prove easier to keep in '92 than in other recent campaigns. At the end of 1991, a spate of negative economic reports led to renewed fears that the recession of the previous spring had not ended. The public's concern about the economy was well known to all five candidates running for the Democratic nomination, not to mention President Bush and his Republican challenger, syndicated columnist Patrick J. Buchanan.

Veteran campaign reporter Paul Taylor of the *Washington Post* noticed early on that the candidates were trying to deal straightforwardly with economic and other policy issues. "In spite of itself," he wrote in February, "this campaign seems to be slouching toward substance."

> Anyone who stayed up Friday night a couple of weeks ago to watch the Democratic candidates debate on PBS knows what I mean: Here were five men going at it for two hours, with a good deal of energy and intellect and a nice mix of vision and policy specifics, on issues ranging from health care to education to industrial policy to taxes and trade. President Bush's State of the Union speech last month... came across to me as the most comprehensive treatment of domestic affairs of his presidency.[25]

To the extent that the candidates were offering substance in their campaign debates and speeches, the media's task of delivering more substantive campaign news was made that much easier. The ingredients for more substantive coverage already existed in the speeches and in the debates, needing only to be harvested.

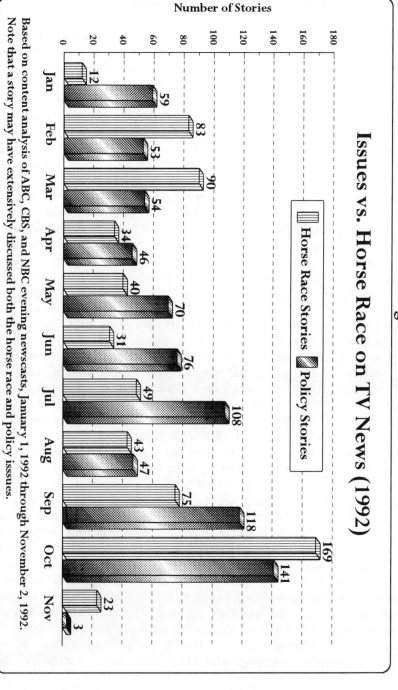

Figure 3-1

Issues vs. Horse Race on TV News (1992)

Number of Stories

Horse Race Stories
Policy Stories

Jan: 12, 59
Feb: 83, 53
Mar: 90, 54
Apr: 34, 46
May: 40, 70
Jun: 31, 76
Jul: 49, 108
Aug: 43, 47
Sep: 75, 118
Oct: 169, 141
Nov: 23, 3

Based on content analysis of ABC, CBS, and NBC evening newscasts, January 1, 1992 through November 2, 1992.
Note that a story may have extensively discussed both the horse race and policy issues.

SUBSTANCE VS. HOOPLA — THE 1992 PRIMARIES

During the 1992 primaries, network news was, in fact, centered more on substance and less on the horse race than in 1988. Figure 3-1 illustrates how issue news predominated for much of the 1992 campaign (although horse race still was heavily featured during the height of the primaries and general election). This represents a substantial change from the previous election. The number of horse race stories broadcast during the peak of the primary season (February and March) dropped sharply from 1988 levels. Conversely, the number of stories focusing on policy issues was up by two-thirds during the first four months of the year, the period when reporters normally focus on the nomination contests.

Overall, the percentage of horse race stories dropped from half the total coverage of the '88 primaries to one-third of the '92 primary news. Meanwhile, the proportion of stories dealing with policy issues more than doubled, from 15% in Campaign '88 to 32% in Campaign '92. In other words, while horse race stories outnumbered substantive issue stories by a margin of three to one during Campaign '88, the networks shifted their priorities in '92 and presented viewers with roughly equal amounts of news about polls and policies.

Those percentages reveal how the networks portrayed the election when they covered it. What they don't show is that during those early months, every network also devoted less air time to Campaign '92 than Campaign '88. Overall, television aired 827 stories on the campaign during the first four months of 1988. Four years later, they broadcast 666 campaign pieces, nearly a 20% reduction. Moreover, the decline was concentrated in the critical first two months of the primary season. Thus, the issue coverage made up a larger slice of a smaller pie. (See Figure 3-2.)

These changes may derive more from the shape of the campaign horse race than from the reformers' efforts to better educate the electorate. Figure 3-3 shows the changes in the amount of horse race news from 1988 to 1992 across the campaign calender. The key factor was the perception among journalists that the Iowa caucuses were not as significant in 1992 as they had been ever since 1976. The reduction in horse race news in 1992 corresponds closely to the amount of coverage given Iowa in 1988 — the caucuses were featured in 110 stories in the first four months of 1988, compared with a mere six stories in 1992. Dismissing Iowa may have saved the cash-strapped network news departments some money in 1992. It also provided a direct demonstration of how the legendary post-Iowa "bounce" is a function of media coverage, rather than actual electoral accomplishment.

Iowa's own favorite son, Sen. Tom Harkin, was considered a sure bet to win an overwhelming percentage of the Democratic vote. Nonetheless, the

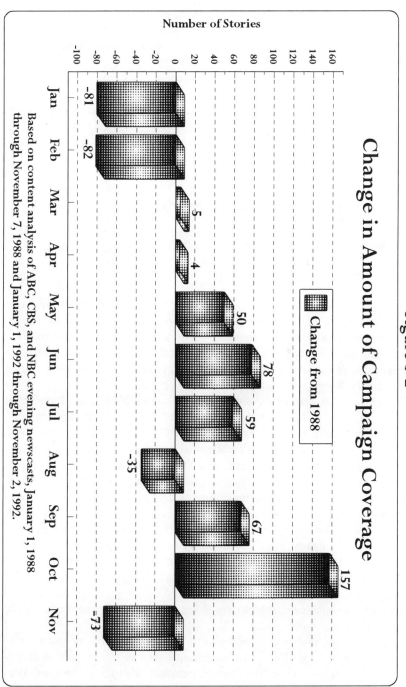

Figure 3-2

Change in Amount of Campaign Coverage

Number of Stories

Change from 1988

Jan −81
Feb −82
Mar 5
Apr 4
May 50
Jun 78
Jul 59
Aug −35
Sep 67
Oct 157
Nov −73

Based on content analysis of ABC, CBS, and NBC evening newscasts, January 1, 1988 through November 7, 1988 and January 1, 1992 through November 2, 1992.

other candidates — Bill Clinton, Paul Tsongas, Bob Kerrey, Doug Wilder, and Jerry Brown — initially decided to campaign there in an effort to benefit from a "better than expected" second-place finish (much as Gary Hart did in 1984).

As it became clear that the networks planned to provide less coverage of Iowa, the candidates redeployed their forces. This retreat drained the last drops of suspense (and potential news value) from the contest. The caucuses were mentioned only twice during January 1992 — a decline of 97% from the previous cycle. The day before the caucuses, ABC's Forrest Sawyer perfunctorily dismissed Iowa's political value:

> For the first time, voters will speak in the presidential campaign when Iowa holds its precinct caucuses tomorrow. President Bush and Iowa's Senator Tom Harkin are considered easy winners, so the first *real* political battle is shaping up across the country in New Hampshire where, with the primary only nine days away, Arkansas Gov. Bill Clinton's lead in the Democratic race appears to be shrinking, and the other candidates have suddenly found themselves in a horse race. [Emphasis in the original.][26]

The fact that Sawyer could so easily shift the Iowa caucuses from the "real" to the "imaginary" column on the basis of reporters' expectations graphically illustrates how much the news media's own presence (or absence) affects the political consequences of each contest. One day before the caucuses, the top political story on all three newscasts was the New Hampshire primary, which was still a week away.

On February 10, Harkin did the expected, winning 80% of the Democratic caucus vote. His victory was the focus of 15 seconds of reporting on ABC and 9 seconds each on CBS and NBC. NBC used the occasion to run a lengthy (3 minutes, 20 seconds) profile of the "prairie populist." Even here, however, the Iowa results were more of a "hook" than a "trigger" — each of the other Democrats received a similar profile during that period.

Harkin's Iowa media payoff thus amounted to just over half a minute of TV news airtime. Tracking-poll data tend to vary from night to night, if for no other reason than sampling error. But Harkin's New Hampshire percentages were rock steady after Iowa, betraying not the slightest hint of a "bounce."[27] Harkin finished a distant fourth in New Hampshire, and his candidacy quickly evaporated. Winning Iowa's delegates failed to provide any help at all to his candidacy; the real reward sought from the caucuses (as is known by politicians and reporters alike) is news media attention. Without it, Harkin's candidacy faded.

Also distracting reporters from the horse race was the presence of an even sexier news story: sex. Driven by saturation coverage of the various allegations against Arkansas Gov. Bill Clinton, personal news about the candidates

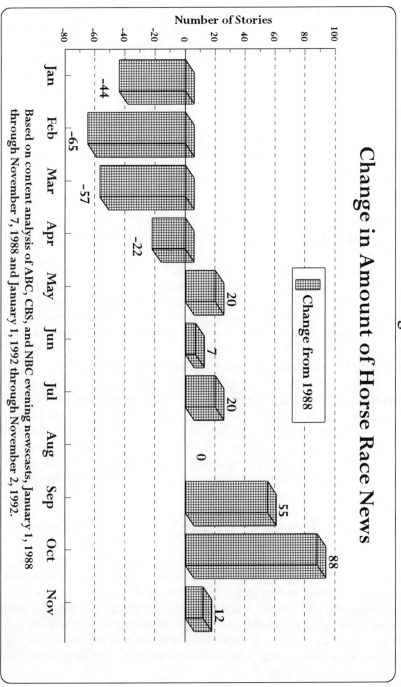

Figure 3-3

Change in Amount of Horse Race News

Based on content analysis of ABC, CBS, and NBC evening newscasts, January 1, 1988 through November 7, 1988 and January 1, 1992 through November 2, 1992.

was the focus of 32% of all campaign news during the '92 primaries, up from 21% in '88. More than one-third (36%) of the 216 stories focusing on candidate news during the primaries featured Clinton's alleged foibles; no other candidate received even one-tenth as much personal scrutiny. Indeed, several of the candidates — Harkin, Nebraska Sen. Bob Kerrey, and Bush's Vice President, Dan Quayle — received less *total* coverage than the number of stories devoted to Clinton's "character issue" alone.

News coverage of Gov. Clinton's character did more than squeeze out coverage of his rivals; it also replaced investigations into his platform and his record in office. During the primaries, 45% of the network news stories featuring Clinton (107 out of 237) mentioned at least one of the various character questions (adultery, drug use, draft dodging, conflict of interest, etc.) that had been leveled against him. By contrast, less than one-third of Clinton's coverage (29% or 68 stories) contained any references to the economy, and just eight stories (3%) mentioned the budget deficit or other budget issues.

Thus, despite the impression of wall-to-wall coverage of Clinton's every word and deed, Democratic primary voters who relied on TV news were much more likely to have heard about his personal foibles than any of the substantive planks in his platform. (A more detailed examination of the media's treatment of Bill Clinton's personal life appears in Chapter 6.)

Substance vs. Hoopla — The 1992 General Election

The Networks: Television's interest in the campaign horse race blossomed in the spring, thanks mainly to the independent candidacy of Texas billionaire H. Ross Perot. Beginning in May, as Figure 3-3 shows, the horse race began receiving *more* coverage than it had during 1988. TV's newfound interest in the 1992 horse race remained high throughout the rest of the campaign. In fact, the only time that it dropped back to 1988 levels was during August, the only month when Perot seemed to be definitely out of the race.[28]

Perot officially announced his candidacy on October 1. That month the networks aired 169 stories about the state of the horse race, more than twice as many as in October 1988 — at a time when the critics were busily clucking over TV's obsession with polls. "With so many polls," *Newsweek's* Jonathan Alter fretted in November 1988, "the result was a horse race story almost every day."[29] During the last weeks of Campaign '92, the new, improved campaign coverage offered viewers an average of not one but *two* horse race stories per night on each of the network evening newscasts. (In his regular *Newsweek* column, Alter was silent about the surfeit of horse race news during the fall of 1992.)

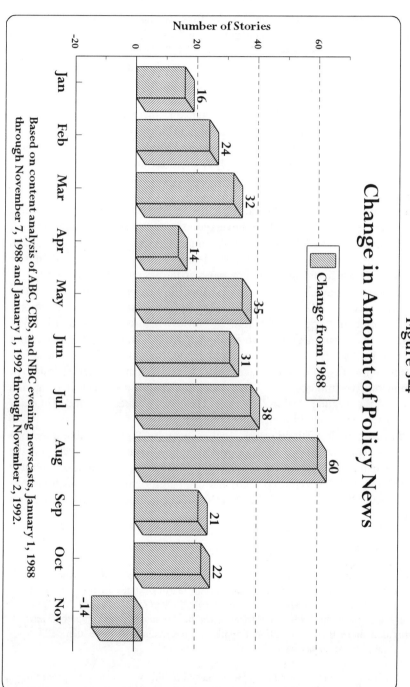

Figure 3-4

Change in Amount of Policy News

Based on content analysis of ABC, CBS, and NBC evening newscasts, January 1, 1988 through November 7, 1988 and January 1, 1992 through November 2, 1992.

Despite the "character issue" distractions during the primaries, and the post-primary surge in horse race news, the networks never flagged in their coverage of policy substance during the 1992 campaign. As Figure 3-4 shows, every full month of Campaign '92 featured more issue stories than the comparable month of Campaign '88. (The small drop in November is due to an artifact of the calender. In 1988, Election Day was on November 7; in 1992, the vote came five days earlier, on November 2.) This uniform gain contrasts with coverage of the campaign horse race, which at varying times either exceeded or lagged the corresponding 1988 levels, depending on the media's perceptions of how close or interesting the race was at any given point.

The shift in favor of substance was clearly intentional, rather than merely circumstantial. The networks had signaled in advance of the campaign that they intended to increase their coverage of the issues, and their regular feature segments (ABC's "American Agenda," CBS's "Eye on America," and NBC's "America Close-Up") routinely departed from the campaign trail to provide contextual and thematic coverage of the issues and candidates.

"American Agenda" in particular provided discussion of policy issues that was untainted by talk of campaign strategy or horse race considerations. ABC's campaign "Agenda" featured 21 stories — three per week, for seven weeks — that focused on the two nominees' records and proposals on major domestic issues. The "Agenda" covered crime, the deficit, drugs, education, the environment, job creation, and health care. "Agenda" stories lasted an average of five minutes, more than twice the length of a typical campaign story. As a regular feature of each Tuesday, Wednesday, and Thursday broadcast, viewers could anticipate each piece.

Adding to their distinctiveness, each campaign "Agenda" item was produced by reporters whose beats were the policy issues themselves, not the political campaign. Their reports offered no hint, for example, of political implication, and they reported facts that campaign reporters would traditionally eschew. For example, on October 20, ABC's Carole Simpson focused on the candidates' urban policies:

> President Bush and Governor Clinton have laid out surprisingly similar proposals for addressing the urban crisis. Bush and Clinton agree that the centerpiece of any plan to revitalize the cities must be economic development. In 1983, Clinton made Arkansas one of the earliest states in the country to give companies tax breaks to locate in so-called enterprise zones.... Today there are more than 450 enterprise zones in Arkansas, which together have provided more than two billion dollars of investment and more than 30,000 jobs, helping Arkansas rank first in job growth....
>
> Bush's most visible urban initiative has been the weed-and-seed program, set up last year.... The idea is to provide federal money to bolster local law

enforcement, to weed out criminals and seed troubled areas with social services. Demonstration projects are underway in 20 cities. According to the
U.S. Conference of Mayors, the weed-and-seed program is showing only
modest results, but Bush wants the program expanded to 50 more communities
next year.[30]

ABC's approach was part of an announced effort to extricate the "news"
from the events of the campaign. "None of this is brain surgery or utterly
original," ABC anchor Peter Jennings told the *Washington Post*. "We must
resist the pressure from senior correspondents to do the Clinton piece today
or the Bush piece today, and not to be seduced by the pictures as we've been
so easily seduced in the past. I don't think any of us ever wants to be in the
flag factory situation again."[31]

It was evident that the reformers successfully tapped into the resentment
in the news industry against candidates who attempted to "use" the media.
This resentment was evident in Jennings's description of ABC's new policy,
when he argued that one goal was to be "less manipulated" by the candidates.[32]

At the 1991 convention of the Radio and Television News Directors
Association (RTNDA), participants exhorted each other "to take control of
the political agenda." Advised one local news director, "Set your own
priorities so that you don't get completely driven by whatever the candidates' priorities become and whatever their strategy becomes." A former
network executive told an RTNDA panel that "If you say, 'On the basis of
my news judgment I have decided that this candidate has nothing new to say
today,' perhaps tomorrow that candidate will."[33]

By the fall of 1992, CNN's Tom Hannon was telling the *Boston Globe* that
"all of [the networks] are better prepared this time to address the substantive
issues *regardless of the media strategies of the campaigns*."[34] (Emphasis
added.) Reported the *Wall Street Journal*: "The network evening news shows
aren't as kind to presidential candidates as they used to be. No more Mr.
Nice Guys, playing things pretty much the way the campaigns want it."[35]

On the contrary, the broadcast networks (and the major newspapers)
planned to offer voters "substance" whether the candidates participated or
not. When we expanded our study during the general election to include
three "prestige press" newspapers, CNN's *PrimeNews* and PBS's *MacNeil-
Lehrer NewsHour*, we found even greater seriousness of purpose.

We worked closely with political scientist Bruce Buchanan, who had
directed the Markle Foundation's exhaustive study of the 1988 race, to
ensure that our study would yield comparable data.[36] We found that the two
categories of coverage that Buchanan counted as "substantive" in 1988 —
policy issues and the candidates' qualifications — together increased from
29% of general election news topics to 38% in 1992. In fact, each of the

five additional news organizations devoted larger portions of their news coverage to substantive issues than did any of the "big three" networks. (See Figure 3-5.)

Newspapers: According to longtime media critic Tom Rosenstiel, now a *Newsweek* correspondent, the major newspapers more than shared TV's desire to assert control over the agenda:

> Many [newspapers] were imbued with a greater desire to change than any of the networks. The *Washington Post* was among the most aggressive. "We do have to find our own agenda," political editor William Hamilton said, to find out what concerned voters and "call into question any candidate" who ignored it. In November, 1991 the *Post* embarked on a series of polls and interviews to register the electorate's mood, which it said would serve as a "guide" for the rest of the coverage.[37]

Fulfilling David Broder's advocacy of a voters' agenda, the *Washington Post* offered its readers more than 6,000 column inches of news that qualified as "substance" during the fall campaign, more than that provided by the *New York Times,* the *Wall Street Journal,* or any other news organization we studied. Still, as a result of the extraordinary total amount of coverage the *Post* gave Campaign '92 (nearly 19,000 column inches in the last 58 days of the campaign), the *Post* ranked only slightly ahead of the networks, and behind the other papers, in the overall *percentage* of substantive news.

Thus, one could justly praise the *Post* for the tremendous amount of issue coverage it made available to its readers. At the same time, the *Post* carried twice as much coverage (more than 12,000 column inches, or nearly two full pages per day for two months) that treated the campaign as either a game or contest, critiqued the strategy and styles of the campaign teams, or lampooned the candidates' foibles in "Style" section pieces, its "Reliable Source" gossip column, etc.

If there was a complaint about the seriousness of the *Post's* election-year coverage (and it is an exceptional newspaper that offers as much substantive information as the *Post* did in 1992), it stemmed from the overall context in which it presented the campaign. *Post* ombudsman Joann Byrd noted in early September that "the *Post* has produced detailed evaluations of the candidates' economic proposals and stories contrasting Bush and Clinton positions on economic issues, abortion and the role of government."[38]

Yet, she continued, the *Post* has also

> been filling a page or two each day with news from the campaign trail: speeches, charges and countercharges, polls, strategy. Some of the most skilled analysts on the *Post* staff have explained the tactics and the reasoning

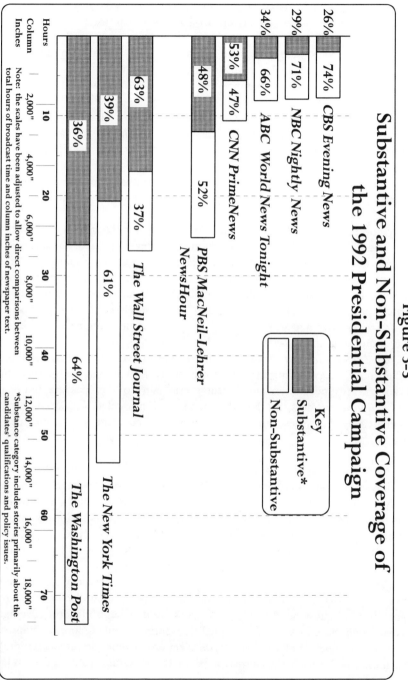

Figure 3-5

Substantive and Non-Substantive Coverage of
the 1992 Presidential Campaign

CBS Evening News — 26% / 74%

NBC Nightly News — 29% / 71%

ABC World News Tonight — 34% / 66%

CNN PrimeNews — 53% / 47%

PBS MacNeil-Lehrer NewsHour — 48% / 52%

The Wall Street Journal — 63% / 37%

The New York Times — 39% / 61%

The Washington Post — 36% / 64%

Key
Substantive*
Non-Substantive

Hours: 10 20 30 40 50 60 70
Column Inches: 2,000" 4,000" 6,000" 8,000" 10,000" 12,000" 14,000" 16,000" 18,000"

Note: the scales have been adjusted to allow direct comparisons between total hours of broadcast time and column inches of newspaper text.

*Substance category includes stories primarily about the candidates' qualifications and policy issues.

and the Election Day stakes. If you wanted to learn to run for public office, you could do worse than to study the pages of this newspaper.

As far as the issues were concerned, "I study the *Post* with the best of them and, as of today, couldn't be trusted in a voting booth."[39]

Byrd wrote her assessment during the first week of the general election, if Labor Day is taken as the starting date. During the following 51 days, the patterns she identified in the *Post*'s coverage remained unchanged. The newspaper offered detailed and occasionally insightful stories about the candidates' programs and platforms, but those stories were usually swamped in a sea of coverage that struck every political note on the scale. The *New York Times* offered a similar balance of substantive and non-substantive coverage, and Byrd's general critique could probably be applied there as well.

By contrast, the *Wall Street Journal* offered by far the highest proportion of substantive campaign news. As Figure 3-5 shows, 63% of the *Journal's* election coverage was focused on its substantive aspects. Economic policy was, of course, the *Journal's* specialty. There was plenty of horse race analysis, to be sure — 2.6 stories per day contained reports about public opinion polls, about half the rate of the *Times* and *Post*. But the context of the *Journal's* coverage was more serious — the issues dominated the horse race, rather than the other way around.

Thus, *Times* and *Post* readers had more substantive information delivered to their doorstep each morning, but it was mixed in with much larger helping of horse race speculation and "theater criticism" of the passing political show. *Journal* readers, on the other hand, were presented with a campaign dominated by the issues, but the total amount of coverage was dramatically lower.

The CNN Experiment: Among the television outlets, CNN's *PrimeNews* was the only newscast to devote a majority of its election coverage (53%) to policy issues and candidate records and qualifications. PBS's highly es-teemed *MacNeil-Lehrer NewsHour* finished a close second with 48% sub-stantive coverage, followed at some remove by ABC (34%), NBC (29%), and CBS (26% — only about half as substantive as CNN). ABC's percentage was boosted, of course, by its "American Agenda" series.

Once again, this comparison refers only to the *proportion* of substantive news. In terms of total air time, *MacNeil-Lehrer* far outdistanced all its competitors in substantive news, partly because its overall election coverage was so much more extensive. In fact, PBS's entry provided more substantive coverage than second-place CNN's *total* election air time, despite airing only five nights per week. Of course, most of this coverage consisted of relatively inexpensive in-studio discussion, as opposed to the commercial networks' heavy use of field reports.

Even in absolute terms, however, CNN's hour-long *PrimeNews* easily outdistanced the "big three"'s half-hour newscasts in providing substantive information to its audience. *PrimeNews* was so issue-oriented as the result of another purposeful attempt to improve election news. CNN received a multimillion-dollar grant from the John and Mary Markle Foundation (which had earlier issued a report criticizing media coverage of the 1988 race) for the purpose of creating additional programming to serve voters' information needs.

Although the Markle grant was used for a variety of innovations, the principal results appeared in CNN's *Democracy in America* series, six hours of special programming on sequential Sundays anchored by Bernard Shaw; and *Promises, Promises*, four hours of Tuesday evening programs anchored by Frank Sesno and devoted to the economy.

The goal of both series was to provide citizens with a depth of information missing in traditional news coverage, and to help voters grapple with the challenge of selecting the best candidate for president. CNN controlled the editorial content of the programs, and veteran correspondents filed the reports. The documentaries were edited into ten-minute segments and rebroadcast during the following week's *PrimeNews*, getting the information out to wider audiences. This material alone accounted for three-fourths of the issue news that we measured on CNN's flagship newscast.

The first three Sunday programs dealt with "The Nation's Agenda." As Bernard Shaw explained it, CNN's agenda consisted of

what we consider the most important problems the United States faces as it nears the 21st Century.... Problems such as the erosion of American competitiveness in the global economy so crucial to our jobs and standard of living; the gridlock in our federal government and the alienation felt by voters; and finally, the urban underclass — angry, seemingly locked out of the American Dream.[40]

The second group of programs — "The Battle to Lead" — dealt with the Republican and Democratic candidates' biographies and records. Coupled with the Tuesday series on the economy, it was one of the most ambitious projects undertaken by a news organization during the 1992 campaign.

The documentary series succeeded in presenting voters with virtually pure substance — more than 90 percent of the airtime for these programs focused on policy issues or candidate qualifications. If the *Democracy in America* series took a markedly substantive approach to campaign coverage, however, it also offered remarkably little information about the candidates' records, proposals, and philosophies regarding the major issues of the day.

The series provided detailed information on three issues CNN identified as among the nation's most urgent problems — government gridlock, race and poverty, and economic competitiveness. While a variety of contending solutions to social problems were explored, the issue-oriented programs did not reveal the candidates' preferred prescriptions. Conversely, the candidate's biographies focused on issues that most illuminated each man's career, rather than those selected as the nation's most pressing challenges in the earlier installments.

This was a serious effort by a news organization and a philanthropic foundation to help establish priorities and a dialogue among competing issues, and to set an agenda based on national needs rather than on political sex appeal. Its failure to connect the issues with equally detailed presentations of the candidates' proposals, however, seems perversely (albeit inadvertently) designed to increase voters' sense of futility rather than their storehouse of relevant knowledge.

The *Democracy in America* series may have been the victim of a journalistic prejudice against straightforwardly broadcasting the issue agendas and platforms of political candidates. The fear of flacking shared by campaign reporters, their antipathy toward reproducing "staged photo-ops" or "manufactured sound bites" in their newscasts, may have led them off the campaign trail and back to network headquarters, where they could report on the issues from "above the fray." However, decoupling the issues from the candidates and the campaign made the discussions less relevant to the voting decision.

HOW SUBSTANTIVE WAS THE SUBSTANCE?

Our mixed review of CNN's election news raises the distinction between the quantity and quality of issue coverage. Thus far we have evaluated the sheer frequency of issue mentions in campaign news. By this measure, the media earned their praise in 1992; audiences were exposed to considerably more talk about "the issues" than in 1988. But how informative was the talk? Was the increase in the quantity of issues matched by an increase in its quality?

Journalists have criticized past presidential candidates not only for ignoring policy issues but also for trivializing them by reducing complicated topics to glib sound bites. It is therefore fair to ask how much better the media did when they took control of the campaign dialogue. To find out, we expanded our analysis of issue coverage during the general election by measuring the level of detail and the context in which each issue was raised. We were particularly interested in how well the media used issue discussions to help voters differentiate among the candidates.

Whenever an issue was mentioned, we noted whether it was linked to any candidate's past record, current plans or proposals, or general philosophy of government. In addition, we sought to measure the amount of *in-depth* issue discussion by noting whether each discussion was mentioned only briefly or discussed at some length; whether the discussion cited any specific details (such as actual dollar amounts of proposed new spending); and whether the context or consequences of an issue position were mentioned (such as the possible effects of a candidate's program).

We were well aware of the demand for brevity in daily campaign report-age, so our criteria were not very demanding. An issue discussion was considered to be "extensive" if it occupied at least 20 seconds of air time or two brief paragraphs of a print article. The requirement for specific details could be satisfied by reporting, for example, that Clinton proposed spending $35 billion to build an orbiting space station. When Clinton's running mate, Senator Al Gore, said the space station plan would provide jobs for highly skilled defense workers displaced by cutbacks, he offered some of the proposal's implications.[41]

Finally, we noted how the issue was raised — by the candidate or other partisan groups, or whether the news organization itself was raising the issue. Discussions of taxes and budget cuts in the ABC report about Bush's economic address on September 10, were examples of issue discussions prompted by one of the candidates.[42] An "American Agenda" report two weeks later focused on "just how much of a role should government play in raising a healthy, happy family.[43] In the first case, ABC was responding to the news of the day. In the second, they were following their own agenda.

Note that we are concerned here only with the depth of issue discussion, not its tone. (The media's treatment of the candidates' competing issue stances is considered in Chapters 6 and 7.) Understanding the basics of the candidates' proposals, however, is a prerequisite for informed voting, since voters cannot intelligently evaluate the praise and criticism of a candidate's program without first understanding its factual components.

By these criteria, most media references (television and newspaper alike) to the candidates' programs resembled bumper sticker slogans — brief, superficial, and without context. We coded 6,280 references during the general election to the three candidates' records, proposals, or stances on more than 90 policy issues. Most of these references were throw-away lines in discussions of campaign strategy or tactics.

Nearly three out of four references (72%) were brief — at most a couple of sentences in either a TV or newspaper story. More than three-fourths (78%) lacked any specifics or details, and almost two-thirds (64%) lacked any contextual references. (See Table 3-1.) *Only 9% of all references to the candidates' issues were reasonably extensive, detailed, and contextually meaningful presentations of their records and proposals.*

Table 3-1

Depth of Media Presentations of Candidates' Issue Stands

	Percent Extensive	Percent Detailed	Percent in Context	Percent All Three	N
All Candidates					
Total	28%	22%	36%	9%	6,280
Record	29	21	33	7	1,876
Proposals	34	35	47	16	1,951
Philosophy	23	12	31	5	2,453
George Bush	31	21	35	8	3,109
Bill Clinton	27	22	39	10	2,630
Ross Perot	22	25	30	8	541

Note -- Based on all mentions of each candidate's record, proposal, or philosophy on specific issues, in eight national news media outlets.

Audiences read or heard more extensive information and context regarding Bush and Clinton than Perot. Specific information was more likely in discussions of new proposals than in summaries of a candidate's record in government or business. Discussions of the two main candidates also differed significantly in their focus: Bush's record was referenced twice as often (1,464 times) as his new proposals (712). Conversely, Clinton's record (390) was discussed less than half as frequently as his plans for the future (946). Perot's proposals, too, were covered far more extensively than his corporate record by 293 to only 22 references.

In presenting the candidates' programs, TV reporters most often chose to cover issues that had been raised by the candidates themselves in their speeches, paid ads, or during public debates. Reporter-instigated explorations of the issues (such as ABC's "American Agenda" or CNN's *Democracy in America* series) were much rarer, accounting for only 29% of TV's issue presentation. In contrast, nearly half (46%) of the references to the candidates' records and proposals in newspaper stories were prompted by the news organization itself.

Because such data do not exist for prior campaign years, it is impossible to say whether these percentages indicate that the media were more aggressive in setting their own agendas than in previous campaigns. Clearly, though, a significant amount of the issue news reaching voters was spurred by news organizations rather than the candidates during Campaign '92.

This accounting also reveals some serious gaps in the media coverage. For example, out of over 3,600 general election stories that appeared in the prestige press and national television, fewer than 100 discussed at length how Clinton handled any particular issues as governor of Arkansas. More precisely, only 93 such discussions exceeded the two paragraph/20-second threshold — 30 on TV and 63 in print.

On the four commercial network evening news broadcasts, discussions of Clinton's record appeared less than once per week; in the newspapers, Clinton's record was referenced every third day. In contrast, nearly seven times as many news stories (641) included detailed allegations about Clinton's draft record, use of illegal drugs, and extramarital affairs.

It is conceivable that the media gave short shrift to Clinton's gubernatorial record not out of malice toward the Arkansas governor but because of the complexity involved in learning about and summarizing a 12-year record whose details were unfamiliar to most national journalists. Still, given the investigative energies devoted to learning about his private life, the relative lack of information about Clinton's official record speaks volumes about the priorities and news judgment of campaign journalists.

The shallowness of the media's issue coverage tells only half the story. Most of the time issues were brought up in election pieces, there was no

Table 3-2

Most Frequently Discussed Policy Issues

	Total Stories	Stories Mentioning a Candidate's Record, Proposal, or Position	
		Number	Percent
Economy	1,431	133	9%
Taxes	1,033	200	19%
Unemployment	801	51	6%
Health Care	546	92	17%
Budget Deficit	532	66	12%
Education	453	101	22%
Environment	403	76	19%
Trade	370	87	24%
Iraq	349	104	30%
Role of Government	333	102	31%
General Foreign Policy	330	72	22%
Job Training	315	47	15%
Defense	292	61	21%
Family	287	23	8%
Abortion	249	55	22%

Note: Based on number of mentions in election stories, in eight national news media outlets.

reference to the candidates' perspectives or policies at all. (See Table 3-2.) For example, the economy was mentioned in 1,431 general election stories at the eight national news organizations we studied. Yet, these three leading newspapers and five broadcast outlets together carried only 133 stories with references to any one of the candidates' economic policies, records, or philosophies. More than nine out of ten times the economy was mentioned, it was discussed without any reference to the candidates who vied to solve the problem in question.

An examination of the most frequently covered issues of the campaign shows that between 69% and 94% of all of the stories about those issues failed to link those issues with the candidates even referentially. Most of the time, readers and viewers faced the issues without any exposure to either the solutions the candidates were proposing or their past records in dealing with them.

Even when the news went into detail about an issue, the candidates were given short shrift. Table 3-3 shows how frequently the media offered "extensive" discussion about each issue (i.e., at least 20 seconds or two paragraphs). There was considerable discussion of the major issues — 557 extended references to the economy's condition, for example, or nearly ten per day during the general election cycle.

Such repeated, extensive features were one of the reasons the media were praised for offering more campaign substance. Yet, in few of the stories containing "extensive" discussions of the issues were the candidates' records, proposals, or philosophies considered. The most frequently covered of these issues involved Gov. Clinton's record and proposals regarding taxes — a debate that drew media attention not because of the importance of a president's tax policies, but because of the *political consequences* of the Bush campaign's attacks on the Clinton record.

In spite of the campaign fireworks, however, Mr. Clinton's taxation policies as Governor of Arkansas, along with the tax proposals he made during the campaign, drew detailed consideration in less than one-fifth of the stories dealing with taxes. Neither of the candidates' records or views on any of the other issues received even that much attention.

News organizations congratulated themselves on their newfound appreciation of the "issues." *CBS Evening News* political editor Susan Zirinsky was pleased that her broadcast had "stepped back. We don't do 'the day.' We look at issues."[44] *Los Angeles Times* Washington bureau chief Jack Nelson, a critic of the press during the primaries, said that "after the two conventions the press was tough [and] it held all the candidates to speak to the issues."[45]

Even as the media devoted more time and space to policy issues, however, they failed to connect those issues with the candidates from whom voters would choose their next president. Newspaper readers and television viewers

Table 3-3

Extensive Discussion of Candidates' Issue Stands

	Total Stories	Extensive Discussion Bush	Extensive Discussion Clinton
Economy	557	22	34
Taxes	358	26	64
Unemployment	215	9	8
Budget	155	4	6
Trade	150	11	8
Health Care	138	22	25
Environment	111	14	16
Role of Government	110	5	8
Iraq	108	21	0
General Foreign Policy	86	2	3

Note: Based on number of times candidates' issue stands were featured, in eight national news media outlets.

could learn plenty about the issues in 1992, but they had to be extremely diligent to piece together the candidates' records on most of them. When the campaign concluded, voters had heard more about "the issues" in Campaign '92 than they had in '88. Yet they were rarely exposed to the details of the candidates' programs. Was that because the media was unwilling to share those details, or were they unable to do so? Were reporters hamstrung by the candidates' own superficial approach to the campaign? To find out, we will compare the news reports to what the candidates themselves were saying.

Notes

Opening quote: Paul Friedman, quoted by Tom Rosenstiel, *Strange Bedfellows: How Television and the Presidential Candidates Changed American Politics, 1992* (New York: Hyperion, 1993), p. 240.

1.   The relevant studies show that voter knowledge does not increase from exposure to day-to-day TV coverage, and increases modestly with day-to-day newspaper reading. Voters do learn from TV coverage of live campaign events, such as convention speeches and debates. This would suggest that the pre-packaged, pre-digested format of the nightly news fails to do what the candidate events accomplish: explain policies and positions in a coherent, contextual fashion that is memorable for voters watching. See, among others, Doris A. Graber, *Processing the News: How People Tame the Information Tide* (New York: Longman, 1984); Thomas E. Patterson, *The Mass Media Election: How Americans Choose Their President* (New York: Praeger Publishers, 1980); Dan Drew and David Weaver, "Voter Learning in the 1988 Presidential Election: Did the Debates and the Media Matter?" *Journalism Quarterly* 68 (Spring/Summer 1991): 27-37; and Bruce Buchanan, *Electing a President: The Markle Commission Research on Campaign '88* (Austin: University of Texas Press, 1991).

2.   When parties were responsible for "getting the word out," failure usually meant the loss of an election and political power for the party, and the individuals involved often lost their jobs. When the media fail to fully inform voters, they often lose nothing of value (although they usually are criticized by members of the defeated political party, whose charges of media bias also absolve them of responsibility for their own electoral failures).

3.   Marvin Kalb, "TV, Election Spoiler," *New York Times*, November 28, 1988.

4.   Ibid.

5.   Richard Harwood, "Pointers From Harvard," *Washington Post*, December 15, 1991.

6.   Rod Granger, "The Campaign Trail: Networks Redefining Their Coverage," *Electronic Media*, February 17, 1992.

7.   Alan L. Otten, "TV News Drops Kid-Glove Coverage of Election, Trading Staged Sound Bites for Hard Analysis," *Wall Street Journal*, October 12, 1992. See also Timothy J. Russert, "For '92, the Networks Have to Do Better," *New York Times*, March 4, 1990.

8.   Ed Avis, "Broadcasters Take Heed of Complaints," *The Quill*, March 1992.

9.   Ken Bode, "Pull the Plug: We Have the Power to Just Say No, to Abandon Our Photo-op Addiction," *The Quill*, March 1992.

10.   Russert, "For '92, the Networks Have to Do Better."

11.   David Broder, "Five Ways to Put Some Sanity Back In Elections," *Washington Post*, January 14, 1990.

12.   M. L. Stein, "Politics from the Voters' Point of View," *Editor and Publisher*, March 2, 1991.

13.   Ibid.

14.   Quoted by Mandy Grunwald in Jeffrey L. Katz, "Tilt? Did the Media Favor Bill Clinton or Did George Bush Earn His Negative Coverage?" *Washington Journalism Review*, January 1993.

15.   Ellen Hume, *Restoring the Bond: Connecting Campaign Coverage to Voters*, A Report of the Campaign Lessons for '92 Project (Cambridge, MA: Harvard University, 1991), pp. 132-133.

16.   Ibid., p. 134.

17.   Quoted by Thomas Winshop, "The New Curmudgeon," *Editor and Publisher*, December 7, 1991.

18.   Broder, "Five Ways to Put Some Sanity Back in Elections."

19.   Hume, *Restoring the Bond...*, p. 133.

20.   Doris Graber, *Processing the News;* Diana Mutz, "Impersonal Influence in American Politics," *The Public Perspective* (November/December 1992): 19-21.

21.   David H. Weaver, "Setting Political Priorities: What Role for the Press?" *Political Communications and Persuasion* 7 (1990): 201-211.

22.   Maura Clancey and Michael Robinson, "General Election Coverage: Part I," *Public Opinion* 7, no. 6 (December/January 1985).

23.   See, among others, Thomas E. Patterson and Robert B. McClure, *The Unseeing Eye: The Myth of Television Power in National Politics* (Toronto: Longman Canada Limited, 1976); Thomas E. Patterson, *The Mass Media Election...*; Michael J. Robinson and Margaret A. Sheehan, *Over the Wire and On TV: CBS and UPI in Campaign '80* (New York: Russell Sage Foundation, 1983); Michael J. Robinson, "Where's the Beef? Media and Media Elites in 1984", in *The American Elections of 1984*, ed. Austin Ranney (Washington, DC: American Enterprise Institute, 1985); S. Robert Lichter, Daniel Amundson, and Richard E. Noyes, *The Video Campaign: Network Coverage of the 1988 Primaries* (Washington, DC: American Enterprise Institute, 1988); and Buchanan, *Electing A President.*

24.   J. Craig Crawford, "On the campaign trail," *Sentinel Quarterly* 6 (Summer 1988).

25. Paul Taylor, "Campaign '92: Thrills and Spills and Substance," *Washington Post*, February 16, 1992.

26. ABC's *World News Sunday*, February 9, 1992

27. For the five nights prior to the Iowa caucuses, Senator Harkin averaged 8.6% in the polls. For the five nights after Iowa, he averaged 8.8%.

28. Perot announced on July 16 that he would not run as an independent in the general election. During late July and August, the media focused on a Bush-Clinton match-up. In early September, however, Perot appeared on a variety of talk shows, hinting that he would re-join the race. "If the volunteers said, 'It's a dirty job but you've got to do it,' I belong to them," Perot told a C-SPAN call-in show on September 11. "Let's try to get the two parties to step up to the plate. If they don't, we'll do what we have to do." (*New York Times*, September 13, 1992.) Perot formally announced his candidacy on October 1, 1992.

29. *Newsweek*, November 21, 1988.

30. ABC's *World News Tonight*, October 20, 1992.

31. Howard Kurtz, "Media Alter Approach to Campaign Coverage," *Washington Post*, September 11, 1992.

32. *The Washington Post*, September 11, 1992. For a detailed, behind-the-scenes look at how ABC News approach Campaign '92, see Tom Rosenstiel, *Strange Bedfellows: How Television and the Presidential Candidates Changed American Politics, 1992* (New York: Hyperion, 1993).

33. Quoted by Rob Puglisi, "Take Control of the Political Agenda in 1992; Election-Year Coverage Debated," *RTNDA Communicator*, November 1991.

34. Quoted by Renee Loth, "Studies Find Tilt in TV Coverage of Campaign," *Boston Globe*, September 2, 1992.

35. Otten, "TV News Drops Kid-Glove Coverage...."

36. Buchanan, *Electing a President.*

37. Tom Rosenstiel, *Strange Bedfellows*, p. 40

38. Joann Byrd, "Recycled Coverage?" *Washington Post*, September 13, 1992.

39. Ibid.

40. CNN's *Democracy in America*, "The Nation's Agenda," September 20, 1992.

41. Warren E. Leary, "Gore Pushes Space Station Plan, Saying It Could Absorb Arms Jobs, " *New York Times*, October 20, 1992.

42. ABC's *World News Tonight*, September 10, 1992.

43. ABC's *World News Tonight*, September 23, 1992.

44. Quoted by Edwin Diamond, "Getting It Right," *New York*, November 2, 1992.

45. Quoted by Debra Gersh, "Introspection," *Editor and Publisher*, November 21, 1992.

Chapter Four

Whose Agenda Is It, Anyway?

The essence of leadership is setting the agenda, and we're in a fight now over who's going to do that.
—Ellen Hume, *Wall Street Journal*, 1988

On September 15, 1992, President Bush and Governor Clinton appeared before the National Guard Association Convention in Salt Lake City, Utah. For both men, it was a relatively routine campaign appearance, where each would reiterate the central messages of their campaigns. President Bush led off the morning with a quip about modern campaign methods: "I was thinking of giving a political speech," Bush joked, "a real stemwinder with catchy sound bites, the usual biting insults. Then I got to thinking: I'm not going to do that; you've already sacrificed enough for your country." The audience laughed appreciatively. "Instead," Bush said, "I'd like to talk about a more serious subject: America's national defense and, really, our place in the world."[1]

Bush's remarks consisted of praise for the National Guard for the relief and assistance they provided after the Los Angeles riots, Hurricane Andrew, and Hurricane Iniki. He pledged that, despite reduced military spending, "maintaining strong, capable Reserve and Guard forces will remain essential to our military strategy." Military downsizing needed to be done in an "orderly and deliberate" manner, Bush said, and he argued that Clinton's proposed reductions in spending were "$60 billion beyond which my civilian and military experts believe is responsible." Bush offered a thematic portrait of an internationalist foreign policy, and vowed that the United States would remain strong and engaged in world affairs:

> For all the great gains we've made for freedom, for all the peace of mind that we've secured for the young people in this country, the world remains a dangerous place. The Soviet bear may be extinct, but there are still plenty of wolves in the world: dictators with missiles, narco-terrorists trying to take over whole countries, ethnic wars, regional flashpoints, madmen we can't allow to get a finger on the nuclear trigger. And you have my word on this: I will never allow a lone wolf to endanger American security. We must remain strong.

> No, our work in the world did not end with our victory in the Cold War. Our task is to guard against the crises that haven't caught fire, the wars that are waiting to happen, the threats that will come with little or no warning. I make this promise: As long as I am president, our services will remain the best trained, best equipped, the best led fighting forces in the world. This is the way we guarantee peace.

Bush concluded his remarks by providing his audience with a sense of what it felt like to be commander-in-chief during a war. He talked about the last-minute doubts he had prior to the start of the Gulf War. ("I remember walking along the Rose Garden [the night the war started] and thinking," Bush said. "I was wondering if our military estimates were really accurate…, if our smart bombs were as smart as [Air Force General] Tony McPeak and other experts told me they were.") He also spoke about the letters he received from the parents of those servicemen and women who were casualties of the war. He stressed the gravity of the decisions a president faces in office:

> But you get letters like these, and you can almost see the faces, faces of youth and innocence. You feel the weight of the job. Sending a son or daughter into combat, believe me, is the toughest part of the presidency. Most presidents never learn that lesson because, thank God, most don't have to ask others to put their lives on the line. But every president might.

> Does this mean that if you have never seen the awful horror of battle, that you can never be Commander in Chief? Of course not. Not at all. But it does mean that we must hold our presidents to the highest standard because they might have to decide if our sons and daughters should knock early on death's door.

Bill Clinton's speech later in the morning struck many of the same points as Bush's. He also praised the Guard for its work following Hurricane Andrew and in Los Angeles. He also offered examples of how, as governor, he had worked with the National Guard. He reported that the Arkansas government acted to "ease the considerable hardships" of Guardsmen mobilized during the Gulf War, by paying state employees an additional salary to compensate for pay sacrificed by Guard duty, and by establishing family assistance centers and support groups. He agreed with Bush about the need for an internationalist foreign policy, using practically identical language:

> We have to shift the focus of our military to meet the real threats that we face today and those we think we are likely to face tomorrow: aggressive tyrants like Saddam Hussein; new regional conflicts; ethnic and racial strife that could spread beyond the borders of particular nations; terrorism and the threat of proliferation of nuclear and other weapons of mass destruction, a major threat we will have to face for several years to come.

He challenged Bush's assertion that his proposed budget cut too much from defense:

> It is true, as the president said this morning, that my five-year defense budget contains somewhat less money than his does. But listen to the difference: $1.36 trillion in my budget, as opposed to $1.42 trillion in his over five years, a difference of only five percent. And we provide in our budget for fewer troops in Europe, less spending on the Brilliant Pebbles portion of Star Wars, but more reliance on new weapons systems, and more reliance on the Guard and the reserve here at home.

Clinton devoted the final minutes of his address to the need he perceived to integrate economic and national security, and to coordinate public and private economic effort. In doing so, he deftly linked concepts of military organization and national commitment with his call for economic change:

> Other nations with which we compete, which are growing more rapidly, nations which realize that economic security is a part of national security, and that in that sense national security has to begin at home, have a totally different approach to the world's challenges.
>
> And we must learn from that, and craft a uniquely American approach. I believe it is time to abandon trickle-down economics, not to go back to tax-and-spend and divide the pie, but to go forward with a theory that says we have to invest, and educate, and train and compete; that we do not have a person to waste; that we need a national economic strategy of partnership between government, business, labor and education, to dramatically increase the incentives for people in the private sector to invest in new plants, and equipment, in research and development, in the commercial technologies that will give us the same lead in the economy that the defense technologies give us on the battlefield, and in training the best educated workforce in America.

If a workforce that is trained well works in the Persian Gulf, believe me, it will work in the factories, on the farms, in the small businesses, on the main streets, in the heartland of the United States of America to bring this country's economy back.

...Today, wherever I go, I find people full of cynicism about whether government can be made to work for them again, except when something bad happens and they see somebody like the Guard. Then they know government works, and they're proud to see their tax dollars are going for you....

My fellow Americans, what is killing this country today is not the size of our challenge but the dimension of our disbelief. And we need faith and conviction that we can confront these problems in an American way that goes beyond the kind of paralysis we've had at home for the last 10 years; that reflects the same sort of spirit and determination and commitment of resources that we saw in Desert Storm.... So that we can be strong abroad, we must again be strong at home.

Bush and Clinton each received extended applause at the end of their remarks. Both received baseball-style caps emblazoned with Guard insignia, and a painting by a Native American artist. Bush's was called "The Silent Warrior," while Clinton received "The Silent Protector." Each depicted an eagle in flight, with Guardsmen and their tools of war etched in the wings of the eagle.

Both speeches were relatively typical campaign addresses, and so too was the coverage they received on the evening news that night — reporters focused not on the substantive significance of either speech, but rather on the event's overall political drama.

ABC's Peter Jennings led his newscast by noting the "rampant specula-tion" that Bush would use the occasion to attack Clinton for his lack of military service.[2] NBC's Tom Brokaw echoed his colleague, saying "It was going to be the showdown of the week in the presidential campaign: Bush and Clinton in Salt Lake City before the National Guard Convention, on Clinton's draft history." But, according to NBC's Andrea Mitchell, "the candidates shadow-boxed over the draft issue, but didn't throw any direct punches."[3] On CNN, co-anchor Susan Rook called it "subtle political warfare."[4]

When they weren't using metaphors to highlight the drama of the mo-ment, reporters were analyzing the strategies and political goals that lay behind each candidates' words. CNN's Charles Bierbauer threaded clips from both candidates' speeches into his analysis:

The Bush campaign strategy is to undermine Clinton's integrity — not by questioning his avoidance of the draft for an unpopular war, but to target

Clinton's reluctant explanation of his acts. The president criticizes Clinton mostly by innuendo, but this is a coordinated attack. Deputy Campaign Manager Mary Matalin fires more blunt quotes across the media faxes, this day charging Clinton's explanations show "habitual delay, deceit and duplicity." Clinton, who shifted his schedule to address the same National Guard conference, ignored the Bush challenge to his draft explanation....

Both campaigns think economics is the key issue in the presidential race. But the Bush campaign thinks the draft question will continue to weaken Governor Clinton, even if the governor does not oblige the president by addressing the draft question directly.[5]

CBS took a different approach to the day's news — covering the Salt Lake City convention while simultaneously branding both men's speeches as irrelevant. Anchor Dan Rather reported the latest economic statistics before he introduced the campaign segment:

Correspondent Richard Threlkeld has been in Ohio, talking to people and looking at what issues do and do not matter to voters. Take Gov. Bill Clinton and the draft. Both Clinton and President Bush were in the west today, *not talking about the economy* — they were talking *around* the subject of the draft at a National Guard convention. [Emphasis added.]

Threlkeld's subsequent story included poll results showing that about eight out of ten voters said the draft controversy would not affect their vote. His summary: "There may well be lots of reasons for voters to wonder if Bill Clinton's the right person to be our next president. But what most voters here in Ohio and elsewhere seem to be saying is: his draft record is just not one of them."[6]

The CBS broadcast seemed tailor-made to fit the reformers' agenda for campaign news. After chiding the candidates for avoiding important issues like the economy, the network put the issue on the agenda itself. Unfortunately, there is one slight problem with this interpretation: Dan Rather notwithstanding, Mr. Clinton *did* speak about the economy for several minutes in his Salt Lake City speech, a fact reported on ABC, NBC, and CNN. So did President Bush, who delivered an economic speech later the same day in Colorado.[7] Yet Threlkeld's story showed an angry voter saying, "The economy's the issue. If Bush wants to keep beating the drums on that draft thing, he's gonna end up losing this election."

The fact is, both Bush and Clinton *had* addressed the economy that day, along with important defense and foreign policy issues. The draft controversy, highlighted by all four newscasts, was not mentioned by Gov. Clinton and only tangentially referred to by President Bush. It led the news, however, because it seemed to offer more drama and potential political significance than any of the policy issues on either candidate's agenda that day.

Despite the fact that the networks led their political news with the draft controversy, all four also made the point that the draft was a non-substantive political concern. But if they considered the draft an irrelevant distraction, the networks had other items to report that night. The day's speeches contained a summary of each candidate's views on foreign policy, defense spending, and the role of the National Guard in a restructured military.

Clinton also addressed U.S. competitiveness during the Guard speech, and Bush did so later in the day, hours ahead of each evening show's deadline. None of those subjects had been completely exhausted as a news topic by mid-September. The networks could have accurately presented both men as engaged in a substantive campaign debate. Instead, they spent more time on the draft controversy that day than did either candidate.

The Salt Lake City speeches are an example of how reporters' news judgments shaped the coverage of the campaign more than events along the campaign trail did. Decisions like the ones the networks made on September 15 account for the major differences between the candidates' agendas and the media agenda.

We systematically examined the candidates' general election speeches, using the same system we used to measure the substance of news content. Our approach was designed to allow a direct comparison of speech content vs. news content. As Table 4-1 shows, the candidates, in their speeches, focused their comments on extensive and detailed discussions of campaign issues. They did not betray a preoccupation with polls, or strategies, or even character questions. Instead, they offered a broad and coherent vision of their platforms, and detailed explanations of their records. They tackled all of the major issues covered by the media, and they offered more details and context of their own plans than the media reported.

More than a quarter of their comments (28%) focused on specific economic issues, compared with 11% of the news coverage. Similarly, nearly a third (31%) of all statements from the candidates' speeches focused on various domestic issues, compared with a mere 7% of news stories. Foreign policy was mentioned by the candidates 9% of the time — hardly a major campaign theme, but still three times as much discussion as news reports offered.

It was fashionable in Campaign '92 for journalists to complain that the candidates were shirking substance. More often than not, however, it was the journalists who failed to pass along the substantive debate to the electorate. A week after Dan Rather intimated that both candidates were ducking economic issues, (when, in fact, neither was), his colleague Rita Braver accused the two nominees of ignoring the public's worries about violent

Table 4-1

Focus of Campaign Discussion

Candidate Speeches vs. Media Coverage

By Topic	Campaign Speeches	Media Coverage
Issue Stances	44%	13%
Records	33	11
Candidate Character	4	5
Campaign Conduct	9	12
Campaign Ability	*	5
Strength in Polls	*	14
Prospects for Election	3	5
General Viability	2	22
General Assessments	5	13
Total	100%	100%

By Issue

Foreign Policy	9	3
Economic Policy	28	11
Domestic Policy	32	7
Non-Issue	31	79
Total	100%	100%

Campaign speeches: Assessments of the three presidential candidates coded from candidate speeches. Includes both assessments of rivals and self-assessments by the candidates.

Media coverage: Assessments of the three candidates coded from ABC, CBS, NBC, CNN, and PBS newscasts, the *New York Times*, the *Washington Post*, and the *Wall Street Journal*.

crime. "Even though Americans are constantly talking about crime, the presidential candidates aren't.... With exactly six weeks left in the campaign, people here [in Baltimore] want the candidates to talk about what they'd do to make things better."[8]

Our systematic survey shows that crime was a major topic in about 30% of the candidates' addresses. Thirty-eight of the 124 candidate speeches we examined contained extensive discussions of crime and proposals to solve it, including speeches Bush delivered in Springfield, Missouri, and Shreveport, Louisiana, on the same day Braver's story aired.[9] Regular CBS viewers had no reason to doubt Braver, however — mentions of the candidates' proposals and records on crime popped up in only four *CBS Evening News* stories during the entire general election campaign.

The Game Beats Substance

The problem was not that the candidates avoided substance during the campaign; the problem was that the available substance lacked the dramatic packaging necessary for it to become "news." Such was apparently the case when the networks focused on the draft controversy on September 15. An even more egregious example took place on October 8, when President Bush spoke at the Port of New Orleans, Louisiana. The president's speech was a philosophical (and autobiographical) defense of his basic economic formula: more jobs and more economic growth through expanded international trade.

> Where once leaders gathered to find ways to evade conflict, now we must meet to find new ways to promote opportunity. And where once our progress was measured only by a crisis averted, in the new world it will be measured by new jobs created. And I learned the lessons of trade... from the only teacher that counts, real world business experience.

> Even back in the days back there in the late fifties and sixties when I was coming here to New Orleans to work with these oil rigs, I learned that the more my company could sell abroad, in Japan in our case or South America or the Middle East, the more jobs we could create for Louisiana roughnecks and drillers and tool-pushers. My company drilled wells off this coast. The skill of our workers made us the very best in the entire world. And as we drilled abroad, we created good jobs for U.S. workers. It was true then, and it is true today....

> Over the years, I sensed that the world was becoming more like us and saw people in China and Europe demand more of our cars, our computers, even our colas. That is why I am so excited by the new era that lies before us, lies ahead for these kids. You know, I know times have been tough here in America, but we must keep in mind, this is a global economic downturn. The

nations of Europe suffer higher unemployment, higher interest rates, higher inflation. But we can and we will lead the way to a new era of prosperity, if we have the courage to do what is right today.

I believe that America is uniquely suited to lead this new world, just as we led the old one. Despite all the pessimism, all the tearing down of the United States of America, don't forget a few facts. We have the world's largest market. We sell more high-tech products than any other nation. Our workers are more productive than the Germans, more productive than the Japanese, more productive than any other men and women in the entire world. And so don't let... that Clinton-Gore ticket tell you how bad everything is.

You know, in the Cold War we used our military might to forge alliances, to push them together all across the Atlantic and the Pacific. Today, we can use our economic strength to forge new trade alliances, push them together. NAFTA is only the first. I see other trade agreements with nations in Europe and Latin America and Asia. As we tear down barriers, we create good, high-paying jobs for American workers, and that is what this nation desperately needs.

You know, there used to be a great distinction, but that old distinction between foreign policy and economic policy has simply vanished. To build a strong economy at home, we must be strong and aggressive abroad.[10]

While the president had discussed trade on previous occasions during the campaign, most notably in his heavily covered address to the Economic Club of Detroit on September 10, this was his most extensive treatment of the subject to date. Few speeches better illustrated Bush's economic philosophy during the fall of 1992 than the Port of New Orleans speech. Yet the speech was mentioned in neither the *Washington Post*, nor the *New York Times*, nor any of the four evening news programs that night, nor *MacNeil-Lehrer NewsHour*. It received one paragraph in the *Wall Street Journal* — the twelfth paragraph of a story headlined, "Bush and Clinton Work at Honing the Themes of Their Campaigns Into Weapons for Debates."[11]

The New Orleans speech was Bush's main event on October 8, 1992, but it failed to make the news. What did? Reporters focused on the latest political conflict. The previous evening, Bush had appeared on CNN's *Larry King Live*, where he was asked by King "What do you make of the Clinton Moscow trip thing?" Bush's response, "I don't want to tell you what I really think, 'cause I don't have the facts.... But to go to Moscow, one year after Russia crushed Czechoslovakia, not remember who you saw — I think, I really think the answer is level with the American people."[12]

That brief exchange caused a political firestorm, overshadowing the rest of what Bush said during the hour-long show, as well as what he said in New Orleans the next day. Bill Clinton, who had been recuperating from a bout of laryngitis, scheduled a press conference for the next day to denounce Bush and defend himself. "Here we are on our way to debate the great issues facing this country and its future and we've descended to that level."[13]

Nearly twenty-four hours after the comment was made, it was the lead story on all four network newscasts. ABC called Bush's comments proof that the campaign was getting "nastier," while NBC said it was proof the campaign was getting "uglier." CNN's Charles Bierbauer said Bush had "loosed a crescendo of innuendo" about Clinton.[14] *MacNeil-Lehrer NewsHour* also led with the story, minus the judgmental language.

CBS's Susan Spencer suggested another reason this exchange struck such a nerve among journalists: "It all seems very familiar to those who remember the president's use of the Pledge of Allegiance issue against Dukakis in]88." She sought out Susan Estrich, Michael Dukakis's 1988 campaign manager, who said, "I feel like I've seen this movie before. I mean, the tactic — when all else fails call your opponent unpatriotic, suggest that he's unpatriotic, use rumor instead of facts—seems like a bad repeat from the last election."[15]

The response in the prestige press the next day was similar. In a news story, the *Wall Street Journal* called Bush's comments "a direct attack on Democrat Bill Clinton's character," and "an apt summary of the message the politically beleaguered president wants the U.S. to hear heading into Sunday's [presidential debate]."[16] The *Washington Post's* editorial (headlined "Anything to Win") termed Bush's tactics McCarthyite: "Chalk up yet another irony in the Bush drive for reelection: the president's complaining about the dirty, ugly character of this year's campaign, even as he propels it toward a new low in sly innuendo and overt mud-heaving."[17]

The *New York Times* agreed, calling the president's campaign style "bitter," "absurd," "nasty," "demagogic," "odd," "fixated," "divisive," "sinister," "sour," and "shrill." The *Times'* editors offered this advice to the president's advisors: "The energy Mr. Bush expends bashing Mr. Clinton could surely be more profitably diverted to putting his own best foot forward."[18]

Yet this episode tells us that the media were as focused on allegedly dirty campaigning as was Bush. Each time a network selects its top story, or a newspaper lays out its front page, it signals its priorities. This incident plainly illustrates how reporters in 1992 acted exactly as Roger Ailes had described them in 1988: "They're interested in polls, they're interested in pictures, they're interested in mistakes, and they're interested in attacks."[19]

When Bush appeared on *Larry King*, he offered neither polls nor pictures. But with his comment about Clinton's Moscow trip, he offered an attack and, in the minds of many reporters, he made a mistake. Without any other new mistakes or attacks manufactured in the past 24 hours (Clinton had laryngitis, after all), the networks ran with what they had. On October 8-9, it was

Table 4-2

Comparing the Media's and the Candidates' Agendas

George Bush

Speeches	Media-Driven Stories	All Campaign News
1. Taxes	1. Taxes	1. Taxes
2. Economy	2. Economy	2. Economy
3. Education	3. Budget	3. Gulf War
4. Trade	4. Gulf War	4. Health Care
5. Budget	5. Trade	5. Trade
6. Unemployment	6. Health Care	6. Budget
7. Health Care	7. Iran/contra	7. Environment
8. Gen. Foreign Policy	8. Education	8. Role of Government
9. Environment	9. Role of Government	9. Education
10. Role of Government	10. Environment	10. Iran/contra

Bill Clinton

Speeches	Media-Driven Stories	All Campaign News
1. Economy	1. Taxes	1. Taxes
2. Education	2. Economy	2. Economy
3. Unemployment	3. Trade	3. Health Care
4. Job Training	4. Health Care	4. Budget
5. Health Care	5. Education	5. Role of Government
6. Taxes	6. Role of Government	6. Education
7. Science & Technology	7. Budget	7. Trade
8. Role of Government	8. Infrastructure	8. Environment
9. Defense Spending	9. Environment	9. Unemployment
10. U.S. Competitiveness	10. Job Training	10. Infrastructure

Speeches: Most prominant issues in Bush's and Clinton's general election speeches, (Sept. 7-Nov. 2) Media-driven stories: Most prominent issues in those stories initiated by news organizations, not events of the day. (Sept. 7-Nov. 2) All campaign news: Most prominent issues in both candidate-driven and media-driven stories.

political reporters — fixated on the conflict and drama of a negative campaign — who relentlessly pursued the Moscow story, innuendo and all.

Voters learned from the media that the Bush campaign had done something disapproved of by the political community. What they had no chance to learn about were the positive and substantive things Bush had also said that day, which were obscured by coverage of the Moscow controversy. For news organizations that had pledged to stick to the issues, on October 8-9, it was politics as usual. One might say that the energy the media expended bashing Bush could have been more productively diverted to reporting on his principal activity that day.

WHOSE NEWS?

When the media did cover the issues, they were usually reading from their own script. As noted in Chapter 3, we coded all references to the candidates' proposals, records, or general views on major policy issues. Often, news stories, only mention of a candidate's stance would be contained within quotes made by one or the other of the candidates in the course of their speeches. On other occasions, however, the story was billed as the news organization's own effort to examine an issue. We called these kinds of issue stories "media-driven," since they were the product of the news organization's own issue agenda and priorities.

For example, a lengthy front-page story in the *Washington Post* focused on the $4 trillion national debt. Its headline: "Politicians Wavering on Debt Crisis Issue; Candidates Fall Far Short on Solutions."[20] The story was the final installment of a three-part *Post* series on the debt, reflecting the newspaper's concern that the debt was an important issue which needed to be addressed by the candidates. Such stories — 29% of all TV news, and 46% of all newspaper stories — formed the core of the media agenda that was, according to the reformers, designed to challenge the candidates to offer more substance of their own.

As Table 4-2 shows, such media-driven stories were more influential than the candidates at setting the overall news agenda of the campaign. The first column reflects the ten policy areas most often mentioned by the candidates in their speeches, presented in descending order of frequency. As one would expect of two nominees with different experiences and ideologies, their agendas differed in many respects.

President Bush focused on trade, the budget deficit, foreign policy and the environment far more frequently than did Gov. Clinton. For his part, the Democratic nominee stressed job training, science and technology issues, defense spending, and U.S. competitiveness far more than did the incumbent. The differences in their agendas reflect their differing approaches to government and their differing priorities.

News coverage of both men, however, stressed a more homogeneous set of issues: taxes, the economy, health care, trade, the budget deficit, the environment, the role of government, and education. Bush stressed all eight of those issues in his speeches, but he also focused on unemployment and foreign policy. When reporters discussed Bush, however, they were more likely to stress his role in the Iran/contra scandal and his performance before, during, and after the Persian Gulf War.[21] Governor Clinton's emphasis on job training, science and technology issues, competitiveness, and defense spending were minimized by news organizations. Reporters instead focused on the same eight issues that dominated Bush's coverage, along with unemployment and infrastructure.

Compare the overall news agenda with a list of issues from those stories that reflected the agenda of the news organizations. With one exception, the issues that defined each candidate in the overall news agenda were the priorities of media-driven stories. If a candidate uniquely emphasized a particular issue area that did not match the agenda of media-initiated stories (such as Clinton's emphasis on technology issues, or Bush's emphasis on foreign policy), that issue was de-emphasized in the overall coverage.

In other words, news organizations apparently did exactly what they said they would do: they determined what the important issues were, and those issues determined the overall news agenda. On issues where candidates deviated from the news agenda, the uniqueness of their agendas was subordinated to the news organizations' own list of concerns. Even on issues where the media's priorities matched those of the candidates, the news offered considerable substance about the issues in general, but few in-depth discussions of the candidates' plans.

IT'S THE ECONOMY, STUPID

There was no dispute among the candidates and the news media on the central issue of the campaign. Economic issues — taxes, trade, unemployment, and the budget — were high on the agendas of all three candidates' speeches, and they were equally prominent in media-driven stories. That said, however, there were substantial differences among the various candidates and the media in what was said about the economy — namely, how it was assessed and what economic measures the next president needed to enact. Because of its singular importance to Campaign '92, the economy provides the best case study of how the media translated the candidates' agendas into their own.

The recession of 1990-91 came and went without generating the heavy network coverage associated with previous recessions, such as the severe downturn of 1981-82. According to government statistics, the nation's economy, as measured by Gross Domestic Product, declined in value between the summer of 1990 and the late spring of 1991. During this period, however, the news media trained their lenses on the Persian Gulf, documenting the massive build-up of U.S. forces and the subsequent war that evicted the Iraqi army from Kuwait.

Given the importance of the Gulf conflict, it is certainly understandable that the recession was given less prominence as a news story. From July 1990 through March 1991 (the months of actual negative economic growth), the "big three" evening newscasts each ran an average of 18 economic stories per month. From April 1991 through October 1992 coverage of the economy boomed to 45 stories per network per month. The coverage peaked in January 1992 at 276 stories, or 9 per night, as the networks' intensive coverage of the presidential candidates began in New Hampshire.[22]

New Hampshire had boasted one of the best economies in the country when the political scribes last descended in January 1988. Now, its statistics were among the nation's worst. The state's unemployment rate (approximately 7 percent) was nearly triple that of four years earlier. Other numbers were equally grim: the state's welfare rolls had tripled since the late 1980s; the food stamp caseload increased dramatically, as did the number of personal bankruptcies. It was frequently noted that in such a small state (1.1 million residents) nearly everyone knew of someone directly touched by the recession.[23]

Political reporters make camp in New Hampshire every four years. The fact that they bypassed Iowa meant that much more time spent in the Granite State in early 1992 — and that meant more time talking to voters about their financial troubles. The New Hampshire economy was "news" not only because the networks were providing exhaustive coverage of the national economy, but because voters' anger about the economy appeared to contain hefty political implications, particularly for George Bush. One voter told NBC that "everybody's out of work, and I just don't think [the president] realizes the problem that the working people have. I think he's just too far above us to understand."[24]

New Hampshire's problems provided the anecdotes reporters used to frame the campaign agenda. ABC's Jim Wooten filed the following report from Manchester on January 13:

> Every four years, [the candidates] come back to New Hampshire, and every four years the knock on New Hampshire is that it's just not the best place for the nation's first primary. It doesn't look like the rest of America — too

small, too rural, too elderly, too conservative, especially for the Democrats. It just doesn't reflect the country.

But this time around it does — the economy is a wreck. For every hour of every day over the last four years, New Hampshire has lost two jobs. In all, 55,000 jobs have disappeared since 1988. Unemployment has tripled, to 7%; bankruptcies up more than 500%. Five of the seven major banks have failed and, for many people, the word "recession" doesn't begin to tell the story....

There is no argument at all as to what this campaign is all about — it's all about one thing, economic recovery, and, although that ought to be playing to the natural strength of the party of Franklin Roosevelt, as yet there is no persuasive evidence that any of these current Democrats have struck a chord with the voters....

Wooten went on to summarize the economic programs of four of the five then-Democratic candidates (he left out Jerry Brown), spending less than thirty seconds on each.[25] He closed by dismissing all four plans, and enveloped the story's policy substance in the horse race: "Since [New Hampshire voters] have heard nothing [in these plans] to excite them, very few have chosen a candidate — and the Democrats' first big test is still wide open."[26]

The Wooten piece is typical of how the networks tried to transmit the substantive agendas of each candidate to the voters. His story spent more time assessing the state of the New Hampshire economy than explaining what each candidate proposed for the national economy. The surrounding context of the story was the horse race — would voter anger about the economy help the Democrats, and which Democratic plan would most inspire voters?

The amount of time spent on each candidate was tiny — 14 seconds for Tom Harkin, 18 seconds each for Bob Kerrey and Bill Clinton. Paul Tsongas received the most time (28 seconds), but his "sound bite" consisted not of a promotion of his own economic policies, but a criticism of the opposition.[27] Thus, even substantive stories were cast in campaign news' one-size-fits all mold: who's up, who's down, and who hit whom.

Network news and the leading newspapers focused on the economy all year long, as did all three presidential candidates, as Figure 4-1 shows. Yet, although each candidate stressed economic issues, there were dramatic differences in their views. While Clinton and Perot voiced deep pessimism about the economy (98% negative and 100% negative evaluations from their speeches, respectively), Bush tried to discuss its strengths. Nearly four-fifths (79%) of Bush's remarks on the economy were positive. An even greater proportion (90%) of his comments reflected optimism about the state of the nation. For their part, Clinton and Perot more often focused on the nation's problems (91% and 88% negative, respectively).

All three men expressed the sentiment that the budget deficit was among the most serious problems facing the nation, but Perot said so most frequently. Clinton and Bush focused on the deficit's importance in only a small percentage of their speeches (25% and 10%, respectively), while Perot stated its importance, on average, several times per speech. The candidates differed on their proposed solutions — Clinton and Perot promoted raising taxes to deal with the deficit, while Bush rejected that idea in favor of spending cuts (which Clinton and Perot also endorsed).

On the tax issue in general, Bush most frequently promised to cut taxes (86%), while Perot more often pledged to raise tax rates (58%). Clinton balanced his remarks between promises to cut some taxes (particularly credits for small businesses and help for lower-income families), and pledges to raise taxes on others (in particular, those earning more than $200,000 a year).

The media coverage of the campaign reflected the candidates' debate, and frequently quoted their positions. But the context in which candidates' positions are presented provides important cues for audiences trying to evaluate competing claims. News reports quoted scores of voters, experts, and interest groups addressing the same issues as the candidates, and offering their own solutions.

On the two major issues on which the candidates disagreed — the economy and taxes — the non-partisan commentary reinforced the positions of those candidates (Clinton and Perot) who argued that the economy was in dire straits (91% of non-partisans agreed), and that tax rates needed to be increased as a method of combating the budget deficit (70% of non-partisans advocated higher tax rates). When he argued that the recovery had begun, the state of the nation was good, and that tax rates were not too low but too high, President Bush was the media's odd man out — separated not just from the other candidates but also from among scores of experts, pundits, and angry voters who were quoted.

Bush was not just outnumbered within campaign news; the broader context of all economic news also lobbied voters against his message. Figure 4-1 depicts the tone of all network economic coverage during the first ten months of 1992.[28] During each of these months, negative assessments of the state of the economy outweighed positive ones — in election and non-election stories alike. During five of those months, the ratio was better than nine-to-one negative. Overall, from New Year's Day through Election Day, 87% of all assessments of the economy on the network evening news were negative.

In such a context, Bush's statement during the final week of the campaign — that while "we've been in an economic international slowdown, it is the

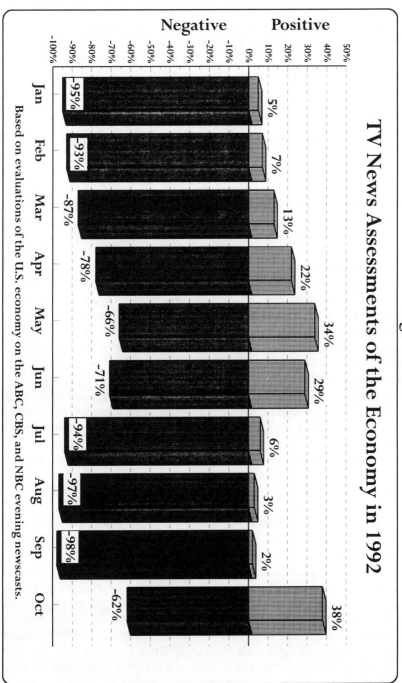

Figure 4-1

TV News Assessments of the Economy in 1992

United States..., with [its] knowledgeable leadership on international affairs and increasing... exports, that's going to lead the way to new recovery"[29] — must have struck voters as proof that their president still didn't know what all the evening newscasters "knew", what all the columnists "knew", and what Clinton and Perot "knew": that despite his wishful thinking, the economy was still in dire straits. "For many voters," reported CBS's Eric Engberg, "who have seen plants close and safe jobs disappear, the highest of the measurable economic indicators is *anxiety*."[30]

The gloom reporters discovered in New Hampshire stayed with the campaign all year long, like a thundercloud over a picnic. Federal unemployment figures were released ten times during the campaign — four times they went up, four times they went down, and twice the figures were unchanged. Up, down, or unchanged, however, the commentary was uniformly negative. On July 2, the Labor Department reported an increase in unemployment, from 7.5% to 7.8%, and all three networks agreed it was bad news. "Unemployment has gone from bad to worse," reported CBS. According to NBC, the "high unemployment... is a dagger aimed at the heart of President Bush's re-election." For its part, ABC noted that "today's news will surely make it harder for Mr. Bush, despite his evident frustration, to continue to claim... that public alarm about the economy is generated by the media."[31]

The next month, however, the rate dropped from 7.8% to 7.7%. ABC's Forrest Sawyer called it "a glimmer of good news," but the story that night was that "many laid-off workers who do find new jobs are worse off than when they started."[32] The September report brought the rate down again, to 7.6%. CBS's Connie Chung cautioned that, "Today's unemployment report from the government appears hopeful on the surface.... But the latest decline is the result of a summer jobs program for teenagers. That program is about to end and... the picture ahead is bleak."[33]

On October 2, NBC reported the third straight monthly drop, down to 7.5%. Chief economic correspondent Mike Jenson told anchor Tom Brokaw that "when you look behind the figure, you find an economy that's just barely growing. Jobs are still hard to find.... [Yet] all the candidates will have their eye on the last important economic report before the election — overall economic growth for July, August and September — and it won't be very good, Tom."[34]

Actually, the Commerce Department's estimate of third-quarter growth *was* fairly good: it showed the economy growing at an annualized rate of 2.7%. To reporters who had broadcast hundreds of stories explaining how bad the economy was, the timing of the report (exactly one week before the election) was a cause for suspicion, not celebration. "There is some doubt about the accuracy of the figures," reported CBS's Dan Rather.[35] The *New York Times* reported that "No one interviewed today suggested that these or any of the other numbers in this [Commerce] report were 'cooked,' although one said the [increase in federal military] spending itself could possibly have been timed for maximum effect."[36] By even raising the question, however, the *Times* was signaling that skepticism was appropriate.

Regardless of the honesty of the numbers, the conventional wisdom reasserted itself within hours (the conventional wisdom is never at a complete loss). The *Washington Post* quoted an expert on its front page: "Anyone who says that 2.7 percent is now our new growth rate is crazy," said Donald Rataczjak, an economic statistic expert at Georgia State University. "This is a surprising number — and it is not sustainable."[37]

Not to be out-gloomed, the *Times* came back the next day with an editorial: "Gross National Letdown."[38] ABC's Jim Wooten caught a plane back to New Hampshire and interviewed a voter who told him that his last three votes for Republican presidential nominees were "the three sorriest mistakes I've ever made." According to Wooten, "The president's problem is that his view of the new economic figures often doesn't tell the whole story of what's happened, or hasn't happened, to thousands of voters who watched his State of the Union address last February."

Melding past and present, Wooten then showed viewers what Ella Flanders had told him on January 7, 1992: "[Bush has] got his head buried. He isn't even beginning to realize what's going on." What did Mrs. Flanders, a widow, think nine months later, on the eve of the election? "He's still got his head buried. He really has." After talking to several other former Republicans, Wooten concluded: "Mr. Bush would have a tough time reclaiming the Smiths and thousands of other New Hampshire voters for whom the grim reality of recession has not changed since the candidates left here last winter."[39]

(A postscript: While Bush was criticized for latching onto the 2.7% growth figure, the final figure, published several weeks after the election, put third-quarter growth at 3.4%, while the fourth-quarter growth rate was 4.7%. Overall, the economy grew by about 3% during 1992, somewhat more than originally predicted by either government or private economists.)

Their coverage of the economy highlights one of the media's worst tendencies: in covering issues, the news tends to ignore problems until they become crises, and then turn them into national obsessions. Among the host of crucial concerns facing the nation in 1992, many — crime, drugs, civil rights, energy policy, and nearly everything having to do with foreign policy — were given only minimal attention.

The campaign news agenda was so dominated by economic issues that even issues that received substantial coverage — health care, the environment, education — tended to be covered from the perspective of job growth (or job losses), taxes, and national economic competitiveness. Instead of arguing that the media benignly reflected national concern over the economy, one could as credibly argue that they stoked the fires of a national panic.

The five issues receiving the most media attention during the general election were purely economic: the state of the economy, taxes, the budget deficit, jobs, and foreign trade. Overall, economic issues were the focus of nearly half (49%) of all issue discussions, compared with all remaining domestic issues (34%) and all foreign policy issues except trade (18%). Four years earlier, only 30% of issue stories focused on the economy, with a greater share devoted to other domestic issues (46%) and foreign policy (24%). Moreover, the pessimism of the economic coverage (both in campaign stories and in more general news) was evident in stories reporting both good and bad economic statistics.

There are drawbacks to crisis-oriented issue coverage. First, as was the case in 1992, other issues are crowded off of the agenda. For example, in its first two years the Clinton administration was faced with a series of foreign policy problems (among them Bosnia, Haiti, the Middle East, and North Korea). Yet the public had little opportunity to learn (from the media) about their future president's views on foreign policy prior to his election.

More importantly, election campaigns are opportunities for an integrated national debate over specific policies, general values, and political leadership. In non-election years, media coverage tends to hopscotch from issue to issue, in patterns dictated by the ebb and flow of events. In campaigns, the candidates present themselves as focal points where the issues intersect (hopefully) in coherent national plans linking a wide range of domestic and international issues.

Campaigns provide an opportunity to set priorities and to debate the connections among various problems and solutions. By focusing on a single issue — even an issue as important as the economy — the opportunity for such a debate is lost, and the mandate for the eventual winner is limited.

Compared with news media reports, the candidates' daily speeches discussed far more issues, and dealt with them far more extensively, and with considerably more detail and context. Candidates extensively addressed an average of nine different issue areas per speech; news stories managed barely one. Most of the top issues were addressed in at least a third of the candidates' speeches. When the candidates raised issues, they were nearly twice as likely as reporters to offer extensive or specific discussions, according to our criteria, and they were dramatically more likely to place the issue in context — 72% of the candidates' issue mentions offered some context, while 64% of news reports failed to do so. (See Figure 4-2.)

President Bush, for example, stressed that his foreign policy experience lent him the ability to negotiate and implement international trading treaties that would offer the U.S. unique competitive advantages. Governor Clinton

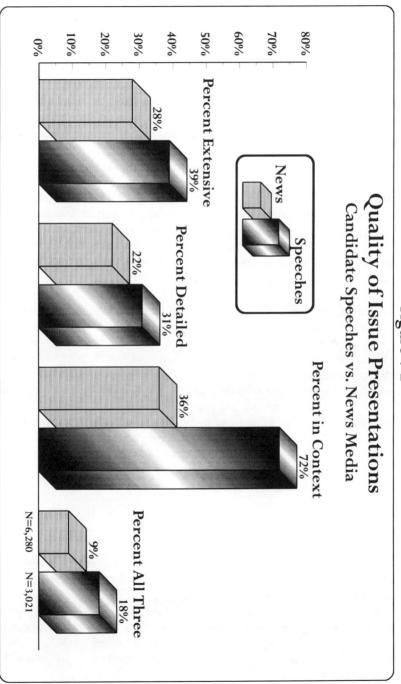

Figure 4–2

Quality of Issue Presentations
Candidate Speeches vs. News Media

routinely discussed the need to consider education — pre-school, primary, and secondary education, as well as continuous career training — as a key component of a national strategy to ensure American economic supremacy. To be sure, it is difficult to convey the complexity and interconnections of the candidates' platforms within the confines of relatively short news stories. Yet, of the three attributes that we looked for (extensiveness, specificity, and context), the candidates' speeches were twice as likely as news reports to supply all three (18% vs. 9%). If the coverage had more closely followed the candidates' own agendas, voters would have been exposed to this material far more frequently and in greater depth.

The problem is not just the old saw that the daily imperatives of "news" necessarily provide an incomplete and distorted view of the candidates and their positions. A newer problem is the conceit that the values of news organizations and journalists should override those of parties and candidates in the service of public education. This conceit is harmless so long as it encourages reporters to ask questions and write stories about the substantive features of campaigns. It is dangerous when reporters begin to use their role to constrain the campaign debate around their own view of the proper campaign agenda.

The candidates will, necessarily, differ on many aspects of the issues — on setting priorities and defining problems, as well as choosing solutions. They will differ because their world views are informed by different philosophies, and their parties represent different interests, which is precisely why voters must select among them.

Journalists cannot independently establish the substantive context of the campaign debate without also affecting the course and outcome of that debate. The media's attempt to do so in 1992 betrayed a lack of appreciation and confidence for voters' role in judging the candidates and the parties, and choosing those who best serve their interests. What voters most need is meaningful information that is useful to them in understanding the issues and differentiating among the candidates.

CONCLUSION: THE VOTERS' AGENDA

In 1991, *New Republic* senior editor Fred Barnes predicted that reporters would attempt to take control of the issue agenda of the 1992 campaign. He argued that those journalists who were urging a more aggressive posture were "so obsessed by the success of Bush's tactics [in 1988] that they want to change the very conduct of presidential campaigns." In a rare criticism of the reform agenda, he continued, "This sounds nice, but my guess is it would stress problems — real or imagined — that lend themselves to programmatic solutions. Reporters would go into "crisis" mode, listing everything in America they think is a problem and asking voters whether government should do something about it." [40]

Barnes was warning his colleagues against trying to protect the public from candidates at the expense of informing the public about them. The burden on journalists who cover campaigns is to provide citizens with an understandable view of the candidates' competing agendas, not to supplant the politicians' perspective with their own.

Ideally, voters would know each candidate's basic message, as well as the opposing ticket's critique of that message. While some voters would undoubtedly prefer to decide based on other candidate characteristics, the basic information about each candidate's platform should be sufficiently disseminated that voters can make their own choices about its relevance.

This was not the case in 1992. As our content analysis shows, news about the general election provided heavy coverage of "the issues," but modest coverage of the candidates' plans and proposals. When news organizations did cover substance, it was frequently overshadowed by the frivolity and hoopla of the campaign.

Despite the reform movement's modest success in raising the general level of issue news, the candidates' pronouncements and activities were still dissected primarily in terms of their meaning for the political horse race. Hence, the focus on the draft, rather than national defense, on September 15, and the focus on the "trip to Moscow thing," rather than international trade, on October 8 and 9.

The media did increase the amount of substantive information available in Campaign '92. What did not increase was the utility of this information to the voter. When covering candidates, the dominant paradigm in 1992 was still the horse race and candidate mistakes (as in '88 and earlier campaigns). The issues that were most often covered were seldom linked with the candidates. Even when they were, the details were often lacking. This was primarily the result of journalists' choices, not the candidates' failures. Their speeches contained far more substance than the news accounts conveyed; they provided the raw material for any number of substantive pieces that were never written or broadcast.

The victim of this sort of media bias is the voter. Citizens can only participate in elections in a meaningful way when they understand what each of the rival candidates stand for, and what their priorities are. They can then reward those candidates who most closely approximate their own views and priorities or punish those whose agenda is most undesirable. If the agenda becomes crowded with alternative platforms that do not correspond to any of the candidates or parties on the ballot, voters may simply become frustrated and alienated.

Among the reasons reporters gave for changing their approach to covering the issues was the notion that the candidates failed to present substantive or meaningful agendas. Our content analysis shows that the candidates were three times more likely than journalists to discuss the issues. The criticism itself implies that reporters can satisfactorily judge the substantiveness and relevance of the candidates' efforts, and fairly render judgment.

This is not a view that is embraced by all. "With all due respect," asked political consultant Mary Matalin when asked about the idea in 1990, "Who are journalists to set the moral standards for politicians?"[41]   More to the point, it implies an inability on the part of voters to successfully decide whether a candidate's platform reflects more political posturing or genuine concern for the nation.

If there is a critique to be made that a candidate is running a particularly superficial or manipulative campaign, it would seem an obvious point for his or her challengers to make. If the partisan challengers fail to blunt the appeal of a candidate's message, that does not necessarily mean that the system has failed and that voters need the assistance of the media. It may mean that the voters have intelligently chosen their own preferred path.

Notes

Opening quote: Ellen Hume, quoted in *Covering Campaign '88: The Politics of Character and the Character of Politics* (New York: Gannett Center for Media Studies, 1988), p. 9.

1.   A transcript of Bush's remarks was retrieved from the government's *Weekly Compilation of Presidential Documents*, pp. 1654-1658.   Clinton's remarks were obtained from the Clinton-Gore '92 Committee.   Both transcripts were compared against a videotape of a C-SPAN broadcast on September 15, 1992.

2.   ABC's *World News Tonight*, September 15, 1992.

3.   *NBC Nightly News*, September 15, 1992.

4.   CNN's *PrimeNews*, September 15, 1992.

5.   CNN's *PrimeNews*, September 15, 1992.

6.   *CBS Evening News*, September 15, 1992.

7.   Speaking to the employees of Jeppesen Sanderson, Inc., Bush reiterated the points of his *Agenda for American Renewal*: smaller government, reduced taxes and spending, and cultivating new overseas markets.   Bush went on to argue that those

steps would boost American competitiveness in the world economy.   Of course, reporters had heard much of this before, so it wasn't "news."

8.   *CBS Evening News*, September 22, 1992.

9.   In his Shreveport speech, Bush took credit for increasing federal anti-crime funding by 43% during his term, for the fact that federal prisoners serve 85% of their sentences, and for a lower national crime rate.   He blamed Clinton for "the biggest increase in the overall crime rate in the entire nation, nearly 28 percent." Violent crime in Arkansas rose 58 percent, Bush said, while Arkansas ranked 46th in per capita spending on prisons, 49th on spending for police officers, and 50th on spending for judicial and legal systems.

10.   *Weekly Compilation of Presidential Documents*, pp. 1879-1882.

11.   *Wall Street Journal*, October 9, 1992.

12.   CNN's *Larry King Live*, October 7, 1992.

13.   Ron Fournier, "Clinton: Bush Statements on War Protest 'Sad, Desperate'," AP Political News, October 8, 1992, Thursday AM cycle.

14.   ABC's *World News Tonight, NBC Nightly News*, and CNN's *PrimeNews*, October 8, 1992.

15.   *CBS Evening News*, October 8, 1992.

16.   *Wall Street Journal*, October 9, 1992.

17.   *Washington Post*, October 9, 1992.

18.   *New York Times*, October 9, 1992.

19.   Quoted by Larry McCarthy, "The Selling of the President: An Interview with Roger Ailes," *Gannett Center Journal*, Fall 1988.

20.   *Washington Post*, September 29, 1992.

21.   Bush frequently cited the Gulf War as one of his accomplishments, but not frequently enough for it to dominate his speeches.   For their part, reporters frequently focused on the question of whether Bush's pre-war policies had improperly (or even illegally) helped the Iraqi regime obtain technological support for their arms program.

22.   References to the networks' economic coverage is based on an examination of all economic stories, whether or not they were related to the campaign.   For the first 10 months of 1992, the ABC, CBS, and NBC evening news shows broadcast 1,410 economic stories, about 15% of which were also campaign stories.   In January 1992, the economy (276 stories) was actually a more prominent story than the campaign (featured in 98 stories).

23.   Walter V. Robinson and Adam Pertman, "Angry and Hurting, N.H. Voters Question Political Loyalties; Buffeted N.H. Voters May Change Their Habits," *Boston Globe*, January 12, 1992; and David Lauter, "Economy Has N.H. Voters Looking to the Democrats," *Los Angeles Times*, January 17, 1992.

24.   *NBC Nightly News*, February 17, 1992.

25.   The following was the complete presentation of one candidate's prescription: **Wooten:** "Sen. Harkin of Iowa offers what sounds like the old New Deal as part of his economic cure."   **Harkin:** "Let's start investing our wealth in building the infrastructure of this country — the roads, the bridges, the sewer and water systems."   Total time: 14 seconds.

26.   ABC's *World News Tonight*, January 13, 1992.

27. Tsongas said, "I think a Democrat who does the quick-fix scenario will, by the time people vote, really be dismissed, because that's what Reagan gave them, that's what Bush gave them." (ABC's *World News Tonight*, January 13, 1992.)

28. Figure 3-6 is based on all TV news coverage of the economy, not just those stories which focused on the campaign. For details about the economic study, see "The Boom in Gloom: TV News Coverage of the American Economy, 1990-1992," *Media Monitor* 6, no. 8 (October 1992).

29. Remarks to the community in Stratford, Connecticut, November 1, 1992. *Weekly Compilation of Presidential Documents*, pp. 2258-2261.

30. *CBS Evening News*, October 28, 1992.

31. *CBS Evening News*, *NBC Nightly News*, and ABC's *World News Tonight*, July 2, 1992.

32. ABC's *World News Tonight*, August 7, 1992.

33. *CBS Evening News*, September 4, 1992.

34. *NBC Nightly News*, October 2, 1992.

35. *CBS Evening News*, October 27, 1992.

36. Robert D. Hershey, Jr., "U.S. Economy Grew at a Rate of 2.7% During 3rd Quarter," *New York Times*, October 28, 1992.

37. Steven Mufson, "Economy's Growth Rate Strengthens; Analysts Surprised; Bush Hails Gain," *Washington Post*, October 28, 1992.

38. "Gross National Letdown," *New York Times*, October 29, 1992.

39. ABC's *World News Tonight*, October 28, 1992.

40. Fred Barnes, "Why Liberals Hate Politics," *The American Spectator*, August 1991, pp. 24-25.

41. Robert Shogan and Thomas B. Rosenstiel, "Latest Wave of Campaign Reform Homes in on Media," *Los Angeles Times*, May 7, 1990.

Chapter Five

Freeze-Frame Journalism

Our coverage is keeping the bastards honest.
— Unidentified television reporter, 1992

Along with concerns about substance and sensationalism, reformers fretted about the fairness of their coverage of the Bush-Dukakis race. "Bias" in campaign news has been an issue since the advent of television journalism, but the fairness debate took a singular turn after the 1988 campaign. Those who wished to reform the campaign process weren't particularly worried about whether *journalists* had said unfair things about either side. Their complaint was that journalists failed to aggressively condemn the Bush campaign for its "unfair" attacks on the Dukakis campaign. By this interpretation journalism's fairness problem was that reporters were too passive and had failed to halt the fall campaign's slide into negativity.

The reformers believed that Bush's TV ads were both negative and misleading. Some sounded their protests at the time. For example, ABC's Richard Threlkeld narrated a piece for *World News Tonight* that condemned Bush's "tank ad" as misleading. The ad in question depicted Michael Dukakis riding in a tank, while an announcer listed various weapons programs the Democrat allegedly opposed. Not so fast, Threlkeld said — Dukakis supports some of those systems, and others ignored by the ad.

In his conclusion, Threlkeld made no bones about his personal opinion of political commercials:

If the government ever gets around to putting a warning label on TV campaign commercials the way they do on cigarettes, maybe it ought to read something like this: If in the heat of a presidential campaign you're tempted to buy something one guy says about the other guy in his TV ads, *caveat emptor* — buyer beware.[1]

Threlkeld's twitting of the candidates would serve as the bugle call, summoning the Fourth Estate to battle.

In 1988, most news reports criticized "the campaign" or "the candidates" without differentiation. ABC's *World News Tonight*, for example, took several field trips during the last week of the 1988 campaign, and wallpapered each of their nightly broadcasts with quotes from voters expressing dissatisfaction with the campaign. "I don't like it," one voter from Peoria, Illinois, told anchor Peter Jennings. "It's dirty, it's rotten, and it's unfair to the people." Another agreed, "There was so much mudslinging, that it seemed like the campaign focused more on that than the real issues, so it makes it really hard for me to make a decision."[2] The impression left by devices such as this, and by the coverage in general: the campaign was bad, voters were mad, but nobody in particular was to blame.

Our own analysis of the general election coverage that year confirms the evenhanded quality of the networks' judgments: both nominees were featured in practically the same number of stories, and each received roughly the same proportion of praise and criticism. But it was this very balance that most animated the reformers. Writing in *Newsweek* shortly after the election, Jonathan Alter averred,

> By almost any standard, Bush slung several tons more [mud] than Dukakis, who for weeks was criticized for not fighting back. But misguided ideas of fairness required that reporters implicate both equally, lest they be viewed as taking sides.... Fear of seeming slanted overcame any interest in reporting a larger truth.[3]

While the overall coverage was balanced, there were distinct differences in the particulars of each man's bad press. Bush was criticized for the perceived excesses in his campaign's conduct. A Democratic pollster dubbed him "George the Ripper." A *Washington Post* reporter thought he saw in the vice president a kind of Jekyll and Hyde duality: "Clint Eastwood-cum-Mister Rogers? Half bully and half grandpa? Tough and tender, doggedly ideological — a man who snarls 'Read my lips' and 'You're history' whenever he's not too busy being 'haunted' by the plight of the deserving poor?"[4]

Dukakis, on the other hand, was criticized for not acting as tough as his Republican counterpart: "For much of the fall campaign, he hesitated to strike back at Bush, stubbornly clinging to his own view of presidential politics.... Dukakis harbored the reformer's disdain for the political packager's art. There would be no Roger Ailes.... in Boston, where the candidate personally reviewed the advertising proposals, rejecting dozens."[5] On this score, disappointed fellow partisans were among Dukakis's biggest critics: "When you run from what you are, they have every right to pin what you are on you," one Democratic veteran told *Newsweek* in October 1988.[6]

To many of the reformers, however, blaming Dukakis for anything seemed unfair, particularly in light of the damage Bush's ads had done to him. By Election Day, Dukakis was seen as the victim of Campaign '88, not one of its architects. "Even though the Vice President was spending thousands more on negative ads than Dukakis, and running them earlier," *Time* scolded after the campaign, "reporters generally blamed both sides for taking the low road."[7] ABC News President Roone Arledge voiced his displeasure, "We have got to reevaluate how we cover campaigns."[8]

Some even saw the somnolence of the press corps as a by-product of conservative attacks on a media ashamed of its liberalism. In a *New York Times* op-ed entitled, "TV's Anti-Liberal Bias," Mark Crispin Miller argued that journalists are "burdened by their own convictions — for, by and large, they are indeed a bunch of liberals. But this ideological slant has worked *against* any 'liberal bias' by the TV news, as reporters bend over backwards not to seem at all critical of the Republicans." [Emphasis in the original.][9]

Reformers were even more piqued when exit pollsters found some evidence that the candidates' ads had successfully framed the voters' agenda. As CBS's Diane Sawyer gave *Evening News* viewers an early glimpse at the exit poll results, she noted that voters' responses to the pollsters matched up with the scripts of campaign commercials:

> We can declare the first victory in this year's campaign: for television communication, because the voters used the exact words that the candidates had used recently in their television campaign. They talked about "concern for the middle class," which is something Michael Dukakis talked about. They talked about the dreaded "L" word, liberalism, which is something George Bush introduced. They talked about "crime" and "experience," and, again, this seems to reinforce the fact that voters didn't go into the booths today with a lot of pounding issues of their own — they really were taking their cues from the candidates.[10]

If voters were echoing the ads in their responses to exit pollsters, reformers concluded, the media must have failed to confront the campaign on its own terms. Their passivity had allowed the misleading messages of an insidious negative campaign to become rooted in the public's collective consciousness.

It would be difficult to overstate journalists' disdain for Campaign '88's political commercials. "The presidential campaign of 1988 left a bad taste in people's mouths," wrote the *Washington Post's* David Broder, because the candidates "force-fed a garbage diet of negative TV ads down the country's throat." Broder advocated that the press needed to make it harder for candidates to successfully implement negative strategies:

> The [strategy of denunciation] is not for reporters: Reporters can report, but not condemn. But columnists, commentators, and editorial writers have the license — and the obligation — to apply verbal heat to those who sabotage the election process by their paid-media demagoguery. And the evidence suggests that such denunciations can have an effect.
>
> Those in the business tell me that there's always a calculation before any candidate "goes negative" on his opponent as to the risk of a backlash. And there are obviously cases where negative ads have boomeranged against those who used them. We should do everything we can to increase the boomerang supply....[11]

Broder was careful to remind his colleagues that editorializing belonged on the editorial page, and that "reporting" should not become entangled with "denunciation." But such a distinction seemed old-fashioned to others riding the reform bandwagon. For most of the reformers, the time had come to deputize journalists, creating an "Ad Police." As NBC's Tim Russert pointed out, "Ads work only if they are believed."[12]

"Ad Watches," as they would become known, would place "denunciation" squarely on the news pages where, it was hoped, they would successfully thwart the politicians' ad machines. In his in-depth study of ABC's 1992 campaign coverage, media writer Tom Rosenstiel commented on the revolutionary nature of "Ad Watches":

> The significance went beyond advertising. Policing what candidates said changed the relationship between reporter and politician. By labeling a candidate's statement as distorted or false, the press went from being a color commentator up in the booth to being a referee down on the field. Implicitly, this role acknowledged that the press not only reflected political events, it shaped them. That fact may be obvious to outsiders, but it is strangely difficult for reporters to accept. Journalists are trained to ignore the consequences of what they do. Worrying about consequences, journalists fear, will lead to self-censorship or bias. So they rationalize that their impact is minimal. Truth boxes conceded the press's power exceeded that.[13]

Although journalists were becoming increasingly aware of the power of their craft, those who vowed to redeem journalism after 1988 (with some notable exceptions) were not opposed to an aggressively adversarial approach. The new conventional wisdom did not find it objectionable that reporters were peppering their news stories with commentary critical of the candidates. Indeed, such criticism (it was hoped) could be the nightstick that journalists used to enforce better campaign standards.

The profession's misgivings after 1988 were far more narrowly focused: the press's concern was that their criticism lacked a sense of priorities or values. Thus, one candidate's (Bush's) reckless use of innuendo and smear tactics was not portrayed as worse than another candidate's (Dukakis's) lack of skill at campaigning. If campaigns were ever to be improved, reporters would have to focus their scrutiny on those aspects of candidate behavior that were most egregious, and they would have to name names. Journalists' own values would have to become actively engaged in their reportage.

The public's anger with the campaign aided those who argued for change. An NBC News/*Wall Street Journal* poll found 68% of Americans considered the 1988 campaign "one of the worst in recent history," while nearly as many (63%) said they were not pleased with their choice of candidates.[14] Reformers within the media read the public displeasure as support for their arguments in favor of change. But for the reformers, "change" meant using the power of journalism to coerce better conduct from the candidates.

As we saw in Chapter 3, those who wished to improve the substantive aspects of campaigns advocated withholding news coverage from candidates whose daily agenda was superficial or irrelevant to voters' concerns. Those who wished to reform the fairness of campaigns targeted the candidates' advertising. "I don't know what the hell we get paid for if we don't make an effort... to keep those guys honest. If we don't, who will?" Richard Threlkeld told an interviewer after the campaign. "The [Bush campaign's] tank ad was the one that broke the camel's back. There had been little bits and pieces [of distortion] in previous ads and we hadn't made a big fuss. But this one seemed so erroneous and flagrant."[15]

Implicit in this response is the primacy of journalism's activist "watchdog" role over its more neutral informative function.[16] Instead of accurately reporting the campaign debate to the public, journalists like Threlkeld saw their most important task as policing the debate to protect the public against the campaign's distortions.

This perspective places journalists in a role that is explicitly critical, implicitly negativistic, and potentially tendentious. Traditional conventions insisted on journalistic neutrality, separating news and commentary, and equating fairness with balance. The reformers emphasized journalistic involvement, saw commentary as an essential component of news, and equated fairness with truth-telling, even when it favored one candidate over another.

This redefinition of professional responsibility carries some obvious risks for journalism's credibility with the electorate. Not the least of these stems from the public's dissatisfaction with the media's performance in Campaign

'88. Whereas most journalists blamed the candidates for the campaign's failings, much of the news audience blamed the media.

According to the *Washington Post's* Richard Harwood, voters thought "the contest has been a nasty and deplorable affair. But only 17 percent of them blame the candidates. The real villains, according to 40 percent of those polled by *Newsweek*, are the 'news organizations covering the campaign.'"[17] More evidence came in a survey by the Times Mirror group, showing that nearly four voters in ten rated the press's campaign performance as only fair or poor.[18] A follow-up poll found that a majority of voters (57%) believed that news organizations tended to favor one side when reporting political issues, and half believed that news reports "are often inaccurate."[19]

A largely unacknowledged danger for campaign journalism was that public complaints about media negativism and one-sided reporting might well be exacerbated by reforms that recast reporters as activist critics and arbiters of campaign behavior.

Reformers saw no need to rein in journalists from making judgments about the candidates. Indeed, they encouraged it. But instead of the occasional ad hoc comment that technically violated the already-frayed norms of traditional objective journalism, they wanted to adopt new standards that institutionalized exactly such judgments. Far from banning judgmental commentary in news stories, they wanted rules designed to ensure the fairness of such judgments. In the absence of "balance" as a standard, the trick was defining fairness in practice, during the best of a campaign.

In the context of ad watches, fairness meant ensuring that the "bad" candidate didn't receive an unintentional boost of good press from carelessly crafted stories. "Be wary," cautioned Ken Bode. "We must not be guilty of simply rerunning the ad as part of the newscast, thereby helping to massage in the original message."[20]

Reporters had learned from 1988, Bode wrote, that Bush's campaign ads that year were "filled not with factual misrepresentations but with *invitations to inferential inaccuracies*. [These] ads were often replayed on news programs analyzing the advertising strategy of the Bush campaign."[21] [Emphasis added.] Bode's tips: label the ad, shrink the screen, freeze the frame, and then deliver the critique. His prescription was duplicated in numerous journalistic "advice columns" during the pre-season, and early in 1992.

Watching ads alone would not be enough to prevent a reprise of Campaign '88, so reformers issued more general guidelines: "Voters need to know when one campaign is distorting the facts and the other isn't," wrote the Barone Center's Ellen Hume in 1991.

It isn't fair for the press to provide a false symmetry simply because it will thereby avoid the charge of bias. Fairness requires, however, that news organizations apply similar standards to comparable candidates, and that candidates have opportunities to respond to journalists' critical analyses.[22]

The Barone Center report advocated that ads should not be the sole focus of journalistic "fact-checkers," but part of an overall effort encompassing "the candidate's speeches, direct mail, and other output, with which [the ads] almost certainly are being coordinated."[23]

Underlying these recommendations was a philosophy similar to the one we described in Chapter 3: Reformers wanted journalists to take a more active role in ensuring a campaign environment amenable to voters' needs. Voters offended by the negativity of modern campaigns would not be allowed to conclude that the offenses were committed equally by both sides if that was not true. Instead, reporters would cast a critical eye toward the campaign ads, speeches, and general conduct of the candidates, and assist voters in separating the black hats from the white.

If a candidate ran a campaign similar to Bush's 1988 effort, the media would be less toothless in its response. They would allow a "fairer" campaign where all candidates could make their case without irrelevant or unfair attacks from each other. Thus, the first order of business for the reformers in Campaign '92 were the "Ad Watches," which would institutionalize scrutiny of campaign ads and highlight distortions and inaccuracies for otherwise unsuspecting viewers and readers.

The journalists who pioneered the "Ad Watches," such as Richard Threlkeld, rejected the notion that "truth-telling" was out of bounds for campaign journalists. But other campaign reporters had a more ambivalent response to the new media activism. CBS's longtime Washington correspondent Bob Schieffer explained the dilemma:

> I have always argued that it is not the role of the journalist to defend one candidate from attack by the other. When George Bush attacked Michael Dukakis, it was Dukakis's responsibility to counter those charges.
>
> I still believe that, but as I have come to appreciate the immediate, searing impact that these charges can have, I have also come to believe that we ought to do a better job of examining these commercials, ferreting out the truth and finding out who is lying and who isn't.
>
> When a candidate turns out to be a liar, that is a perfectly legitimate issue and voters have a right to know about it.[24]

Some reluctant journalists, like Schieffer, eventually signed on to the new system, but with the relatively narrow purpose of exposing outright "lies." Such a mission more closely resembled traditional notions of "watchdog" behavior. This reassured those who worried that journalists were straying dangerously close to a position where they would act (or appear to act) as partisan players in the electoral game.

The reformers, however, understood that the real issue wasn't "lies" (deliberate errors of fact or misrepresentation) at all. Modern political advertising was sophisticated and well-researched, particularly at the presidential level. As Ken Bode pointed out, the problem was an ad's "invitations to inferential inaccuracies" — technically truthful statements that reporters feared were being misinterpreted by the public.

The implied goal of "Ad Watches" was to ensure a "correct" interpretation of campaign ads. Thus, in 1992 the media's "Ad Watches" not only pounced on explicit falsehoods, they also offered their own interpretations of campaign commercials, which effectively altered the public's perceptions of the candidates who ran them.

The "Ad Watch" technique was first "test marketed" by regional newspapers during the 1990 congressional campaign cycle. Fellow journalists applauded the initial results. Assessing the 1990 efforts, the Barone Center pronounced "Ad Watches" a commercial as well as a political success. The Center's report quoted Carole Kneeland, part of the 1990 "Ad Watch" team at KVUE-TV in Texas: "Viewers have called and written us thanking us, and we've had both candidates and political operatives tell us… that the question came up a few times 'will this pass the KVUE truth test?'"[25]

Political consultants, always receptive to new trends, had their own reaction: "The press gives us ammunition we can use on the air," said Democratic consultant Frank Greer, who produced ads for Florida gubernatorial candidate Lawton Chiles. "Most people won't read or see one article, but we can put it on the air and run the hell out of it."[26] When Greer produced the Clinton/Gore advertising in 1992, he used "Ad Watch" material to counter the Bush campaign's commercials.

The "counter-attack ad," featuring commentary (sometimes out of context) from journalists' own "Ad Watch" stories, was an unintended consequence of the reform effort.[27] But, having played to rave reviews in Peoria, "Ad Watches" were ready for Broadway. Both the broadcast networks and the major newspapers instituted them as regular features in Campaign '92 (although the frequency of their appearance varied).

FIGHTING FIRE WITH FIRE

One problem for the networks' truth-in-advertising squads, when they began patroling the airwaves in 1992, was the dearth of obvious wrongdoing. There had never been much outright lying in political ads, and the candidates' media consultants were smart enough to anticipate the networks' new aggressive policy. As a result, the "ad police" were often reduced to hassling the candidate passers-by, questioning their presence in the rough neighborhood of presidential campaigns. In this regard, the networks blurred the two critiques of 1988: one against negative ads per se, the other against misleading ones. By painting with broad brush strokes, however, the networks' "ad police" sometimes resembled vigilantes more than sheriffs.

In late February, CBS's Eric Engberg began his network's ad news (CBS's "Reality Checks" had not yet been formally introduced). His target, however, was not a misstated fact, but advertising in general, and his tone was contemptuous:

> They're back! ...Negative attack ads, universally deplored as a vile and corrosive force in presidential politics, once again rule the airwaves in key primary states... It matches the overall tone of a campaign dominated by sideshows like infidelity and draft-dodging, not issues. The latest to pull off the high road and reach for a brickbat: George Bush, now running an ad in Georgia that uses an ex-Marine commandant to attack Pat Buchanan's opposition to the Gulf War....
>
> The negative trail, with emphasis on patriotic themes, is a familiar one for Mr. Bush, who used flags and the Willie Horton furlough effectively against Dukakis in '88, and who gave all of his opponents this time a warning. [QUOTE FROM BUSH: "It's a dog-eat-dog fight, and I will do what I have to do to be re-elected."]...
>
> Four years of "never again" hand-wringing over an '88 campaign that left voters disgusted has brought forth more of the same.... But the tactic could backfire this year. The voters appear hungry for big changes, and a discussion of where the country is headed, not just another political food fight.[28]

The specific target of Engberg's report was a Bush ad featuring retired Marine commandant Gen. P. X. Kelley, whose tag line was, "The last thing we need in the White House is an isolationist like Pat Buchanan." Engberg stated no specific complaint about the ad, other than to note that it was an example of a negative commercial. The story also aired brief "actualities" of other candidates' ads, but Engberg made no reference to any of them — and alleged no specific wrongdoing — in his script.

Along with three other commercials, the Kelley spot was also targeted by NBC in one of its first "Ad Watches" of the new political season (March 3, 1992). The story started by scrutinizing a Buchanan commercial then airing in Georgia:

LISA MYERS: Pat Buchanan has been hammering George Bush with an ad attacking the National Endowment for the Arts.

Buchanan Ad: In the last three years, the Bush administration has invested our tax dollars in pornographic and blasphemous art too shocking to show. [The film is of several men wearing leather and dancing. The script appears on screen in red letters superimposed over the film itself.]

Lisa Myers: That's misleading. [The word "Misleading" appears in red, obscuring much of the Buchanan ad.] First, the Bush administration had absolutely nothing to do with the film in that ad. It was produced with $5,000 from a grant bestowed during the Reagan administration. And there's another problem:

Kathleen Hall Jamieson, Political Ads Analyst: The Buchanan ad distorts the record of the National Endowment for the Arts by suggesting that this film is a typical instance of funding. It's not.

Lisa Myers: The vast majority of NEA money supports groups like the Chicago Symphony and programs such as "Live from Lincoln Center." [The story shows clips of the Symphony and an opera performance by Luciano Pavarotti.] The Bush campaign also has taken liberties, with ads trumpeting the president's leadership.

Bush Ad: Now he has an agenda to strengthen our economy, and make America more competitive in the world, to change welfare, and make the able-bodied work.

Lisa Myers: That's misleading. [Again, the word is superimposed onto the ad.] Here's why:

Bob Greenstein, Welfare Policy Specialist: In the three years he's been president, he's not submitted a single significant proposal in the welfare reform area.

Lisa Myers: Another Bush ad also generated controversy:

Gen. P. X. Kelley [in Bush ad]: When Pat Buchanan opposed Desert Storm, it was a disappointment to all military people.

Lisa Myers: Wait a minute. Today, the Buchanan campaign produced a speech General Kelley made in December 1990, when troops already were in the Gulf, in which he seems to oppose going to war. [A photo of Pat Buchanan and a press release zoom out of the center of the ad to encompass the entire screen.] Kelley claims he was quoted out of context.

Gen. P. X. Kelley: I have supported President Bush from the day he gave the first order to deploy forces to the Gulf, until the last day of the war.

Lisa Myers: And now the Democrats. Paul Tsongas, who preaches honesty, plays fast and loose with the truth in attacking his rivals' support for a middle-class tax cut.

Sen. Paul Tsongas [in Tsongas ad]: And they want to give me a tax credit that they're going to have to borrow from my children.

LISA MYERS: That's misleading. [AGAIN, THE WORD IS SUPERIMPOSED ON THE AD.] Both Bill Clinton and Bob Kerrey would pay for their tax cuts by raising taxes on the rich.

KATHLEEN HALL JAMIESON, POLITICAL ADS ANALYST: That means there's no cost to our children.

LISA MYERS: In this latest round of ads, the theme seems to be distraction, distortion, and deception. And as the stakes get higher, it's likely to get worse.

The Myers spot is a fairly typical network "Ad Watch." It was among the earliest, but its structure and tone were duplicated throughout 1992 on ABC, CBS, and NBC as well as CNN. Additionally, the main target of her story, Buchanan's ad about the NEA, was one of the most-frequently criticized of the primary season. The ad used film from a controversial documentary, indirectly funded by government grants, called "Tongues Untied," about gay black men in America.

During much of 1990 and 1991, a well-publicized debate took place about whether the NEA should seek a "no obscenity" pledge from grantees, or whether art projects should be publicly financed at all. President Bush himself had not participated in the debate, which pitted some Republican members of Congress against the arts community. In the ad, however, Buchanan sought to hold Bush accountable for how NEA grant money had been distributed during his administration.

As Myers correctly pointed out, the grant for "Tongues Untied" was made in 1988, during the last year of the Reagan administration. She could also have made the point that presidents have no direct responsibility for distributing grant money, which is done by a peer review process. But Buchanan's ad also sought to make a larger point about national values that, while obviously debatable, is certainly relevant to broach in a national campaign.

Buchanan's complaint (and that of other cultural conservatives) was that Bush's appointee to head the NEA, John Frohnmayer, was not predisposed to shut off money to projects such as "Tongues Untied," and that he was not concerned about the moral messages of government-funded art projects. Bush, too, seemed little troubled by the controversy, maintaining Frohnmayer as head of the endowment until just a few days before the Georgia primary.[29]

In her story, however, Myers made no reference to this broader debate about the propriety of government financial assistance to allegedly obscene or pornographic art. Implicitly, her report actually seemed to dismiss the validity of attacks on the NEA — specifically, when she showed how "the vast majority of money" goes to projects such as the Chicago Symphony and PBS's "Live from Lincoln Center" program.

The piece correctly labeled the Buchanan ad as "misleading" insofar as it suggested that either Bush personally or his appointees authorized the controversial grant. But it also implied that the basic message of Buchanan's ad — that Bush's NEA allowed government money to flow to arts projects out of step with mainstream America — was also wrong. Such a conclusion was not only unsubstantiated by the evidence she presented, it is not an *empirical question* (which can be settled by facts, data, and observation), but rather a *normative question* (whose answers are dependent on individual beliefs and values). After all, the Buchanan ad did not state that "Tongues United" was "typical" of NEA-supported projects. And there had been enough similar controversies, such as the funding of Robert Mapplethorpe's homosexual and sadomasochistic photographic images and of "performance artists" who featured controversial sexual themes — to justify the ad's statement that tax dollars had supported such art "in the last three years." Myers's implied point — that the NEA was not guilty of doing anything objectionable, and any questionable grants are far outweighed by its good works — was her opinion, not fact. Its inclusion undercuts the non-partisan posture of the "Ad Watch."

One of the on-camera sources in this story was Kathleen Hall Jamieson, dean of the University of Pennsylvania's Annenberg School of Communications, and a leading expert on campaign ads. Dr. Jamieson later praised Myers's piece in her book, *Dirty Politics*:

> By 1992, the press had learned one lesson of 1988. As a result, voters rejected a drama-filled but atypical instance of arts funding that played on fears of gays. Where the press had abetted the Horton story, it discredited the tale of a president funding pornography. On CNN (February 28, 1992), Brooks Jackson pointed out that the film had been funded by the Reagan, not the Bush, administration at a total cost to the tax payers of $5,000. NBC's Lisa Myers went a step further (March 3, 1992) to note that the film was not typical of NEA projects.
>
> As she made this claim, Myers displaced the ad's images with shots of the Chicago Symphony and Pavarotti on PBS. These, she argued, were more representative of the Endowment's mission and expenditures. Both NBC and CNN distanced audiences from the ad by boxing it on the screen and dampened the power of the ad's visuals by imposing the words "misleading" or "false" over the ad copy in appropriate places.[30]

Three focus groups of undecided Georgia voters watched the ad, and Jamieson recounted their reactions to it. Their comments showed that they had learned the messages — both factual and editorial — of Myers's "Ad Watch":

"What matters to me," said a middle-aged male construction worker, "is that the ad doesn't tell the truth." "Bush didn't support that film. It happened under Reagan. This kind of advertising is what's wrong with politics." "But it does tell you a lot about Buchanan," said the college student. "Yeah," responded the construction worker. "He's a low life." "If that's all he's got to say about what he'd want to do when he is president, he hasn't got much more to say," commented a secretary.

"How, what makes you think the ad is untrue?" asked the focus group leader. "It was on the news," said the construction worker. "CNN" said the school teacher. "No, it was one of the other ones," added the construction worker. "It said the film was funded by someone else while Reagan was president and that what the agency [National Endowment for the Arts] does now is funds symphonies and opera."[31]

According to Jamieson's account, it was the construction worker who made the most specific arguments against Buchanan during the discussion. He was also the only participant who clearly had watched Myers's report.[32] Specifically, he regurgitated both of the points made by Myers in her NBC story — that the film was funded "while Reagan was president" and that the NEA "funds symphonies and opera." He also added an opinion about Pat Buchanan that could be regarded as Myers's subtext: "He's a low-life."

Was Myers "wrong" in her claims? Not as far as we know, but some of her comments were statement of opinion rather than of fact. Her points appear conclusive because of the story's tone and structure, which present her in the role of omniscient narrator. But her "Ad Watch" (and others, by other reporters) could be criticized as easily as a political commercial. The trademark of network "Ad Watches" is their low tolerance for any comment that could be construed as "invitations to inferential inaccuracies." It is a tough standard for both commercials and news stories to meet. To wit:

Myers's critique of the first Bush ad is misleading. The text that appeared on the screen discussed a speculative agenda of a second Bush administration. The expert states, correctly, that Bush had not "submitted a single significant proposal" on welfare in his first three years. But that is hardly proof that he would not do so in a second term.

Further, source Bob Greenstein does not draw into question the other element of the Bush ad — his "agenda to strengthen our economy, and make America more competitive." By tarring the entire agenda with the label "Misleading," Myers needed to provide proof that the quote she excerpted was indeed misleading. She only offered evidence about one part of the quote, and even that did not substantiate her claim.

•   Myers's inclusion of Bush's "Kelley" commercial implies that it is as misleading as the others, although she never states so directly. She deliberately includes this spot with the other ads, interrupts it with an objection ("Wait a minute") just as she did with the others, and says a speech shows General Kelly may have opposed the war he claims to have supported. That claim, however, came from Pat Buchanan, Bush's campaign nemesis, and General Kelley took vigorous exception to the charge that he was lying.

Myers, who had access to the ad, the general, and the general's speech, took no position on the ad's truthfulness — even though she had no compunction about evaluating the accuracy of other ads. Here, she seems to want to have it both ways — she includes the ad in a roster of objectionable commercials, but won't choose between Pat Buchanan and P. X. Kelley. If "Ad Watches" were supposed to help citizens sort out competing claims, this one just enhances the confusion.

•   The statement by Jamieson, critiquing the Tsongas ad, is as open to interpretation as is Tsongas's original statement. Tsongas stated that, to pay for a tax cut, "they're going to have to borrow from my children." That's true to the extent that it is a diversion of money away from deficit reduction.

The comment that "there's no cost to our children," implies that following generations will suffer no consequences if deficit reduction is delayed in order to provide immediate tax relief. One could just as easily argue — and Tsongas did — that any delay in deficit reduction has very real costs to the next generation ("our children"), not "no cost." In any event, such a comment is more opinion than fact, as illustrated by the robust debate over the deficit during the 1992 campaign.

•   Myers's closing comment that "in this latest round of ads, the theme seems to be distraction, distortion, and deception," unfairly implies that all the candidates' recent advertising was similar in tone and accuracy to the four she selected for criticism. And her comment that "as the stakes get higher, it's likely to get worse," reflects not fact, but rather a perception about how modern campaigns are conducted. In a story that was designed to be a fair and factual evaluation of the ads, her broad-brush summary is highly opinionated.

In fairness, the problem with "Ad Watches" is not that they are filled with inaccuracies or misrepresentations. Myers's story was hardly unusual. But neither Myers's piece, nor other "Ad Watches" produced by other news organizations (nor the candidates' own advertising), can satisfy the impossible standards created by the "ad police," who needed to justify their beat by handing out tickets.

Just one of the statements in Myers's story — that "Tongues Untied" was funded by NEA while Reagan, not Bush, was president — caught Buchanan in a bona fide falsehood. The remainder of the piece merely replaces the inferential claims of the ads with equally interpretive counter-claims. As the focus groups showed, however, an interpretive news story is generally more believable than an interpretive political advertisement, where the partisan motives of the ad's producers may be more apparent to the viewer.

Let's not single out Myers; other pieces were worse. The Engberg story, for example, linked Bush's relatively innocuous ad featuring Gen. Kelley with grievances about Bush's conduct during the 1988 campaign. ("The negative trail, with emphasis on patriotic themes, is a familiar one for Mr. Bush, who used flags and the Willie Horton furlough effectively against Dukakis in '88....")

The mildness of the Kelley ad, and the campaign environment that week (Buchanan was lobbing rhetorical grenades at Bush on an almost daily basis), made Engberg's dig seem a bit gratuitous at best. In his story, none of the ads were challenged on their accuracy or their fairness. Instead, all negative ads were dismissed as "vile and corrosive," without regard to their truth or falsity, their accuracy or their relevance. Compared with Engberg's slash-and-burn-approach to political analysis, Myers's occasional overstatements seem sugar-coated.

Myers's "Ad Watch" focused on individual commercials, examining each for their messages. Other stories, such as Engberg's piece, focused on the candidates more generally — their past as well as present campaigns. Engberg was hardly alone when he used Bush's relatively mild "Kelley" ad to charge the president with negative campaigning. By 1992, most of Campaign '88 had faded from public memory, but small aspects — among them, Bush's negative ads — lingered in the media's collective consciousness.

Thus, many journalists, including the *Boston Globe*'s Robert Turner, saw little wrongdoing but lots of irony in Buchanan's campaign ads:

[Bush] campaign spokeswoman Torie Clarke blasted the ad's "disgusting lies." ... It was Bush's White House spokesman, Marlin Fitzwater, who capsulized the message on Buchanan: "He's a town bully kind of guy."

But Bush was the attack dog — the town bully — of 1988. That is a fact. Americans believe it, and he is stuck with it. If this doesn't suit his 1992 campaign, he can try to modulate it, but he can't deny it.

The last thing he can do is convince anyone he is horrified by the TV ads of candidates who went to school in his own classroom.[33]

The "fact" that Bush was "the town bully of 1988" was a key consideration when the 1992 "Ad Police" were rounding up suspects. But could that "fact" really be considered a consensual view of reality shared by most Americans of all political persuasions? Or is it the consensus view among political journalists in the national media, whose backgrounds and perspectives are as distinctive as their experience of the 1988 campaign? Even if Bush supporters agreed with the general point that their candidate was the aggressor in the last campaign, they could hardly be expected to accept his pejorative phrasing.

The above examples clearly cast doubt on the assumptions behind TV's "Ad Watch" style of reporting. One of the criticisms of campaign ads was that the "facts" they claimed to provide were illusory, built upon a foundation of shaky evidence. The conceit was that journalists could replace the ad-makers' illusions with a certifiable reality.

Yet, as professionals in the advertising and television industry know, TV news spots — like political ads — are spliced together from highly selective pieces of sound and video, scripted and narrated by professionals, and packaged not for completeness and detail, but to evoke images and emotions.

In an interview with the *Washington Post* in 1988, then-*CBS Evening News* producer Brian Healey agreed that television news was designed to evoke emotions in much the same way political commercials did. Ad makers, Healey said, "are using techniques and styles that give you a mood and a feeling — which is what we try to develop in our stories."

A media consultant agreed: "What is completely similar is that both advertising and television news are very controlling. They don't let you decide for yourself what to think. They tell you how to feel. The network news is theatrically produced to provide that feeling...."[34] For TV news to condemn advertising for lacking objectivity, nuance, or context is at least as ironic as George Bush accusing Pat Buchanan of being a mean campaigner.

TV news fails the same tests as candidate advertising. Some claims made in Lisa Myers's NBC story were shaky not because this was a poorly done piece by the standards of television news, but because it met that standard, with all the conventions and limitations this implies. It was short (2 minutes, 20 seconds). It spent relatively little time on each ad (Buchanan's "Tongues Untied" received the most time, 48 seconds). It made its points by using broad generalizations supported not by a careful marshaling of evidence, but by a carefully worded script, the inflection of the narrator's voice, and powerful visuals — much like the style of political commercials themselves.

Television news, of course, has different goals from those of political commercials. Ads are designed to sell a candidate; news is designed to inform the public. But individual news stories often resemble individual commercials: a producer decides to make a particular point, writes a script, and then illustrates the "story" with sound and pictures.

A piece such as Engberg's — whose point was to decry all political ads, and remind viewers of Bush's 1988 sins — is no more designed for completeness than, say, Buchanan's heavy-handed NEA ad. Buchanan's sin was to pick an illustration that was factually at odds with his larger point. But his larger point was, at root, a statement of opinion (as was Engberg's) — involving assertions that, in and of themselves, cannot be falsified by the use of empirical data.

Even if taken on their own terms, TV's "Ad Watches" failed by virtue of their infrequence and irregularity. While the networks aired far more of them in '92 than in '88, they hardly maintained pace with the political advertisers. NBC, which ran the most "Ad Watches," finished the entire year with fewer than a dozen. CBS and ABC ran even fewer (although CBS's "Reality Checks," a feature of their general election coverage, turned their spotlight on radio ads as well as TV).

Their sporadic nature meant that TV's "Ad Watches" were susceptible to the vicissitudes of network news judgment. During the general election, as we will see, that meant that, while Bill Clinton's ads were routinely examined and criticized in the major newspapers, he largely avoided the surveillance of TV's ad police.

THE GENERAL ELECTION AIR WARS

During the general election our study expanded to include CNN's *PrimeNews*, PBS's *MacNeil-Lehrer NewsHour*, the *New York Times*, the *Washington Post*, and the *Wall Street Journal*. We also obtained videotaped copies of the three candidates' television ads. Heavy use of "Ad Watches" during the fall of 1992 boosted the percentage of news stories about campaign advertising above 1988 levels, but the focus of such stories remained surprisingly similar.

After 1988, Bruce Buchanan found that "the largest number of [advertising] stories emphasized strategic guile."[35] In 1992, while newspapers such as the *New York Times* and the *Washington Post* devoted considerable resources to their "Ad Watches," the lack of explicit falsehoods in most commercials meant that reporters had little to critically analyze other than the candidates' motives and strategic goals.

Our study found nearly 200 stories devoted to coverage of campaign advertising, more than half of which appeared in the *New York Times* and

The New York Times
                                                      October 9, 1992

The Ad Campaign

Perot: Raising Alarm on the Deficit

The Perot campaign began broadcasting three 60-second commercials about the state of the economy on Thursday. They are being shown on eight cable networks and on ABC, CBS, and NBC — mostly during sporting events — between now and Monday. A representative advertisement is titled "Red Flag."

On the Screen: A red flag, rippling slowly, fills the screen, providing the backdrop for white-lettered text that rolls upward. A deep-voiced announcer reads the script, accompanied by the militaristic roll of a snare drum. At the end of the ad, the campaign's red "Perot" logo briefly flashes.

Producer: The 270 Group.

Script: "While the cold war is ending, another war is now upon us. In this new war, the enemy is not the red flag of communism, but the red ink of our national debt, the red tape of our government bureaucracy. The casualties of this war are counted in lost jobs and lost dreams.

"As in all wars, the critical issue to winning is leadership. In this election, you can vote for a candidate who has proven his leadership by making the free enterprise system work. Creating jobs. Building businesses. A candidate who is not a business-as-usual politician, but a business leader with the know-how to expand the tax base, reduce the national debt, and restore the meaning of 'Made in the U.S.A.'

"The issue is leadership. The candidate is Ross Perot. The choice is yours."

Accuracy: The ad accurately conveys Mr. Perot's belief that the most dangerous threat to the country is its growing debt. His opponents, President Bush and Gov. Bill Clinton, say unemployment is an even more pressing problem.

As in the 30-minute "infomercial" broadcast by Mr. Perot on Tuesday, which will be repeated Friday, the 60-second ads never mention Mr. Perot's tough prescription for eliminating the deficit, which includes higher income taxes, a large increase in gasoline taxes and deep cuts in entitlement programs.

Mr. Perot's claim that his success in the business world would be transferable to government is, of course, unprovable. He has no prior political experience.

Scorecard: Mr. Perot is at his best when tsk-tsking about the economy, a practice that allows him to cast blame on both the Republicans and the Democrats. By stressing that the main threat to the country is now red ink, not the Red Army, Mr. Perot diminishes the liability of his dearth of foreign policy experience. By not appearing or being heard in any of the three ads, Mr. Perot may be acknowledging that his on-again, off-again campaign has made his message more powerful than its messenger.

                                                      Kevin Sack

Washington Post. Together, those two papers ran 38 campaign "Ad Watch" boxes — 16 at the *Post* and 22 at the *Times*, an average of one every three days. (The large number of remaining ad stories focused on the candidates' strategies for buying time, targeting markets, or crafting messages.) The four networks also ran "Ad Watches," but on a more infrequent and irregular basis. The *Wall Street Journal* and PBS's *MacNeil-Lehrer NewsHour* did not run "Ad Watches" per se, but discussed advertising in their regular stories.

   MacNeil-Lehrer did demonstrate an interesting alternative to the "Ad Watch" approach. On two occasions, it aired an extended feature called "Fact or Fiction," which invited representatives from the Bush and Clinton campaigns to discuss their grievances with their rival's ads. On September 25, for example, Clinton-Gore communications director George Stephanopoulos and Bush-Quayle issues advisor James Cicconi spent 30 minutes debating two ads that together lasted only a minute and a half.

   The Bush campaign charged that Clinton's radio ad (saying the president would cut benefits for a million disabled veterans and 30 million Medicare recipients) was a lie. The Democrats charged that a Bush ad (listing Arkansas tax increases on beer, mobile homes, cable TV, and groceries signed by Clinton) was hypocritical and misleading. The length of the discussion provided a rare glimpse at the campaigns arguing over the fine print of their records and proposals — something that was rare not just in other news organizations' "Ad Watches," but in media coverage of the campaign generally.

   What set the *MacNeil-Lehrer* segments apart is that they offered opportunities for the campaigns to complain directly about their rivals, and for a campaign accused of a falsehood to rebut the charge. For example, Cicconi charged that the Clinton ad lied, and that Bush had no plans to cut Medicare. Stephanopoulos countered that the cut was described in an appendix to Bush's *Agenda for Economic Renewal.* Cicconi responded that the "cut" was just a cap on future increases, and that it was similar to a proposal made by Democratic Budget Chairman Leon Panetta.

   While the discussion did not end with the two sides agreeing, the exchange was far more illuminating than a traditional news story. It also left the viewer with a sense that the "truth" may not be easily established — unlike the typical "Ad Watch," which purported to present the truth after less than 30 seconds of investigation.

   As we discovered with the networks during the primaries, few "Ad Watches" found flatly incorrect statements or assertions in any candidate's advertising. Instead, they took candidates to task for exaggerated or incomplete claims, or for steering the debate away from certain issues. For example, the *New York Times* carried an "Ad Watch" that purported to analyze a Perot ad entitled "Red Flag." (See opposite page.)

As the "Accuracy" part of the story makes clear, the "Ad Watch" could not deal with the truth or falsity of any of the ad's claims, since it expressed little more than the opinions of the Perot campaign. The ad was not susceptible to "fact-checking" because it did not incorporate data as part of its argument. Instead, it merely offered an assertion (that the deficit was the most important issue), and invited those who agreed to vote for Perot, and those who disagreed to vote for another candidate.

Lacking facts to check, the reporter instead tweaked Perot for failing to include his "Solutions" (which would be the subject of a 30-minute program aired a week later), and for "tsk-tsking about the economy." This was probably not what Bode had envisioned when he advocated "Ad Watches."

The "Scorecard" section amounted to little more than speculation about how the ad may or may not help Perot's candidacy. ("By stressing ... red ink, not the Red Army, Mr. Perot diminishes the liability of his dearth of foreign policy experience.") Strategic assessments such as these were the tactic of second resort in most of the newspaper "Ad Watches," when their first option — fact checking — failed to provide sufficient grounds for criticism.

The Perot ad is interesting because it was the type of campaign commercial that "Ad Watches" were supposed to encourage. It is hardly a negative ad — the closest the script comes to criticizing Perot's opponents is when he is described as "not a business-as-usual politician." Its focus is hardly trivial or irrelevant — for years, journalists had been criticizing politicians of both parties for evading the budget deficit as an issue. But "Ad Watches," of course, had no way to deal with positive, issue-oriented ads on their own terms. Their premise was that the candidates were going to run superficial and negative campaigns.

When an ad appeared that, on its face, would seem to suit the reformers perfectly, journalists blinked. While perfectly willing to criticize negativity and target all misleading statements, it was apparently too much for reporters to abandon objectivity to move in a *positive* direction. Thus, the *New York Times* (and the *Washington Post*, in a similar "Ad Watch") changed the subject from what Perot was saying to what he was not saying, from the ad's accuracy to its strategic import.

The *Post* and *Times* deserve credit for their policy of printing and analyzing most of the three major candidates' commercials. But their format demanded that they find something to critique, even in the case of ads that were bland and unobjectionable. Thus, their "fact-checking" frequently devolved into a strategic analysis of the ads' role in the campaign.

Ironically, the new format often produced just the sort of story Bruce Buchanan found dominant in 1988, when he called it "strategic guile." As we noted earlier, the media have long depended on the game paradigm to organize campaign news, despite the fact that this has often been criticized as distracting and superficial. As Kathleen Hall Jamieson observed,

> The strategy schema is cynical. It takes nothing at face value. Its world is Machiavellian. And since it assumes that most candidates are pandering sophists, it minimizes the disposition of the press to elicit or the viewer to discern the important differences the candidates would bring to the process of governance.[36]

The dominance of the strategy schema was evident in the newspapers' "Ad Watches." Lies, half-truths, distortions, attacks, and innuendo fit well within the media's strategy paradigm. When a candidate such as Perot offered a commercial that appeared to meet all of the "Ad Watch" standards, reporters seemed to limit themselves to only two choices: try to discover Perot's true motivation, or dismiss the ad as unilluminating.

While newspapers fought to publish a meaningful analysis of each ad, the networks' policy was to ignore all but the most egregious commercials. During the general election, the four broadcast networks collectively ran only a handful of "Ad Watches" on their flagship evening newscasts.[37] CBS aired two "Watches" that focused on the candidates' radio ads. Additionally, stories by campaign trail correspondents occasionally incorporated the candidates' advertising as part of their round-up of the day's events. But, on TV, the "Ad Watches" often lost the nightly competition with other newsworthy material to earn a spot in the broadcast.

The practical effect of these limitations was not politically neutral. It worked in favor of the Clinton campaign, whose ads were hardly ever scrutinized by the "big three," and against the Bush campaign. During the general election, we identified 152 instances when network reporters drew into question or refuted campaign statements. Mostly they targeted ads, but occasionally they corrected a comment from a debate or speech. More than half (52%) of these corrections targeted the Bush campaign; the remaining 48 percent were evenly divided between the Clinton and Perot camps. Specific comments about campaign commercials focused on Bush's ads three-fifths of the time, with the remainder split between his rivals.

One source of this disparity is a Bush ad released on October 1, which quickly became the most controversial one of the general election. Cryptically titled "Federal Taxes," it was the only commercial subjected to critical reports on all eight national media outlets. This ad was controversial because it attempted to place a price tag on what it called "Clinton economics" by estimating the increases in federal taxes for some representative citizens. It was modeled after an ad run by British Prime Minister John Major's Conservative Party in their 1992 campaign. It was immediately denounced by both the Clinton campaign and the major news organizations.[38]

The *Wall Street Journal* not only wrote the toughest story but placed it on the front page: "Reaching across the Atlantic for inspiration, President Bush is airing a new attack advertisement against Bill Clinton on taxes — and it's a real stretch," the *Journal* piece began. "The problem," the story continued, "is that Mr. Clinton has proposed to *cut* taxes for the sort of workers featured in the ad."[39] [Emphasis in the original.] Explained the *New York Times*: "The Bush campaign uses figures that cannot be reconciled with Mr. Clinton's figures. Bush aides acknowledge that they were making a leap of logic: that Mr. Clinton would not have enough money to keep his campaign promises and would therefore tax the middle class rather than revising his plans."[40]

For the only time during the campaign, the networks all focused on the same ad. ABC's Jeff Greenfield noted that "the numbers don't come from Clinton's plan at all. They come from the Bush campaign's very questionable assumptions about Clinton's plan."[41] NBC's Lisa Myers echoed the *Journal*: "In fact, Clinton has proposed cutting taxes for the sort of people in this ad."[42] CBS's Susan Spencer brought up the ad as part of her daily report on Bush's campaign: "The Clinton campaign is genuinely worried about this ad. As one source said, 'What if people actually believe it?'"[43]

The response ad from Bill Clinton was on the air the next morning, ensuring that voters would not have fully digested the original Bush message. But the Clinton campaign's use of the "Ad Watches" in their counterattack was as noteworthy as its speed. As Tom Rosenstiel writes, the Clinton campaign immediately began lobbying reporters to label the Bush ad false.

The Clinton team's plan (which turned out to be successful) was to incorporate the toughest of the "Ad Watches" in their response: "George Bush… says all these people would have their taxes raised by Bill Clinton. Scary, huh? 'Misleading' says the *Washington Post*. And the *Wall Street Journal* says 'Clinton has proposed to cut taxes for the sort of people featured in [Bush's] ad.'"[44]

As a formality, an "Ad Watch" scrutinizing this Clinton ad appeared in the next morning's *Post*, but based on its previous day's edition, it found little to criticize: "This commercial, produced in 24 hours, underscores Clinton's determination to respond quickly to negative ads."[45] Rosenstiel reports:

> By the next morning, TV stations and reporters had a Clinton response ad to Bush that quoted that morning's papers. The episode amounted to the swiftest and most elaborate use by a politician yet of the press's new role as policemen for political advertising.[46]

The "Ad Watches," however, failed to take note of the Bush campaign's justification of their data (other than to note that they were based on "assumptions" of how, given the deficit, Clinton would decide various tax and budgetary issues). On Monday, October 5, 1992 — 72 hours after the Clinton response ad was released, and long after the rest of the media pack had moved on — *MacNeil-Lehrer* invited George Stephanopoulos and James Cicconi back for a second "Fact or Fiction." Cicconi argued that for Clinton to reach his goal of $150 million in new revenue he would have to increase taxes on more than just the top 2% of income-tax payers:

> The fact is we have looked at the Clinton plan, the Clinton proposals. These are his proposals out there. He says he's going to levy a 36 percent income tax rate on the top 2 percent. That starts — contrary to what he's saying publicly — at people making $64,000 a year. To get the total amount in income taxes in his plan, he'd have to drop that rate to $53,000, and to get the total $150 billion, to make up for the phony revenue in there, he'd have to drop that rate to $36,000.

Stephanopoulos had a chance to rebut that assertion:

> Clinton will raise taxes on the very wealthy, those with adjusted gross incomes in families over $200,000, individuals over $150,000. Every single one of our revenue estimates are based on those figures. Mr. Cicconi does an interesting little trick there: number one, he counts the top 2 percent, not the $200,000 and the $150,000, which is what our revenue estimate is based on. Number two, he slips in the words "taxable income." Now you, me, everybody else in the world considers their salary their income, their adjusted gross income, which is what you make before your deductions for your house, for your loans, and for everything else, for charity, everything else that brings it down to taxable income.[47]

Again, this format provided considerable opportunity for both campaigns to make their case. (The discussion continued for several minutes.) Cicconi was able to explain how the Bush campaign had calculated their figures. Viewers would decide whether they found the explanation reasonable. Stephanopoulos systematically stated his complaints with both the ad's math and Cicconi's justifications. He also made his case for the program the Bush commercial criticized. None of the "Ad Watches" carried as much information. Instead, they dashed to the bottom line, leaving audiences without a contrary point of view to consider.

As we noted earlier, "Ad Watches" frequently criticized, and rarely praised, candidate commercials. The criticism — and there was plenty — was disproportionately aimed at the Bush campaign's ads. Fully two-thirds of the media criticism of the commercials was aimed squarely at the Bush

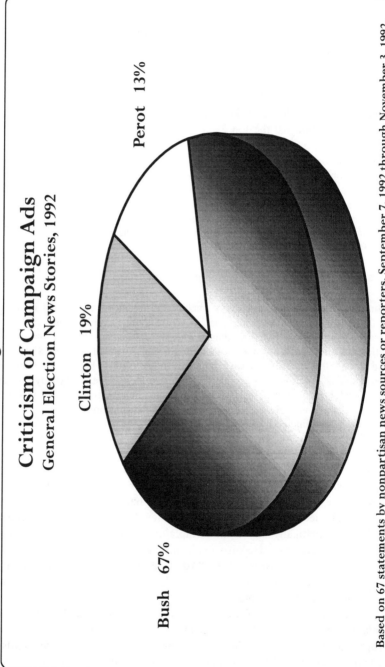

Figure 5-1

Criticism of Campaign Ads
General Election News Stories, 1992

Perot 13%

Clinton 19%

Bush 67%

Based on 67 statements by nonpartisan news sources or reporters, September 7, 1992 through November 3, 1992.

campaign (in no small measure because of the heavy criticism of his "Federal Taxes" ad). (As Figure 5-1 shows, Bush received more than three times the criticism levied against Clinton, and more than four times that aimed at Perot.)

Ironically, the networks' decision to act as "ad police" made the battle of campaign commercials seem more negative than it actually was. That is, the ads that showed up on the evening news were collectively more negative than the full range of paid ads that the campaigns aired. Overall, the candidates ran 34 negative ads out of a total of 81 commercials (42%).[48] Thirty-five of those ads were selected by the news organizations we examined for analysis in one or another of the "Ad Watch" columns. Nearly three out of five spots chosen for "Ad Watches" (59%) were negative ads. Positive ads, such as Perot's "Red Flag," Clinton's "Trust," (Clinton: "It's exhilarating to me to think that as President I can help to change all our people's lives for the better, and bring hope back to the American Dream") and a two-minute ad called "Presidency" produced by the Bush campaign at the end of the campaign, seldom popped up in "truth boxes."

"Ad Watches" were an experiment that were given their first national try-out during the 1992 campaign, and they did have some success at cleaning up the airwaves. Some falsehoods, such as Buchanan's, were caught and labeled. Other falsehoods may have been prevented by consultants' fore-knowledge that the "ad police" were on the beat. Campaigns took the time to document their claims. The Bush campaign's Cicconi, for example, had prepared an argument in favor of the "Federal Taxes" spot if it was challenged. It was challenged, but he was only allowed to make his case on *MacNeil-Lehrer* several days after the complaints appeared.

TV's "Ad Watches" weren't systematic but depended on the vicissitudes of the day's news. That was fair to neither the viewers nor the candidates. The *Washington Post* and *New York Times* "Ad Watches" offered their readers a far more representative batch of ads, but the wider selection revealed that most of the ads were relatively problem-free. Without "corrections" to make, the ad watchers were stymied, and reverted back to the pre-1992 system of analyzing ads for their strategic political value.

ROSS PEROT'S THIRTY-MINUTE WORK-OUT

An October 2, 1992, editorial in the *Wall Street Journal*, dressed up as a memorandum to the chief executive officers of the three major networks, stated its position bluntly: "Gentlemen: If your policies on political commercials weren't so restrictive, we all might have been spared the Ross Perot spectacle."[49] The *Journal's* complaint reflected not just their opinion of Perot, but the unusual nature of the Perot candidacy. Almost without exception, Perot's campaign consisted of free television appearances and paid advertising.

Indeed, before he re-joined the presidential race on October 1, Perot stated his desire to offer his economic proposals to the public in paid 30 minute broadcasts. But the networks turned him down because he was not a declared presidential candidate. So, Perot obliged the networks, declaring, "I may be the first guy in history that had to declare he was a candidate so he could buy TV time."[50]

Perot's candidacy had been conceived in February, on CNN's *Larry King Live*. Perot was so pleased with his appearance that waiting callers to his Dallas headquarters months later would not hear Muzak, but Perot and King chatting about the issues. Perot announced that he would run if volunteers put his name on the ballot in all 50 states, and he promptly donated office space and telephones for the fledgling movement.

By June, some polls had Perot leading both President Bush and Gov. Clinton in trial heats. In July, however, stung by bad press (mainly about his business practices, his verbal gaffes, and his unorthodox style), Perot announced that he would not be a candidate after all. "Our objective is to improve our country, not disrupt the political process," Perot told his volunteers. "I believe it would be disruptive for us to continue our program. So therefore I will not become a candidate."[51]

By fall, however, he was back, his book outlining his prescriptions for an ailing U.S. economy (*United We Stand: How We Can Take Back Our Country*) topped best-seller lists across the country. Perot reappeared on television talk shows to argue that the deficit was America's single most important issue, and the major party candidates were not dealing with it in a straightforward manner.

Audaciously, he offered the other candidates a chance to "prove" their seriousness. Both Clinton and Bush sent emissaries to Dallas to meet with Perot and his volunteers on September 28. Three days later, Perot declared that their efforts were not sufficient for the volunteers, and he declared his candidacy. A week later, his first infomercial — "Plain Talk about Jobs, Debt, and the Washington Mess" aired on CBS. He drew 16 million viewers, enough to lead the Nielsen ratings for the time slot, ahead of NBC's *Quantum Leap* and ABC's *Full House*.[52]

Perot's first two addresses ("Problems" and "Solutions") were generally regarded as useful and substantive exercises that attracted much voter attention. Using charts and a pointer, Perot walked voters through a primer on the budget and recent economic trends. He paid for repeat broadcasts, in order to allow viewers who missed the first time to watch.

According to the ratings, they did. As the *Washington Post*'s TV critic, Tom Shales, noted, "For years, professional worrywarts and furrow-browed academics have been saying that TV shortens viewers' attention spans... But millions of viewers are sitting there watching a funny little man with a pointer talk about the economy for half an hour or more at a time."[53]

Those who tuned in generally approved of Perot's show. Audience research by Video Storyboard Tests found that 35% rated his first infomercial "informative," 25% said it was "entertaining," and one-third said the program was useful in helping them decide their vote — all far better than the normal response to political advertising. The audience for the first show was estimated at approximately 20% of the viewing audience.[54]

Initial media reaction to Perot's speeches was more skeptical. "Perot promised 'solutions' in future programs, but avoided them last night," reported the *Washington Post* in a typical newspaper account. "He spoke of the rising gasoline prices but did not mention his proposed 50-cent increase in the gas tax. He illustrated the growth of entitlement programs but steered clear of his proposal to trim cost-of-living increases for Social Security and Medicare."[55] CBS also reported the ad was "a laundry list of problems," but that solutions were promised "in future episodes."[56]

When "Solutions" aired, however, it was generally ignored by the newspapers as more of the same. CNN's *PrimeNews* spent 23 seconds noting that Perot had spoken. "In the ad, Perot calls for raising taxes and cutting spending to erase the federal government deficit. Included in that tax package: a 50-cent increase in gasoline taxes over five years."[57]

CBS and NBC, however, both provided extensive coverage. CBS interviewed a historian who faulted the premise of Perot's candidacy: "It's this confusion that if you succeed in business, therefore you can succeed in politics. And that is simply not the case."[58] NBC caught up with Bill Clinton, and asked his reaction. Clinton confessed he didn't watch the Perot show: "I got home too late, and I was tired." Reporter Jim Cummins also talked to voters, most of whom said they liked the show. "I thought Perot did very well," said one. "He was forthright, he was honest."[59]

Mostly, political reporters contemplated the size, scope, and potential effect on the race that Perot's ads were having. The *New York Times* reported that, "If Mr. Perot's advertising budget were annualized, it would exceed that of companies like Chrysler and RJR Nabisco."[60] The size of his audience also surprised reporters. Some experts advocated that Bush or Clinton also adopt a 30-minute format to explain their platforms, or else "people [may] assume that they don't have a message."[61] But as one reporter noted, "If either Mr. Bush or Mr. Clinton could attract the kind of network audience that Mr. Perot does, the 30-minute commercial might make sense for them at this point, too. But they probably could not."[62]

Perot's appeal was considered puzzling. "He isn't warm, he isn't cuddly, he isn't an old dear, and Heaven knows he doesn't appear to have great prowess as a performer," wrote the *Post*'s Tom Shales. "But people, bless their pea-picking hearts, like this guy and the way he comes across on TV." Shales sought the advice of former NBC News president Reuven Frank, who offered some pop psychology: "Perot is a mythological creature, self-created, who's come along to satisfy the need for myth at a time when people have given up on rational solutions." Frank also sounded envious. "It's virtually unheard of for political ads to out-rate first-run entertainment programming. Perot keeps doing it."[63]

Later Perot efforts were criticized when they retreated from policy toward the personal realm, such as one 30-minute program filled with encomia from his wife and children. ("He is my hero," said his son, Ross, Jr.; daughter Suzanne added, "He really has this warm, soft, sweet, sweet, caring side.")[64]

Reporters also began fact-checking Perot's doom-and-gloom economic diagnosis. "In contrast to his allegations against political foes, Ross Perot's straight-talking television commercials have built a persuasive case about what ails the U.S. economy. There's just one problem," wrote the *Wall Street Journal*. "A number of the startling assertions he makes in those half-hour and one-hour commercials aren't true. In case after case, Mr. Perot exaggerates the facts to make his point, usually making the country's situation look far worse than it is."[65]

The fact-checking was part of a more general anti-Perot tide that swept news reports during the final week of the campaign. A *Washington Post* editorial declared that, "Ross Perot would have been better off to have left it at quitter....

> In the TV ads through which he has mainly chosen to campaign, he too is avoiding those real issues he accuses the media of ignoring. His was supposed to be the candidacy that legitimized the hard decisions the country has to make to reduce the budget deficit, but most of his ads have been about himself, his family, the nation's problems — anything but his proposed solutions. Those aren't what supersalesman Ross Perot is selling in the final days of this campaign.[66]

Criticism was hardly confined to the editorial pages. NBC's Lisa Myers filed the following report on October 26:

LISA MYERS: Perot's bizarre allegations raise more questions about his character, truthfulness and fitness to be president....

Sources close to Perot told NBC News that while running his company, EDS, in the '80s, Perot had a device on his phone to tape callers without their knowledge, and sometimes used it on business calls. At EDS, Perot was so notorious for not telling the truth that well-placed sources say, among senior officials, lying was known as "Rossing."...

Ed Rollins, who ran Perot's campaign for 45 days, says Perot sees the world as he wants to see it.

ED ROLLINS: He used to talk about the phone banks. He'd say, "Well, the phone banks are calling, and they're ringing off the hook." I'd walk down to the phone banks, and there'd be very little activity.

LISA MYERS: Yet few dare tell Perot his prism is distorted.

ED ROLLINS: And I found the whole experience — there was never a reality check. And my sense is there hasn't been a reality check with Ross Perot for a very long time.

LISA MYERS: ...The dark side of Perot can be ruthless: investigating and attempting to discredit enemies, business adversaries, even those who merely oppose him....

The temperamental outbursts that have become part of his campaign pale when compared to the abuse he has heaped on once-close aides like Tom Luce....

Another troublesome tendency: Perot's habit of seeing conspiracies where none exist. He blows up when reporters get near his plane for fear terrorists will get the I.D. number. He believes the Secret Service is controlled by the CIA. Now, the supposed dirty tricks against his daughter.

...Not even tens of millions of dollars in ads are likely to wipe out the questions raised in the last 24 hours.[67]

Two days later Lisa Myers offered a final "Ad Watch," examining the truthfulness of Perot's claims. She concluded that, "In some cases, Perot's ads mislead or stretch the truth." Her closer: "The conflict between fact and fiction goes to the heart of the Perot campaign. While watching his multi-million-dollar blitz: Buyer Beware."[68]

Ultimately, what appeared to most fuel journalists' pique was that Perot flouted the rules of conventional campaigning. *Newsday*'s Gaylord Shaw noted that, with the Perot campaign, "There were no pressrooms and press officers, advance men. There weren't a whole lot of folks around Perot who knew what was going on." That was a problem because, as Shaw put it, "A lot of things we do are based on interviews with people around the candidates."[69] The *New York Times* believed there was a strategic rationale behind his closeted personae:

By controlling his message and limiting his access to the media, the experts said, Mr. Perot has eliminated the potential for gaffes like his earlier reference to a meeting of blacks as "you people." By not engaging his opponents, he has manufactured an image of seriousness and statesmanship. By not campaigning, he has insured that most news reporters will be about his advertising, allowing him, like the Wizard of Oz, to portray himself as he wishes.[70]

Perot's stated belief was that campaigns ought to be conversations directly between the voters and the candidates. He organized his own campaign around mass market advertising, he said, because his goal was not to "stage" rallies or "manufacture" sound bites for the evening news. Journalists, however, seemed surprised that the logical replacement for campaign trail events (particularly for a candidate with no grass-roots party machine to massage) was a direct-communication campaign via television.

The media should have seen the Perot campaign coming. After all, their complaints about "photo-ops" reflected their understanding that the campaign trail was a stage, and that most of the speeches and rallies were created not for local audiences, but for television to disseminate to the country. "The dirty little secret of all of us on the campaign planes is that the day New Hampshire is over, personal campaigning does not matter," said one political reporter. "It doesn't matter that Bill Clinton wowed an audience of 1,500 in Atlanta, or that he was terrific in his visit to a senior citizen center in Fresno."[71]

What mattered after the TV revolution is what went on the evening news, not what happened on the campaign trail itself. Perot, who seemed not to care what went on the evening news, decided not to participate in the charade. He aimed his campaign at voters, using television to reach them in their living rooms. Such a strategy, however, cut out journalists' mediating role, and they didn't appreciate it. As the Perot experience showed, the further candidates maneuvered away from the media's reach, the more determined the media effort to block them became.

The reformers had something quite different in mind — a campaign in which *they* controlled the means of image production. "Ad Watches" and "Reality Checks" offered journalists a chance to retain a role in the campaign discourse. By having the last word on campaign pronouncements, journalists could (and did) influence the way in which the public interpreted the campaign. It offered a means for journalists to stay relevant in a campaign when the candidates seemed so determined to avoid their control. "Ad Watches" promoted the idea that journalists were truth-tellers, when in fact what they offered was mostly alternative interpretations of a candidates' claims.

The rationale for "Ad Watches," however, was that the candidates' negative and misleading messages were primarily responsible for any unfairness in past coverage. That was a flawed assumption. The candidates' ads, for example, appeared in barely 7% of Campaign '88 news stories. Most of the coverage was framed by the journalists themselves — who decided what to cover, who to quote, and how to frame their stories. The 1992 "Ad Watches" illustrate the fact that journalism is not neutral in its effects — not every ad was checked, and those issued by the Bush campaign were disproportionately criticized. "Ad Watches" did some good during Campaign '92, but they failed to live up to their advance billing. They didn't fix the media's fairness problem. *Caveat emptor*: Let the viewer beware.

By focusing on the candidates as the source of the media's problems, reformers largely neglected the public's prevailing concern about fairness: that journalists were too negative, too adversarial, and often let their own point of view invade stories. During the 1992 primaries and general election, both Clinton and Bush would face heavy negative coverage from the national media, and their supporters would express growing concerns about the fairness with which the media went about its work.

Notes

Opening quote: "The Press and Campaign '92: A Self-Assessment," Times Mirror Center for the People and the Press, supplement to the *Columbia Journalism Review*, March/April 1993.

1. ABC's *World News Tonight*, October 19, 1988.
2. Both quotes, ABC's *World News Tonight*, November 3, 1988.
3. Jonathon Alter, "How the Media Blew It," *Newsweek*, November 28, 1988.
4. Paul Taylor, "A 'Gap Between Image and Reality'; Rhetoric Bears Little Resemblance to Candidates' Pasts," *Washington Post*, November 5, 1988.
5. Edward Walsh, "What Campaigns Tell of Leadership; Slowness to Respond to Attacks Reflects Dukakis's Faith in Self," *Washington Post*, November 6, 1988.
6. "The Smear Campaign," *Newsweek*, October 31, 1988.
7. Laurence Zuckerman, "The Made-for-TV Campaign," *Time*, November 14, 1988.
8. Ibid.
9. Mark Crispin Miller, "TV's Anti-Liberal Bias," *New York Times*, November 16, 1988.
10. *CBS Evening News*, November 8, 1988.
11. David Broder, "Five Ways to Put Some Sanity Back in Elections," *Washington Post*, January 14, 1990.
12. Timothy J. Russert, "For '92, the Networks Have to Do Better," *New York Times*, March 4, 1990.
13. Tom Rosenstiel, *Strange Bedfellows: How Television and the Presidential Candidates Changed American Politics,* 1992 (New York: Hyperion, 1993), p. 273.
14. *NBC Nightly News*, November 6, 1988.

15. Quoted by David Broder, "Should News Media Police the Accuracy of Ads?" *Washington Post*, January 19, 1989.

16. See Ted J. Smith III, "The Watchdog's Bite," *American Enterprise* (January/February 1990): 63-70.

17. Richard Harwood, "Call Them Mugwumps," *Washington Post*, November 6, 1988.

18. "The People, Press & Politics: October Pre-Election Typology Survey," conducted for Times Mirror by the Gallup Organization, Inc., October 1988.

19. *The People and the Press, Part V: Attitudes Toward News Organizations; An Examination of the Opinions of the Press, the General Public and American Leadership*, Times Mirror, November 1989.

20. Ken Bode, "Guidelines for Covering Ads as News Stories," *Electronic Media*, February 17, 1992.

21. Ibid.

22. Ellen Hume, *Restoring the Bond: Connecting Campaign Coverage to Voters — A Report of the Campaign Lessons for '92 Project* (Cambridge, MA: Harvard University, 1991), p. 141.

23. Ibid., p. 144.

24. Bob Schieffer, "Trivializing the Irrelevant," *The Quill*, October 1990.

25. Hume, *Restoring the Bond*, pp. 98-102.

26. Quoted in "The Press Plays Referee on Campaign Ads," *National Journal*, October 27, 1990.

27. "It seems that the candidates use the newspaper's analysis of their opponents' ads in their counter-ad. They flash the headlines and quote the reporting. But not always accurately. In total role reversal, journalists can be quoted out of context." Ellen Goodman, "Two Political Negatives Don't Make a Positive," *Newsday*, October 23, 1990.

28. *CBS Evening News*, February 26, 1992.

29. Ann Devroy, "Bush Maneuvers to Ease Conservatives' Concerns; Steps Aimed at Depleting Buchanan Arsenal," *Washington Post*, February 23, 1992.

30. Kathleen Hall Jamieson, *Dirty Politics: Deception, Distraction, and Democracy* (New York: Oxford University Press, 1992), pp. 264-265. CNN's "Ad Watch" was similar to Myers, although Brooks Jackson placed the Bush campaign's P. X. Kelley ad first on his hit list that day. When he got to Buchanan's ad, he spent more time discussing the indirectness of its government funding, and did not deal with the merits of the NEA:

JACKSON: Meanwhile, Buchanan is running one of the roughest political ads we've ever seen.

BUCHANAN AD: In the last three years, the Bush administration has invested our tax dollars in pornographic and blasphemous art, too shocking to show.

JACKSON: Look what this says:

BUCHANAN AD: Bush used your tax money for this.

JACKSON: That's false. The fact is, the federal grant for this film was made in 1988 when Ronald Reagan was president. Bush didn't become president until 1989. Furthermore, the filmmaker got only $5000 from the Rocky Mountain Film

Center, which got its money from the American Film Institute, which got its money from the National Endowment for the Arts.

Let's watch a little more of how Buchanan is appealing to southern conservatives:

BUCHANAN AD: This so-called art has glorified homosexuality, exploited children, and perverted the image of Jesus Christ. Even after the good people protested —
JACKSON: Although Buchanan accuses Bush of misusing tax money, Buchanan himself is using your tax money to produce and show this ad. His campaign has received more than $1 million in federal subsidies, so far.

31. Jamieson, *Dirty Politics...*, p. 264.

32. Particularly, the construction worker said he didn't think he saw the story on CNN, which did not juxtapose the sadomasochistic ad with the shots of the Chicago Symphony and Pavarotti, as NBC had done. The NBC story alone made both of the points that the voter used to form his judgment: the funding was approved during the Reagan administration, and the grant was not typical of NEA projects.

33. Robert L. Turner, "The Ads that Haunt Bush," *Boston Globe*, March 3, 1992.

34. Quoted by Lloyd Grove, "TV News, Ad Images Melding," *Washington Post*, October 20, 1988.

35. Bruce Buchanan, *Electing a President: The Markle Commission Research on Campaign '88* (Austin: University of Texas Press, 1991), p. 68.

36. Jamieson, *Dirty Politics*, pp. 187-188.

37. CNN's special election unit produced several "Ad Watches," but most were not aired on *PrimeNews*. Even at an hour's length, their election "newshole" was usually consumed mainly by excerpts from the *Democracy in America* series.

38. Rosenstiel, *Strange Bedfellows*, pp. 271-272, 285-289.

39. John Harwood and Jeffrey H. Birnbaum, "President Is Hoping A British-Style Ad Will Turn the Tide," *Wall Street Journal*, October 2, 1992.

40. "Bush: Attacking Clinton's Tax Proposal," *New York Times*, October 2, 1992.

41. ABC's *World News Tonight*, October 2, 1992.

42. *NBC Nightly News*, October 2, 1992.

43. *CBS Evening News*, October 1, 1992.

44. "Scary," Clinton/Gore for President, October 1, 1992.

45. "30-Second Politics," *Washington Post*, October 3, 1992.

46. Rosenstiel, *Strange Bedfellows*, p. 288.

47. PBS's *MacNeil-Lehrer NewsHour,* October 5, 1992.

48. The total number of ads includes all "spots" (under five minutes) aired by the campaign committees during the general election phase of the campaign. Some of the Bush and Clinton ads aired prior to Labor Day, but were included since some of those ads continued to run after the start of our sample period.

49. "Prime Time for Perot," *Wall Street Journal*, October 2, 1992.

50. Quoted by Timothy Noah, "Perot May Declare Candidacy to Buy TV Ads Promoting His Economic Plan," *Wall Street Journal*, September 21, 1992.

51. *CBS Evening News*, July 16, 1992.

52. It was not unusual for CBS's regular 8:00 show, *Rescue 911*, to beat NBC's *Quantum Leap*, but ABC's *Full House* had been winning the time slot during the first several weeks of the 1992-93 season.

53. Tom Shales, "Uncanned Ham: Perot's Shows," *Washington Post*, October 27, 1992.

54. Laura Bird, "Perot's 'Plain Talk' Wins Many Viewers, Mixed Reviews," *Wall Street Journal*, October 8, 1992.

55. Howard Kurtz, "Perot Ad Hits 'Trickle Down' GOP Economics," *Washington Post*, October 7, 1992.

56. *CBS Evening News*, October 7, 1992.

57. CNN's *PrimeNews*, October 17, 1992.

58. *CBS Evening News*, October 17, 1992.

59. *NBC Nightly News*, October 17, 1992.

60. Elizabeth Kolbert, "Perot Spending More on Ads Than Any Candidate Before," *New York Times*, October 28, 1992.

61. Kathleen Hall Jamieson, quoted by Elizabeth Kolbert, "Perot's 30-minute TV Ads Defy the Experts, Again," *New York Times*, October 27, 1992.

62. Elizabeth Kolbert, "Perot's 30-Minute TV Ads Defy the Experts, Again," *New York Times*, October 27, 1992.

63. Tom Shales, "Uncanned Ham," *Washington Post*, October 27, 1992.

64. Quoted from "The Best of Ross Perot by His Family." The Perot infomercial series consisted of: "Problems," a Perot speech in which he detailed the nation's economic troubles and introduced his flip charts; "Solutions," a second speech in which he reviewed the problems and presented his solutions; "The Perot Biography," a two-part interview with Perot media advisor and former ABC reporter Murphy Martin in which Perot summarized his childhood and business career; "The Best of Ross Perot by His Family," which consisted of interviews with Perot's wife, Margot, and their five children; "The Ross Perot Nobody Knows," which consisted of interviews with individuals Perot had helped over the years; "How to Build a Business and Create Jobs," another Perot interview with Murphy Martin, in which Perot offered advice to new businessmen and more of his economic theories; and "Deep Voodoo, Chicken Feathers, and the American Dream," an election-eve speech in which Perot summarized the economic records of George Bush and Bill Clinton, and reviewed his own economic plans.

65. David Wessel and Gerald F. Seib, "In Straight-Talking TV Spots, Perot Stretches the Truth to Make His Point," *Wall Street Journal*, October 28, 1992.

66. "Ross Perot's World," *Washington Post*, October 27, 1992.

67. *NBC Nightly News*, October 26, 1992.

68. *NBC Nightly News*, October 28, 1992.

69. Debra Gersh, "Introspection: Journalists Examine Presidential Campaign Coverage and the Impact Ross Perot Had on Coverage," *Editor and Publisher*, November 21, 1992.

70. Kevin Sack, "For TV, Perot Spends Heavily on Wart Removal," *New York Times*, October 25, 1992.

71. *Time* correspondent Walter Shapiro, quoted by Howard Kurtz, "Clinton Does a Fadeout from Media Coverage," *Washington Post*, May 22, 1992.

Chapter Six

The Media's Character Test

*We live in a world where if anybody says anything about you that's bad, you
folks will publish it and worry about whether it's true later*
— Gov. Bill Clinton, 1992

While "Ad Watches" were the centerpiece of the reformers' efforts
to provide fairer coverage after 1988, fair coverage involves far
more than policing commercials. The debate over the fairness of
TV news has been going on since the early 1960s. Conservatives began
complaining first — one of the most memorable scenes from the 1964
Republican convention, involved former president Dwight D. Eisenhower's
complaint about "sensation-seeking columnists and commentators."

In 1969, then-Vice President Spiro Agnew raised the stakes when he
criticized the "nattering nabobs of negativism... a small band of network
commentators and self-appointed analysts," who, he said, jeopardized the
public's right "to form their own opinions" by their practice of instantly
analyzing (i.e., criticizing) presidential addresses and other forms of direct
communication between the public and their leaders.[1]

The media roundly criticized Agnew for his speech. One news executive
called it an "unprecedented attempt by the vice president of the United
States to intimidate a mass medium which depends for its existence upon
government licenses."[2] But Agnew's speech added considerable fuel to a
sometimes heated debate about the credibility and fairness of the news
media's coverage of politics — a debate that is still with us. As we noted in

Chapter 2, liberal politicians made the accusation bipartisan when they launched their own attacks on the fairness of journalism in the 1980s.

Today, politicians of both the right and the left routinely criticize the establishment media for coverage that allegedly slants, distorts, ignores, or otherwise misrepresents reality. This accusation against the press has been echoed in all recent presidential campaigns, from Democrats and Republicans alike, and it involves far more than how frequently and effectively campaign advertisements are criticized.

The issue of "bias" is also a hardy perennial for the many media scholars who have studied the tone and balance of campaign news, examining the coverage received by a variety of candidates in different election contexts. The accumulated evidence of these studies demonstrates that, while some candidates have been blessed with positive coverage and others cursed with highly critical coverage, there is little evidence of a systematic partisan or ideological consistency in the distribution of good and bad press.

After some elections, conservatives have pointed to instances when Republican or conservative candidates received critical coverage, as examples of a pro-liberal (or anti-conservative) bias in the news media. Although individual cases may present circumstantial evidence of such a bias, there have also been many cases where Democratic or liberal candidates have received unfavorable coverage.[3] Similarly, there are enough instances where Republicans and conservatives have been pilloried to preclude notions of a systematic pro-conservative bias, as alleged by some liberal media critics.

If ideology and partisanship are not the primary ingredients in determining the tone of a candidate's news coverage, scholars have identified factors that play a greater role in the distribution of good and bad press. Generally, the media perceive themselves as "the loyal opposition," whose function is to question and challenge those in authority.[4] During election campaigns, this tendency asserts itself as an anti-frontrunner bias. Hence, Thomas Cronin explained the media's early scrutiny of Sen. Edward Kennedy's presidential candidacy in late 1979 and early 1980:

> Unwittingly or not, the media often levels front-running candidates. In a variation of the adversary relations theme, it is as if the press and television have a greater obligation to probe, scrutinize, and pick apart the latest celebrity. Pulitzers don't go to journalists who deflate dark horses, but to those who expose the leaders. Hence, the notion of the primaries as a multi-media survival course, perhaps better suited to knocking people off than permitting the best to rise.[5]

A series of studies since then has found that candidates who are perceived by the media as frontrunners tend to receive more news coverage, but also more critical coverage, than their competitors. "The degree of scrutiny a candidate receives increases in direct proportion to his standing in the polls," CBS's Bill Plante acknowledged a few years ago.[6] The frontrunners' nearest rivals also receive substantial attention. Such candidates (whom Michael Robinson termed "plausibles") are treated as the frontrunners' foils, whose function within news stories is to personalize the alternatives to the apparent winners, and to stand ready to assume the mantle of frontrunnership.[7]

Candidates with little or no chance of winning their party's nomination receive the most variable treatment: some, such as Bruce Babbitt in 1988, are featured in an occasional positive story and otherwise ignored; others, notably Gary Hart in his post-scandal candidacy in 1988, are mentioned only in an occasionally negative story. Most minor candidates are usually granted the media's version of Last Rites, a final series of stories repeating the positive or negative spin which has dominated their coverage, and which finally declares their candidacies moribund.[8]

Some of these so-called "hopeless cases" are denied even minimal coverage of their candidacies. In 1992 Larry Agran, the former mayor of Irvine, California, qualified for the Democratic primary ballot in New Hampshire and 26 other states. He also participated in some of the candidate forums (including a well-received speech to the U.S. Conference of Mayors).[9] Campaigning in New Hampshire, Agran created a stir when two consecutive nightly tracking polls showed him with measurable support among Democratic voters (ahead of former California Gov. Jerry Brown, although still behind Paul Tsongas, Bill Clinton, Bob Kerrey, and Tom Harkin).[10]

While not a heavyweight, Agran — who had recently held elective office, was energetically campaigning in New Hampshire, and who, without media attention, was receiving the support of a measurable percentage of voters — was clearly not part of the typical "fringe" that surfaces in New Hampshire every four years (in 1992, more than 62 candidates appeared on the ballot). Although no conventional analysis could envision Agran's winning the presidency, the same could be said for Pat Buchanan, Jerry Brown, and others who received far more attention.

Agran's efforts, however, were essentially ignored by the evening news. The *CBS Evening News* profiled the former mayor on September 20, 1991 (anchor Dan Rather called him the "Democratic candidate who without question is the least known") and never again mentioned his name. ABC's *World News Tonight* mentioned Agran twice — once in December and once in March — both times to explain who the extra person was in the picture at different forums with the other candidates. The *NBC Nightly News* never mentioned Agran or his candidacy by name. At times, Rodney Dangerfield has been treated with greater respect.

The networks' treatment of Agran mattered not just because it ensured his continued anonymity. Some state laws directed election officials to assess a candidate's national media attention in order to decide who belonged on the primary ballot. Maryland's ballot, for instance, reserved spots for candidates who are "recognized in the media throughout the United States or in Maryland."[11] The idea was to preclude politicians from playing favorites, but it drew the ire of those left out. "This raises questions of the power of the national media to control, not just politics, but life," protested former U.S. Senator Eugene McCarthy.[12]

In 1968, McCarthy's presidential campaign drew considerable media attention, particularly after his strong showing in that year's New Hampshire primary. In 1992, however, McCarthy was shunted alongside Agran, Lenora Fulani, Tom Laughlin (TV's "Billy Jack"), and other minor candidates who were generally ignored by the news media.[13]

For Agran, the coup de grace came when a New Hampshire sixth-grader chose to portray him in a mock debate as part of a class exercise. His teacher refused, saying that it would confuse the class.[14] The student was later interviewed on "All Things Considered," where he summed up Agran's plight in a savvy sound bite for correspondent Linda Wertheimer, "[Agran] can't get television publicity, which is what everyone watches. And if you don't see the candidate on TV, they're not a candidate."[15] Hearing of the incident, Agran wanly commented that "maybe we ought to lower the voting age to twelve."[16]

For those "frontrunners" and "plausibles" who do receive TV attention, the situation is better, but not by much. Candidates who make the media's final cut are usually subjected to considerably more bad press than good. Likely winners are depicted as dangerous manipulators of an unwary public, while likely losers are dismissed as incompetent bumblers.

The main reason for this profusion of bad press is not that voters offer their support only to deeply flawed individuals. Nor is politics a part of our national life populated solely by rogues and scoundrels. Rather, the reason lies in the media's (particularly television's) definition of its own role. "We are progressive reformers," wrote the *Washington Post's* Paul Taylor, "deeply skeptical of all the major institutions of society except our own."[17]

The "bias" of campaign journalism manifests itself in negative caricatures of practically any candidate whom journalists believe has a chance of actually winning either a nomination or election. As Edward Jay Epstein wrote in his classic study of network news over a quarter of a century ago:

> The working hypothesis almost universally shared among correspondents is that politicians are suspect; their public images probably false, their public statements disingenuous, their moral pronouncements hypocritical, their motives self-serving, and their promises ephemeral. Correspondents thus see their jobs to be to expose politicians by unmasking their disguises, debunking

their claims and piercing their rhetoric. In short, until proven otherwise, political figures of any party or persuasion are presumed to be deceptive opponents.[18]

In 1980, for example, Michael Robinson and Margaret Sheehan found that only about a fifth of *CBS Evening News* campaign reports were directional in nature (the balance being neutral or ambiguous in their treatment of the candidates). Of that directional news, however, a large majority (65%) was negative. Cynicism and criticism was threaded through CBS's coverage of all of the major candidates that year.

The authors concluded that, in 1980, the networks operated under the assumption that,

if the correspondents could not say something critical about the active candidates, they tended to say nothing at all. Network news does not say or imply all that much about candidates: most news is neutral or ambiguous, but when the networks do paint images, the sketches suggest the cynical caricatures of Daumier, not the ennobling portraits by David.[19]

In the case of presidential campaigns, that usually meant tougher press for the leader of the pack, as reporters focused their resources on plumbing through the records, backgrounds, platforms, and psyches of those most likely to win the presidency. For example, Robinson and Sheehan found that the network delivered most of the bad press to the perceived frontrunners, President Carter and former Governor Reagan.

Studies of subsequent campaigns reinforced this conclusion. In 1984, the networks treated Sen. Gary Hart to favorable press early on. Once his momentum had carried him from dark horse to frontrunner, they delivered the blows that staggered his candidacy on the eve of the Super Tuesday primaries.[20] During the 1984 general election, no one received worse press coverage than the Reagan/Bush ticket,[21] whose lead in the polls averaged more than 15 points in October 1984.[22]

During the 1988 primaries, our study found that Democratic frontrunner Michael Dukakis consistently received more negative coverage than his nearest rival, Rev. Jesse Jackson. Republican frontrunner George Bush received heavy criticism (72% negative) prior to the Iowa caucuses, where he placed third behind Sen. Robert Dole and Rev. Pat Robertson. After Iowa, however, when Bush was no longer considered the frontrunner, he received his first good press of the primary season (79% positive). After Bush's New Hampshire victory a week later, his positive coverage dropped considerably for the remainder of the primary season.[23]

During the general election, however, Dukakis — an underdog candidate whose hopes faded with every passing day — received press coverage that was as negative as Bush's. Journalists' didn't make it up, of course — the criticism of Dukakis was mostly that he conducted an inept campaign, and he did, after all, lose. But the belittling nature of his coverage betrayed the image of journalists kicking a downed man.

In October, for example, ABC's Sam Donaldson confronted Dukakis with a poll that placed the governor eight points behind Bush. "Are you depressed by the polls, Governor?" he bellowed. "Feel good," Dukakis responded without enthusiasm, climbing into his car. "How can you, sir?" the reporter demanded. Dukakis, Donaldson implied in his closer, was just going through the motions. "Candidates who appear to be losing can't quit. Dukakis has to press on: for his supporters, for his party, and because there's always a chance he can turn it around."[24]

An end-of-campaign report by NBC's Tom Pettit epitomized the dismissive tone of Dukakis's coverage. "Dukakis, who had danced his way through the mine fields of the primaries blowing his own horn, seemed unprepared for the fall campaign.... For two weeks in August, he went about his duties as governor, touring the state, giving out grants. While Bush was burning up the campaign trail, Dukakis was fiddling with state functions."

As Pettit's narration continued, the video showed Dukakis in several distinctly un-presidential poses. "This is the Democratic nominee for president," Pettit intoned with heavy irony, "at an agricultural event in Whately, Massachusetts, displaying keen knowledge of gardening." He then ran a clip of Dukakis discussing his personal experiences with compost. Pettit: "This is what you call a turning point: Dukakis discussing composting, while George Bush was out being ferocious."[25] The story ran two days before the election, but its tone was unmistakable: the campaign was over and Dukakis's meanderings had lost it for the Democrats — again.

As we noted earlier, the equity of Bush's and Dukakis's bad press stimulated many of the reform efforts launched after 1988. It also foreshadowed a break with traditional patterns of media coverage. Formerly journalists — wittingly or unwittingly — meted out good and bad press based on their perceptions of the race: who is the frontrunner, and how firm is his lead?

"Scrutiny" followed the leader of the pack like a dark shadow. In part, this was because the frontrunner was the "celebrity" of the field. It was also because challengers, as a general matter of strategy, tend to direct their criticism toward the frontrunner, providing reporters with ample raw material for critical news stories.

Additionally, frontrunners are the presumptive winners of a presidential race. Subjecting them to a higher degree of scrutiny makes sense, if only to ensure that news organizations use their resources wisely. As one CBS newsman put it, "There's no point in picking on the dead."[26] If the press's efforts caused a frontrunner to lose his footing, journalists could assure themselves, it was better for the public to find out sooner, rather than later. And there is never a shortage of frontrunners-in-waiting — during some nomination races, new frontrunners seemed to appear more regularly than some big-city buses.

If the anti-frontrunner bias is a clumsy application of journalism's adversarial stance to the electoral process, it was at least "fair," insofar as all frontrunners could expect similar treatment. Most underdogs who were lucky enough to surge into the lead would find their "honeymoons" brief (e.g., Carter in 1976; Bush in 1980; Hart in 1984; Bush in 1988). If the practical effect was a build-'em-up-knock-'em-down syndrome that first raised and then dashed voters' hopes and candidates' reputations, well, those were the rules of the game. At least the media were, in Barbara Matusow's phrase, "equal opportunity destroyers."[27]

But the practice of targeting frontrunners proved an ill fit with the culture of reform that swept journalism in 1988. As we have seen, the mechanical notion of "balance" was eschewed in favor of "fairness," which would be determined by those with the campaign's best vantage point — campaign trail reporters. And rather than resorting to mindlessly picking apart the frontrunner — which was less of a norm than a habit — journalists would try to "fairly" judge each of the candidates on their own merits.

As it turned out, the two frontrunners during the 1992 presidential primaries — President Bush and Governor Clinton — received worse press than their nomination rivals. At least in Clinton's case, however, many journalists expressed misgivings about the tough scrutiny he faced. A concern for "fairness" was certainly one source of these misgivings.

More important, though was the fact that much of Clinton's bad press was centered not on his campaign proposals, nor how he conducted his governorship in Arkansas, but on questions surrounding his personal character — sex, drugs, and draft dodging. The Clinton character stories instigated a crisis for reporters in the midst of their efforts to reform coverage of the 1992 campaign.

UNFORTUNATE FRONTRUNNERS

TV news is more than the projection of reality onto a television screen. Journalists' daily routines involve innumerable value judgments: What events merit coverage? What topics of a candidate's speech are most important? Which quotes would make the most interesting story? Who should be asked for a response? Which labels (liberal, pro-growth, anti-nuclear, radical, fundamentalist, etc.) would help the audience place the candidate (or interest group or idea) in the proper context? How these decisions are made by journalists shape the final version of "reality" that TV viewers see at home.

For example, a story about a hypothetical Bush campaign speech on the environment might contain a quote from the speech and a counterpoint from an environmental activist criticizing his policy. Or it could contain Bush's quote and an approving response from a member of the audience. It could involve a 15 second "tell story" in which the anchor capsulized the "who, when, and where" of the speech; a more thematic two-minute field report quoting the speech at some length; or an in-depth five-minute feature, examining both the speech and Bush's broader environmental record.

The story could be played "straight" ("Today, George Bush spoke at a national park about the need to protect the environment..."), or it could be "slanted" to convey skepticism about Bush's motives ("With polls showing voters disapprove of his environmental policies, Republicans invaded this national park today so Mr. Bush could once again declare that he is the 'environmental President'...").

Which choices the journalist and news organization make will decide how "positively" or "negatively" the story "spins" the Bush speech. Among other factors, these selections will be influenced by how much time the journalist has to prepare; on whether or not an environmental group is actively trying to promote an opposing viewpoint; and on the journalist's "gut" impressions regarding the Bush campaign's motives and the credibility of his environmental policies. Over the course of an entire campaign, these decisions form the accumulated media "spin" about a candidate — determining, in no small measure, the public image voters will take with them to the polls.

Applying a yardstick to good and bad press involves more than analyzing a series of anecdotes. It can best be accomplished by using the tool of content analysis, a scientific method for producing an objective and systematic description of communicative material (such as books, speeches, newspaper articles, and television broadcasts). Its applications are varied — for example, content analysis is often used by intelligence agencies to scrutinize the media of closed regimes, in order to gain an understanding of their politics and motives.

The procedures of content analysis are straightforward: trained researchers read or watch every relevant piece of material, noting each instance when the content of the news story matches one of the predetermined research categories. That may mean noting each mention of a candidate's name or policy issue, or each statement of praise or criticism. The researcher may also note any associated descriptive material, such as: who made the mention (was it a reporter or a news source), what was the target of praise or criticism (campaign advertising, economic policy, foreign policy), etc.

In order to be scientific, such analysis requires explicit rules and procedures that control for a researcher's subjective predispositions. The sample must include all relevant stories, not just a haphazard collection of pieces that happen to support the researcher's position. Categories and criteria must be rigorously defined and applied consistently to all material.

The categories must be valid measures of the concepts being studied (for example, it is valid to measure a candidate's "visibility" by counting the number of times he or she is mentioned in a news story; it is *invalid* to base "visibility" on the number of times he or she is reported to be leading in public opinion polls). The system must also be reliable, meaning that additional researchers using the same criteria should reach the same conclusions. Researchers must be trained to understand the categories used in the study, and to recognize them in news stories.

Because it is both systematic and reliable, content analysis permits the research to transcend the realm of impressionistic generalizations, which can be distorted by individual preferences and prejudices. For the past quarter century, media scholars have relied on content analysis as a principal tool of mass media research in general, and campaign journalism in particular. Building on the research designs of Richard Hofstetter in 1972, Thomas Patterson in 1976, and Michael Robinson in 1980, they have honed and sharpened the tool of content analysis to dissect the who, what, when, where, and why of campaign news.

Our analysis of good and bad press was based strictly on the opinions expressed by any independent observers quoted in the story, or on the stated views of the reporters themselves. We coded each comment separately, identifying the source, target, and direction of the evaluation. This method of data collection greatly enhanced our ability to describe the details and dynamics of the coverage.

Thus, for example, we could note whether the story praised Bill Clinton's policies but criticized his personal life, whether the reporter's own expression of opinion differed from that of the voters who appeared, etc. Most importantly, all such details could be aggregated across all stories, to differentiate Clinton's overall coverage on each policy issue from his "character" coverage, to determine how he was evaluated by voters, pundits, and reporters respectively.

For each time period, we calculated the proportion of positive and negative opinions expressed about each candidate, relative to the total of directional opinions. Therefore, each candidate's "good press" score ranged from entirely negative to entirely positive coverage (zero to 100% positive).[28] No ambiguous or neutral statements were included in this category.

Figure 6-1 compares the number of network TV stories that featured each candidate during the first four months of 1992, while Figure 6-2 compares the percentages of good and bad press received by each. As the chart makes clear, the frontrunners in both parties — Clinton and Bush — received the

Figure 6-1

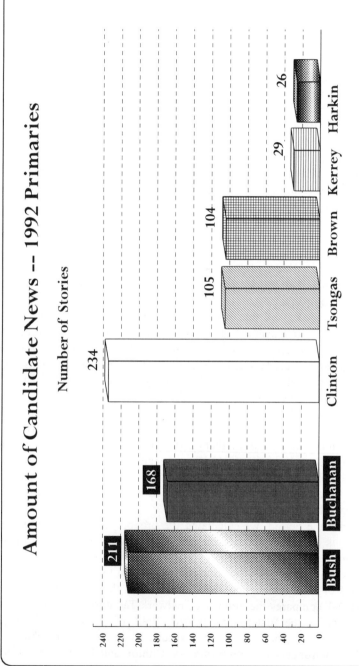

Amount of Candidate News -- 1992 Primaries

Number of Stories

Bush	211
Buchanan	168
Clinton	234
Tsongas	105
Brown	104
Kerrey	29
Harkin	26

Based on content analysis of election stories on ABC, CBS, and NBC evening newscasts January 1 through April 30, 1992.

Figure 6-2

Good Press/Bad Press

Major Candidates -- 1992 Primaries

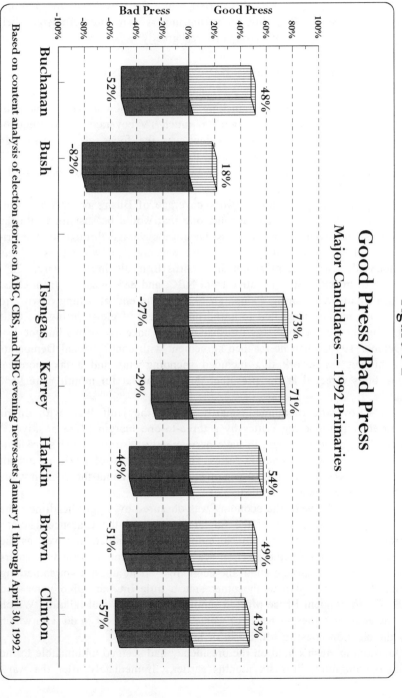

Based on content analysis of election stories on ABC, CBS, and NBC evening newscasts January 1 through April 30, 1992.

most critical coverage during this period, while their rivals for the nomination all fared better. But while both frontrunners were often criticized, their paths to the nomination otherwise differed greatly.

THE REPUBLICAN PRIMARIES: BAD NEWS FOR BUSH

As the incumbent and as a punching bag for attention-starved Democrats, President Bush received nearly twice as much TV coverage as his Republican rival Pat Buchanan. The president was the focus of 211 campaign stories during the primaries, compared to 108 for Buchanan. (Another 157 news stories featured Bush in his role as president but did not focus on the election.)

Throughout the primaries, network coverage of Bush's re-election effort conveyed a relentlessly negative tone, one that would be sustained into the fall. Bush received overwhelmingly negative coverage throughout the primaries — 18% positive and 82% negative coverage, the worst press of any candidate all year. The president drew barbs from all three networks: 72% negative from ABC, 80% negative from NBC, and 88% negative from CBS.

Bush's bad press during Campaign '92 was the end of a long downward slide in his media image that followed his moment of glory during the Gulf War. But the hostile tone was foreshadowed by coverage of his budget deal in October 1990, when he reached agreement with congressional Democrats on a budget framework that included spending cuts and a tax increase. Sound bites directed at the president during that fateful month were 96% negative.

Bush's coverage rebounded smartly during the Gulf War, with on-air supporters outnumbering critics by a three-to-one margin (77% positive).[29] But the budget deal appears to have permanently destroyed Bush's credibility with the media on economic issues. Throughout most of 1991, his overall TV coverage was highly (62%) negative. On stories about the economy, his bad press score was astronomical: 90% negative.

For most of the year, the economy was obscured by bigger headlines: the Gulf War, the dissolution of the Soviet Union, and the Clarence Thomas Supreme Court nomination. In November and December, however, as the networks geared up for the election season, their attention turned to voters — and voters were talking about the economy. "If he doesn't get something going, I'd have to listen to the other side a little bit," an Ohio voter told CBS. Correspondent Bruce Morton summed up the political fallout: "Which way the economy goes — better or worse — will have a lot to do with which way the election goes: to Mr. Bush, or to a Democrat."[30]

Questioning Bush's hold on the presidency had seemed unthinkable to the political community just six months earlier. Immediately after the war's successful conclusion, pundits called Bush a shoo-in. CBS's Bob Schieffer noted that "most of the pros believe that the only thing that can keep George Bush from winning a second term is if Norman Schwarzkopf turns out to be a Democrat."[31] An Iowa farmer told ABC's Chris Bury that "If Bush [doesn't] trip now, the only one that can run against him is if they get the Good Lord down, and I don't think He could win this next election."[32]

Credit goes to ABC's Jeff Greenfield, one of the few who struck a contrarian note. Just one week after the cease-fire in Iraq, he observed that "the best thing the Democrats have going for them is that nobody thinks they can win. When it comes to political predictions, it's amazing how often nobody's right."[33]

Almost as rapidly as the Desert Storm hit, it was blown away by new headlines that generally tilted against the president. Bush's hospitalization in May for an irregular heartbeat brought intensive scrutiny to Vice President Quayle. NBC's Jim Miklaszewski quipped, "The very thought of 'President Dan Quayle' caused a few hearts to skip a beat."[34]

The dissolution of the Soviet Union on Christmas Day brought to a formal end more than 40 years of the Cold War and certified that foreign policy would be a secondary issue during the upcoming election. The landslide loss of Bush's Attorney General, Richard Thornburgh, in a Pennsylvania Senate election, brought new questions about Bush's political vulnerability.

Pundits blamed Bush's new weakness on the state of the economy, and reporters found former supporters of the president defecting to the Democrats. An angry California businessman told CBS's Richard Roth that, "The country and its economy is in a crisis — we've got all kinds of human issues that are in crisis. We do not see bold leadership and the kinds of plans that will fix that."[35] The businessman, Roth said, along with other Republicans, was going to co-host a fund-raiser for Democrat Bill Clinton.

The whispers of rebellion became full-throated cries on December 10, when conservative commentator Pat Buchanan announced his campaign against Bush for the Republican nomination. The networks placed the story in the context of voter unhappiness with Bush. CBS's coverage of the announcement virtually ignored Buchanan himself, instead stressing Bush's problem with New Hampshire Republicans. After profiling a former Bush supporter who was switching to Buchanan, Engberg concluded,

New Hampshire Republicans are overwhelmingly conservative. And the economic agony, on top of suspicions about Mr. Bush's commitment to conservative values, gives Buchanan plenty of running room with the right....

Buchanan doesn't need to win in New Hampshire to damage the president. A 35 to 40 percent showing, the White House knows, would create a strong impression that conservatives ... are deserting George Bush and that he's in trouble in his own party.[36]

Engberg aired just one clip of Buchanan's announcement, which meshed perfectly with the "new" conventional wisdom of an uncaring or unsympathetic president: "What," Buchanan demanded, "is the White House answer to the recession that was caused by its own breach of faith? It is to deny there is a recession. *Well, let them come to New Hampshire!*"

On opening day, Buchanan received his own shot of bad press. NBC's Lisa Myers, for example, interviewed a conservative activist, who said economic troubles in New Hampshire meant that "Mickey Mouse could run against George Bush and pick up 25 or 30 percent of the vote." Maybe so, Myers noted,

> But Mickey Mouse doesn't have some of Buchanan's problems. Buchanan has no experience as a candidate — witness his bafflement over what to do today when confronted with a baby. [BUCHANAN SEES BABY AND JUST SMILES AT IT.] And the landscape is littered with his, at best, insensitive remarks about blacks, gays, and Jews.... Buchanan once called AIDS nature's "retribution" against homosexuals.... Buchanan does not have a prayer of beating Bush, but he may be able to embarrass him. And even more dangerous to Bush, he could raise doubts about the president that Democrats could exploit.[37]

Myers also showed the "Let them come to New Hampshire" quote. Her story contrasts with Engberg's in its focus on Buchanan, but shares with it a complete lack of representation of Bush's point of view. Even when Myers criticized Buchanan for his "insensitive" remarks, she did so on her own, rather than relying on quotes from either Bush or his surrogates. In both stories, numerous charges were made against Bush, by Buchanan and others. In neither did Bush or his allies have a chance to respond to his depiction as an insensitive president and a hollow conservative.

This typifies the coverage Bush received during the primaries. Our good press measure does not include statements from partisan sources, such as Bush, Buchanan, or any of the Democrats who were running. But in profiles of the Democratic contenders, as well as in Buchanan's coverage, numerous charges were made against Bush for which no response was offered. For example, an NBC report about a debate among Democratic candidates included the following:

ANDREA MITCHELL: Frequently citing his own Vietnam war experience [Nebraska Senator Bob] Kerrey said George Bush was too timid about helping the Soviet republics, too aggressive toward Saddam Hussein.

SENATOR KERREY: And when Secretary of State Baker tried to clarify what it was all about in November 1990, saying it was "jobs, jobs, jobs," I didn't believe that, and, if it's true, where are those jobs?[38]

If Bush had a response to that charge, it went unreported on NBC that night. Similarly, voters who were unhappy with the economy said their piece. On ABC, correspondent Jim Wooten filed the following story, which focused on Buchanan:

JIM WOOTEN: [Buchanan] blames Bush for just about everything that's gone wrong in economically desperate New Hampshire, and people *are* listening. They blame Bush, too.

WOMAN: It comes right from him. He's got his head buried. He isn't even beginning to realize what's going on.

JIM WOOTEN: Although Buchanan offers few solutions himself, it doesn't seem to matter. He is primarily a vehicle for the rage and the worries of many New Hampshire voters.

MAN: Look at Bush. "I will not raise taxes, I will not raise...." What happened!?

JIM WOOTEN: There's a very real question now as to whether the president has enough time to soothe the anger and the anxiety that seems to be fueling Buchanan's challenge, and to discourage the traditional willingness of voters here to transform their primary into a political protest.[39]

As with the earlier stories, there was no opportunity for Bush to respond to either the voters' charges or Buchanan's.

A major reason Bush's press coverage was so negative was that his presidency was no longer being debated. The other candidates were relatively new to the national stage, and reporters' choice of sources conveyed the fact that they had both supporters and detractors. Buchanan's coverage, for example, was relatively balanced (48% positive, 52% negative), in spite of stories like Myers's, which essentially accused him of bigotry.

Bush, on the other hand, was a weakened frontrunner whose plight was illustrated by stories chock full of sagging poll numbers, critical quotes from voters and policy experts pooh-poohing of his policies, and critical quotes from political pundits who disapproved of his campaign's futile efforts to resurrect his popularity.

The "failed president" story pre-empted further media debate on George Bush. The American people, speaking through public opinion polls and man-on-the-street sound bites, had already spoken. By January, all that was left to this story line were the post-mortems explaining why he had failed — not a promising framework for an incumbent beginning his reelection campaign. In late January, for example, NBC offered this analysis of Bush's presidency:

LISA MYERS: It's tough to lead when you don't know where you want to go. Call it a vision — George Bush doesn't seem to have one. Domestically, he's at best a broker who works out deals with Congress. Beyond education, the environment and his crime bill, he hasn't really addressed major domestic problems such as health care. Even judged by the words of his own inaugural address, he comes up short:
PRESIDENT BUSH AT INAUGURAL: My friends, we have work to do. There are the homeless, lost and roaming....
LISA MYERS: Yet Bush has never visited a homeless shelter, and homelessness continues to increase.
PRESIDENT BUSH AT INAUGURAL: ... there are the children who have nothing...
LISA MYERS: Today, one million more children live in poverty.
PRESIDENT BUSH AT INAUGURAL: ... There are those who cannot free themselves of enslavement to whatever addiction: drugs, welfare, the demoralization that rules the slums.
LISA MYERS: Today, while casual drug use is down, hard-core addiction is not. Two million more Americans are on welfare, and despair rules the inner city.[40]

During the primaries, 93% of source comments criticized Bush's handling of the domestic economy, and an identical 93% of those discussing non-economic domestic issues (like homelessness, poverty, welfare, and drugs) also found Bush's efforts wanting. Only on foreign policy did a majority (57%) of comments reflect approval of Bush's presidential performance.

As a frontrunner, Bush was the target of nearly all of the media's scrutiny. It made no sense for the networks to spend resources investigating and scrutinizing Buchanan, since he had no realistic chance of winning the nomination. The bad press came from media attempts to "illustrate" Bush's political predicament, rather than a continuing debate on his presidency.

As we will see with Gov. Clinton's coverage, the best way for a politician to halt such bad press is to exceed journalists' expectations in the primaries and caucuses. A "better-than-expected" electoral performance confounds the assumption of unpopularity and sends journalists scurrying to illustrate the new, improved, and suddenly popular candidate.

Unfortunately for Bush, the conventional wisdom among reporters was that Buchanan could not possibly win. This made it very difficult for Buchanan to lose the media's expectations race, or for Bush to win it. During the primaries, reporter's own on-air assessments of the president's campaign strength were mostly (58%) negative. In contrast, Buchanan's candidacy was portrayed as strong or successful by 62% of reporters' comments.

The reason for this disparity was not that reporters were ignorant of the fact that Bush was winning all of the real contests and nearly all of the delegates. Rather, they measured each candidate against a separate standard of expectations, and Bush's hurdle was set far higher than Buchanan's. Even Bush's landslide victories on Junior and Super Tuesdays (he averaged approximately 70% of the vote in those contests) were not seen as victories over expectations. The "news" instead was the protest vote that kept dogging his campaign from one primary state to the next.

After Super Tuesday, Dan Rather assessed the results: "The president now has an overwhelming lead in delegates needed for renomination but... still hasn't been able to put a stake through the heart of Mr. Buchanan's 'We-can't-afford-Bush' campaign."[41] The presumption that Buchanan was merely a protest candidate meant that the cycle of Bush's coverage could not be broken by a primary victory, not even a landslide victory.

Despite winning every contest and easily securing the nomination, Bush was never able to beat the media's expectations during the primaries. He was thus doomed to exist in a media purgatory, cast as the weakened frontrunner. Most weakened frontrunners eventually lose or are forced from the race. To avoid this fate, they must recast their candidacies as "revived" or "reinvigorated" in the media story line.

Bush was far too strong politically among Republicans to be beaten, but he was also unable to shake off a 30% protest vote. By the time Buchanan drifted from the race, Bill Clinton had emerged as the all-but-inevitable Democratic nominee, whose own bout with "frontrunner-itis" had left him strengthened rather than weakened.

THE DEMOCRATIC PRIMARIES: CLINTON'S ROLLER-COASTER

During 1991, the frontrunner for the Democratic presidential nomination — both in terms of network news visibility and public opinion polls — was New York Governor Mario Cuomo. Although news about the nascent campaign was minimal during the pre-season, Cuomo was featured in more network news stories (21) than any of the six declared Democrats (the runner-up was Iowa Sen. Tom Harkin, featured 14 times).

Even before he appeared to have formed any intentions about running, the networks began to turn a critical eye toward the governor's record and prospects. "Even Cuomo's friends concede he can be insular, suspicious, self-righteous, and arrogant," reported CBS's Richard Threlkeld.[42] Journalists quickly added "indecisive" to Threlkeld's list. ABC's Cokie Roberts reported in November that "Democratic leaders are getting tired of Mario Cuomo waiting in the wings, distracting attention from the action on stage."[43]

By mid-December, Cuomo's unwillingness to state whether he would or would not run for the nomination had exasperated many news reporters. "What did the governor say today?" NBC's Tom Brokaw reported on the eve of the New Hampshire filing deadline. "Just this: 'I am just about at the point where you really can't avoid saying something reasonably decisive.' Translation? Who knows?"[44] The *CBS Evening News* even ran a clip from Jay Leno, ribbing "Cuomo's new public service campaign: A mind is a terrible thing to make up."[45]

The sarcasm foreshadowed the sharp scrutiny that lay in wait for frontrunner Cuomo. Then, at the last minute, the governor opted against running. Cuomo's abdication left the media with an intolerable situation: a presidential campaign with no designated frontrunner. Within days, the cognoscenti had begun to settle on Arkansas Governor Bill Clinton. On Christmas Eve, the *Los Angeles Times* wrote,

> Alone — so far — among the Democratic presidential contenders, Clinton has demonstrated an ability to frame a message that not only mobilizes his base, but reaches beyond it. Largely on the strength of that ability, Clinton has received an early nod from the political Establishment as the lead candidate in the Democratic race. "He is doing best at what's most important — message making, clarity, what he's up to, what the country has to do," said one uncommitted Democratic strategist. "He's much further along on that."[46]

It took a while longer for the networks to catch on. On January 14, CBS's Richard Threlkeld commented, "It's presumptuous before the first primary to say there's a frontrunner, but even his rivals would have to concede that right now Clinton's the man to beat for the Democratic nomination."[47]

The first days after a candidate becomes the designated frontrunner are usually dominated by good press, as reporters attempt to illustrate why a particular individual is gaining support. For Gov. Clinton, the early part of January was no exception. "He spent much of the last decade making things better in Arkansas schoolrooms," reported Threlkeld.[48] "In eleven years as governor, he has offered innovative programs to remake a state which ranked almost last in everything," added Lisa Myers. "The result: slow but steady progress on education, better than average economic growth."[49]

But Clinton's days as a media darling were already numbered. On Friday, January 24, Arkansas executed convicted murderer Rickey Ray Rector. Death penalty opponents criticized the execution, arguing that Clinton should have granted Rector clemency because he had undergone a lobotomy and was mentally impaired. The same day, newspapers began dribbling out the story of Gennifer Flowers, who claimed that she had had a long-standing affair with Clinton.

Sex quickly trumped death as a focus of media criticism. On Sunday, January 26, Clinton, accompanied by his wife, went on CBS's *60 Minutes* to defend himself. On Monday, Gennifer Flowers held a press conference in New York and offered irresistible sound bites: "Yes, I was Bill Clinton's lover for 12 years, and for the past two years I have lied to the press about our relationship to protect him. The truth is, I loved him. Now he tells me to deny it. Well, I'm sick of all the deceit and I'm sick of all the lies."[50]

Flowers's charges marked the start of a three-week period during which Clinton endured his worst press of the campaign (see Figure 6-3). After pursuing her charges, the networks began reporting on a letter written by Clinton in 1969, in which he thanked an Army recruiter for "saving me from the [Vietnam War] draft."

ABC's Jim Wooten received his copy of the letter from Clinton Jones, who was an official with the University of Arkansas' ROTC program while Bill Clinton was there. "Jones, a Democrat, says he took the letter from the files only because he was still angry at Clinton for breaking his promise to join the ROTC," reported Wooten. Jones gave an on-camera interview, declaring, "He signed a contract and did not honor it."[51]

The pairing of the allegations, with the draft charge surfacing mere days before the New Hampshire primary, meant that Clinton was suddenly a much weaker frontrunner. Even before the vote, reporters began to speculate: "The Democrats' worst nightmare about New Hampshire is "what if?" reported Threlkeld.

> What if Clinton finishes badly? What if Tsongas is no more than a flash in the pan? There's already a bustling little write-in effort underway here for Governor Mario Cuomo of New York.... In Washington, Sen. Lloyd Bentsen is also waiting for the New Hampshire results.... and Congressman Richard Gephardt... and so on.[52]

With some weekend polls showing Clinton sliding toward third place, behind Sen. Bob Kerrey, it looked like curtains for the beleaguered governor.[53]

Then, on primary day, Clinton won what the correspondents called a "strong second place." Clinton declared victory, calling himself "the Comeback Kid." The phrase was featured in headlines the next morning. *Newsweek* called the governor "restored" to at least co-frontrunner status, but warned darkly that "he may undergo scrutiny on other generational character issues."[54] *Newsweek* was half right: Clinton faced additional scrutiny, but on the same issues — the draft and adultery. As the campaign moved into Georgia, CBS's Threlkeld visited an American Legion Post:

RICHARD THRELKELD: Rick Edgar, a Vietnam vet who works over at the Lockheed plant, knows he won't be voting for Bill Clinton. He doesn't like what he's heard about how Clinton avoided the draft.

RICK EDGAR: There's all kinds of ways to beat the system legally, but he lied, he misrepresented himself and he said he was too smart to go over there.

RICHARD THRELKELD: It's the same with most everybody here.

HUGH HIGLEY: I don't like draft dodgers. I don't care who they are, or where they come from. I saw [dodging during] the Korean War and all the way through and it kinda sticks in my craw.

JIM FORD: I'm one of the old Archie Bunker boys, and I just won't tolerate that.

RICHARD THRELKELD: Only Jack Rolland is willing to cut Bill Clinton a little slack.

JACK ROLLAND: In the Vietnam era we had a lot of people who did practically the same thing.

RICHARD THRELKELD: There are 26 million American veterans. If what you hear from the ones in Kennesaw [Georgia] is any guide, come November the Vietnam issue is going to hurt Bill Clinton if he's the Democratic nominee.[55]

Working in Clinton's favor, however, was the fact that, unlike President Bush, he had several chances to beat the "expectations" reporters had set for him. His second-place showing in New Hampshire, for instance, was stronger than polls had shown over the weekend. His victory in Georgia over Paul Tsongas was by a wider margin than forecast. And his victory in Florida was also something of a surprise, giving him a sweep of all of the Southern primary states on Super Tuesday.

The scandal coverage had the effect of lowering reporters' expectations of how well Clinton would perform. This allowed him to argue that his "relatively" strong showings proved that, while the press pursued character questions, "real people" were considering his record and platform.

When Clinton won the Michigan and Illinois primaries, he settled in for his first truly positive news coverage of the year. He received kudos for surviving the media gauntlet. "One politician who didn't quit when the going got tough is the new leader of the Democratic pack," reported NBC's Tom Brokaw.[56] Tsongas's withdrawal from the race on March 19 appeared to open the path for Clinton's nomination. The honeymoon was interrupted by Jerry Brown's victory in the Connecticut primary five days later. Beating expectations helped Clinton de-legitimize the character issue; losing an expectations race re-legitimized them.

The Connecticut primary placed Clinton in the same awkward spot Bush had occupied all year. As an opponent, Jerry Brown was a highly unlikely nominee, and thus eminently beatable. But the fact that Clinton was beaten by Brown in Connecticut seemed to indicate a weakness in his candidacy. During the two weeks prior to the New York primary, Clinton received his worst press (75% negative) since the advent of his character troubles in January. Voters, the networks reported once again, had a problem with Clinton's character:

RICHARD THRELKELD: If New Yorkers haven't exactly embraced Clinton, they're no different than the rest of the electorate. In the CBS News/ *New York Times* poll, when people were asked whether Clinton has more honesty and integrity than most people in public life, more than half said no.

VOTER #1:   Clinton, every time you turn around, what else? I don't know what else they're gonna find out about the guy.

RICHARD THRELKELD: And, despite Clinton's best efforts, there are a lot of New Yorkers who've come to regard him as "Slick Willie."

VOTER #2:   He's always got a grin on his face, which I think is ridiculous for a man running for president. I mean, there are very important things in this world going on.[57]

Adding to the governor's woes, the media revisited the draft issue on the eve of the primary. Reporters discovered that Clinton had received an induction notice from his draft board before joining the ROTC. Clinton acknowledged the induction notice, but wondered why reporters thought it significant. Jim Wooten's story on ABC was the toughest:

JIM WOOTEN: Why has he never told anybody he was ordered to report for duty before he applied for the ROTC? Because no one asked, he says.

GOVERNOR CLINTON: I want you to understand something. I would gladly have told you this if it had even occurred to me that this was relevant to the story.

JIM WOOTEN: But eight weeks ago, in New Hampshire, he was given at least an opportunity to mention his induction orders from the spring of '69. When we asked if he thought his draft was imminent that summer:

GOVERNOR CLINTON [FEB. 10, 1992]:   Oh, I always assumed that that would happen, yes, I do think that. That's what I always thought would happen, too. I thought sometime in the fall I was gonna be drafted.

JIM WOOTEN [FEB 10, 1992]:   And, you thought that because you were told that?

GOVERNOR CLINTON [FEB. 10, 1992]:   [LONG PAUSE] Well, I mean, I just knew that my time was up, and that's why I was at home, just trying to figure out what else I would do. I just, you know, they didn't say you will be called on this date —

JIM WOOTEN: But we now know his draft board *had* called him, for a date certain, and then, he says, had given him an extension. While this omission does not contradict his earlier explanation, it may reinforce any public perception of the governor as unwilling to tell the whole truth, or the whole story, at one time.[58]

In private, Wooten was much harsher in judging Clinton on the draft story. He had been the among the first reporters to see Clinton's 1969 letter, and he asked him about it in New Hampshire. Tom Rosenstiel recounts the interview:

> There was a lot Wooten was trying to discern. Why was the letter dated December 3, 1969, two days after the federal lottery was held, in which Clinton, with lottery number 311, escaped the draft? Had he known his lottery number when he wrote the letter? Clinton claimed not to have. And what made Clinton so sure he would be drafted? Had he received an induction notice? No, Clinton answered. That answer, Wooten would discover three months later, was a blatant falsehood.... Almost everything Clinton had said on the [draft] subject, Wooten feared, was a lie.[59]

Wooten's was the most extensive network story that night about the draft controversy, and his recollection of his earlier meeting with Clinton in New Hampshire appears to explain his tough tone. But Wooten was not the only reporter to believe that Clinton had prevaricated in response to the various character questions that were posed to him. According to Rosenstiel, many reporters also "believed that Clinton had been dishonest about the Flowers affair."

> The lesson [that the media] took from New Hampshire was that the draft story and Gennifer [Flowers] were not resolved. Wooten and other reporters thought too many questions were unanswered. Clinton had gotten away with lying, twice. "He should have just come clean and said, 'Like the majority of Americans in 1969, I opposed the war and did everything I could within the law not to die in it,'" *USA Today* reporter Adam Nagourney stated. In the end, the Gennifer and draft story blended into one incident, an example of a man who would not level with people, and perhaps with himself.
>
> Not long after, Democratic National Committee strategist Paul Tully... told Walter Robinson of the *Boston Globe*: "Clinton's biggest problem now is that 90 percent of the press corps think he is a liar."[60]

The new draft questions were not enough to prevent Clinton from prevailing in New York. Once again, the political world had held its breath, waiting for Clinton to finally fall from his tightrope. Once again, he surpassed the

Figure 6-3

Clinton vs. His Rivals
Good Press -- 1992 Primaries

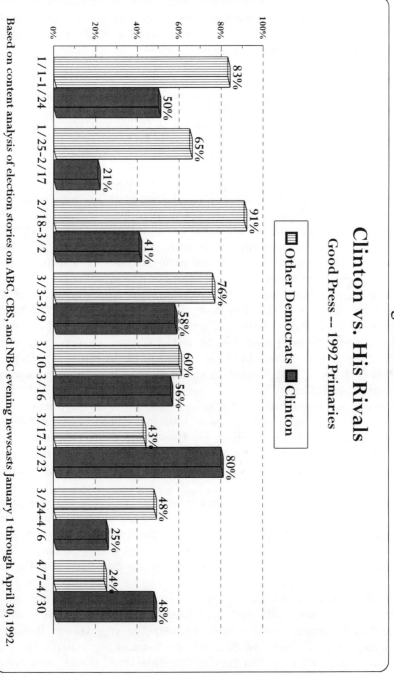

Based on content analysis of election stories on ABC, CBS, and NBC evening newscasts January 1 through April 30, 1992.

lowered expectations. After New York, Andrea Mitchell calculated that "it is now mathematically impossible for [Jerry Brown] to get the nomination." The honeymoon that was pre-empted by Connecticut began again. NBC's John Chancellor told viewers not to worry about Clinton's electability:

> The Bush campaign is going to attack any Democratic presidential candidate this fall, but Clinton's armor seems quite thick. He has a remarkable ability, an eerie ability, to recover from personal attacks. That would help in the fall campaign. Given Bill Clinton's performance so far this year, maybe it's time for Democrats to look at his strengths instead of his weaknesses. He's earned it — he's done awfully well so far.[61]

As Figure 6-3 shows, the weeks following the New York primary marked only the second time that Clinton's level of good press was higher than that of his Democratic rivals. (The first was after his wins in Illinois and Michigan, a brief run of good press that was ended by his Connecticut loss.) But Clinton's level of bad press was not unusual for a frontrunner. What was unusual was its heavy emphasis on his personal character, and the relative lack of emphasis on his gubernatorial record or policy positions.

Table 6-1 compares the topics of Clinton's coverage with those of the Republican frontrunner, President Bush. News coverage of Bush focused on the state of the economy, taxes, and jobs. Clinton's coverage had two main topics: the allegations of draft dodging and of adultery, crowding out coverage of his policy positions. In all, just over half of the stories that featured Clinton (118 out of 234) focused on one or more of the various "character" allegations against him.

There is no denying that Bill Clinton's early press coverage was tough. Despite the widespread belief in early 1992 that Clinton enjoyed the personal support of many journalists, his Democratic rivals collectively garnered far more praise than the beleaguered governor. As a group, they received 60% positive evaluations, compared to only 43% for the eventual nominee.

Clinton himself faced more criticism than praise (57% negative press, 43% positive press). His chief rival, former Massachusetts Senator Paul Tsongas, averaged 73% positive press over the course of the campaign. Senators Tom Harkin and Bob Kerrey, two also-rans who spent only a short amount of time in the limelight, also fared better than Clinton (54% and 71% positive respectively). (See Figure 6-2.) At 49% positive, even Jerry Brown fared better than Clinton.

For all his problems with the "character issue," however, Clinton fared far better than the opponent who ultimately mattered most — George Bush. As we noted earlier, Clinton had electoral opportunities to confound the presumption among reporters that his character "problems" would prove politi-

Table 6-1

Featured Subjects in TV News Coverage of 1992 Frontrunners
1992 Primaries

Bush Stories			Clinton Stories	
1.	Economy	39	Adultery	46
2.	Taxes	25	Draft Dodging	46
3.	Jobs	13	Taxes	14
4.	Budget	8	Conflict of Interest	12
5.	Gulf War	7	Economy	12
6.	Abortion	6	Personal Drug Use	11
7.	Trade	6	Job Training	6
8.	Environment	5	Education	5
9.	Japan	5	Abortion	4
10.	Russia	5	Environment	4

Note -- Based on content analysis of ABC, CBS, and NBC evening newscasts, January 1, 1992 through April 30, 1992. Stories may have included multiple issue mentions.

cally lethal. In addition, though, mainstream news organizations treated charges of personal misdeeds far more gingerly than charges of economic mismanagement. Both sets of allegations, were often discussed in the context of diagnosing the political standing of one or the other frontrunner, so that they did not call for a response from the campaigns. But Clinton's campaign was able to respond to the character charges in about half of the TV news stories that raised them.

Further, reporters often noted the allegations against Clinton and, in the same story, dismissed them as irrelevant or out of bounds. The ambivalent nature of the character coverage reflected the debate within journalism over how far reporters should go in investigating a candidate's private life, and whether or not such stories yielded anything of significance to the public's storehouse of relevant knowledge.

CHARACTER COPS

The mainstream media's entanglement with the character issue began in May 1987, when Gary Hart, the favorite for the 1988 Democratic nomination, abandoned his candidacy after stories surfaced that he had spent the weekend alone with Donna Rice. The initial report appeared in the *Miami Herald*, which had staked out Hart's Washington, D.C., town house. After five days of frenzied activity, the *Washington Post* informed the Hart campaign that it had confirmed a second liaison and possessed both the name of the second woman and photographs of Hart leaving her home. The *Post* called Hart's campaign on Thursday, May 7. The next morning, Hart quit the campaign, deploring a system that "reduces the press of this nation to hunters and presidential candidates to being hunted."[62]

With Hart gone, it was the media's turn to answer questions. "Is this what journalism is about, hiding in a van outside a politician's home? Is it 'investigative reporting' to write that a woman may have spent the night there — or may not, since we're not sure we watched all the doors?" protested Anthony Lewis in the *New York Times*. "The loss of respect for privacy has exacted a terrible price in American politics."[63]

After the hasty exit of another candidate (Sen. Joseph Biden, after allegations of college plagiarism) and a nominee for the Supreme Court (Douglas Ginsburg, after admitting to smoking marijuana), the *Washington Post's* David Broder warned his colleagues that "the press is on shaky ground.... Political journalism is not a way of satisfying the random curiosity or the voyeuristic inclinations of reporters or readers," he wrote. "It's time to slow down and take another look at what we're doing, before more damage is done to the reputations of the candidates and the credibility of the press."[64]

Nearly every reporter, columnist, and editor who spoke out publicly in 1987 agreed that the press needed to use caution when investigating a candidate's personal life. But some also welcomed the new role, arguing that it was a long overdue step that would let voters more fully judge the men or women who would vie for the presidency in the future. "No one should mourn the death of the old ground rules," wrote *Newsweek's* Jonathan Alter.

> Under the elitist dispensation that prevailed in years past, the Washington press corps decided that it was fine to conceal details of politicians' private lives on the assumption that mere citizens could not be trusted with such information. The result was that potentially important character traits were ruled out of bounds for scrutiny.[65]

Notwithstanding such high-minded rationales, however, polls showed that the public, thought that competition among news organizations, or the belief that such stories would attract large audiences, was the main reason behind the press's new found attention to personal character.[66]

Journalists' claims that 1992 would see more "substantive" media coverage was taken by many to mean that the media would be wary of conducting another sexual inquisition. In the beginning, the questions surrounding Clinton's marriage were mentioned, but delicately. A *Time* cover story tiptoed around the gossip: "He admits that his 16-year marriage has gone through some troubled times but says it is now solid. Friends, and even some foes, note that no one has ever been able to pin down anything."[67]

Gennifer Flowers's public statement did not predispose *Time* to take another look. In a piece entitled "Who Cares, Anyway," Lance Morrow wrote, "The nation cannot afford to waste good candidates. There are not so many to spare.... Given the size of the job that needs to be done, it is time for America to get serious. At the very least, turn off the television set. And grow up about sex."[68]

The reformers who suggested so many prescriptions after 1988 offered surprisingly few guidelines on how reporters should approach stories such as Gary Hart's (and, now, Bill Clinton's). Most avoided the issue entirely. To its credit, the Barone Center's report gave "the gossip culture" equal attention with the other media controversies. But even this document offered only general guidance: reporters should treat rumors more carefully, it advised, and they should safeguard against being manipulated by one campaign against another.

The Barone Center report stated that some investigation into a candidates' private life is justified, including evidence of ongoing adultery, and certainly any personal behavior that involved public funds or job performance. But the report, which offered so much specific guidance on other media issues, did not provide clear guidelines of what threshold character issues needed to pass before journalism could properly begin to investigate them. The document hints that the reason for the fuzziness was disagreement among panel members about which aspects of "character" were appropriate topics of public scrutiny.[69]

If so, the panel members were only reflecting the sharp divisions among the journalistic community at large — divisions that broke into the open after Ms. Flowers's charges were widely disseminated. It hadn't helped that the first reports appeared in the *Star*, a supermarket tabloid. While the major media obviously resisted plunging into the story, the effect the charges were having on the Clinton campaign made them "newsworthy" even to more traditional journalists.

That effect, however, was itself created by the efforts of news organizations: those few who were disseminating the charges, and those reporters who were interrogating the Clinton campaign about them. This "trickle-down" effect offended those who felt that the charges lacked proper substantiation, and that the ever-widening number of newspapers who were publishing them were trading on journalism's good name.

Some of the exchanges were quite pointed. *New York Times* columnist A. M. Rosenthal blamed what he called the "vermin" and "whores" of the "poison-pen press" for conducting an "inquisition on politicians' sexual history." Personally, he wrote, "the only candidate for public office I would automatically disqualify on sexual grounds would be a rapist or a virgin."[70]

The *Boston Globe*'s Tom Oliphant wrote of his hope that the Clintons would "prevail over a naked attempt by pornographers, learned thumb-suckers and go-along hacks to hijack democracy."[71] The strong language from influential columnists, and the Clinton campaign's obvious displeasure with the story (one aide called the Flowers's story "the press's crack cocaine"[72]) caused many reporters to flinch.

Public disapproval may also have caused some second thoughts. A 1991 pre-election survey had asked voters which aspect of a candidate they thought news organizations should pay the most attention. Only a tiny fraction (7%) chose personal character. The bulk of voters split between choosing the candidate's issue stands (46%) and past experiences and qualifications (42%).[73] Voters in New Hampshire seemed to echo the poll results. One told *Newsweek*, "We're voting for president, not pope.... We just don't care about Clinton's personal life. We're more interested in hearing more about his plan."[74] ABC's Chris Bury talked to voters after a Clinton speech:

CHRIS BURY: Many who heard [Clinton] were aware of the character questions:

VOTER #1: Prior to hearing him, I was very concerned about them, and I think I would not have voted for him. After hearing him, I think he expressed in very concrete terms how he cares for people.

VOTER #2: His character has been at such a test the last couple of weeks, but he didn't let that dominate tonight at all. That wasn't the issue — the issues were.

CHRIS BURY: Some people do care about issues such as Clinton's attempts to avoid military service in Vietnam. At a high school in Tilton, some of New Hampshire's youngest voters said it bothered them.

STUDENT: If you're against the war, that's fine, you can protest, or whatever. But when your country calls on you to serve for it, I think you should serve your country.

CHRIS BURY: But after a Clinton speech to retirees, no one we talked to cared:

SENIOR CITIZEN: I'm a World War II veteran. I didn't put much credence to it at all. I really don't feel it's an issue.[75]

Stories like Bury's helped to further de-legitimize the character questions. They retained their "news value" not because journalists thought they were important, but because reporters continued to perceive their effect on the horse race. Whenever the Clinton campaign stumbled during the primary season, the media would refresh the character story as a means of providing an explanation.

Indeed, the perceived effect of the charges on the campaign horse race provided traditional news organizations with their original rationale for publishing them. Flowers's story, in and of itself, never reached the standards necessary for publication as set by the traditional media, as Larry Sabato points out in *Feeding Frenzy*:

Gennifer Flowers was a name unfamiliar to the public but well known to many in the political press. For many months she and several other women had been romantically linked to Governor Clinton by his opponents, and even by some neutral observers in Arkansas. Given the centrality of the post-Gary Hart character issue, most major broadcast and print-news organizations had sent reporters — some had dispatched teams of them — to Arkansas, to investigate. *Not one news outlet uncovered enough evidence to warrant a single published or broadcast story.* The claims simply did not check out, were unprovable, or suffered from other fatal flaws. Therefore, one might presume that well-prepared news organizations, having already thoroughly investigated these allegations, would discard them as without merit once they reached print in a sleazy, suspect publication. [Emphasis in the original.][76]

News organizations that had earlier rejected the charges printed them after Clinton and Flowers began discussing them in public. Because of the actions of news organizations with a lower threshold, the Clinton campaign was forced to react. The campaign's reaction, and rampant speculation about the effect of the allegations on his political standing, were "news" according to the conventional yardstick used during campaigns. Even the *New York Times*, which gave the story less attention than any major news organization, provided coverage (although the news editors restricted both the space and visibility they gave to the story).

One of the most frequent justifications for media investigations into a candidate's private life is that the candidates who appear on primary ballots are no longer screened by party leaders, and may not have been subjected to any thorough scrutiny by anyone. Under the current nomination rules, such "scrutiny" must be carried out by voters. Voters, however, can only consider information that has been made available to them. Thus, they need access to all relevant aspects of each candidate's biography in order to make informed, thoughtful decisions.

The problems with this position are twofold. First, as we saw in Clinton's case, media scrutiny of his character *supplanted* rather than supplementing scrutiny of his record and proposals. As Table 6-1 shows, the extent to which reporters abandoned the chore of discussing the substance of Clinton's candidacy was considerable.

This development gave rise to second thoughts among some journalists. The *Washington Post's* Howard Kurtz wrote, "If [the media's] professed goal during the primaries was to keep the spotlight on important issues, the verdict is clear: we failed miserably."[77] ABC's anchor Peter Jennings put it this way, "[The need to do things differently] hit me in New Hampshire when I realized that the press only cared about Gennifer Flowers and the people only cared about the economy."[78] The "reality check" that New Hampshire residents supposedly provided to reporters was not immediately evident in network news coverage, although it may have pushed Jennings and ABC toward adopting a more substantive fall format (see Chapter 3).

Second, as Clinton himself pointed out, the media — composed of hundreds of organizations, each with their own rules and thresholds of proof — were unable to apply consistent "standards" to him or any other candidate. From his perspective, on the receiving end of dozens of different questions, the inquiry was both capricious and arbitrary.

This situation created an environment that neither enabled the public to learn the reality behind the charges, nor allowed the candidate to clear his name. "I have said things to you tonight," he told CBS's Steve Kroft during the *60 Minutes* interview, "that no American politician ever has." He continued:

> I think most Americans who are watching this tonight, they'll know what we're saying; they'll get it, and they'll feel that we have been more than candid. And

I think what the press has to decide is: Are we going to engage in a game of "gotcha"?... I can remember a time when a divorced person couldn't run for president, and that time, thank goodness, has passed. Nobody's prejudiced against anybody because they're divorced. Are we going to take the reverse position now that if people have problems in their marriage and there are things in their past which they don't want to discuss which are painful to them, that they can't run?[79]

The media's coverage of his character seems to have permanently colored Mr. Clinton's view of the press. According to one book about the campaign, Clinton felt "victimized... by a cynical press motivated mostly by 'commerce and naked power.'"[82] *Newsweek*'s Peter Goldman and his co-authors were granted unusual access to the major candidates, which enabled them to witness the campaign "from a privileged inside position," on the condition that "our findings would be held in strict confidence" until after the election.[81] They recorded Gov. Clinton's private fulminations in New Hampshire:

"I mean, no one has ever been through what I've been through in this thing," he told his traveling companions. "*No* one. Nobody's ever had this kind of personal investigation done on them, running for president, by the legitimate media." By their own ordination, the press had become the arbiters of character in American politics, and, Clinton complained, their standards had become "a moving target."

..."I think that it is almost blood lust," [Clinton continued]. "I think it is an insatiable desire on the part of the press to build up and tear down. And they think that is their job — and not only that, their divine right."[82]

Beyond the obvious self-interest in both his public and private remarks, Clinton was right. The media lack both the coordination and the incentive to devise a set of standards that could govern their approach to personal character issues. Instead, each news organization set its own rules, but those with the toughest standards were unable to avoid the competitive pressures to publish or broadcast once the charges began flying.

Perhaps the most inventive mechanism for disseminating the charges against Clinton was one that can be dubbed the *Nightline* maneuver. That program's producers scheduled a show on the propriety of the media's coverage of rumors, where the *Star* article was discussed. Although the show was not technically focused on the charges, it was the first nationally broadcast news program to contain extensive discussion of them.

Journalism seemed at war with itself over the Clinton character charges. Although many journalists apparently believed that Clinton's blanket denial of Flowers's charges was dishonest, they were also uncomfortable about pursuing allegations into his sexual conduct.   Similarly, the allegations surrounding Clinton's draft history and college-era drug use were seen as "generational" issues, and some journalists argued that there needed to be greater tolerance for the personal actions of politicians Clinton's age.   As Ellen Hume argued,

> You can't just litmus-test people out because they did drugs or they were against the war or they had a lot of affairs back then. To deny that generation its own history and to deny people a chance to grow up and really work through some of these spasms of growth that we've had culturally and individually, I think is very dishonest.[83]

While a truce was declared at the end of the primaries, no permanent peace pact was ever signed. Journalism would appear destined to revisit its own character questions in the future. Over the course of the campaign, however, the argument that the media had been excessive in its coverage of Clinton's character would prevail.   During the general election, reporters focused more intensely on Clinton's record and proposals.

Furthermore, when new charges arose — particularly those surrounding the Clintons' Whitewater real estate investment, and possible conflicts of interest involving Hillary Rodham Clinton's law practice — the national media offered little coverage. Instead, those allegations — unresolved in 1992 — rose to the fore in 1993 and 1994. The Whitewater stories of Clinton's presidency — coupled with new and more serious charges of sexual misconduct involving state employees — undermined the effectiveness of his government, and distracted both the government and the country from pressing policy concerns.

These issues could have been more completely resolved during the 1992 primaries, but the media — divided as they were — could neither conclude the investigations nor permanently drop the matter. Although he did not agree at the time, Bill Clinton was perhaps fortunate that his primary-season "hazing" focused on questions of his personal character. The media were of two minds on the relevance of such inquiries, and residual guilt may have been one factor in the relatively mild treatment he received during the general election.

No such qualms were evident in the media's coverage of George Bush. His coverage during the primaries reflected the dominant media view that his was a failed presidency. As a frontrunner during the primaries, Bush's bad press was anticipated by the media's treatment of previous frontrunners. As we shall see, however Bush received nearly as tough press during the general election, when he was an undisputed underdog. The disparate treatment of the two nominees that fall was the culmination of the media's aggressive posture toward politicians in the wake of the 1988 campaign.

Notes

Opening quote: Bill Clinton on *Donahue*, October 8, 1992.

1. See Austin Ranney, *Channels of Power: The Impact of Television on American Politics* (New York: Basic Books, 1983), pp. 31-63 and James Deakin, *Straight Stuff: The Reporters, the White House, and the Truth* (New York: William Morrow and Company, 1984), pp. 285-291.

2. Ranney, *Channels of Power*, p. 33.

3. Edith Efron, *The News Twisters* (Los Angeles: Nash Publishing, 1971); Michael J. Robinson and Margaret A. Sheehan, *Over the Wire and On TV: CBS and UPI in Campaign '80* (New York: Russell Sage Foundation, 1983); Michael J. Robinson, "The Media in Campaign '84, Part II: Wingless, Toothless, and Hopeless," *Public Opinion* 8, no. 1 (1985); C. Anthony Broh, *The Horse of a Different Color: Television's Treatment of Jesse Jackson's 1984 Presidential Campaign* (Washington, D.C.: Joint Center for Political Studies, 1987); and S. Robert Lichter, Daniel Amundson, and Richard Noyes, *The Video Campaign: Network Coverage of the 1988 Primaries* (Washington, D.C.: American Enterprise Institute, 1988).

4. Michael J. Robinson, "Television and American Politics, 1956-1976," *The Public Interest* (Summer 1977): 19-21.

5. Thomas E. Cronin, "Looking for Leadership, 1980," *Public Opinion* (Feb-Mar. 1980): 17.

6. Quoted by Robinson and Sheehan, *Over the Wire and On TV*, p. 116.

7. Robinson and Sheehan, *Over the Wire and On TV*; Robinson, "Where's the Beef? Media and Media Elites in 1984," in *The American Elections of 1984*, ed. Austin Ranney (Washington, D.C.: American Enterprise Institute, 1985); S. Robert Lichter et al., *The Video Campaign*; Richard E. Noyes, S. Robert Lichter, and Daniel R. Amundson, "Was TV Election News Better This Time?" *Journal of Political Science* 21 (1993): 3-25.

8. For an excellent discussion of the patterns of candidate coverage based on reporters' assessments of their viability, see Robinson and Sheehan, *Over the Wire and On TV*, pp. 66-90.

9. Richard L. Berke, "Mayors Appear Unmoved by the Major Candidates," *New York Times*, January 23, 1992.

10. Robert W. Stewart, "Brief Lead Over Brown in Polls Boosts Agran Camp; For 2 Days, Ex-Irvine Mayor Enjoys an Edge Over Ex-Governor Among N.H. Voters," *Los Angeles Times*, January 28, 1992. For an in-depth comparison of how

local and network media treated the Agran campaign in New Hampshire, in Joshua Meyrowitz, "Visible and Invisible Candidates," *Political Communication* 11 (1994), 145-164.

11. Fern Shen, "Three Tell Md. Court They Deserve To Be Included on Primary Ballot; Presidential Hopefuls Try to Show They've Had Media Attention," *Washington Post*, January 30, 1992.

12. Ibid.

13. Fulani was the candidate of the New Alliance party, but was competing in some of the Democratic primaries.

14. Nancy Roberts, "Sixth Grader Prohibited from Playing Agran in Mock News Conference," Associated Press Political News, January 31, 1992, P.M. Cycle.

15. NPR's *All Things Considered*, January 31, 1992.

16. Roberts, "Sixth Grader Prohibited..."

17. Paul Taylor, *See How They Run: Electing the President in an Age of Mediaocracy* (New York: Alfred A. Knopf, 1990), p. 23.

18. Edward Jay Epstein, *News from Nowhere: Television and the News* (New York: Vintage Books, 1974), p. 215.

19. Robinson and Sheehan, *Over the Wire and On TV*, p. 115.

20. William C. Adams, "Media Coverage of Campaign '84: A Preliminary Report," *Public Opinion* 7, no. 2 (April/May 1984): 9-13; Robinson, "Where's the Beef?"

21. Robinson, "Where's the Beef?"; Robinson, "Wingless, Toothless, and Hopeless."

22. Opinion Roundup. *Public Opinion*, (October/November 1984): 40.

23. Lichter et al., *Video Campaign*.

24. ABC's *World News Tonight*, October 26, 1988.

25. *NBC Nightly News*, November 6, 1988

26. Quoted by Michael J. Robinson and S. Robert Lichter, "The More Things Change...: Network News Coverage of the 1988 Presidential Nomination Races," in *Nominating the President*, eds. Emmett H. Buell, Jr., and Lee Sigelman (Knoxville, TN: University of Tennessee Press, 1991).

27. Barbara Matusow, "Fear and Loathing '88," *Washingtonian*, April, 1988.

28. This is the formula we used for calculating good press/bad press in both our 1988 and 1992 studies. The procedures remained the same for both campaigns, in order to allow a direct comparison of the percentages of good and bad press.

29. Data on network news coverage of President Bush before 1992 is based on a separate study conducted by the Center for Media and Public Affairs for their regular newsletter, *Media Monitor*.

30. *CBS Evening News*, November 18, 1991.

31. *CBS Evening News*, March 5, 1991.

32. ABC's *World News Tonight*, March 9, 1991.

33. ABC's *World News Tonight*, March 7, 1991.

34. *NBC Nightly News*, May 5, 1991.

35. *CBS Evening News*, December 6, 1991.

36. *CBS Evening News*, December 10, 1991.

37. *NBC Nightly News*, December 10, 1991.

38. *NBC Nightly News*, December 16, 1991.

39. ABC's *World News Tonight*, January 15, 1992.

40. *NBC Nightly News*, January 28, 1992.

41. *CBS Evening News*, March 11, 1992.

42. *CBS Evening News*, November 22, 1991.

43. ABC's *World News Tonight*, November 24, 1991.

44. *NBC Nightly News*, December 19, 1991.

45. *CBS Evening News*, December 20, 1991.

46. David Lauter, "Clinton on Roll, but Centrist Stance Could Be a Liability," *Los Angeles Times*, December 24, 1991.

47. *CBS Evening News*, January 14, 1992.

48. *CBS Evening News*, January 14, 1992.

49. *NBC Nightly News*, January 23, 1992.

50. ABC's *World News Tonight*; *NBC Nightly News*, January 27, 1992.

51. ABC's *World News Tonight*, February 12, 1992.

52. *CBS Evening News*, February 14, 1992.

53. Peter Goldman et al., *Quest for the Presidency, 1992* (College Station, TX: Texas A&M University Press, 1992), pp. 126-150.

54. "Wondering Who's 'Electable,'" *Newsweek*, March 2, 1992.

55. *CBS Evening News*, February 28, 1992.

56. *NBC Nightly News*, March 18, 1992.

57. *CBS Evening News*, March 31, 1992.

58. ABC's *World News Tonight*, April 6, 1992.

59. Tom Rosenstiel, *Strange Bedfellows*, pp. 71-80.

60. Ibid., pp. 45-80.

61. Both, *NBC Nightly News*, April 8, 1992.

62. Tom Morganthau, "The Sudden Fall of Gary Hart," *Newsweek*, May 18, 1987.

63. Anthony Lewis, "Degrading the Press," *New York Times*, May 5, 1987.

64. David Broder, "The Press is on Shaky Ground," *Washington Post*, November 15, 1987.

65. Jonathan Alter, "Character Cops on Patrol," *Newsweek*, May 18, 1987.

66. A Gallup poll conducted for *Newsweek* asked "Why do you think news organizations have focused so much attention on charges of marital infidelity on the part of Gary Hart?" Thirteen percent selected "Because they think that voters should know about the character of a presidential candidate"; 12% selected "Because of competition among news organizations;" and 69% selected "Because they know such stories attract large audiences." See *Newsweek*, May 18, 1987, p. 25.

67. George J. Church, "Is Bill Clinton For Real?" *Time*, January 27, 1992.

68. Lance Morrow, "Who Cares, Anyway," *Time*, February 3, 1992.

69. Ellen Hume, *Restoring the Bond: Connecting Campaign Coverage to Voters — A Report of the Campaign Lessons for '92 Project* (Cambridge, MA: Harvard University, 1991), pp. 103-125.

70. A. M. Rosenthal, "The Clinton Couple," *New York Times*, January 28, 1992.

71. Tom Oliphant, "The Scandal Machine — A Campaign Intruder that Must Be Defeated," *Boston Globe*, January 29, 1992.

72. Eleanor Clift, "Character Questions," *Newsweek*, February 10, 1992.

73. Survey conducted by Princeton Survey Research Associates for the Times Mirror Center for the People and the Press, October 3-6, 1991.

74. Bill Turque and Nancy Cooper, "We're Voting for President, not Pope," *Newsweek*, February 3, 1992.

75. ABC's *World News Tonight*, February 14, 1992.

76. Larry Sabato, *Feeding Frenzy: How Attack Journalism Has Transformed American Politics* (New York: The Free Press, 1993), p. 264.

77. Howard Kurtz, *Media Circus: The Trouble with America's Newspapers* (New York: Times Books, 1993), p. 262.

78. Remarks made at a forum sponsored by the Joan Shorenstein Barone Center on the Press, Politics and Public Policy, held July 12, 1992 in New York, and quoted by Howard Kurtz, "Network TV Anchors Sharply Criticize Campaign Reporting," *Washington Post*, July 13, 1992.

79. Excerpts from an interview of Arkansas Gov. Bill Clinton and his wife Hillary, by Steve Kroft of CBS's *60 Minutes*, as published in the *Washington Post*, January 27, 1992.

80. Goldman et al., *Quest...*, *1992*, p. 118.

81. Ibid., pp. *viii-xv*.

82. Ibid., p. 118.

83. NPR's *Morning Edition*, February 21, 1992.

Chapter Seven

Credibility in the Balance

We should shoot out the windows on both sides of the street, while walking down the middle.
— Eric Engberg, CBS News

Even before the primaries ended in June, the media had begun to cover the campaign from the perspective of the coming general election. This meant that Bill Clinton, now assured of the Democratic nomination but trailing badly in some polls, was no longer considered the frontrunner. But neither was Republican nominee, George Bush, considered the favorite. Instead, during the spring of 1992, the media's top prognosticators were obsessed by the steadily strengthening candidacy of Texas billionaire Henry Ross Perot.

The media's early treatment of the inscrutable businessman appeared a close fit with the anti-frontrunner trend of the primary season. Perot began to receive coverage as a prospective candidate in late March. He rapidly qualified for the ballot in several states and reached double digits in presidential preference polls. As his candidacy grew in strength, the national media began to investigate the "Perot phenomenon."

For television reporters, illustrating his strengths meant stressing the positive side of his campaign. Thus, a number of news reports in April and May showed ordinary citizens praising Perot. "I just think he's a man of integrity, and we need that," one voter told ABC's Jim Wooten. "He just doesn't seem to have all the political crap that everybody else has," added another. "He's just one of these guys that says let's go *do* it, as opposed to talking about it," said a third.[1]

No other candidate received news coverage filled with such numerous and fervent citizen endorsements, an advantage that was reflected in Perot's TV news image. Through the end of May, Perot's good press score stood at 63% positive, compared with only 45% positive for Clinton and a mere 17% positive for Bush. That is, among all the sound bites from non-partisan sources who evaluated Ross Perot, nearly two out of three offered words of praise. Only a minority of such sources bolstered Bill Clinton's candidacy, and viewers rarely heard anything but discouraging words about George Bush.

So long as his press notices were friendly, Perot's poll numbers soared. In late March, a CBS News/*New York Times* poll gave him 16% of the vote in a three-way matchup with Clinton and Bush. By May, that figure had risen to 25%.[2] The apex of Perot's candidacy came on June 3, 1992, when large numbers of primary voters in several states told exit pollsters that they would have voted for him had he been on the ballot. "If Ross Perot, candidate of no political party, had been on the California ballot yesterday," marveled the *New York Times*, "he might conceivably have defeated an incumbent president in the Republican primary and the frontrunner in the Democratic primary."[3]

Despite the fact that no third-party candidate had ever won the presidency, the poll results validated the media's perceptions of Perot as the leader of a new three-way race. Journalists had spent the entire primary season spreading the news about voters' contempt for George Bush and their mistrust of Bill Clinton. So it hardly seemed unusual that voters would gravitate toward a "white knight" like Perot. Believing that the exit poll was not the crest of the Perot candidacy, but the portent of a greater surge yet to come, the *Times* all but declared the end of two-party politics in America:

> Ross Perot has already triumphantly demonstrated something recently unimaginable: It is now possible to mount a plausible campaign for president without backing from any political party at all.
>
> Parties are not dead, but as a medium in presidential politics they can be superseded by electronic means. Ross Perot rides the new medium to connect with the other tide, of voters dissatisfied with the two-party system and its candidates. He has already demonstrated how to use back-channel television — interview and talk shows — to denounce politics as usual.[4]

A *Time*/CNN poll taken June 3-4 offered further evidence of a Perot surge. It showed Perot with 37% of the general election vote, compared with 24% each for Clinton and Bush.[5] The poll found more voters with a favorable impression of Perot (40%) than either Bush or Clinton (36% and 35% respectively). In only a few weeks, Ross Perot had established himself as a potent political force, if not the man to beat. As journalism's conventional wisdom adjusted to the idea, a new frontrunner was anointed.

Inevitably, journalists began to shift the tone of their coverage — having built Perot up, it was time to knock him down. Fewer stories focused on the volunteers' praise for the un-candidate, and more scrutinized his background and character. NBC's Lisa Myers reported in late May that associates "paint widely divergent portraits of [Perot]. Some see him as bold, decisive, inspirational. To others he is manipulative, bullying and deceitful."[6]

A month later, Myers returned with another Perot story that left out words like "bold" and "inspirational." "Ross Perot loves to lecture reporters about getting the facts straight," she reported. "However, in a number of important instances, [his] version of the facts does not mesh well with either the public record or others' recollections of events."[7] A spate of network TV stories depicted Perot as "emotionally maladjusted,"[8] and as "some kind of super-snoop,"[9] with a "penchant for military solutions, covert operations, and intimidation,"[10] and a "willingness to ignore constitutional rights of privacy and due process."[11]

Polls showed Perot's candidacy losing steam even before his ill-fated July 11 appearance before the annual NAACP convention. At the convention, Perot offended the audience by using language that was interpreted as condescending and perhaps racist. One delegate told CBS that she "was so upset that he would insult us. This is the leadership of the black community in this country, and he has the utter gall and audacity to come in here and call us 'you people.' Where the hell has he been?"[12]

On television news, Perot's bad press was mounting. His proportion of negative sound bites rose from 34% in early June to 47% in late June to a withering 76% during the first half of July. In the course of a month, the tone of his coverage had made a complete turnaround, going from two-to-one positive to three-to-one negative.

Four days after the NAACP debacle, Perot's campaign manager Ed Rollins resigned from the campaign after an unrelated dispute. The problem with Perot, concluded ABC's David Brinkley, was that "he wants to run his own campaign — his ego has become involved.... The result is that [the political professionals] think he's half-crazy, and it is [crazy] — running your own campaign is somewhat like trying to be your own dentist. [It] doesn't make any sense."[13] The next day, Perot was officially (if temporarily) out of the race he had never officially joined.

Throughout the early phase of his candidacy, Perot's good press followed the established path of a rising star: a candidate develops support while receiving mainly good press; then, when he reaches frontrunner status, he receives increased media criticism and loses support. This is the same pattern described by content analysts ever since 1980. Candidates from John

Anderson to Gary Hart to George Bush (in both 1980 and 1988), Bob Dole, Jesse Jackson, and Paul Tsongas have alternately benefited and suffered from its consistent application over the years. In the general election of 1992, however, reporters would play the political game differently than they had in years past — raising anew the old questions of partisan bias and jeopardizing the public's faith in the media's impartiality.

The Last Frontrunner

After Perot's hasty retreat, the frontrunner's mantle was wrapped firmly around the shoulders of the newly nominated Bill Clinton. In one of the last polls taken before the start of the Democratic convention, President Bush still held a slight lead (36% to 32%) over Gov. Clinton, with the fading Perot in third with 26%.[14]   Five days later, Perot had left the race entirely, and Clinton, buoyed by the favorably covered Democratic convention, jumped to a stunning 23-point lead over Bush in the CBS News poll (58% to 35%).[15]

The numbers indicated that Clinton had inherited practically all of Perot's backers, doubling his support in less than a week. Other polls showed a similarly wide gap between the two nominees.[16] While Clinton's lead would ebb somewhat over time, it turned out to be permanent. Following the Democratic convention in July, President Bush became the undisputed underdog of the general election campaign.

Network news reporters' on-air comments about the horse race illustrated their bleak assessment of Bush's prospects. As Figure 7-1 shows, even in the afterglow of the Republican convention — which saw Bush rise between 5 and 8 points in most national polls[17] — network reporters' assessments of the campaign horse race reflected skepticism about Bush's chances (62% negative). Assessments of Clinton's prospects never dipped below 50% positive, while positive assessments of Bush's prospects never rose above 40%.

As the general election campaign wore on, it became evident that reporters increasingly thought Bush's cause was lost. On the first Sunday in September, Forrest Sawyer began ABC's newscast by noting recent polls showing Bush trailing in Texas, Connecticut, and Ohio. "Republicans solidly won those states the past three presidential elections," Sawyer reported, "and, most troubling for Mr. Bush, is a *Time* magazine poll, which shows he is in trouble in key suburban counties in battleground states, voters the president needs to win."[18]   On September 29, Bush's proposal for six campaign debates was assessed by CBS's Dan Rather as the desperate act of a campaign running out of options:

Figure 7-1

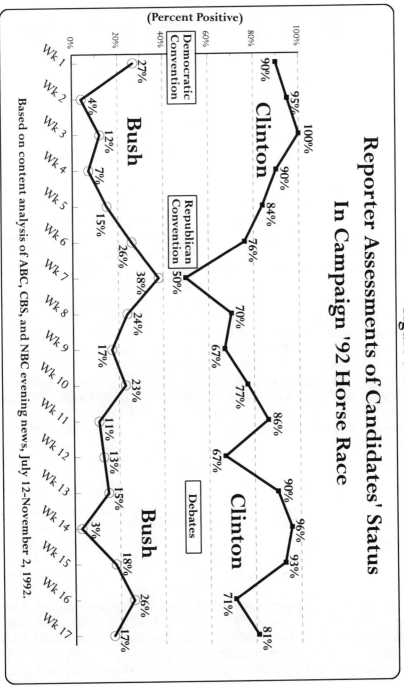

Reporter Assessments of Candidates' Status
In Campaign '92 Horse Race

(Percent Positive)

100%
90%
80%
60%
40%
20%
0%

Democratic Convention

Clinton

90%
95%
100%
90%
84%
76%

Republican Convention

70%
67%
77%
86%
67%

Debates

Clinton

90%
96%
93%
71%
81%

Bush

27%
4%
12%
7%
15%
26%
38%
24%
17%
23%
11%
13%
15%
3%
18%
26%
17%

Bush

Wk 1
Wk 2
Wk 3
Wk 4
Wk 5
Wk 6
Wk 7
Wk 8
Wk 9
Wk 10
Wk 11
Wk 12
Wk 13
Wk 14
Wk 15
Wk 16
Wk 17

Based on content analysis of ABC, CBS, and NBC evening news, July 12-November 2, 1992.

The president is trying desperately now to turn his campaign around because so many numbers, at least for the moment, seem to be against him. The poll numbers: Mr. Bush is trailing in all the national surveys. The calender numbers: Just 35 days now until the election. The economic numbers, including new ones: A report today says consumer confidence in the economy now is lower than it was before any of the past five presidential elections. People fear the economy is getting worse, not better.[19]

Reporters were careful not to openly forecast a Bush loss, but their running assessments of the campaign horse race made the point clearly enough. Out of 515 reporter assessments of Bush's campaign position, only one in six (17%) found a silver lining in the cloud darkening his reelection prospects. Conversely, 82% of all reporter assessments of Clinton's campaign strength and prospects were positive.

To reporters, Clinton's prospects looked best immediately after the Democratic convention (95% and 100% positive, respectively, during the two weeks that followed), and during and after the presidential debates (96% and 93% positive). It was also during the debates that Bush's campaign was rated its weakest (3% positive vs. 97% negative horse race assessments).

In spite of the Bush campaign's dire straits, the tone of his evaluative coverage was consistently more hostile than the tone of Clinton's coverage. Even in 1988, the worst that underdog Dukakis had to suffer was coverage that was *equally* as bad as Bush's. By contrast, Bush now faced coverage that was far more critical of him than of frontrunner Bill Clinton.

The story was the same everywhere on the dial. On NBC, Bush's good press score was 16 points lower than Clinton's (46% to 30% positive), while on ABC the gap was 18 points (54% to 36%). And frontrunner Bill Clinton's proportion of good press on CBS was actually twice as high as that of underdog George Bush. On CBS, evaluations of Clinton averaged 55% positive, while those of Bush averaged just 27% positive (a gap of 28 points).

This flies in the face of the patterns of coverage documented by every content analysis that has ever distinguished between judgments of candidates' viability (horse race coverage) and their desirability (good/bad press). Each campaign contains its own dynamic of media coverage, but none has ever seen an acknowledged frontrunner get better press than the underdog throughout the course of a general election campaign. This suggests that 1992 was no ordinary election year, as far as the media were concerned.

The clearest comparison is with 1984, when the Reagan-Bush ticket led Mondale-Ferraro wire-to-wire. After studies showed that the Democratic ticket had gotten far more positive coverage than the Republicans that year, the disparity was attributed to traditional anti-frontrunner rather than partisan (anti-Republican) bias. Michael Robinson and Maura Clancy described the good press gap documented by their research as "compensatory journalism" — the tendency of reporters to bash top dogs and boost underdogs. An election-eve report by NBC's Chris Wallace typified the anti-Reagan tilt that year: "Today's sentimental journey through California ended the highly staged, low-risk campaign of a big frontrunner... a cynical campaign, manipulative.... Protecting a big lead, the president offered pomp and platitudes...."[20] In 1992, by contrast, the media didn't compensate for the frontrunner's lead — they magnified the underdog's misfortunes.

If the networks' general election coverage broke the anti-frontrunner mold, it ran true to form as far as George Bush was concerned. At no point during the campaign did a majority of evaluations favor Bush. (See Figure 7-2.) His best week of TV news coverage (48% positive) came after the third and final presidential debate. A voter interviewed on NBC said that he felt "happy for Mr. Bush. He presented himself and his case in a much more efficient manner last night."[21] Two nights later, NBC's Lisa Myers offered a rare bouquet: "Even critics concede that, on a personal level, George Bush is an inherently decent man... devoted to his family, to his country, to public service.... Bush is deeply loyal to those he serves, and to his own staff, even when things go wrong."[22]

Even during that week — Bush's best showing of the campaign — the praise was offset by a slightly greater amount of criticism (48% positive vs. 52% negative). The day after the debate, CBS found an angry voter who declared that Bush "ought to be addressing the economy, [not] attacking [the other] candidates." Another, described as a lifelong Republican, said he would be voting for Bill Clinton. "I see the Republican party, in general, moving to the far right."[23]

Thus, the bad press that had haunted Bush throughout the primaries shadowed him during the summer and fall as well. During the summer of 1992, Bush received only 30% positive evaluations, compared with 53% positive evaluations for Clinton. After the formal Labor Day kick-off of the general election, the situation remained virtually unchanged — 31 percent good press for Bush, compared with 52% for Clinton. For the president, this actually represented an improvement from his shockingly bad primary season TV coverage (18% positive, 82% negative), but tough nonetheless. A 40-odd week long streak of bad press can be dispiriting for any campaign.

For Clinton, who had faced the worst press of any Democrat during the spring (43% positive vs. 57% negative), the improvement was particularly noticeable. Not only were a majority of comments about the Democratic nominee positive (a ten-point increase to 53%); compared to Bush, his press notices were practically sycophantic.

Clinton's TV coverage was particularly positive during and after the Democratic convention. Following his acceptance speech, CBS's Mark

Phillips interviewed a voter from Peoria, Illinois, who declared that "I am a Clinton fan as of this morning."[24] NBC's Tom Brokaw painted the Democratic convention as the picture of success: "Bill Clinton and Al Gore got what they needed from New York City — a unified Democratic party, a harmonious convention — so today they loaded their message onto a bus and moved out of the Big Apple and headed for the heartland."[25]

The bus tour, which paired enthusiastic Clinton supporters with political reporters looking to illustrate Clinton's jump in the polls, helped sustain Clinton's post-convention good press. The following ABC story was typical:

RON CLAIBORNE: At every stop on his bus tour, Clinton insisted he had found Perot backers who have now come over to his side:

GOV. BILL CLINTON: In that last crowd I had two more people come up and say "I was for Perot, now we're gonna support you."

RON CLAIBORNE: And in fact there are both Perot people and turned-off Republicans in the cheering crowds that greet him at each campaign appearance.

VOTER #1: I'm a Republican, but we're gonna work for you.

VOTER #2: I probably will vote for Bill Clinton.

RON CLAIBORNE: And you're a Republican?

VOTER #2: I'm a Republican, that's correct.

VOTER #3: I've been pretty unhappy of late so I've been a Perot supporter, and felt quite disappointed when he pulled out.

RON CLAIBORNE: And now?

VOTER #3: Well, I'm wearing the Clinton tag today.

VOTER #4: I was more inclined to vote for Bush until the other night when I heard the speech and I was very impressed with the speech, and now maybe I'm a Clinton supporter.[26]

Clinton's other major dose of good press came after the second presidential debate on October 15, 1992. The debate's format was a town-meeting-style question-and-answer session with randomly selected voters. Both Clinton's performance (he was "judged to have done very well," stated Peter Jennings) and the general impression that the debates weren't moving voters the president's way led reporters to speculate that the Democrats were heading toward not just victory, but a landslide. ABC's John McWethy talked to employment agencies in Washington, D.C., and found that mid-level administration officials were abandoning ship: "The president and his top aides are keeping up a brave front, but behind the scenes, aides admit there is frustration, confusion, and what appears to be a growing rush for the door."[27]

On CBS, Richard Threlkeld reported that, after the second debate, "the Clinton campaign is [now] daring to dream about victory in November,

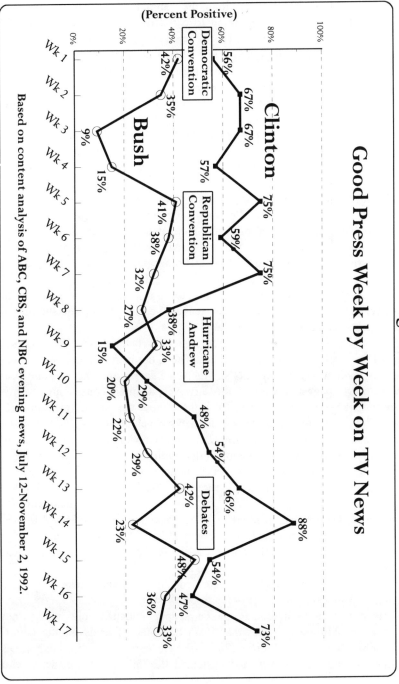

Figure 7-2

Good Press Week by Week on TV News

Based on content analysis of ABC, CBS, and NBC evening news, July 12-November 2, 1992.

maybe a great big victory.... Along the campaign trail for the first time people in the crowds are beginning to call Bill Clinton 'Mr. President.'"[28] On the night of the last debate, NBC's report showed auto workers cheering him on: "Don't let Bush give you any of that crap about how you're gonna lose our jobs, 'cause you're not," one man told the nominee. "You're gonna create more jobs for us people. Kick ass tonight, buddy!" "We're both Vietnam veterans," chimed in his friend, obliquely referring to the draft controversy, "and we're supporting you."[29]

What is most unusual about the good press Clinton received is that it is so incongruous for a frontrunner — particularly one whose lead is so firmly established. As Figure 7-2 shows, Clinton's weekly level of good press averaged above 50% for much of the summer and fall. It sank to Bush's level only once, in late August and early September.

Part of the reason for this dip was heavy coverage of Hurricane Andrew, which reduced the amount of airtime devoted to the campaign.[30] What remained on the air was less the day-to-day business of campaigning, and more feature stories that struck out at both candidates, increasing the bad press for each. Bush's level of good press also dropped during this period — from August 30 to September 19, his TV news evaluations sank to 26% positive, even lower than the 30% he received earlier during the summer and the 31% he would receive in the fall.

This anomaly of the frontrunner as media favorite was by no means limited to major network newscasts. The Clinton advantage was equally evident when we examined CNN, *MacNeil-Lehrer*, and the prestige press. On the news pages as well as the airwaves, Clinton consistently received more positive press notices than Bush throughout the general election. (See Figure 7-3.) Clinton fared best on the news pages of the *Wall Street Journal* (68% positive) and least well on CNN (43% positive). Bush's press was lopsidedly negative at every major outlet, with his worst reviews coming on CNN's *PrimeNews* (22% positive vs. 78% negative).

Overall, from Labor Day to Election Day, Bush was criticized by 71% of news sources and praised by only 29% at the eight news organizations we monitored. Clinton was praised by 52% of sources and criticized by 48%. At four out of eight national news organizations (CBS, CNN, the *Post,* and *Journal*), Clinton's level of good press *doubled* that of Bush. The closest Bush came to his rival was on *MacNeil-Lehrer*. Yet even on PBS's nightly news show, which is widely respected for its evenhandedness, Clinton led Bush by 15 percentage points (45% to 30% positive).

It is important to note that the newspaper statistics only include news articles, not editorials — not that Bush had many friends on the editorial page either. Over three-fourths (78%) of *New York Times* editorials and 93% of those in the *Washington Post* criticized the incumbent president, whose

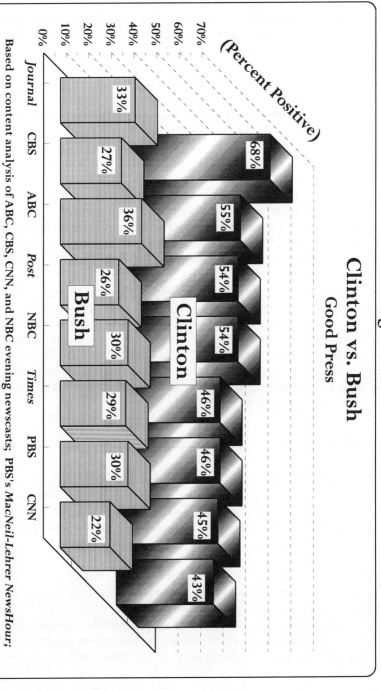

Figure 7-3

Clinton vs. Bush
Good Press

(Percent Positive)

Based on content analysis of ABC, CBS, CNN, and NBC evening newscasts; PBS's *MacNeil-Lehrer NewsHour*; the *New York Times*; *Washington Post*; and *Wall Street Journal*, September 7-November 3, 1992.

only consistent support came on the fiercely Republican *Wall Street Journal* editorial page (59% positive). Conversely, the *Times* and *Post* were usually supportive of Clinton (60% and 81% positive, respectively), while the *Journal* was frequently critical of him (67% negative).

Thus, the overtly editorial comment at the *Times* and *Post* reinforced the overall impression from their news pages that Clinton would make a better president than Bush. Only at the *Journal*, where the ideological schism between political news and editorial pages is well-known, did these two aspects of campaign coverage diverge.

Opinion is the stock in trade on the editorial page, where there is no expectation of balance from opposing viewpoints. In news articles, however, the assessments made by reporters and quotes from their sources weighed heavily against Mr. Bush. "Bush has been in office 12 years and the country has gone down instead of up," one voter told the *Journal*.[31] The *New York Times* quoted a California newspaper editor who complained, "George Bush [is] far too weak. He doesn't stand for anything, and he hasn't done anything." Similarly, a political strategist called Bush "the voyeur of domestic policy, who just sits and watches events march past."[32] The *Journal* offered an economist's assessment of Bush's plan for an across-the-board income tax rate reduction: "The only word for it is stupid."[33]

With this kind of handicap, it is difficult to imagine how any underdog could overtake his frontrunning opponent. Numerous studies have shown that presidential approval ratings are highly dependent upon the tone of the incumbent's media coverage.[34] Throughout the fall, every major source of information in the mainstream media reinforced the notion that this incumbent deserved to be turned out.

A LIBERAL BIAS?

The imbalance we found in the 1992 general election news coverage was pronounced, sustained, and overt. Not surprisingly, Republicans noticed this. The Bush campaign and its supporters charged the media with consciously attempting to undermine his candidacy. In the final days of his campaign, Bush personally made the point repeatedly. Why, he wondered, on ABC's *Good Morning America*, "if the media were so fair, why do we get these thunderous calls of applause when you say, 'Annoy the Media: Re-Elect Bush,' and why are you in the media holding little brainy seminars about 'Have we been fair?' You've never done that before."[35]

Other conservatives agreed. "The vast majority of reporters, certainly most all of them who write about politics in Washington, would have a cow if somehow or other Bill Clinton were to lose this election," conservative columnist Robert Novak said at a Barone Center symposium. "The young reporters I've talked to [think] he is the answer to all their dreams."[36]

During the campaign, reporters were skeptical of such complaints. "The losing party always whines," responded ABC's Cokie Roberts. "When you say the Bush campaign was a disaster, it's simply a fact. It's not our fault."[37] Some saw gamesmanship at work. "When one side starts saying the other side is getting the benefit of the press, you know... the side making the charge is trying to manipulate the press," commented the *Washington Post's* Lou Cannon in October, "and two, that side is probably losing."[38]

Indeed, strategy was a factor in some of the Republicans' complaints. In the *Columbia Journalism Review*, Christopher Hanson noted that "even top Republicans concede that some of their attacks on the press were contrived for political effect. As [Republican party chairman] Rich Bond told the *Washington Post*, putting pressure on the media was rather like a coach 'playing the referees' in hope of winning by intimidation."[39]

Even after the election was lost, however, Republicans continued to maintain that the game was rigged. Writing in the *National Review*, one-time NBC newsman Lorrin Anderson excoriated his former colleagues for acting as "spear-carriers for the Democrats."[40] L. Brent Bozell, chairman of the Media Research Center (and finance director for Pat Buchanan's presidential campaign), wrote in the *Wall Street Journal* that the press's condemnation of the Republican convention revealed a double standard:

> The speeches and pronouncements at the Democratic National Convention were filled with poison arrows aimed at the Republicans. Jesse Jackson compared Dan Quayle to King Herod of baby-killing fame; California Rep. Maxine Waters called Mr. Bush a racist and then refused to apologize for it; Ronald Reagan was blamed for everything under the sun, including the AIDS-related death of convention speaker Elizabeth Glaser's child. No one in the networks found this offensive. Not once did a single reporter ever use the terms "negative," "sleazy" or "mean" to describe the Democrats.[41]

Besides the campaign coverage, Republicans cited other evidence: a 1992 poll found that 44% of American journalists identified themselves as Democrats, compared with only 16% who said they were Republicans. (A comparable poll of U.S. citizens found that 34% called themselves Democrats vs. 33% who were Republicans.)[42] Similarly, a May 1992 Times Mirror survey found that 55% of national media journalists rated Bill Clinton favorably, compared to only 38% who had a favorable opinion of George Bush.[43]

Conservatives also recited a long list of perceived past slights: the alleged hostility of journalists towards the Reagan presidency; the "feeding frenzy" that greeted Dan Quayle after his selection as Bush's running mate in 1988; and their allegedly one-sided coverage of disputed accusations involving Supreme Court nominee Clarence Thomas in the fall of 1991.

Even some members of the "media elite" were having second thoughts. A lengthy article in *Time* magazine posed the question, "Are the Media Too Liberal?" The author, senior correspondent William A. Henry III, essentially answered "Yes."[44] Henry later commented,

> I pointed out that hardly any big-league journalists planned to vote for Bush and that most of the White House press corps openly loathed and belittled him, assertions that I expected to make headlines elsewhere or at least ripples. They didn't. Journalists didn't seem shocked by these facts and the public didn't seem surprised.[45]

As for the candidate himself, a full year after he left the presidency — long after any political benefits of "press-bashing" had evaporated — George Bush continued to state his belief that his re-election prospects were hurt by press coverage of both his presidency and the economy in 1992:

> I couldn't cut through the fog, the barrage. I give the Clinton campaign credit for those three famous words, "The economy, stupid." ...The media would find someone unemployed who'd say, "Well, he [Bush] may say things are getting better, but not for me and my family." And I'd sympathize with that individual worker — but the larger fact, as we now see, was that the economy was doing far better than the Clinton campaign or the press, particularly the network-TV shows, portrayed it.[46]

Our statistics confirm both of Bush's points. First, as we pointed out in Chapter 4, the state of the economy was indeed overwhelmingly (and often incorrectly) portrayed as negative or poor on the network newscasts. Second, on television and in print, Bush received the most negative press coverage of *any* national candidate during 1992. Even Dan Quayle, his much-maligned vice president, fared better than his boss: 61% negative coverage for Quayle vs. 79% negative for Bush.

The fact that Bush's treatment was so negative, however, does not necessarily imply that an across-the board ideological bias existed in the coverage. For example, his primary season nemesis Pat Buchanan (an impeccably credentialed conservative) fared far better than Bush on TV news (48% positive for Buchanan vs. 18% positive for Bush).

It is particularly difficult to accept the notion of a generalized "liberal bias" after considering the network coverage of President Clinton's own term of office. The Center for Media and Public Affairs has found that 73% of all network news evaluations of the president during 1993 and 1994 involved criticism, compared with only 27% positive sound bites.[47] Ironically, these are the same proportions of good and bad press that Bush received from the networks in 1992. Clinton's coverage as president was far more negative than what he received either during the primaries (43% positive) or the general election (52% positive).

While some individual reporters were undeniably Clinton fans during the campaign (*Time*'s Strobe Talbott, NBC's Carl Stern, and ABC's Kathleen de Laski all received high-ranking positions in Clinton's administration), his presidency was treated to the same brutal negativity that President Bush faced during his final year in office. The bad press that the new president received in office — on gays in the military, taxes, Haiti policy, Somalia, health care reform, and a host of other issues — belies the notion that the media were generally acting as an advocate for Clinton's ideology or platform.

Other Democrats besides Clinton have also received highly negative press coverage, as our previous studies have documented. Among them are former presidential candidates Michael Dukakis,[48] Gary Hart,[49] and Richard Gephardt,[50] former Speaker of the House Jim Wright,[51] and former president Jimmy Carter.[52] Such countervailing examples provide sufficient evidence to reject the notion that 1992 proves a generalized anti-Republican or anti-conservative bias.

Indeed, the stylized, highly structured, and personalized setting of a presidential election is poorly suited to test this argument. Allegations of ideological bias are probably more relevant to unstructured and open-ended stories, such as social movements, which offer more "blanks" for reporters to fill in with their preconceptions and personal convictions.[53]

On its own terms, however, the magnitude of the imbalance in 1992 raises important, and uncomfortable, questions for the media. While conservatives clearly had partisan motives for charging bias, a number of independent reporters and academics also spotted an anti-Bush trend. Dan Thomasson, Washington bureau chief for Scripps Howard newspapers, said "The columns were full of preferential treatment to Clinton... It was all very adulatory toward Clinton. Reporters didn't ask the tough questions. Every time Bush said something there were three qualifiers. I had to stop my reporters from doing it."[54] Reporters' "bias, enthusiasm, and emotion... brought about a tilt that was more pervasive and obvious than I've ever seen," added *Time*'s long-time White House correspondent Hugh Sidey.[55] A post-election *New York Times* headline conceded that, "Maybe the Media DID Treat Bush a Bit Harshly."[56]

The academics agreed. Political scientist Larry Sabato, a prominent analyst of political news, concluded, "Any fair, objective reading of the coverage of 1992 is going to conclude there was very, very substantial bias in the Democratic direction."[57] This view was echoed by Everette Dennis, director of Columbia University's Freedom Forum Media Studies Center: "Pejorative coverage of the Republican convention by much of the press was reprehensible."[58]   Most compelling of all, in a systematic content analysis that paralleled our own, scholars at Harvard's Barone Center also documented an especially harsh tone to Bush's network news coverage, relative to all other candidates.[59]   Marion Just, director of the Barone Center's Democracy '92 study, concluded that on TV news, Bush was "blamed for everything from the economy to the weather."[60]

None of the scholars who examined the coverage in Campaign '92 concluded that the imbalance offered proof of a systematic pro-liberal bias.   It was clear to all, however, that George Bush faced unusually negative treatment from the establishment media.   As Sabato concluded in a revised edition of his widely cited book, *Feeding Frenzy*, "Seemingly, everywhere one looked in the summer and autumn of 1992, Bush and Quayle were being bashed and Clinton and Gore were being hailed by the media."[61]

If it is unfair to heap praise on one political party and criticism on the other, it is equally unfair to distort an individual candidate's image by focusing exclusively or inordinately on his or her negative aspects.   Even if a one-sided debate does not affect voters' beliefs and values, it narrows the range of information available to them and distorts the political environment within which they process that information.

There is considerable evidence that the public's dissatisfaction with President Bush in 1992 was at least partly the product of his negative coverage. Washington University's Mark Joslyn and Steve Ceccoli matched our TV news data against National Election Study survey data from the 1992 general election.   They found that the respondents' amount of news consumption and the tone of the news coverage had "identifiable effects on respondents' judgments of the candidates."

Using NES feeling thermometers as their gauge of public sentiment, Joslyn and Ceccoli concluded that voters'

> judgments reflected the weekly changes in news tone, responding favorably in positive weeks and less favorably in negative periods.   The net tone of news coverage forms a verbal context from which respondents sample political reality.   A predominately negative context translated into less favorable feelings for a candidate, whereas a positive context increased favorable ratings.[62]

The news effects were strongest for Bush's ratings in September (in a negative direction) and Perot's in October (in a positive direction).

This result is consistent with our own studies that link Bush's public approval ratings to the tone of his media coverage.   Throughout the 48 months of his presidency, public attitudes toward Bush's job performance (as measured by Gallup polls) consistently shifted in the direction of his sound bite ratings, especially when the news coverage was both intensive and one-sided, as it certainly was during the 1992 campaign.   These shifts in his public approval rating followed, rather than preceded, shifts in Bush's television coverage. This suggests that the evaluative tone of Bush's news coverage was partly responsible for shifts in public attitudes toward him.[63]

In modern election battles, virtually the entire campaign experience is mediated. It would be highly unlikely that dramatic and long-lasting differences in candidate portrayals would fail to have corollary effects on some voters' attitudes. As Patterson writes, "The stories that the journalists tell of the candidates are not harmless little tales that mix fact and fiction. They are narratives with real consequences, because they affect the images that voters acquire of the candidates. The press is the message."[64]

Even more devastating to Bush's reelection prospects than his personal media image was the context in which his presidency was presented to the electorate. The state of the economy is by far the best predictor of national election outcomes. And the media played a major role in recasting Bush's public image from triumphant author of Gulf War victories to inept architect of economic disaster.

Beginning in the fall of 1991, the media agenda began to focus heavily on the allegedly parlous condition of the American economy. During the year that preceded the presidential election, economic coverage on the network evening news doubled from the previous 12 month period. As notable as the upsurge in economic news was its unrelievedly negative tone. Unemployment was the leading economic topic for 11 straight months from October 1991 through August 1992. The second most prevalent topic was the recession or economic stagnation.[65]

When sources specifically commented on economic conditions, over 90% of their on-air assessments were negative. (For example, one worker told CBS, "We're in a depression.... There's no work. There's no jobs."[66]) Throughout the entire third quarter of 1992, a remarkable 97% of all sources turned thumbs down on the economy's performance.[67]

Everett Ladd, director of the Roper Public Opinion Center, calls this "uninterrupted stream of negative press and commentary on the nation's economy ... the most important political 'event' on the 1992 campaign."[68] Ladd notes that in 14 consecutive national surveys taken throughout the campaign, at least three-quarters of the public rated the condition of the economy as "bad" — including 77% of those polled on election eve.

In fact, as we noted earlier, the economy was growing rapidly at precisely the time the public was processing the frequent media reports to the contrary. The recession, which was relatively mild and brief in historical terms, ended after the first quarter of 1991. By the third quarter of 1992, the GDP was growing at the robust rate of nearly 4% in real terms.

Yet our studies found that network news correspondents continued to bemoan the putative recession even as the expansion picked up steam. In fact, they mentioned the "recession" more frequently in the second quarter of 1991, after it had ended, than they did during the first quarter, while it was actually occurring.[69]

Thus, even as the network truth squads were scrutinizing every statement by the presidential candidates for errors and misinterpretations, they were implanting an inaccurate and highly misleading image of the economy in the minds of voters, with momentous consequences for the election. As S. M. Lipset, the dean of American political sociologists, later concluded, "The problem for Bush... was that many people thought conditions were worse than they were.... What defeated the Republicans was perception."[70]

But a greater irony was yet to come. It lay in the media's sudden discovery of economic growth *after* election day. From November 3 through the end of the year, over 60% of economic evaluations on TV news were favorable.[71] If ever a single piece of evidence demonstrates that the news is as much a prism of journalistic perceptions as a mirror on external reality, this must be it. It is also an argument for greater humility from journalists who presumed to protect the public from politically inspired misapprehensions, all the while creating misperceptions on a far greater scale than anything corrected in an "Ad Watch."

SHIFTING STANDARDS

Candidates tend to see a polarized world along the campaign trail: Republicans vs. Democrats; liberals vs. conservatives; "us" vs. "them." It is no wonder that, when they encounter unfavorable news coverage, they begin to see the media as one of "them." But ideology and partisanship are of little consequence to journalists, who see a different world — one composed mostly of individuals (both virtuous and villainous) and their unique stories.

Discovering those stories, and illustrating them with selected facts, quotes, and anecdotes, is the workaday business of journalists. Their *modus operandi* are *intended* to distort reality — to make it more condensed, interesting, understandable, and dramatic. They can also unintentionally shade the news in a way that political combatants interpret not as colorful writing and vivid narration, but as partisanship and adversarial distortion.

Thomas Patterson argues that a certain kind of "journalistic bias" — reporters' penchant for interpreting events and individuals through the prism of the horse race or other superficial themes — leads them to resort to "fanciful imagery" that is designed not to illuminate, but rather to illustrate their own view of the race.[72]

Our substantive research provided copious examples of such gratuitous juxtapositions. After Paul Tsongas's worse-than-expected performance on Super Tuesday in 1992, for instance, reporters reached for an irresistible metaphor after his campaign plane slipped off the runway onto wet ground. "Paul Tsongas's airplane got stuck in the mud today, and so did his campaign," intoned ABC's Judy Muller.[73] "Paul Tsongas's campaign seemed to be going nowhere, just like his plane," echoed NBC's Andrea Mitchell.[74]

Such images inevitably contain partial truths — piecemeal impressions that are designed to illustrate reporters' preconceptions of how politics works and who's winning or losing. Like the more positive portrayals of "bandwagon" candidates who are suddenly portrayed as masterful and inspiring, such images reduce candidates to caricatures. Reporters who resort to them are motivated not by partisanship, but by their professional incentive to tell a good story. The biases such rhetorical devices introduce are inadvertent, the result of journalists following their own professional dictates without regard to the larger consequences.

The effect, however, can be quite partisan. Particularly when the candidates are not otherwise well-known to the public, these media-constructed images can have a powerful effect on voters. As Patterson writes, "Reporters' vision of politics as a strategic game and the narratives they use to tell this story introduce *random partisanship* into the campaign.... The voters, as V. O. Key noted, 'are not fools.' But their decisions can be foolish when they are forced to choose without adequate guidance." [Emphasis added.][75]

Patterson's argument reflects his analysis of general election coverage in news magazines since 1960. He documents a structural "bias" that is inadvertent in origin, unselfconscious in execution, and random in impact. And so it was for nearly 30 years. After 1988, however, journalists — especially broadcast journalists — began to consider the consequences of their work. They resolved to be much more deliberate in shaping their role next time around.

The interregnum between Campaign '88 and Campaign '92 proved a crucial time for news organizations burdened by their perception that politicians had gained the upper hand in manipulating and controlling media images. What was different about 1992 was the degree of self-awareness that the media elite possessed about their own role in the campaign, and the aggressiveness with which they played their newly scripted part.

The national news media, responding to the complaints about the 1988 campaign, consciously changed the rules of its campaign coverage. The basis for this change was a pair of sincere but self-serving assumptions: that candidates were primarily at fault for the trivial and negative nature of modern campaigns, and that it was journalism's job to turn things around. The public's misgivings about the press coverage was seen as part of a generalized discontent with campaigns in general. Therefore, reformers believed the press could burnish its own image by enforcing better standards on the political players.

The two main efforts of journalists — to craft their own more substantive agenda, and to police the accuracy of campaign commercials — betray the arrogance of their approach to Campaign '92: They believed that complaints about the media coverage of past campaigns were, at root, complaints about the campaign process, which could be ameliorated only if journalists assumed a more powerful role in the process.

Superficially, at least, the media achieved their goal of giving more coverage to policy issues. Even so, the voters were seldom informed about the details of the candidates' policy prescriptions. (ABC's "American Agenda" series and PBS's *MacNeil-Lehrer NewsHour* stand out as impressive exceptions to this trend.) As we learned in Chapter 4, the candidates' stump speeches actually proved more substantive than either television or newspaper campaign news.

The news agenda was heavily weighted with economic and domestic policy concerns, and foreign policy received less coverage than it did during the "trivial" campaign of 1988. The major news organizations had their own policy priorities, which they substituted for the candidates' agendas when the two conflicted. And both newspaper and television coverage continued to be suffused with talk of strategy, tactics, and speculation about the horse race.

It is even more difficult to credit the media with restoring "fairness" to campaign news. What was perceived as "unfair" about 1988 was the ability of George Bush to control the news agenda with attacks on his opponent. Those attacks were seen by reporters (among others) as lacking the necessary substantiation to be considered fair.

In 1992, campaign journalism's new goal was to check the ads, check the facts, check the rhetoric, and discipline candidates who roamed too far out of bounds. Instead of accurately presenting the contrasting claims of partisan advocates, the new fairness meant telling voters which claim was accurate.

In practice, this new approach to fairness put the media firmly in charge of defining political reality. In a nod to this self-appointed function, CBS News instituted a new feature called the "Campaign '92 Reality Check." All four networks dedicated at least some resources to "Ad Watches," as did the *Washington Post*, the *New York Times,* and other major newspapers. Candidate assertions were frequently contradicted by reporters. Tactics that reporters perceived as unfair were so labeled. Campaign trail reports no longer presented one campaign's point of view, balanced by the other side's rebuttal, but rather the reporter's own critique.

These "corrections" often amounted to substituting journalists' own "spin" on how an ad should be interpreted, rather than correcting factual errors. And they were disproportionately aimed at George Bush. We noted 360 instances during the general election in which print or broadcast reporters called into question or refuted campaign statements. More than half of these (56%) focused on the Bush campaign, compared with only 28% for the Clinton campaign and 16% for Perot. Bush's own statements were challenged far more frequently than Clinton's (103 to 58), while the Bush campaign's ads were labeled as misleading twice as often as Clinton's (51 vs. 26).

This doesn't mean that Bush's ads were necessarily twice as misleading as his opponent's. It only means that they were more often so labeled by news organizations.[76] In fact, some reporters expressed misgivings afterward that they had policed just one side of the street. "If you look at the statistics, the economy didn't stink as badly as we allowed Clinton to say it did," said Scripps Howard's Dan Thomasson. "We didn't hold Clinton accountable and we should have."[77]

Moreover, the imbalances in 1992's coverage were not solely the results of reporters' attempts to enforce higher standards of campaign conduct. If that were so, they would still have presented relatively balanced coverage of the candidates' respective issue positions, character, and job performance.

Although Bush was most heavily criticized for his campaign conduct, however, the coverage did not become more balanced when we excluded all such comments from our analysis. Indeed, the gap between the two nominees during the general election actually increased: Bush's good press rose to 33% positive, but Clinton's jumped even more, to 58% positive. If reporters had never published a single criticism of any candidate's campaign conduct, there would still have been a major imbalance in the coverage: a three-to-two positive ratio of comments about Clinton vs. two-to-one negative on Bush.

Thus, journalists were most critical of the campaign waged by the candidate whose policies they approved of the least. In fact, as Table 7-1 shows, news articles reflected mostly criticism of the president on a broad array of domestic policy issues. Only on his character and his approach to foreign policy did Bush receive better press than Clinton. On all major domestic issues of the campaign — the economy, abortion, health care, education, and the environment — the news gave Clinton credit for better policies than the president. In general assessments of their performance in office — Bush as president, Clinton as Arkansas governor — Clinton received glowing reviews (71% positive); Bush got scorched (only 22% positive).

Reporters' license to judge after 1988 was justified by the allegedly excessive campaign conduct of the candidates, particularly George Bush. It was permissible to single out candidates for criticism, according to the reformers, if their tactics were offensive or their charges erroneous. Reporters, it was argued, had special standing to criticize campaign excesses

Table 7-1

Good Press by Topic

September 7 - November 3, 1992
(Percent Positive)

	Bush	Clinton
Total	29%	52%
Abortion	20%	48%
Economy	19%	44%
Education	22%	88%
Environment	30%	37%
Foreign Policy	54%	35%
Health Care	21%	34%
Presidency	22%	Governorship 71%
All Substance	24%	47%
Personal Character	29%	15%
Campaign Conduct	6%	16%

Note -- Based on content analysis of ABC, CBS, CNN, and NBC evening news-casts; PBS's *Macneil-Lehrer NewsHour*; the *New York Times*; *Washington Post*; and *Wall Street Journal*, September 7 through November 3, 1992.

because of their daily presence as witnesses on the campaign trail. In practice, though, the new tone that reporters adopted in their stories permeated all categories of their evaluations — candidate conduct, domestic policy, economic policy, foreign policy, and general job performance.

A survey of journalists taken in October 1992 found that more than half (55%) believed that Bush's candidacy was hurt by the way he was covered by the media. But when asked why, most cited his record as president or the prominence of the economy as an issue in the campaign, rather than the tone or fairness of the campaign coverage.[78] After all, if fairness consisted of giving every candidate the coverage he deserved, and Bush was the worst candidate, then why should journalists be faulted for giving him the most negative coverage?

As *Newsweek*'s Jonathan Alter put it just before the election, "The main reason the president has received a bad press is that he's done badly.... A Bush victory... would indeed annoy — even depress — many journalists, who overwhelmingly believe that he has not been a good president."[79] Campaign conduct was not, in 1992, the high-profile issue it was in 1988. Bush's bad press was not compensation for an unfair campaign; it was rooted in journalists' perceptions of a job poorly done.

While most reporters thought Bush's problem was his failure as a president, a few (about 9%) thought that their peers were biased against Bush.[80] Some said it was personal: One reporter covering the White House put it this way: "Reporters feel condescension and contempt for Bush. There really is that attitude. They're openly derisive."[81] "Some reporters are smitten with Clinton," ABC White House correspondent Brit Hume told the *Washington Post*. "There are things written about Bill Clinton and Al Gore that I've never seen written [about other politicians before], even by opinion reporters. I think there has been a double standard."[82]

Others thought the bias stemmed from reporters' boredom with the president and his party. "Frankly, Bush is old hat," one reporter commented before the election.[83] "After 12 years of a Republican-controlled White House, many in the Washington press corps admit that they'd like to see some new faces at press conferences," reported the *National Journal*.[84] Former CBS and NBC newsman Roger Mudd thought that the press carried with it an "anti-incumbency bias":

> I think you'll find because the press so enjoys a story, an exciting story, particularly one in which one in power is about to fall from power, that is reflected in the coverage. That makes a good story, and I think that's where the bias comes in, is the press generally favors the underdog, someone who's going to topple someone who's in power, and I think President Bush was a victim of that this year.[85]

All of these various explanations — Bush was a failed president, reporters didn't like him personally, or they wanted to see a change — miss the point. The important question is not what motivated journalists to shower Bush with negative press coverage. Rather, it is why news organizations allowed such feelings to influence their coverage.

Under the old rules, "mindless objectivity" would have ensured that voters were treated to rough approximations of good and bad news about each candidate, or equivalently bad press about both. In 1992, the reformulated norms allowed reporters more leeway in expressing themselves. "The notion that a reporter should have a point of view, usually camouflaged, has very much invaded television, and print [journalism] as well," *New Yorker* media critic Ken Auletta told the *Washington Post* in 1994.[86]

Journalists were encouraged after 1988 to retreat from the campaign trail, provide more analysis and perspective, and keep the news from becoming hostage to the campaigns' competing agendas. In large part, this was accomplished. But the force behind such a shift in approach was concern over the conduct of the campaign. Reporters gave themselves license to referee the contest and make it "fairer." But in attempting to clean up the campaign environment, they created an environment in which their own values and beliefs took on far greater importance.

Journalists began to see themselves as responsible for the conduct of the campaign, and for the quality and correctness of the information provided to voters — by any source. The reforms, however well-intentioned, stimulated a range of unintended consequences, not the least of which was an opportunity for journalists to begin to consider the consequences of their stories — for voters, for the candidates, and for the process.

Reporting on the candidates' agendas might not be sufficient, the reformers concluded, so journalists were advised to consider those issues that also demand attention and cover them. Even if the candidates don't lie outright in their television ads, reporters were warned, they might leave the public with wrong impressions. Journalists were advised to ensure that the public retain the right impressions. Journalism's *modus operandi* changed from finding stories and telling them to the public, to using the media's now formidable power over public opinion as a tool to police the contest.

Fairness — ensuring that everyone received the coverage they deserved — replaced objectivity or balance as the ideal of good journalism. "Objectivity," wrote the *Post*'s Joann Byrd, was merely "a pretentious fantasy that made stenographers of reporters and produced irresponsible journalism."[87] Byrd conducted her own unscientific review of the *Post*'s campaign coverage. She concluded that, out of 813 campaign items (pictures, headlines, and news stories), 184 were negatives for or about President Bush, vs. 52 for or about Gov. Clinton. Positive items broke the other way — 195 for

Clinton, 175 for Bush. Subtracting Byrd's numbers, one gets a net score of +143 for Bill Clinton, and a -9 for George Bush. While clearly no fan of the old system, she concluded that, "Fairness — which was supposed to substitute for objectivity — is, it turns out, a very subjective successor."[88]

A generation ago, a network executive told a government commission that television was "a mirror of public attitudes and preferences."[89] The notion that TV's cameras merely show viewers the real world, warts and all, was problematic even then. Today it is laughable. Under the old rules, journalists were indeed expected to act more like court stenographers than judges. The old rules were clumsy, and sometimes they broke down. But they provided an independent standard that served as a check on the preferences and preconceptions of both individual reporters and news organizations.

A new generation of campaign journalists chafed at the constraints and contradictions of old-fashioned standards of objectivity. They sought new standards that would permit them to right the "wrongs" they had witnessed during earlier campaigns. In 1992, they got their chance. The result was that leading news organizations shifted from recording reality to reshaping it. They set out to become partisans on behalf of the process. They ended up becoming partisans on behalf of their own preferences.

MEDIA CHEERS, PUBLIC JEERS

When their campaign experiment ended, most journalists expressed their approval. The Times Mirror post-election survey found that four out of five journalists rated the 1992 coverage as "good" or "excellent." The survey also reported that many of the top media people interviewed volunteered that the coverage was much improved from 1988. Two-thirds of reporters rated coverage of policy issues and particularly the economy as at least good; more than a quarter (27%) said that coverage of the economy was "excellent."[90]

The president of the American Society of Newspaper Editors, Seymour Topping, said proudly, "I think the country owes a debt for a job well done to the press, certainly in the latter stages of the campaign."[94] Media critic Edwin Diamond praised the press for "Getting It Right":

As Campaign '92 winds down, it's clear how the old media-information complex — the three traditional networks, the prestige newspapers like the New York Times, and the news magazines — has changed the way it covers presidential elections. The results have been dramatic, particularly at ABC, CBS, and NBC: The networks have produced perhaps their best contextual campaign reporting of the 40 years since television started bringing presidential races indoors to living-room screens.[92]

According to the Times Mirror survey, more than three-fourths of reporters (77%) agreed that media scrutiny of the candidates' commercials had a
positive effect on the campaign process. "Ad Watches," said a television
newsman quoted by the Times Mirror report, "is the primary reason why no
Willie Horton ads or their cousins have appeared in this campaign." Nearly
as many (76%) thought that the press's coverage of the candidates' positions
on the issues was good (59%) or excellent (17%).[93] Reuters' Gene Gibbons
said afterwards that, "This was an interesting story from start to finish. It
was more substantive than some of the past campaigns I've covered. I think
we did come to grips as a country with some of the issues we have to face.
It was a real watershed."[94]

There was only one problem with this crescendo of self-congratulation:
The public seemed deaf to the paeans of praise from the nation's pressrooms.
A post-election survey of voters by the Times Mirror Center found that only
36% gave the press a grade of "A" or "B" for its campaign coverage. If that
seems less than a glowing endorsement, consider this: The electorate gave
higher average grades to talk show hosts and campaign consultants.[95]

In September, Ted Koppel's *Nightline* went on the road for a *Viewpoint*
special: "Politics and the Media: Reporting or Distorting?" The program
began by quoting voters resentful or dissatisfied with the news media, none
of whom appeared ready to offer the press the "debt for a job well done"
demanded by Seymour Topping:

VOTER #1: Most of the people who work in the media are biased in a liberal
direction.

VOTER #2: Of course they've been biased.

VOTER #3: I think they're just going after what they think people, you know,
want to — you know, the crap that people like to feed on, instead of the
real issues.

VOTER #4: I could care less about Bill Clinton dodging the draft.

VOTER #5: Sometimes I feel like it's a lot of propaganda.

VOTER #6: They say what the candidates say, and that's the line you read in
the newspaper.

VOTER #7: I think there's a lot of exploitation.

VOTER #8: And I think it's getting a little bit out of hand.[96]

Why didn't the public appreciate the media's efforts? According to Times
Mirror, a majority (54%) believed that the press had too much influence on
which candidate becomes president. During the primaries, nearly three in
five voters (58%) thought the media had too much influence on the selection
of a Democratic nominee.[97] Moreover, most of the electorate believed that
journalists "often" (49%) or "sometimes" (35%) let their own political
preferences influence the way they report the news.[98] After the election,

more than one-third (35%) asserted that the media had been unfair to Bush; a quarter (27%) said Perot was treated unfairly; and a fifth (19%) said Clinton's coverage had been unfair. [99]

These polling data reveal an embarrassing and troubling gap between press and public perceptions. The fact that journalists' own assessments differed so drastically from the public's suggests that the reformers' prescriptions were better suited to journalists' complaints than to those of the voters they claimed to serve.

For more than a decade, leading journalists protested their manipulation at the hands of politicians like Ronald Reagan. They complained that candidates like George Bush could virtually commandeer the airwaves with negative or misleading ads, and so "use" the media for political effect. Throughout the Reagan years, however, voters did not appear to sympathize with reporters' complaints. Even though journalists had begun to censure Bush before the 1988 vote, he paid no apparent price in popular support for offending the media's sensibilities.

Some newspeople concluded that the voters deserved the sort of campaign that journalists were condemning. "The fault, dear voters," wrote the *New York Times* Anthony Lewis in 1988, "is not in our politicians but in ourselves."[100] By this way of thinking, it was necessary for journalists to save the electorate from its own worst instincts. During 1992, however, the media's efforts to tame politics made them a more visible target for voter complaints. Reporters' aggressiveness in "refereeing" the contest seems to have alienated not just the candidates they punished, but also their constituents.

Well below half of all Republican voters (41%) said they thought coverage of President Bush was fair. Nearly two-thirds of Republicans (65%) and nearly half of all independents (47%) thought the press had too much influence over the campaign. Rank-and-file Democrats were more pleased in the fall; only 29% complained about the press's influence. But they had been equally upset during the primary season. In February, at the height of Bill Clinton's character problems, 55% of Democrats said they, too, thought the press had too much influence.[101]

Some in-house press critics, like *Newsweek*'s Jonathan Alter, accused the voters of being unreasonable and ungrateful for the services the media had rendered. "Bush supporters see it as somehow presumptuous and premature to raise substantive questions about how Clinton would handle the office if he reaches it. Perot supporters act as if it's unfair to ask their man any difficult questions...." But, he wrote, the voters "can't escape us [journalists.] We'll be around long after Bush, Perot and Clinton have slunk offstage. No term limits, either."[102]

But media analysts outside the profession were alarmed by the increasingly low regard the public professed for the press. "Even if journalism does not need the public's adulation to play its essential role," wrote Larry Sabato in 1993, "it does require voters' respect, and their basic belief in the high quality of both its information and its underlying fairness."[103]

In 1992, journalists concentrated on changing those aspects of campaign coverage that they were most concerned about, rather than those the public sees as most important. The result was media coverage of the campaign that only journalists applauded, despite the fact that its treatment of the issues remained superficial while its coverage of the candidates became even more opinionated and less balanced.

Meanwhile, broad segments of the public have come to view the press as a partisan player in the political process, rather than as a fair and honest broker of both sides' positions. As politicians know, if voter dissatisfaction is left untended, unhappy citizens will eventually find other alternatives. As a result, displeasure with the establishment media's coverage of the campaign, a number of citizens have taken flight, toward newer and more genuinely populist alternatives.

Notes

Eric Engberg, quoted by James McCartney, "Used and Abused," *American Journalism Review*, April 1995.

1. ABC's *World News Tonight*, May 11, 1992.
2. Based on CBS News/*New York Times* polls of registered voters, with the first poll conducted March 26-29, 1992, and the second conducted May 6-8, 1992. Source: "Public Opinion and Demographic Report," *American Enterprise* (July/ August 1992): 84.
3. "The No-Party System," *New York Times*, June 3, 1992.
4. Ibid.
5. "Perot the Front Runner," *Time*, June 15, 1992.
6. *NBC Nightly News,* May 20, 1992.
7. *NBC Nightly News*, June 17, 1992.
8. ABC's *World News Tonight*, July 2, 1992.
9. *CBS Evening News*, June 27, 1992.
10. *CBS Evening News*, June 23, 1992.
11. ABC's *World News Tonight*, June 23, 1992.
12. *CBS Evening News*, July 11, 1992.

13. ABC's *World News Tonight*, July 15, 1992.

14. *CBS Evening News*, July 12, 1992.

15. *CBS Evening News*, July 17, 1992.

16. "Public Opinion and Demographic Report," p. 82. A *Los Angeles Times* poll taken at the same time showed a 20-point Clinton advantage; ABC New found a 29-point edge for Clinton; and a Harris poll found a 30-point gap.

17. Ibid. The six polls taken in early August, before the Republican convention, showed Bush averaging about 34% of the vote; seven polls taken immediately after the convention showed Bush bouncing to just over 40% of the vote, a typical convention bounce, although nothing like Clinton's 20-point jump.

18. ABC's *World News Tonight*, September 6, 1992.

19. *CBS Evening News*, September 29, 1992.

20. Maura Clancey and Michael J. Robinson, "General Election Coverage: Part 1," *Public Opinion* (December/January 1985): 33.

21. *NBC Nightly News*, October 20, 1992.

22. *NBC Nightly News*, October 22, 1992.

23. Both, *CBS Evening News*, October 20, 1992.

24. *CBS Evening News*, July 17, 1992.

25. *NBC Nightly News*, July 17, 1992.

26. ABC's *World News Tonight*, July 18, 1992.

27. ABC's *World News Tonight*, October 16, 1992.

28. *CBS Evening News*, October 16, 1992.

29. *NBC Nightly News*, October 19, 1992.

30. Elizabeth Kolbert, "In Bid for Attention, Weather Wins," *New York Times,* September 19, 1992.

31. David Shribman, "Young Voters Are Crowding Clinton's Corner, Portending GOP Loss of a Former Stronghold," *Wall Street Journal*, October 19, 1992.

32. R. W. Apple, Jr., "Bush's Downhill Political Journey in California," *New York Times*, October 11, 1992.

33. Alan Murray, "Clintonomics: Democrat's Plan Relies on Public Spending to Spur Investment," *Wall Street Journal*, October 19, 1992.

34. Fred Smoller, "The Six O'Clock Presidency: Patterns of Network News Coverage of the President," *Presidential Studies Quarterly* 16 (1986): 31-49; "Enter Clinton... Exit Bush *"Media Monitor* 7, no. 2 (February 1993); S. Robert Lichter and Richard E. Noyes, "In the Media Spotlight," *American Enterprise* 2, no. 1 (January/February 1991): 49-53.

35. ABC's *Good Morning, America*, October 28, 1992.

36. Quoted by Graeme Browning, "Too Close for Comfort," *National Journal*, October 3, 1992.

37. Quoted by Jeffrey L. Katz, "Tilt," *Washington Journalism Review,* January/February 1993.

38. Quoted by Browning, "Too Close for Comfort."

39. Christopher Hanson, "Media Bashing," *Columbia Journalism Review*, November/December 1992.

40. Lorrin Anderson, "Here Now, the News...; Media Coverage of the 1992 Presidential Campaign," *National Review*, November 16, 1992.

41. L. Brent Bozell, "Annoy the Media, Elect Bush," *Wall Street Journal,* November 2, 1992.

42. Both surveys included in David H. Weaver and G. Cleveland Wilhoit, "Journalists — Who Are They, Really?" *Media Studies Journal* (Fall 1992): 63-79.

43. Times Mirror Center, "The Campaign and the Press at Halftime," June 4, 1992.

44. William A. Henry III, "Are the Media Too Liberal?" *Time,* October 19, 1992.

45. William A. Henry III, "Why Journalists Can't Wear White," *Media Studies Journal* (Fall 1992): 19.

46. Victor Gold, "George Bush Speaks Out," *Washingtonian,* February, 1994.

47. Data on network news coverage of President Clinton in 1993 and 1994 is based on a separate study conducted by the Center for Media and Public Affairs for their regular newsletter, *Media Monitor.* See "They're No Friends of Bill," *Media Monitor* 8, no. 4 (July/August 1994).

48. Noyes et al., "Was TV Election News Better This Time?"

49. Lichter et al., *Video Campaign.*

50. Lichter et al., *Video Campaign.*

51. "Keeping an Eye on Congress," *Media Monitor* 3, no. 9 (November 1989).

52. Robinson and Sheehan, *Over the Wire and On TV.*

53. For a fuller consideration of underlying issues involved in debates over media bias, illustrated by case studies, see S. Robert Lichter, Linda S. Lichter, and Stanley Rothman, *The Media Elite* (New York: Hastings House, 1990).

54. Quoted in "Insiders' Guide to Campaign Coverage," in *The Media and Campaign '92,* published by the Freedom Forum Media Studies Center at Columbia University, pp. 114-115.

55. "Assessing Coverage: A Survey of Campaign Correspondents," in *The Media and Campaign '92,* published by the Freedom Forum Media Studies Center at Columbia University, p. 128.

56. Elizabeth Kolbert, "Maybe the Media DID Treat Bush a Bit Harshly," *New York Times,* November 22, 1992.

57. Quoted by Thomas C. Palmer, "Reputation for Bias Seems Well Earned," *Boston Globe,* January 3, 1993.

58. Everette E. Dennis, "Memo to the Press," in *The Media and Campaign '92,* published by the Freedom Forum Media Studies Center at Columbia University, p. 10.

59. Ann N. Crigler, Marion R. Just, and Timothy E. Cook, "Local News, Network News and the 1992 Presidential Campaign." Paper presented at the Annual Meeting of the American Political Science Association, Chicago, September 3, 1992.

60. Renee Loth, "Studies Find Tilt in TV Coverage of Campaign," *Boston Globe,* September 2, 1992.

61. Sabato, *Feeding Frenzy: How Attack Journalism Has Transformed American Politics* (New York: The Free Press, 1993), p. 255.

62. Mark R. Joslyn and Steve Ceccoli, "Media Messages and Voter Judgments, Is There a Link? Estimating the Impact of News Consumption and Content on Voters' Judgments During the Final Months of the 1992 Campaign." Paper prepared

for delivery at the Midwest Political Science Association 52nd Annual Meeting held in Chicago, IL, April 14-16, 1994.

63. The overall strength of the relationship was r=.64. This correlation fits well with Smoller's analysis of media coverage and public opinion towards Presidents Nixon through Reagan. (See Fred Smoller, "The Six O'Clock Presidency"; S. Robert Lichter and Richard E. Noyes, "In the Media Spotlight"; and "Enter Clinton... Exit Bush," *Media Monitor* 7, no. 2 (February 1993).

64. Patterson, *Out of Order*, p. 125

65. "The Boom in Gloom," *Media Monitor* 6, no. 8 (October 1992): 2.

66. *CBS Evening News*, April 5, 1992.

67. "It's Still the Economy, Bill," *Media Monitor* 7, no. 5 (May 1993): 3.

68. Everett Ladd, "The 1992 Election's Complex Message," *American Enterprise* (January/February 1993): 49.

69. "Reporting on Recession," *Media Monitor* 5, no. 5 (May 1991): 6; "Recession or Recovery?" *Media Monitor* 6, no. 4 (April 1992): 3.

70. S. M. Lipset, "The Significance of the 1992 Election," *P.S.: Political Science and Politics* (March 1993): 7.

71. "The Boom in Gloom."

72. Patterson, *Out of Order*, pp. 116-122.

73. ABC's *World News Tonight*, March 11, 1992.

74. *NBC Nightly News*, March 11, 1992.

75. Patterson, *Out of Order*, pp. 131-133.

76. As Tom Rosenstiel points out, *NBC Nightly News's* "Ad Watch" project, the most ambitious of the three networks, was interrupted when Lisa Myers was reassigned to the Perot campaign. "She did only a handful of truth boxes, but Myers for one felt that the Clinton campaign was often as guilty of distortion as Bush's. They just complained more loudly about the other guy. 'They were terribly aggressive. It became excessive.'" *Strange Bedfellows*, p. 290.

77. Quoted in "Insiders' Guide to Campaign Coverage."

78. "The Press and Campaign '92: A Self-Assessment," Times Mirror Center for the People and the Press, supplement to the *Columbia Journalism Review,* March/April 1993.

79. Jonathan Alter, "Go Ahead, Blame the Media," *Newsweek,* November 2, 1992

80. "The Press and Campaign '92: A Self-Assessment."

81. James Gerstenzang, *Los Angeles Times* White House correspondent, quoted by William A. Henry III, "Are the Media Too Liberal," *Time*, October 19, 1992.

82. Quoted by Howard Kurtz, "Republicans and Some Journalists Say Media Tend to Boost Clinton, Bash Bush," *Washington Post*, September 1, 1992.

83. Quoted by Graeme Browning, "Too Close for Comfort."

84. Graeme Browning, "Too Close for Comfort."

85. PBS's *MacNeil-Lehrer NewsHour*, November 3, 1992.

86. Quoted by Howard Kurtz, "The Jaded Crusader," *Washington Post,* December 15, 1994.

87. Joann Byrd, "73 Days of Tilt," *Washington Post*, November 8, 1992.

88. Ibid.

89. Robert D. Kastmire, NBC vice president, quoted by Edward Jay Epstein, *News from Nowhere* (New York: Vintage Books, 1974), p. 13.

90. "The Press and Campaign '92: A Self-Assessment."

91. Quoted by Debra Gersh, "Introspection: Journalists Examine the Presidential Campaign and the Impact Ross Perot Had on Coverage," *Editor & Publisher*, November 21, 1992.

92. Edwin Diamond, "Getting It Right: The Networks and the Campaign," *New York*, November 2, 1992.

93. "The Press and Campaign '92: A Self-Assessment."

94. Quoted by Debra Gersh, "Introspection: Journalists Examine the Presidential Campaign and the Impact Ross Perot Had on Coverage," *Editor & Publisher*, November 21, 1992.

95. Times Mirror Center for the People & the Press, November 15, 1992.

96. ABC's *Viewpoint*, "Politics and the Media: Reporting or Distorting?" September 16, 1992.

97. Times Mirror Center for the People & the Press, June 4, 1992.

98. Times Mirror Center for the People & the Press, September 22, 1992.

99. Times Mirror Center for the People & the Press, November 15, 1992.

100. Anthony Lewis, "A Corrupted Process," *New York Times*, October 13, 1988.

101. Times Mirror Center for the People & the Press, November 15, 1992. Also according to the February poll, 40% of all respondents said Clinton was most responsible for his own problems; 48% said his problems were caused by the press. A similar survey of reporters found that 12% of national reporters said Clinton's troubles were caused by the press, and 63% said they were his own fault. See Times Mirror Center for the People & the Press, February 28, 1992 and June 4, 1992.

102. Jonathan Alter, "Go Ahead, Blame the Media," *Newsweek*, November 2, 1992.

103. Sabato, *Feeding Frenzy*, p. 298.

Chapter Eight

The Talk Show Campaign

Is this how the presidency is to be won in 1992: in confessional pleas to the priests of pop, uttered amid commercials for deodorants, depilatories and sanitary napkins?
— Jonathan Yardley, *Washington Post*

Many of the complaints about the media coverage of Campaign '92 were echoes of grievances accumulated from past election years. It was nothing new that the candidates felt unfairly treated. The media's treatment of the campaign as a game, focusing on its rules and tactics but neglecting its consequences, had increasingly aggrieved voters and candidates over the course of several campaigns.

This time, however, journalists deliberately took steps to improve both the coverage and the campaign itself. The national media ratcheted up its criticism of the candidates, deploring those tactics that they considered improper or excessive. They padded their coverage with their own analyses of the campaign issues (mainly the economy). They applauded their own efforts. They thought the coverage — their work — was far better in 1992 than it was in 1988.

But voters, who remained far less satisfied, had an opportunity in 1992 to take their business elsewhere. Cable television and talk radio, which had grown throughout the '80s, stimulated perhaps the most far-reaching reform of '92, and one that was totally unplanned. The so-called "New Media" offered candidates a format far less mediated than the traditional "Old Media," and offered the public a chance to size up the candidates on their own. The insurgent talk shows became the establishment media's campaign rivals in 1992, and citizens voted with their remote controls. Eventually, the networks hopped on the bandwagon, and old standards of broadcast journalism, such as NBC's *Today* show, altered or jettisoned their traditional formats in favor of New Media-style call-in shows.

The talk show campaign, as it came to be known, offered more than just freedom of choice. In 1992, the country had a chance to compare two very different styles of campaign news. Traditional news mediated the campaign, distilling a candidate's messages into brief stories reflecting the journalists' news judgments. The talk shows offered voters a chance to render their own judgments of the candidates — and their own judgment of the traditional media.

STEALING THE SHOW

The three broadcast networks, pillars of the media establishment, had been growing increasingly possessive of their function as intermediaries between the candidates and the public. Among the more recent studies to that effect, none resonated more than a report written by Harvard researcher Kiku Adatto. Comparing network evening news coverage of Campaign '88 with that of 1968, she found "dramatic changes in the way television covers presidential politics."[1]

One statistic from her study was frequently cited because it illustrated so succinctly the shifting standards of campaign news. "The average 'sound bite,' or bloc of uninterrupted speech," she calculated, "fell from 42.3 seconds for presidential candidates in 1968 to only 9.8 seconds in 1988."[2] Among the media critics who seized on this number was Michael Dukakis, who complained, "If this thing is reduced to which one of the two candidates, in the course of a 14- or 16-hour campaign day, can say something that is the cleverest for 9.8 seconds, then we've got a problem."[3]

Adatto was onto something, and her statistic struck a nerve among journalists. "The 9-second sound bite is the phoniest of academic contrivances," complained Ken Bode. Such bogus complaints were designed, he charged, to distract reformers from their real mission. "No one who works in television believes that Americans should rely exclusively on the 22 minutes of evening network news to get their information on presidential campaigns." The evening news, Bode continued, had to report on "all of the domestic and international news of the day." They could not be expected to be as complete in its campaign coverage as, say ABC's *Nightline*, CNN's *Inside Politics,* or C-SPAN's *Road to the White House.*[4]

Bode's response is valid as far as it goes, but it misses Adatto's point. Sound bites weren't shrinking because newscasts had more domestic and international news to report, or because the newscasts themselves were growing shorter. Sound bites were dwindling because television's role had shifted from displaying the campaign to critiquing it. Adatto reported that "political reporters began to sound like theater critics, reporting more on the stagecraft than the substance of politics."[5] Only a tiny fraction of stories (6%) focused on the candidates' deliberate image-making in 1968. That proportion leaped to 52% — a majority of campaign stories — by 1988.

Campaigns had not become nine times more manipulative; it was television's presentation that was radically altered. The candidates' words and ideas were relegated to the sidelines so that reporters could devote their time to illustrating and exposing what they saw as the cynicism of modern campaigns. "The more the campaigns sought to control the images that appeared on the nightly news," Adatto wrote, "the more the reporters tried to beat them at their own game, to deflate their media events by magnifying a minor mishap into a central feature of the event itself."[6]

Television journalists were no longer content merely to transmit the campaign as it happened. Producers and correspondents now sought to screen the campaign for unwitting citizens, showing them footage that illustrated their own insights about the campaign. Adatto criticized television for focusing too much on the images and mechanics of politics, thus losing sight of the substance and the reality. The real problem with nine-second sound bites was not that they gave short shrift to any given news event; it was that they shunted aside the newsmakers in favor of the journalists.

As we have seen, though, one of the main critiques reformers offered of the campaign coverage was that it didn't do *enough* image-debunking. NBC's Tim Russert, for example, had proposed that reporters label the "photo-ops" as such. "Believe me," he wrote, "the staging would stop."[7] Adatto was right: network reporters, whose own stock-in-trade consisted of pretty pictures and colorful quotes, had become preoccupied with the candidates' image-making, and it was clouding their perspective.

Adatto released her research in 1990, in the midst of the media's debate about its proper role, and long before the networks had settled on their final strategies for Campaign '92 coverage. So one might reasonably have expected that the networks would place a high priority on giving the candidates enough uninterrupted airtime to express their ideas in a more fully-developed and informative fashion. To the contrary, our study found that the candidates' sound bites shrank once again during the 1992 primaries, to an average of only 7.3 seconds each — a 25% reduction from 1988, and down 83% from 1968.[8]

The "big three" networks' coverage of the primary campaigns totaled 26 hours 11 minutes of airtime. Of that, the eight candidates were heard just

13% of the time, and other sources (such as voters and political experts) took up 15% of the airtime. Reporters' own voices occupied the remaining 72% of election news airtime — approximately 19 hours for reporters, compared with about 25 minutes for the average presidential candidate. As Adatto found in 1988, the networks were still spending most of their airtime critiquing the campaign, rather than displaying it.

In 1968, television reporters still placed the candidates in the spotlight and relegated themselves to the sidelines. Typical stories showed clips of the candidates speaking for extended periods of time, with many quotes lasting more than a minute apiece. By 1992, reporters had moved themselves to center stage, minimizing the amount of time the candidates were on-screen, and broadcasting their own (usually negative) analysis of the combatants.

No wonder the survivors from the primaries, Bill Clinton (whose TV coverage was 57% negative) and George Bush (82% negative) both felt abused by the network newscasts. Late in the spring, they were joined by Ross Perot, a man completely at ease breaking the norms of conventional political discourse. For the candidates, the Old Media had become, in the words of Paul Taylor, "discourteous hosts."[9] Lengthy talk show sessions offered an opportunity for them to avoid the negative commentary of political reporters, and simultaneously convey their ideas to the public — in "bites" longer than 7.3 seconds.

THE NEW KIDS IN TOWN

It took an unconventional politician like Ross Perot to create the talk show campaign. In bringing the New Media into electoral politics, however, he was taking advantage of new channels of persuasive communication whose political relevance had become increasingly obvious since 1988.

The New Media began this evolution long before the 1992 campaign, as advances in satellite and cable technology allowed more — and more varied — national programming. While most of these additional outlets offered entertainment rather than news, their effect was to diminish the broadcast networks' hold on their audiences. The audience share of the "big three" has dropped from more than 90% of all households in the late 1970s to less than 60% of households today.[10]

This trend resulted in declining audiences for the networks' news and public affairs programming as well, while creating opportunities for rivals to emerge (the best known of which is the Cable News Network). Today, viewers interested in public affairs programming have a variety of television choices, ranging from the exhaustive and serious C-SPAN to the youth-oriented MTV News.

The revolution in news delivery has encompassed more than just television. The repeal of the "Fairness Doctrine" (FCC regulations designed to ensure equal time for all sides on public affairs debates) encouraged radio stations to develop "news/talk" programming with a distinct point of view (the most widely heard program of this type being *The Rush Limbaugh Show*).

Formerly, such programming had been impractical, because of the Fairness Doctrine's requirement that opposing viewpoints be given an opportunity to respond. But news/talk caught on quickly, and the number of stations with the new format boomed, rising from 308 stations in 1988 to 500 in 1990, including many stations with large regional audiences, such as Atlanta's WSB, Baltimore's WBAL, and Chicago's WGN.[11]

In addition, the accessibility and affordability of personal computers has enabled tens of thousands of individuals to link themselves electronically, using communication networks such as on-line services and the Internet. The proliferation of information sources in the late 1980s and early 1990s meant that Americans could more easily learn about those topics — ideas and individuals alike — that the Old Media covered infrequently or from a limited vantage point.

Given the size of their audience, it was inevitable that the New Media would one day clash with the Old Media in the realm of politics. For talk radio, the moment came in early 1989, as Congress was considering a 51% pay increase for its members, federal judges, and senior executive branch officials. Traditional news organizations gave little coverage to the issue, since the increase was automatic unless both houses of Congress voted it down, and the House of Representatives had no plans to vote on it at all.

When talk radio's listeners learned about the pay hike, however, thousands flooded telephone lines to complain on the air. Hosts urged listeners to show their ire by mailing teabags to their congressional representatives in symbolic reference to the Boston Tea Party.

The response was overwhelming — then-Speaker Jim Wright reluctantly scheduled a vote on the measure, and the House of Representatives voted it down, decisively. Their success in the pay raise fight made it clear that talk radio was emerging as both a powerful pulpit for its hosts, and a forum through which the public could more directly engage the issues of the day.

For the first time in the television age, information had reached around traditional media organizations and found a mass audience ready to listen and act. Mike Siegel of Seattle's KING radio helped coordinate the effort with about twenty other radio hosts. "We heard that the Democrats were going to the Greenbriar [a resort in West Virginia] for their retreat. We looked up the phone number, passed it around, and told our listeners to call." The listeners did call. Afterward, Siegel observed that, "I think *that*, more than anything else, convinced these guys that they weren't going to hide from us."[12]

This unexpected use of mass media as a tool of political mobilization did not sit well with many legislators who had come to an uneasy accommodation with more traditional forms of broadcast journalism. One member of the congressional leadership, Democrat Vic Fazio of California, complained about the New Media's populism: "We became cartoon cannon fodder for trash television and for talk radio.... We fell prey to the deception of the rabble rousers."[13]   Some in Congress briefly considered reinstating the Fairness Doctrine, in order to make it more difficult for radio hosts to act as advocates in future policy debates.[14]

The New Media's successful sinking of the pay raise illustrated more than a breach between political elites and a populist media; the media's own ranks were demonstrably split. The Old Media, after all, hadn't considered the pay raise a story worth covering, and many of the traditionalists agreed that the raise (which would trigger raises for several classes of senior government officials) was a good idea. For example, the *Washington Post*'s David Broder opposed what he called "the know-nothing demagoguery of ... hometown radio talk shows."[15]

Although talk radio was becoming popularly identified with the political right, the alliance of forces on this issue showed that its populist impact was not limited to one side of the spectrum. Thus, Ralph Nader, a staunch ally of the talk show forces (and whom Broder had called a "national nag"), commented that "You have a two-tiered media in this country now. People like Broder, the national columnists, and the TV-network correspondents, earn more than most congressmen. [Their support for the pay raise shows] just how insular, how far from reality, Washington has become."[16]

But the pay raise fight itself was less consequential to many than the shift in media power that it foretold. At the time, columnist Joe Klein speculated that perhaps the New Media could one day be the tool of a populist rebellion:

> There is always the fear that some unscrupulous bozo will find the magic words and mobilize a furious rising of the heretofore uninterested, routing incumbents with a mindless, half-crazed populism. The pay-raise revolt was a whiff of that.[17]

For many in the establishment, Klein's prophecy may have seemed fulfilled in 1992, with Ross Perot as the "unscrupulous bozo", and his "volunteers" the vanguard of the "half-crazed" populist rebellion.

Just as talk radio's notoriety was enhanced by its successful thwarting of the pay raise, Perot's two-phased candidacy in 1992 provided the breakthrough talk TV had been waiting for. Philosophically, Perot was a kindred spirit with the New Media. One of the fundamental components of his candidacy was Perot's belief that citizens were no longer acting like "owners of the country," a situation he believed could be remedied by instituting electronic democracy.

As Perot described it, the "electronic town hall" would serve two functions: first, it would televise forums to educate citizens about all sides of current issues, designed in such a way that citizens could question the participants. Second, once voters had heard the complete debate and considered the choices, they could express their preferences by voting. While their votes wouldn't be binding, Perot said, the citizens' preferences would "kind of clear Congress's heads about whether or not to listen to folks back home."[18]

Perot's faith in direct citizen communication was apparently one of the main reasons he chose to announce his campaign on *Larry King Live*. "We've got an hour tonight to talk about the real problems that face this nation and you, in effect, have sort of an electronic town hall," he told King. "I think we can serve the country by really getting down in the trenches, talking about what we have to do, and then doing it."[19] While the hour-long session was nationally televised, it took weeks for most of the traditional media to discover Perot's campaign — it didn't "break" in the *New York Times* until March 7, and the *Washington Post* held off until March 18.[20]

By the end of March, a quarter of the public — who had little opportunity to learn about Perot's candidacy from either network television[21] or the major newspapers — were telling pollsters they supported Perot for president.[22] As with the teabag revolt, an end-run had been made around the establishment media, who in March were focused on the party primaries and their cast of Clinton, Bush, Tsongas, Brown, and Buchanan — not Perot.

Upon discovering candidate Perot, however, the Old Media appeared to feel neglected by him. Perot conducted his candidacy by appearing on television interview programs, and held very few traditional campaign events. Political reporters wishing to cover Perot were reduced to watching him on TV along with millions of other citizens. The network morning shows — whose interviews were as frequently dominated by chefs, psychotherapists, and Hollywood celebrities as by politicians — offered Perot a forum that more resembled *Larry King* than *Meet the Press*.

On June 11, 1992, for example, NBC's *Today* devoted its entire two hour program to interviewing Perot, or rather, to interacting with him — he was questioned by both the hosts and by viewers who picked up the phone. The experiment drew considerably more viewers than a typical *Today*.[23] The next morning, the major newspapers all covered Perot's TV appearance (the *New York Times* ran three stories), significantly extending its reach.

Traditional journalists were not about to embrace the Texas tycoon; the tone of the next day's reports mixed astonishment with a touch of disdain:

Folksy even as he gazed intensely into the camera, Perot rambled through an avuncular mix of anecdotes, colorful phrases and "good news, bad news" summaries that make up his electronic version of a stump speech. He quoted lyrics from "Annie" and "America the Beautiful," and reflected on the difference to a farmer between a soft rain and a hard rain.[24]

Besides the convulsive effect he had on the campaign itself, Perot's candidacy triggered a fair amount of fretting over journalism's place in the campaign process. "The networks better wake up or they'll find themselves marginalized," warned Marvin Kalb.[25] "The whole structure of the media, like that of other institutions, is coming unglued," wrote Jonathan Alter, somewhat hyperbolically. "News used to filter down from the country's most powerful news organizations. Today... when the *National Enquirer* sneezes, the *New York Times* catches a cold."[26]

The *New Republic's* Michael Kinsley argued that traditionalists could learn something from the public's choice of questions. Still, he professed two worries:

> First... untrained amateurs are no match for skilled professionals in exposing a candidate's flaws and weaknesses. And second, that semi-journalists like [Phil] Donahue and [Larry] King, not to mention non-journalists like Arsenio [Hall], unhealthily — or at least surrealistically — muddy the distinction between serious politics and trivial show biz. There is, no question, something eerie about the same show discussing men-who-would-be-president one day and women-who-ate-their-husbands the next.[27]

If Ross Perot had been the only candidate to use the talk shows aggressively to disseminate his views, the phenomenon would probably have been more of a footnote than a feature of Campaign '92. Before long, however, Perot was joined on the talk show circuit by both of the major party nominees, who also sought the chance to speak more directly to citizens. Even before he wrapped up the Democratic nomination, Bill Clinton took two turns on the syndicated *Donahue*, the doyen of daytime talk. The difference between those two appearances provided another early warning signal about public disaffection with the direction of campaign journalism.

On April 1, 1992, host Phil Donahue had angered both Clinton and his audience by grilling Clinton about his personal character — inhaling marijuana smoke and having an affair with Gennifer Flowers.[28] When Donahue turned to a woman in the audience for a comment, she angrily ticked off several of the nation's problems, then berated the host: "I can't believe you spent a half an hour of airtime attacking this man's character." The rest of the audience cheered her loudly.[29] To "balance" the presentation, the next day Donahue questioned rival Jerry Brown about his sexual preference (Brown: "If you want to know, do I go out with girls, yes I do.") and his religiosity. At one point, Brown complained, "This is like an acupuncture of political attacks."[30]

The host's performance seemed a parody of reporters' worst excesses. In his effort to play the "serious" journalist rather than the lightweight entertainer, Donahue must have expected the same public gratitude that Seymour Topping and Jonathan Alter did. His aggressive and personal questioning of the candidates about personal matters with little relevance to national issues brought vocal protests from the audience (the alleged beneficiary of this type of questioning). It may have been a new low point for a campaign that had already seen more than its share of embarrassments.

Three days later, however, Phil Donahue returned with an innovative program that was among the campaign's finest moments. Both Clinton and Brown agreed to return for another hour. Their agreement was that the host would say nothing, and the two candidates would simply discuss the issues. That is precisely what they did. Both began with short biographical statements and then engaged in a cordial conversation about the need for political reform, the Reagan-Bush legacy, health care, the environment, and the differences between Republicans and Democrats. Each yielded the floor graciously to the other without the help of a moderator. Afterward, Donahue himself observed, "This looks like the most civil encounter of the campaign."[31]

It is interesting to note that, when the only participants were candidates, the discussion was entirely based on the issues and totally cordial. During debates and other joint encounters, it was not unusual for the candidates to aggressively confront each other. (Three weeks earlier, in fact, Brown had confronted Clinton in a debate in Chicago: Brown: "He is funneling money to his wife's law firm, for state business!" Clinton: "You ought to be ashamed of yourself for jumping on my wife! You're not worth being on the same platform with my wife!" Brown [wagging his finger]: "I'll tell you something, Mr. Clinton...!") [32]

In standard encounters, a moderator was supposed to maintain order. On Donahue — in spite of their competitiveness and their ambition — when the candidates (with cameras rolling) were forced to take responsibility for the conduct of their debate, the finger pointing ceased.

After the primaries ended, Bill Clinton returned to the talk show circuit, in need of a boost to his flagging prospects. Despite outlasting his Democratic rivals, his campaign had come to a standstill. The primaries had turned out to be more bruising than he had expected. Continuous media scrutiny of his character made it far more difficult than it otherwise would have been to overcome the lightly regarded Tsongas and Brown.

The traditional media's obsession with "character" made it difficult to convey to mass audiences what Clinton saw as his essential message: A lifelong commitment to making government work for people, and an opportunity for the Democrats to demonstrate they could once again be trusted with the White House. And there was no sign that this was going to change.

Now, with the primaries over, Clinton should have been able to commandeer the spotlight during the run-up to the Democratic convention. Instead, he was eclipsed in the headlines and on the nightly news by the spectacle of Perot's multi-million-dollar talk show campaign. As Clinton explained it later, "What I was saying was still not being reported. The media were more interested in the horse race. That's when we decided to go full steam ahead in a new way."[33] It was time, Clinton aide Mandy Grunwald advised, to visit the *Arsenio Hall Show*.[34]

"I thought 'Arsenio' was some kind of poison you took," Clinton campaign manager James Carville later quipped.[35] Clinton's June 3, 1992, appearance on the late-night comedy program, much celebrated at the time, put the media establishment on alert: the New Media were going to be more than just Perot's playground in Campaign '92. The following week, Clinton appeared for an hour on NBC's *Today*, where he took viewer calls in the post-Perot format.

On June 12, the Democratic National Committee bought a half-hour of prime time for Clinton to conduct a town-hall-style meeting. The show cost $400,000, its content was indistinguishable from the morning call-in shows, and it fared poorly in the ratings.[36] Clinton followed up his paid town meeting with free appearances on *CBS This Morning* and MTV, and his campaign scrapped plans to buy another half-hour block of airtime. "If you gave me $3 million today, I wouldn't spend a penny on TV. We can't get any more than we are getting [now]," said deputy campaign manager George Stephanopoulos.[37]

While Clinton was finally getting his message across to voters, his wooden speaking style drew jeers from the TV critics, who panned his stilted first outing on *Today*. The *New York Times* complained "he lapsed into bureaucratese... and his answers, complete with subparagraphs, sometimes seemed to come right out of a Democratic Leadership Council White Paper."[38] The *Washington Post* found "Clinton's appearance... so dull that it bordered on soporific."[39] With repeated outings during the late spring and early summer, however, the Democratic nominee grew more relaxed and comfortable with the format, developing a well-honed delivery style that would serve him well in the fall.

That left George Bush as the lone holdout among the three candidates. There were some concerns about the protocol of a sitting president hitting a talk show circuit populated by "authors hustling their books, faded movie stars grasping for one last jolt of celebrity and transvestites telling their pathetic tales."[40]

There was also the danger from the crazies who might call — a *Today* show caller asked Ross Perot on the air if the Texas billionaire "ever had the desire to mind-meld with Howard Stern's penis?"[41] Perot, unflustered, began talking about government gridlock, but the White House — knowing that the prestige of the presidency was one of their man's few remaining assets — certainly didn't want a replay of that scene with the eminently more flappable Bush in the guest chair.

Thus, Bush's advisors settled on a safe opening play: they scheduled a prime time news conference. During the 1988 campaign, Bush was frequently criticized for dodging reporters, although he held regular press conferences after becoming president. This time, according to CNN's introduction, the "three broadcast networks [ABC, CBS, and NBC] suspect this will be more political than presidential. They are refusing to carry it, period."[42]

It wouldn't have helped Bush much, anyway. Of 19 questions and followups, 15 focused on politics, and six of those focused on Ross Perot. UPI's Helen Thomas, for example, used her presidential access as a way to discover more about the elusive billionaire: "Mr. President... since you've known Mr. Perot for so long, is he an insider, an outsider? Is he a man of principles...?"[43] Even in the East Room, Bush couldn't escape Perot's shadow.

Shortly after that, the president agreed to dip a first toe into the talk show waters, while insisting on a presidential format. On July 1, Bush appeared for 90 minutes in the White House Rose Garden with *CBS This Morning* hosts Harry Smith and Paula Zahn, along with 125 citizens plucked from a White House tour line. It was certainly more successful than the press conference: the questions from audience members were mostly straightforward questions about policy, rather than politics. They were also mostly about the president himself, not Ross Perot.

Questions from the hosts, however, were more pointed. At one point, Bush complained that "it's the correspondents that have [questions about] the controversy about Iraq or the polls or what I want to say about Ross Perot, when the American people want to know what I'm doing about the problems."[44]

Journalists noticed the same thing but interpreted it differently. Audience questions were "gentle and polite,"[45] "rarely confrontational,"[46] and "respectfully asked."[47] It is, wrote Richard Berke in the *New York Times,* "no wonder that... Mr. Bush and Gov. Bill Clinton — encouraged by Ross Perot's initial success in such formats — often bypass national reporters, leaving their jobs to ordinary citizens.... Most are too timid to ask pointed questions and often let candidates off the hook by not following up."[48]

The first round of talk shows made it clear that reporters and voters had different agendas. As Berke noted, "Reporters dwell on the process, asking about polls, tactical strategy and, of course, the story of the day.... An overwhelming number of people ask candidates how they would solve problems that affect the questioner."[49]

Implicit in the ordinary citizens' choice of questions were two criticisms of traditional interview methods. First, the public may genuinely *prefer* that candidates be questioned about their policies. In their choice of questions, voters were signaling reporters what interested them and what didn't. For reporters still clinging to the notion that they are the public's surrogates, the public's starkly different notions of what they wanted to ask the candidates should have been revealing.

Second, citizens may have been asking about substance because they hadn't learned enough about what the candidates stood for to cast an informed vote. The media coverage, focused on the polls, the horse race, and Clinton's character, hadn't offered them that information in a clear and understandable fashion.

The agenda of reporters' questions, as described by Berke and others, mirrors what we found about the agenda of news reports: while issues were addressed and candidate biographies were probed, nearly all stories were contextually framed by the campaign horse race, and the details and implications of the candidates' programs were ignored. The essentials of a candidate's policies were only indirectly passed along to audiences, after they had been plumbed for their potential political consequences, which are the main focus of most news reports.

Even at the end of the campaign, voters were still frustrated by the lack of clear information about the candidates in the press. "I am angry," one voter wrote to the *Washington Post*'s ombudsman. "You are not giving me enough information to make up my mind.... I want my vote to be an honest vote." "It's not a question of whose side you're on," said another. "We want to make a decision based on all the facts. Papers are controlling our decisions by not giving us enough information."

A third reader complained that, "Journalism is a noble profession, but all the journalists seem to have the same slant on anything.... You don't tell us what we want to hear; you have to go out and search."[50] The problem was, as Michael Kinsley put it, "the pros are obsessed with the process while the amateurs are obsessed with substance."[51] In the summer and fall of 1992, the amateurs were rebelling against the pros.

The candidates understandably gravitated toward talk shows as a method of conveying their messages to the public in as undiluted a fashion as possible. Citizens liked the talk shows because they provided an opportunity for the candidates to answer *their* questions and speak to *their* interests.

While traditional news routinely focused on a candidate's warts, talk show viewers got a more complete view of each individual.

Journalists were divided in their reaction. Many applauded the new format as an appropriate complement to their day-to-day coverage, while some blamed talk shows for luring the candidates away from more adversarial interviews. "Call-in and talk shows are interesting and sometimes helpful," wrote CBS's Dan Rather in a October 29 *Washington Post* op-ed, "but they simply aren't enough to offer an informed electorate."

> Like our fellow citizens, we journalists are people who question. We people simply have more time to prepare questions, more practice and more experience asking them — at least, we have more experience asking those questions that need to be asked even when other people may be uncomfortable asking them. And as journalists, we people can analyze the answers we get — and we can measure those answers against the facts.[52]

The frequency of candidates' talk show appearances subsided during July and August, displaced on television by the national nominating conventions, but the pace resumed in the fall. From September 1 through November 2, the candidates appeared on 34 nationally televised interview programs (most individually, but some jointly) in venues ranging from *Larry King Live* to *Donahue*, with a total airtime of 16 hours 43 minutes (*sans* commercials).[53]

We analyzed the content of every exchange in these shows throughout the general election. We measured the talk shows' interviews with the candidates against the same standards as traditional news shows in order to establish a bottom line: were talk show more or less substantive than traditional news, and were they more or less balanced in their portrayals of the candidates?

THE BOTTOM LINE

How did the talk shows measure up against traditional journalistic venues such as Dan Rather's *CBS Evening News*? Our content analysis found that TV talk shows focused more consistently on the issues than did any of the traditional media outlets. As a matter of fact, the *CBS Evening News* finished at the bottom of the list.

As we noted in Chapter 3, the national news organizations we studied spent about two-fifths of their time focused on matters of substance. Using the same criteria, we found that nearly three-fourths (74%) of the talk show segments focused on policy issues or candidate qualifications. This "seriousness" rate was nearly twice as high as that of the national news media's traditional formats.

Talk shows look even better when compared solely against their broadcast news competitors. (See Figure 8-1.) The traditional flagships of broadcast journalism — the network evening news programs — offered their viewers substantive discussions just under 30% of the time. Thanks to its unique resource of major foundation funding, CNN's *PrimeNews* provided much more substance. But *PrimeNews* was still a laggard when compared to the talk shows — 5.6 hours of substance, compared with 12.3 hours on the talk shows.

Only the *MacNeil-Lehrer NewsHour* (12 hours of substance, just under half of its 25 hours of campaign-related news) rivaled the talk shows in the amount of airtime devoted to campaign substance. The "big three" network evening news shows, which offered nearly 24 hours of campaign coverage, aired only 7 hours' worth of substantive material.

Many of the talk shows, of course, were produced by the network news organizations themselves. The data illustrate how the networks' morning talk shows and their evening newscasts provided different views of the campaign to different audiences. The traditional evening newscasts tended to focus on the polls, the horse race, and non-substantive controversies such as Clinton's draft record, Bush's negative commercials, Perot's alleged paranoia, etc.

Lengthy conversations with the candidates about policy issues appeared in the morning, during programs such as *Today, Good Morning America,* and *CBS This Morning,* and in occasional prime time shows like *20/20* and *Prime Time Live.* The latter shows, with their longer formats, had an opportunity to reveal more of the candidates to their viewers, while the evening news clung to its role of campaign arbiter.

The talk shows displayed the candidates for voters; the evening news offered analysis and discussion of the candidates, but kept the principals mostly off-screen. During the fall campaign, as they had in the spring, network reporters consumed 71% of the broadcast airtime, with the remainder split among the candidates, the voters, policy experts, political strategists, etc. George Bush received a total of less than 66 minutes, speaking time on three network evening newscasts (just over 26 minutes on NBC, just under 21 minutes on ABC, and an even 18 minutes on CBS). Bill Clinton was given 55 minutes of speaking time, while Ross Perot was heard from for just 23 minutes — the standard length of a network situation comedy, minus the commercials.

The complaints about short sound bites after the primaries had prompted the *CBS Evening News* to institute a new policy in July: "No more of those cute eight-second sound bites," decreed executive producer Erik Sorenson. During the summer, CBS established a minimum 30-second threshold for sound bites.[54]

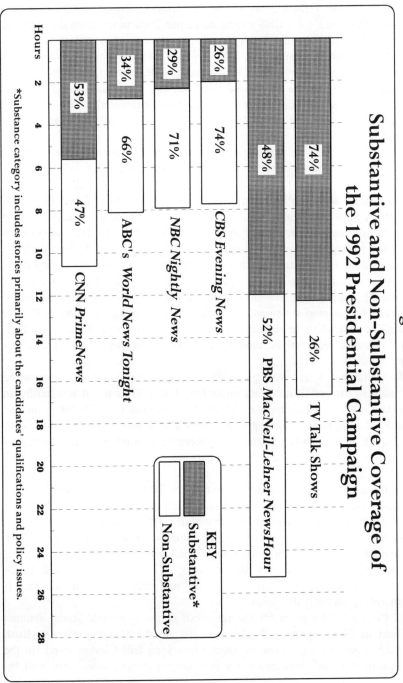

Figure 8-1

Substantive and Non-Substantive Coverage of
the 1992 Presidential Campaign

*Substance category includes stories primarily about the candidates' qualifications and policy issues.

This midstream reform generated an unintended consequence: rather than trimming their own role, CBS's field correspondents more often dropped the candidates' words entirely from the story. Rather than broadcast a 30-second clip, the correspondent would instead summarize the candidate's remarks and then quote others — campaign aides, voters, experts — anybody not covered by the 30-second rule. By fall, Sorenson scaled back his edict to a 20-second minimum, with exceptions permitted. "We said we'd probably adjust it after the Republican Convention and we did," he explained.[55]

To be sure, CBS's intentions were good — the producers were trying to change the procedures of news reporting in order to better inform voters. But what Adatto found to be routine in 1968 (when 63% of all quotes were longer than 30 seconds)[56] proved to be impossible in 1992. Fewer than 10% of CBS's sound bites during the general election exceeded 20 seconds, and only 1% exceeded 30 seconds. (To be fair, ABC, CNN, and NBC never even attempted to lengthen their sound bites, or at least never said so publicly.)

Thus, journalists on the flagship evening newscasts were either unwilling or unable to give up their role as campaign interpreters. Two-minute stories that use 30-second clips are heavily dependent on reporting what the candidates are saying, and reporters are reduced to narrating the scene. Briefer bites allow journalists to abandon the candidate's context and substitute their own. Network reporters seemed were loathe to give up that role in Campaign '92.

On September 8, for example, CBS correspondent Mark Phillips wanted to show how the candidates were mimicking Harry Truman. It was hardly an important story, but Phillips got almost three minutes to make his point. In his story, Clinton and Bush were represented by a pair of two-second sound bites (each 18 seconds shorter than Sorenson's publicly proclaimed new minimum):

MARK PHILLIPS: They are arguing about Harry Truman constantly.
GOVERNOR CLINTON: I will do what Harry Truman did —
PRESIDENT BUSH: I am going to do what Harry Truman did —
MARK PHILLIPS: And what would Harry Truman say today about his reborn popularity? Ask the man who wrote the book:
DAVID MCCULLOUGH (TRUMAN BIOGRAPHER): [Truman] never tried to be anything but Harry Truman. And anyone who tries to imitate him is therefore missing the point.
MARK PHILLIPS: The point for George Bush seems to be that Harry Truman won in 1948, against all odds and despite the fact that George Bush voted against him.... And no matter how long Bill Clinton stands in the rain in Truman's hometown, the comparison doesn't work very well for

him, either. In fact, earlier in the campaign, he preferred the Kennedy image, even digging out an old snapshot of a meeting he'd had once with JFK.... Here are two candidates reaching for stature out of the past, perhaps because they feel the lack of it in the present.[57]

Phillips could not have created his essay using 20- or 30-second sound bites. Neither can campaign trail correspondents do much besides report on their candidate's speech-of-the-day if they are forced by producers to use only lengthy sound bites. While the networks occasionally used lengthier excerpts in straightforward reports about the candidates (we clocked an 82-second Bush sound bite on NBC on September 29), most of the time the spotlight stayed on the reporters themselves.

A policy of lengthy sound bites, strictly implemented, would have shifted the balance of power back to where it stood in 1968, when candidates were the centerpieces of campaign news. Short sound bites are a mechanism that allow the reporters, not the candidates, to have the final say. As illustrated by Mark Phillips's piece, reporters don't construct too many positive stories with those cute eight-second sound bites.

On talk shows, the situation was radically different. The candidates were allowed to speak until they were finished answering the questions, and viewers heard the entire answer — not just the meager hors d'oeuvres dished out by network reporters. Toward the end of October, for example, an Atlanta woman called *Larry King* to ask Bill Clinton about welfare reform:

LARRY KING: Okay, the caller is from Atlanta. Hello?

CALLER: Good evening, Larry. Governor Clinton, good evening. Glad to see you in my home state of Kentucky. I have a question on how you plan on reforming the welfare system so that it's no longer a lifestyle for some people but just a helping hand so they can get on their own two feet. And how do you feel about the way New Jersey has reformed their welfare system?

GOV. BILL CLINTON: Thank you. Let me say, first of all, I have been working on this issue since about 1980. If you look at the people on welfare, about half the people on welfare really do view it as a second chance. They're on welfare for a while because they're down on their luck and then they get right off. But about half the people stay longer. And about 25% of the people stay for years and years and years. They are, by and large, young women and little children with no education. And so what I think we should do is to make the welfare system a second chance, not a way of life, and here's how I would do it.

First, I would fully implement the law I helped to write that was signed late in 1988 but has never been implemented in America. We would invest in people on welfare and their education and their training. We would support their children through medical coverage and child care, and then we would require them to take jobs. Then, I would go one step further than that. I would say that once you educate somebody, once you support their kids, if they can't get a job in the private sector after a certain amount of time, then they ought to have to do community service work to keep drawing an income from the government. You should promote work and independence.

And there's a lot of community service work to be done. We need workers in child care centers, for example. We need people working with the homeless. We need people doing work to help folks stay in their homes, if they want to stay out of nursing homes — persons with disabilities, persons who are older. There is all kinds of people work that needs to be done that we could use folks on public assistance to do until they can move into private sector employment. So that's what I think we ought to do.

The New Jersey experiment — I want to see how it comes out. I can say that we've tried a lot of these experiments. In Wisconsin, for example, they tried lowering the welfare benefits of people if their kids dropped out of schools. It seems to have made no difference. In New Jersey, they want to reward people who don't have extra children and penalize people who do and see if it makes any difference. I think the states ought to be free to experiment. But if you want to really change it, what you've got to do is empower people on welfare to go to work without hurting their children. That is, train them and take care of the kids through health care, and then require them to do it. Make work the rule at the end of the rainbow for welfare. That is the answer to this issue.[58]

Clinton's answer took 2 minutes 17 seconds to deliver, and he was talking fast. Only once during the general election did Clinton receive more than a minute on the evening news, when he was interviewed by Tom Brokaw on November 2. In no news story was a Clinton comment allowed to run anywhere close to a minute. If ABC, CBS, or NBC had given Clinton (or Bush, or Perot) nearly two and a half minutes of uninterrupted speaking time on a single issue, it would have been exceptional. On programs such as *Larry King Live*, it was the rule.

It was also not unusual for Clinton to use his uninterrupted two-plus minutes to speak about a policy issue. We examined the stated evaluations about each candidate on the talk shows with those on the regular news. Analyzing the shows comment by comment, we found talk show discussions to be consistently more focused on substantive policy issues than on other aspects of the campaign.

As Table 8-1 shows, fewer than one-fourth (24%) of the evaluations reported in the traditional news media focused on the candidates' issue proposals (13%) or records (11%). Substantially more attention (41%) was paid to their poll standings, prospects for election, or general viability in the campaign horse race. Talk shows reversed this order, spending over twice as much time on each candidate's issues and record (42%) as on his status in the horse race (19%).

We did not find that coverage of the candidates' issue proposals, records, and philosophies was more extensive, detailed, or contextually relevant on talk shows than on traditional news shows. In fact, the percentages are about the same: 72% of traditional news mentions of issues were brief, as were 75% of the references on talk shows; 78% of traditional news coverage of issues lacked specific details, as did 84% of the talk show coverage; and 64% of traditional news mentions and 68% of talk show mentions lacked contextual references to help make the issues more understandable.

Indeed, by slight margins the issue discussions in news programs tended to offer more information than the discussions on talk shows (although talk shows offered more linkage between problems and a candidate's programs to solve them). As we noted in Chapter 4, the candidates are far more detailed and extensive in their treatment of the issues when they completely control the event, as with their campaign speeches.

Talk shows, evidently, share many of TV's imperatives for entertaining and lively — and brief — segments. But "brief" on the evening news meant two-minute stories, in which candidates received an average of 8½ seconds each (barely a second more than they received during the primaries). Talk show segments were equally brief — about two or three minutes apiece — but the candidates were featured nearly the entire time. Neither format offered too much depth, but the candidate-oriented focus of talk shows meant that viewers were hearing more of the candidates' describing their own programs.

Talk shows are a unique category, a hybrid of "mediated" and "direct" communication between the candidates and the audience. The evening news offers a heavily mediated campaign, in which news organizations interpose themselves between the candidates and the public, providing the latter with a distilled version of events. The candidates' TV commercials, on the other hand, offer direct communication from the candidates, since the public sees the ads exactly as produced by the campaigns.

On talk shows, the candidates and their campaigns do not control the event, although some rules can be arranged in advance — President Bush, for example, insisted that his interviews on *Good Morning America* focus strictly on policy issues.[59] But the candidate cannot prevent the hosts and

Table 8-1

Focus of Candidate Discussion

Traditional Media vs. TV Talk Shows

By Topic	Traditional News Media	TV Talk Shows
Issue Stances	13%	19%
Records	11	23
Candidate Character	5	4
Campaign Conduct	12	20
Campaign Ability	5	3
Strength in Polls	14	4
Prospects for Election	5	5
General Viability	22	10
General Assessments	13	12
Total	100%	100%

By Issue

	Traditional News Media	TV Talk Shows
Foreign Policy	3%	7%
Economic Policy	11	19
Domestic Policy	7	13
Non-Issue	79	61
Total	100%	100%

Traditional news media: Based on content analysis of ABC, CBS, CNN, NBC, the *New York Times*, *Washington Post*, and *Wall Street Journal*, September 7 - November 3, 1992.
TV talk shows: Based on content analysis of 34 candidate interviews on nationally televised talk shows, September 6 - November 2, 1992.

citizen questioners from asking aggressive or hostile questions, and all three candidates were put on the spot in 1992.

Unlike the evening news, however, where reporters could tweak the candidates *in absentia*, on the talk shows the candidates could respond — often live and unedited. The candidates don't control the questions, but they do control their answers; no matter how tough the question, candidates could be assured that voters would see and hear their response. On traditional television news, reporters always had the last word. On the talk shows, the candidates had greater leeway to express their own messages.

Because they did the most talking, the tone of the TV talk shows was established by the candidates. Given the ubiquitous hand-wringing about the "negativity" of their campaign conduct, we were surprised to discover that the candidates did not stress the negative aspects of their opponents nearly as much; instead they emphasized their own positive qualities.

President Bush used his TV appearances to praise himself more than criticizing his two opponents: 62% of his comments were positive, vs. 38% negative. Governor Clinton was similarly expansive, with 56% positive remarks and 44% criticisms of others. Ross Perot (70% positive) ran a frontrunner's strategy, virtually ignoring his two rivals. Overall, the three candidates offered a much more positive (61%) than negative (39%) campaign on the talk shows.

Again, this contrasts sharply with the more traditional television news portrayals of the campaign. The three evening newscasts mostly selected the negative sound bites that the candidates uttered on the campaign trail. On the evening news, Bush was shown saying something negative about one or both of his rivals 63% of the time. Similarly, 71% of Clinton's evaluative sound bites were negative as were 70% of Perot's.

Thus, evidence from the talk shows indicates that the candidates actually comported themselves much better than their abbreviated nightly news appearances suggested. Our examination of their actual speeches also confirms this. While TV news showed the candidates criticizing each other 72% of the time, on the campaign trail they balanced their positive and negative remarks (a collective 46% positive vs. 54% negative). Thus, when TV news depicted the candidates, their brief appearances disproportionately focused on their negative remarks. The talk shows gave citizens a view of the campaign that more closely resembled the reality of the campaign trail.

This does not mean that talk shows were an oasis for candidates. The journalists who thought the talk shows' appeal was their guarantee of a "friendly if not downright sycophantic reception"[60] must not have been regular viewers. Both the hosts and callers frequently challenged the candidates, voicing negative evaluations 77% of the time.[61] The positive cast of the talk shows was caused not by friendly callers or sycophantic hosts, but by the fact that the candidates themselves were given time to discuss their positive attributes. Their defense of their own beliefs and behavior, which were less likely to be heard on TV news, dominated the talk shows.

On October 28, for example, Bill Clinton appeared on the *Today* show, where he was confronted on the draft issue by an angry caller from New Jersey. In the exchange, which lasted nearly five minutes, Clinton was frequently criticized but always responded by stating his own position forcefully:

KATIE COURIC: Governor, on the line now is Sue from Hillside, New Jersey. Good morning, Sue.

SUE FROM HILLSIDE: Good morning.

GOV. BILL CLINTON: Good morning, Sue.

KATIE COURIC: What's your question?

SUE FROM HILLSIDE: My question deals with the character issue. I'm about 46 years old and had my first child as a single parent because my husband at the time was serving in Vietnam. If you weren't affluent, or didn't have a college background when you came out of school, you were drafted into the army and had to do your service. I used to get letters from overseas about draft dodgers. I want to know how you can justify asking me or anybody else to vote for you, because when the time came that our country needed someone to support it, it was easier for you not to support it.

GOV. BILL CLINTON: Well, you know the facts, Sue. I didn't agree with the Vietnam war, and I didn't want to go. I did not dodge the draft in the sense of violating the law —

SUE FROM HILLSIDE [INTERRUPTING]: Excuse me, my husband did not agree with it either —

GOV. BILL CLINTON [INTERRUPTING]: Well, I'm sorry.

SUE FROM HILLSIDE: — but because he was called, he had to go. In your instance, you were unable, you were able to not go.

GOV. BILL CLINTON: That's right, I joined an ROTC program, and I didn't feel right about having the deferment, either, so I gave up the deferment. I went back into the draft, and I was classified 1A again. Then the lottery came in, and I got a high number. For months I still didn't know if I'd be called, but ultimately I was never called. I would have gone if I had been called, even though I didn't believe in it. I do think if we have a draft again there shouldn't be so many deferments for people who have educational options.

But, I would remind you, if that's your criteria, Vice President Quayle was in the National Guard; Secretary of Defense Cheney had deferments; most of President Bush's major spokespersons did not go —

SUE FROM HILLSIDE [INTERRUPTING]: That's not my, my criteria is not that. My criteria is that they were unable to be in the position you were, and whether they had deferments —

GOV. BILL CLINTON [INTERRUPTING]: No, they were all in the same position in my, they all had deferments.

SUE FROM HILLSIDE: Yes.

GOV. BILL CLINTON: And I gave up my deferment and got back in the draft because I felt bad about it, too.

KATIE COURIC: But didn't you give up your deferment —

SUE FROM HILLSIDE [INTERRUPTING]: I, I, did not, from the facts that are in, and the changes in, your position, what you're telling me right now is different than what's been in the papers, and I just disagree —

GOV. BILL CLINTON [INTERRUPTING]: No, no, it's been in the paper. It's been in the papers.

SUE FROM HILLSIDE: I have a problem with you demonstrating against the country while the country's at war. I mean, I'm a middle-class person who works hard, and I found that very resentful at the time.

GOV. BILL CLINTON: Well, let me say, you're entitled to your opinion, and I respect it. I demonstrated because I didn't agree with the policy, and because I was trying to keep people like your husband alive, and because I thought that the war was wrong. I still believe that.

And I would just point out, I'll say what I said again at the beginning of the program, 24 retired admirals and generals, many of whom were Vietnam veterans, have supported my campaign. The man who was the Chairman of the Joint Chiefs of Staff under Presidents Reagan and Bush, Admiral Crowe, has endorsed me. The deputy commander-in-chief of Operation Desert Storm, and most important to me, thousands of Vietnam veterans all over this country have come to my rallies, expressed support, written me letters — three of them have even sent me their battle ribbons because they believe it's time to put that war behind us, and they think it was either a mistake, or it ought not to be the issue, and they're concerned about the future.

If you disagree, I certainly respect your position, but it seems to me the conversation we've just had only proves that we should have put that war behind us long ago. If we keep dealing with what happened 25 years ago, we're never going to be able to face the future. But I have to tell you, I still believe the war was a mistake, and I can't help the way I felt then, and even now I can't say that I think I was wrong, then. I agree that there were too many deferments for educational reasons. I had one because I didn't want to be drafted, but I gave it up. I couldn't help it that I got #311 in the lottery — if I'd have gotten #3 or #100, I would have been called, and I would have gone.

KATIE COURIC: But didn't you give it up to maintain your political viability, Gov. Clinton?

GOV. BILL CLINTON: No. No, I gave it up because I didn't think it was the right thing to do. I entered the ROTC because I didn't want to go to Vietnam, because I didn't agree with it, and I gave the ROTC deferment up because I didn't feel good about it, and I wanted to go back in the draft, and that's exactly what I did. The records reflect that I had a 1A classification when the lottery came in, and I got a high number. I couldn't have known I was going to get a high number. And, uh, even for months after that I thought I might be called — the number was just never called. I had no way of knowing President Nixon was going to de-escalate the war. The facts are clear on that.

But I didn't, uh, the lady is right: I was opposed the war, I didn't agree with it, and I've said so. I believe that if more people had taken that view, fewer Americans would have died, we would have gotten out earlier, and it would not have changed the course of events in Vietnam that subsequently occurred.[62]

As if Sue wasn't tough enough for the governor, the next caller, Larry from Indianapolis, asked Clinton about his taped phone conversations with Gennifer Flowers (Larry: "I think the issue of truth is very important in this campaign"), and the Democratic nominee was forced to defend himself again.[63]

The fact that the callers were tough does not imply that Clinton would have been better advised to sleep in that Wednesday morning. Indeed, his appearance on *Today* was an effective opportunity for him to confront those questions and answer them, without having his answers edited or otherwise altered by reporters. And, unlike the nightly news, there were occasional softballs from callers, such as this earlier exchange from the same *Today* program:

KATIE COURIC: We're going to go to another call now, to Suzanne in Boston. Suzanne, good morning.

SUZANNE: Hi.

COURIC: Hi. What's your question for Gov. Clinton?

SUZANNE: My question is brief, but I also first want to be sure to say that, although Katie and Bryant like to point out just the opposite, support for Mr. Clinton is *not* soft. People around this country are absolutely wild, crazy and happy about —

COURIC: What's your question?

SUZANNE: My question is that —
COURIC [INTERRUPTING]: And are you a relative? [CLINTON LAUGHS]
SUZANNE: [LAUGHING] No, I'm not at all.[64]

President Bush, too, received his share of both friendly and not-so-friendly phone calls. One woman called *Larry King* to say it was "such an honor to be able to speak to you. I've been an admirer of yours for years." Bush smiled and thanked her. A few minutes later, however, a caller aggressively challenged the president:

Mr. Bush, I think you are out of touch. I am not happy with you. For two years, you did not recognize that people were hurting out here and we were in a recession. I feel like you have not come clean on Iran/contra, and I'm tired of your party and you preaching to us about family values.

Listening to the tirade, Bush quipped, "I'll put you down as 'doubtful,' fella." At King's urging, he then responded to the substance of the accusations.[65]

Nor were the hosts cowed by their political guests. Paula Zahn and Harry Smith, co-hosts of *CBS This Morning*, began their last pre-election interview with President Bush by repeatedly challenging his assertions about the state of the national economy:

PAULA ZAHN: We want to welcome President Bush to our broadcast again. Welcome. Thanks for being with us.
PRESIDENT BUSH: Glad to be back.
PAULA ZAHN: I want to start off with a question about the economy. We have just seen the growth rate come through at 2.7 percent for the third quarter. A lot of economists are suggesting that that number is artificially high, because Americans, in fact, have had to reach deeper into their savings to buy household goods, and that also there were increased military expenditures. Is that correct?
PRESIDENT GEORGE BUSH: I was — I don't know all the technical details — but I was wondering if an economist who has been wrong on the prediction could find some reason to take good news and make it into bad, and obviously you've found some. We've been growing at 2.7 percent. We've grown for six quarters, and yet the opposition in this campaign has tried to convince this country we're in a deep recession. A lot of people are hurting, but —
PAULA ZAHN [INTERRUPTING]: But what they've done is taken —
PRESIDENT GEORGE BUSH [CONTINUING]: — but we're growing, and that is the key factor, and we don't want to go back and set it back by outrageous policies.

PAULA ZAHN: But they're using government statistics: factory orders for
durable goods, down for the third straight month — that's the longest
sustained drop we've seen over an 18-month period. Consumer confidence is down for four months in a row. Are you saying that those
numbers are wrong?

PRESIDENT GEORGE BUSH: Unemployment claims are down, on average.
Productivity is up. I mean, you can find the negative statistics, and,
obviously, that's what the opposition has tried to do. The only way they
can win is convince everybody — Clinton and Gore — that the country's
in a recession. And it isn't, it is growing, and that came out as great
news, and then you had everybody scrounging around — including the
economists who are wrong now, and who've been wrong in the past —
trying to explain it away. I don't know about these —

HARRY SMITH [INTERRUPTING]:   But you have to admit it is the slowest recovery
since the Great Depression.

PRESIDENT GEORGE BUSH: But it is *not* in a depression and it's not in a
recession, and it's not negative growth like we had in previous times. In
1981 and '82 we had deep negative growth. So, I believe you ought to
just put it in perspective and, look, I'm not saying it's perfect. I'm
saying we have the best agenda out there to make it better. But it is
growing, and it was very good news for this country, who's been ham-
mered by everything being bad.

PAULA ZAHN: So, are you saying then, that your economic policies for your
first four years in office have worked, and you will stay the course if
you're re-elected?

PRESIDENT GEORGE BUSH: I am going to certainly improve things if I'm re-
elected, and I'm saying that we have been caught up in a global
slowdown. Do you know, Paula, that this economy is doing better than
Japan? It is doing better than Germany and the rest of Europe. It is
doing better than Canada. And Governor Clinton would have you
believe the whole thing is all my fault. It isn't. What I'm saying is,
"We're growing. Please don't let the fear-mongers tell you we're not,"
and that the way to get out of it is to do my Agenda for American
Renewal.

PAULA ZAHN: What has been your fault? What do you claim responsibility
for in terms of the economy?

PRESIDENT GEORGE BUSH: Well, I told you I made a mistake on taxes, but I
don't know how you assign blame. I'll take my share of the blame, for
anything — captain of the ship does not assign blame to somebody else.
But we're, we had been in a global recession. Now we're in a global
slowdown. Countries are growing — we've been growing for six straight
quarters, but 92% of the news — and you've managed to find some
negative statistics about growth —

PAULA ZAHN [INTERRUPTING]: These are government statistics!

PRESIDENT GEORGE BUSH: I know it, but I'm just saying, you emphasize the negative all the time. I mean, the country emphasized the positive when they heard we were growing at 2.7%. That is good news. That is very good. It puts the lie to the recession.

HARRY SMITH: But if I'm sitting at home right now, and I know that over the last five years wages and benefits have been so so slow to grow, and I am having more trouble buying what I could have bought five or ten years ago, and I'm listening to you and I'm saying, "I don't feel it. I don't feel it where I am."

PRESIDENT GEORGE BUSH: Well, then, you've got to look at what kind of program it's going to take to make the growth more robust. And the last thing you need is a program that's going to tax, and then take the money and do what Gov. Clinton says is "invest," have government "invest." Government never creates any meaningful jobs — it's the private sector. And that's why my program of stimulating small business through a series of tax matters that I've tried to get through the gridlocked Congress, and I will get through the new Congress, is the answer.[66]

In this format, Bush — aggressively questioned by the hosts — had an opportunity to respond to each charge. He made his case that the economic slowdown was global, and thus outside of his control; that the Democrats were portraying the economy as far weaker than the statistics indicated; and that he had a program to boost the recovery.

Smith and Zahn repeatedly challenged the president, citing statistics that (they argued) showed that the recovery was weaker than normal and that wages and benefits were virtually stagnant. They also noted that some economists credited the economic growth statistics that Bush cited as an artifact of one-time factors. The segment was hardly a "softball" for Bush, but neither was it as negative as a typical evening news story. In spite of the tough questioning by the hosts, it was Bush's responses — not the questions — that dominated the discussion.

As an alternative to traditional news, the talk shows had their weaknesses. On the evening news, the campaign was a steady presence throughout the fall. In contrast, the candidates' talk show appearances were episodic — Bush and Clinton were absent from morning TV during September, but during the final week of the campaign, one or the other popped up every single morning.

Overall, the talk shows offered a balanced view of the major party nominees, but individual programs were obviously dominated by the sole candidate who appeared. Only those few shows that offered simultaneous interviews — Talking with David Frost, PrimeTime Live, and the Brokaw Report — could offer programs that were individually balanced. Of course, if undecided viewers wanted to balance their view of the campaign, there was no shortage of programs — particularly in the last week — featuring one or another of the candidates giving their basic pitch.

The strength of the talk shows was their ability to supplement the horse race view of the campaign routinely portrayed on the evening news and in the newspapers. Seldom did a voter ask a question about polls, strategy, or tactics. The focus of most talk show exchanges remained squarely on policy issues.

What the talk shows contributed was the candidates' unfiltered view of the campaign, and that appears to have been a success at informing voters. According to research conducted at the University of North Carolina, exposure to the New Media (primarily talk shows), accounted for a far greater increase in public knowledge about the candidates' positions on policy issues than did either print media or conventional TV news.[67]

The campaign, as seen on the evening news, was highly negative. On the talk shows, most of the discussions were weighted in a positive direction. The candidates stressed their positive attributes for audiences who had seldom been exposed to the candidates' better qualities. Thus, Thomas Patterson concluded that

> the new media, in combination with the debates and the return of Ross Perot, "saved" the 1992 campaign. Until these developments, voter disillusionment was higher even than it had been at the same stage in 1988. The new media helped to energize the campaign, give the public a sense of greater participation, and improve people's opinions of the candidates.[68]

Many reporters also approved of the talk shows. A Times Mirror poll found that more than two-thirds of journalists (68%) thought the talk shows were having a positive effect on the campaign.[69] "There's not a program I've watched where I've not learned something new about the candidates," NBC's Tim Russert told the *Washington Post*. "It exposes people who wouldn't normally be exposed to politics. It's healthy as hell for the media and the political process."[70]

Although most journalists agreed with Russert and praised the talk shows as a positive "supplement" to their traditional campaign coverage, many also adopted a defensive posture. If citizens could capably question the candidates, some critics wondered, what role remained for traditional journalists?

Reporters responded by stressing their "watchdog" role — because they had researched the issues, studied the candidates' records, traveled extensively with them, and had more experience quizzing politicians, they were the best-equipped questioners the public could hope for. ABC's Sam Donaldson complained, "*Larry King* is not designed to really interrogate someone, but to schmooze with them."[71] During an interview, reporters can assess the completeness, consistency, and veracity of candidates' answers, and ask follow-ups if needed. "I don't think Larry King evaluates the truth or falsity of what candidates say," noted the Barone Center's Ellen Hume.[72]

But the difference between the establishment media position and the New Media on this score was not that great. As far as we know, nobody argued that talk shows should displace the Old Media as the primary source of campaign news for voters. Similarly, reporters generally applauded the talk shows' success at revealing the candidates' personal side to voters.

The real conflict was over how far journalism, in pursuing its "watchdog" role, had drifted from its original mission. After all, the news media are supposed to serve as the public's surrogate eyes and ears. When the watchdog adopts a separate agenda, it is no longer guarding the public's interests. As Bill Clinton commented shortly after the election,

> I think the watchdog function is fine. But it's often carried to extremes in a search for headlines. For instance, the missing pages from my State Department file — here was a deal where *Newsweek* bit on a rumor. So you had these serious reporters who just wanted to grill me about that — when the economy is in the tubes, when 100,000 people a month are losing their health insurance.... And I'm supposed to take these people seriously as our sole intermediaries to the voters of this country? Sure, they should do their watchdog function, but anyone who lets himself be interpreted to the American people through these intermediaries alone is nuts.[73]

The traditional journalists were partly correct — they have a role to play as watchdogs, and they need to maintain a vigilant eye on government institutions, business leaders, politicians, and other powerful interests in society. But the politicians and the public were also correct in replying that the growing excesses and irresponsibility of journalists poses a risk to their ability to carry out its basic mission. "Campaign reporters had fallen into a trap, as beat reporters often do, of resembling the insiders more than their own readers and projecting their interests and those of the insiders onto their audience," concluded journalism professor Philip Meyer.[74]

Consumers of traditional news were being exposed to less of the candidates' own words, and more of the reporters' commentary. Post-'88 reforms merely accelerated this trend and validated it in the minds of reporters. Meanwhile, voters were watching and reading news constructed around themes that bore little relationship to their own interests. Adding insult to injury, their own questions — when they finally got a chance to ask them — were derided by reporters as "timid" and overly "gentle."

In researching an article on the campaign coverage, Jeffrey Katz asked a reporter about complaints from voters. "They tell us they want analysis, background, interpretation, and when we do that and it's not entirely in keeping with their view of the world, they say we're biased," the reporter replied. Thanks to her issue research and travels with the candidates, she boasted, "I'm probably one of the best informed voters in America, and yet when I say the slightest thing someone disagrees with, I'm the one who's biased."[75]

Katz then read the reporter's comments to a citizen disenchanted with the media. "That is exactly the extraordinary arrogance of the media today," exclaimed the non-journalist. "Who in God's name cares that this woman feels as though she's well informed?... The press is literally a very small group of voices with a very, very narrow frame of reference."[76]

Talk shows will be too episodic and infrequent to ever provide a useful substitute for conventional news coverage. Unless candidates appear jointly, the conversations are also one-sided, depriving voters of the ability to compare their choices. Nevertheless, the establishment media could have learned a lot from the 1992 talk show experience.

Based on our viewing, talk shows were hardly "amplification chambers for the most estranged of the estranged,"[77] as one disgruntled academic put it — their callers were mainstream citizens who asked mainstream questions about real-life problems. The best hosts echoed that agenda, quizzing candidates about what they would do as president.

At their worst, the talk shows emulated their traditional counterparts — they asked the candidates to explain the polls and the process. "Today's numbers, that we've just gotten," CNN's Frank Sesno informed George Bush on November 1, "among likely voters, show Bill Clinton with 43%, which is up one from yesterday; you with 36%, which is down three from yesterday and Ross Perot at 15%. So, how do you attribute that — has the drive stopped?" The president had to remind Sesno that "you don't live or die by an overnight poll."[78]

Obviously, the polls are interesting and provide journalists as well as candidates with a daily snapshot of where the race is and how voters are (or are not) responding. For the most part, polls ought to be in the background of election news — informing the reporters, but not becoming the focus of their reports. Implicit in the public's embrace of talk shows was their rejection of traditional campaign news, which remained firmly rooted in this horse race perspective. Journalists could do worse than adopting the voters' vocabulary in their questioning of the candidates.

The strength of talk shows was their relative lack of "mediation," a format that allowed voters to obtain a fuller sense of the candidates themselves. In their TV appearances, the three candidates were the primary communicators, most conversations focused on substantive policy matters, and the audiences at home were the primary evaluators of the candidates' performances. As a replacement for traditional news, talk shows had their own weaknesses. But as a supplement to the efforts of traditional news organizations, the American public was well-served in 1992. The best "reform" of 1992 appears to have been the least intentional.

Notes

Opening quote: Jonathan Yardley, "Campaign '92: Can We Talk?" *Washington Post*, October 12, 1992.

1. Kiku Adatto, "Sound Bite Democracy: Network Evening News Coverage, 1968 and 1988." Research Paper R-2, The Joan Shorenstein Barone Center, June 1990, p. 4.

2. Ibid. p. 4.

3. Christopher Daly, "Dukakis Looks Back with Discontent; '88 Nominee Assails Emphasis on 'Sound Bite' in Campaign Coverage," *Washington Post*, November 26, 1990.

4. Ken Bode, "Pull the Plug: We Have the Power to Just Say No, to Abandon Our Photo-Op Addiction," *The Quill*, March 1992.

5. Adatto, "Sound Bite Democracy," pp. 4-6.

6. Ibid., p. 12.

7. Russert, "For '92, the Networks Have to Do Better," *New York Times*, March 4, 1990. Russert really didn't want all staging to cease — he just wanted the candidates to stop posing for their own pictures. NBC's own reporters, however, would continue to choose photogenic sites for their closing remarks ("stand-ups"), even when those sites had little or no relationship to the content of the news story. See Tal Sanit, "Stand and Deliver: The Art of the Pseudo-Stand-Up," *Columbia Journalism Review*, July/August 1992.

8. The Barone Center study reported that sound bites on ABC, CBS, and NBC averaged about nine seconds throughout the primaries, unchanged from 1988. This may reflect measurement differences or the fact that their study period began in February, one month after our starting period. In any case, the point remains the same: The snatches of sound voters heard from the campaign trail stayed extremely brief, "in spite of considerable journalistic attention to the sound bite problem," as project director Marion Just put it. See Marion Just, "Democracy '92," *Politcal Communicaton Report*, February 1993, p. 8.

9. Paul Taylor, "Political Coverage in the 1990s: Teaching the Old News New Tricks," in *The New News v. The Old News: The Press and Politics in the 1990s,*

edited by Suzanne Charlé (New York: A Twentieth Century Fund Paper, 1992), p. 40.

10. William Sposato, "Fox Muscles Its Way Past CBS in Ratings War," Reuters Business Report, April 18, 1995. For the 1994-1995 season, ABC, CBS, and NBC shared 57% of sets in use, an all-time low.

11. James C. Roberts, "The Power of Talk Radio," *American Enterprise*, May/June 1991.

12. Quoted by Joe Klein, "Talk Politics," *New York*, February 27, 1989.

13. Quoted in "Hill Steamed Over Radio's Tea Time: Many in House and Senate Blame Talk Show Host Drive Against Proposed Pay Raise for Turning Public Sentiment Against Plan," *Broadcasting*, February 13, 1989

14. Ibid.

15. David Broder, "The Pay Raise Fiasco: Everybody Lost," *Washington Post*, February 12, 1989.

16. Quoted by Klein, "Talk Politics."

17. Klein, "Talk Politics."

18. CNN's *Larry King Live*, February 20, 1992.

19. CNN's *Larry King Live*, February 20, 1992.

20. The *Los Angeles Times* was the only major newspaper to run the "Perot for President" story, February 22, 1992.

21. *NBC Nightly News*, for example, ran just 3 Perot stories in March, with a total airtime of 4 minutes 15 seconds. *CBS Evening News* ran 2 stories about Perot, totaling 3 minutes 11 seconds. ABC's *World News Tonight* made no mention of Perot's candidacy until April. None of the network newscasts mentioned Perot before March 20, a full month after his King appearance.

22. "Public Opinion and Demographic Report," *American Enterprise* (May/June 1992): 109.

23. According to Paul Taylor, Perot's first hour on *Today* drew a 4.9 Nielson, and his second drew a 5.3. (Each rating point represents 921,000 homes). The typical *Today* rates a 3.8 Nielson. See Paul Taylor, "Teaching the Old News New Tricks," p. 42.

24. David Von Drehle, "Perot Targets Affluent Retirees; Texan Says He Would Seek Volunteers to Give Up Social Security," *Washington Post*, June 12, 1992.

25. Quoted by Sharon Moshavi, "Is Campaign '92 Bypassing Network News?" *Broadcasting*, June 15, 1992.

26. Jonathan Alter, "How Phil Donahue Came to Manage the '92 Campaign," *The Washington Monthly*, June 1992.

27. Michael Kinsley, "Ask a Silly Question," *The New Republic*, July 6, 1992.

28. Steve Daley, "Clinton-Donahue Spat Eclipses Foreign Policy Focus," *Chicago Tribune*, April 2, 1992.

29. *CBS Evening News*, April 1, 1992; and Douglas Jehl, "Clinton Takes A Grilling in New York and Gains an Audience," *Los Angeles Times*, April 2, 1992.

30. Jerry Roberts, "Donahue Fails to Ruffle Jerry Brown's Feathers," *San Francisco Chronicle*, April 3, 1992.

31. *Donahue*, April 6, 1992 [transcript from Federal News Service, Federal Information Systems Corporation].

32. ABC's *World News Tonight*, March 16, 1992.

33.   Barry Golson and Peter Ross Range, "Clinton On TV," *TV Guide*, November 21, 1992.

34.   Howard Kurtz, "The Woman Who Put Clinton on 'Arsenio,'" *Washington Post*, August 10, 1992.

35.   Ibid.

36.   According to Paul Taylor, the Clinton show "drew a 4.5 national rating, well below the 6.4 rating of an NBC News special on guns in the same slot the week before." See "Teaching the Old News New Tricks," p. 43. According to the Nielson figures cited by Taylor, the number who tuned in was approximately 4.1 million households; before the broadcast, the campaign said it had hoped for an audience of 7 million. See A. L. May, "Clinton's 30 minutes of TV Tonight May Be Crucial," *Atlanta Journal and Constitution*, June 12, 1992.

37 .   Gwen Ifill. "For Clinton, Attention Grows, Problems Remain," *New York Times*, June 21, 1992.

38.   Elizabeth Kolbert, "Perot Takes Issue, While Clinton Takes On Issues," *New York Times,* June 12, 1992.

39.   Howard Kurtz, "Canned Candidates; Talk Shows Are Forums for Pat Answers," *Washington Post*, June 12, 1992.

40.   Jonathan Yardley, "Campaign '92: Can We Talk?" *Washington Post*, October 12, 1992.

41.   John Elvin, "Stern Stuff," *Washington Times*, June 12, 1992.

42.   Bernard Shaw, CNN Coverage of the President's News Conference, June 4, 1992.

43.   CNN Coverage of the President's News Conference, June 4, 1992.

44.   Howard Kurtz, "On Television, Candidates Need a Fastball to Hit One Out of the Park," *Washington Post*, July 2, 1992.

45.   Ibid.

46.   Elizabeth Kolbert, "From the Rose Garden, the Bush TV Show," *New York Times*, July 2, 1992.

47.   Douglas Jehl, "President Meets the Public in Talk Show-style Politics," *Los Angeles Times*, July 2, 1992.

48.   Richard L. Berke, "Why Candidates Like Public's Questions," *New York Times*, August 15, 1992.

49.   Ibid.

50.   Joann Byrd, "Fundamental Stuff," *Washington Post*, November 1, 1992.

51.   Michael Kinsley. "Ask a Silly Question." *The New Republic*, July 6, 1992.

52.   Dan Rather, "Don't Write Us Off," *Washington Post*, October 29, 1992.

53.   The study included the following programs: ABC's *Good Morning America*, *PrimeTime Live,* and *20/20*; CBS's *CBS This Morning*; NBC's *Brokaw Report* ("Decision '92: 58 Days"*)*, and *Today*; CNN's *Larry King Live*, *Newsmaker Saturday* and *Newsmaker Sunday*, PBS's *Talking with David Frost*, and the syndicated *Donahue.*

54.   Richard L. Berke, "Presidential Candidates to Get 30-Second Minimum on CBS," *New York Times*, July 3, 1992.

55.   "Shrinking Sound-Bite Policy," *Electronic Media*, September 7, 1992.

56.   Adatto, "Sound Bite Democracy," p. 22

57.   *CBS Evening News*, September 8, 1992.

58. CNN's *Larry King Live*, October 28, 1992.

59. "Candidates Call the Shots; New Strategy: Get Air Time, but Set Terms," *Atlanta Journal and Constitution*, October 3, 1992.

60. Yardley, "Can We Talk?"

61. Of all evaluations by hosts and callers, Bush was rated negatively 76% of the time, and Clinton faced criticism 78% of the time. Perot, in contrast was mostly praised — 64% positive evaluations, vs. 36% negative.

62. NBC's *Today*, October 28, 1992.

63. NBC's *Today*, October 28, 1992. Larry, it turns out, lied to *Today* show producers in order to get to Clinton; he had said his question was about jobs. (Reported by Lois Romano, "The Reliable Source," *Washington Post*, October 29, 1992.)

64. NBC's *Today*, October 28, 1992.

65. CNN's *Larry King Live*, October 7, 1992.

66. *CBS This Morning*, October 29, 1992.

67. Philip Meyer, "The Media Reformation: Giving the Agenda Back to the People," *The Elections of 1992*, ed. Michael Nelson (Washington, D.C.: Congressional Quarterly Press, 1993), p. 91.

68. Patterson, *Out of Order*, p. 170.

69. "The Press and Campaign '92: A Self-Assessment," Times Mirror Center for the People and the Press, supplement to the *Columbia Journalism Review*, March/April 1993.

70. Quoted by Howard Kurtz, "The Talk Show Campaign," *Washington Post*, October 28, 1992.

71. Quoted by Howard Kurtz, "Network Correspondents Test Candidates," *Washington Post*, September 18, 1992.

72. Quoted in "Candidates Call the Shots; New Strategy: Get Air Time, but Set Terms," *Atlanta Journal and Constitution*, October 3, 1992.

73. Golson and Range, "Clinton on TV."

74. Meyer, "The Media Reformation," p. 91.

75. Jeffrey L. Katz, "Tilt?" *Washington Journalism Review*, January/February 1993.

76. Ibid., p. 26.

77. Todd Gitlin, "Larry King is Still No Walter Cronkite," *Newsday*, October 8, 1992.

78. CNN's *Newsmaker Sunday*, November 1, 1992.

Chapter Nine

Putting People First

The trouble lies deeper than the press, and so does the remedy.
— Walter Lippmann, 1922

The news media were not always the ripe target for critics that they are today. To some extent, the current surge of criticism was unavoidable. The media's dizzying and highly visible rise over the past quarter century virtually guaranteed that they would provoke resentment. Further, much of their ascent was fueled by social changes, technological advances, and political events beyond the control of individual newspeople or news organizations. But journalists must share the responsibility for their own responses to these developments.

Like many another new elite, members of the national media were at first ambivalent about their change in status but soon came to embrace it. Their new self-confidence included the growing conviction that this newfound influence should be used for social betterment. Most took it for granted that their prescriptions reflected a posture of disinterested idealism, rather than the self-interested motives they routinely ascribed to other contenders for influence.

Nowhere was this change in attitude more evident than on the campaign trail. Once content with their traditional role as spectators and chroniclers, journalists began to resent candidates who manipulated the media for their own advancement. They retaliated by calling attention to the candidates' stagecraft, hoping public exposure would end the practice. But the 1988 campaign proved the last straw; it provided the impetus for major news organizations to accept the judgment of in-house reformers that journalists should use their power to reform the political process. The great experiment was on.

Armed with the conviction that they were acting on behalf of an abused electorate, the media strode into the center ring of the 1992 presidential campaign. News organizations focused on their own issue priorities, subordinating the candidates' agendas. Journalists threw off the constraints of "objectivity," the better to aid voters by reporting which candidates were right and which were wrong. All this was done in the public's name, and with the best of intentions. The idea was to make campaigns cleaner and more substantive — more user-friendly for voters — by aggressively holding the candidates accountable for their conduct.

The aggressive journalism succeeded at pleasing its practitioners, but it failed to offer voters the substantive campaign they craved. The horse race still enveloped much of the coverage. Substantive policy problems *were* frequently discussed, but the candidates' proposed solutions were not. The candidates' advertising was checked and scrutinized, but the coverage not only remained negative, it became less balanced and more laden with commentary.

George Bush was plagued all year by the networks' insistently gloomy portrayal of the economy, in spite of statistical evidence to the contrary. During the primaries, a media feeding frenzy over Bill Clinton's character crowded out information about his substantive record. Even as journalists congratulated themselves, angry candidates and dissatisfied citizens fled the traditional media and met instead on talk shows — to talk directly to each other about the nation's problems and the candidates' proposed solutions.

Even though the media made a valiant effort to fulfill their pledges of greater scrutiny and substance, the coverage failed to improve because reporters did not change their overarching paradigm of election news. Their routine coverage continued to focus on winning and losing, strategy, tactics, gamesmanship, etc. While news organizations tried to fine tune particular aspects of their coverage, they did not alter their own big picture. And, as 1992 made clear, it was the media's big picture of elections that was — and remains — so at odds with voters.

Campaign journalism still stressed the *inside story* — the backroom wheeling and dealing, the clash of personalities, and the dirty little secrets that get aired along the campaign trial. Reporters failed to question their assumption that the privileged inside story was real, while the speeches, position papers, and other public events were merely a facade. They did demand a greater role in creating the story, and in that they succeeded. Indeed, the tales they told during Campaign '92 were often riveting, if sometimes arcane. But the media's inside story bore little relevance to voters' lives and civic responsibilities.

Few voters are political junkies. Their forays into civic life are not marked by preoccupation with political maneuvering. Instead, they are concerned with the condition and prospects of their own families and communities. Voters' information needs during election years are far different from those of reporters steeped in inside gossip and campaign minutiae. Journalists who focus on the process don't ask the questions, or write the stories that answer the questions, that ordinary citizens most frequently ask.

At the end of the 1992 campaign, on *Larry King Live*, a caller told Bill Clinton that his small trucking business "can't get any help from the banks because they don't want anything to do with the trucking industry. We would like to be able to expand and grow. How can we look for any help in your administration?"[1] The businessman had a practical question about how Clinton's election would affect his own interests. Clinton gave him an answer. Reporters hadn't.

THE MEDIA: FOCUS ON THE HOME FRONT

Citizens and their elected leaders have a communications problem, but the media are hurting, not helping, the situation. After 1988, voters *were* dissatisfied with the media and the campaign. The Barone Center was on target when it charged that "the public is losing its grip on the democratic process. Elections, the litmus tests of democracy, are becoming mud-wrestling contests that are irrelevant to the realities that face the candidates once elected."[2] David Broder and others were absolutely right to believe that the process, including the media, had to undergo reform so that the public would again feel invited to participate rather than just observe.[3]

Sadly, voters did not renew their faith in journalism during the 1992 campaign. By arousing such suspicions about their own impartiality and seriousness, journalists' efforts to assume a greater voice in the campaign created a public backlash.

Polls found that nine out of ten Americans thought that newspapers "would rather take cheap shots at candidates' personal lives than help voters understand the issues." Nearly three in four felt the national media have gotten out of touch with what most Americans really think." And almost two-thirds agreed that the media "favor some candidates over others."[4] Voters had lost faith in news media that had lost sight of them.

The reformers correctly perceived the disconnect between the public and the nation's politics, and the need for systemic reform. The problem was that the solutions they proffered were ill-suited to reconnecting citizens and candidates. Taken as a whole, their prescriptions demanded a more intrusive and aggressive role for journalists — more *mediation*, at a time when the public desired more *direct* communication with their elected leaders. Voters felt shut out of a process that seemed to talk about them, and claimed to speak for them, but rarely spoke *to* them.

Further, by becoming "partisans in behalf of the process," journalists became as responsible as the candidates, consultants, and pundits for the tone and shortcomings of the campaign. Instead of changing the system, they became more closely identified with it. In 1992, as they stooped to criticize the candidates' ads and campaign conduct, reporters took that much more time away from the issues, and added that much more negativity to the process. You cannot stay clean after joining in a mud fight.

In spite of voter dismay, the newfound aggressiveness adopted by leading news organizations has persisted since 1992. Unlike his predecessors, President Clinton enjoyed no media "honeymoon." He faced mostly bad press from the start of his term. During his first two years in office, our studies show, he has been subjected to three times as much criticism as praise on the network evening news shows.[5] Only a small fraction of the criticism has focused on the president's lingering character problem — most news reports rebuked specific administration policies or the president's general leadership ability.[6]

The national media's coverage of the 1994 midterm election campaigns was even more superficial than in 1992. Applying the same criteria to evening news coverage as we had in presidential races, we found that barely one out of five assessments of the candidates focused on the substance of their records or proposals. The majority concerned the campaign horse race — this despite the Republicans' much-publicized "Contract with America," which detailed a substantive legislative platform signed by most G.O.P. House candidates.[7]

Republicans and Democrats engaged in a vigorous debate over the "Contract" in 1994, while television news focused on polls, projections, and their latest round of "Ad Watches." For a media dogged by perceptions that it is part of an entrenched establishment, it is perhaps no coincidence that the most positive national news coverage went to three beleaguered incumbents — New York Governor Mario Cuomo, Texas Governor Ann Richards, and Massachusetts Senator Edward Kennedy.[8]

Finally, just as President Clinton was denied a media honeymoon, the ambitious 100-day agenda of the Republican 104th Congress received heavily negative media coverage. Both the broadcast networks (71% negative evaluations) and leading newspapers (70% negative from the *New York Times*, 65% negative from the *Washington Post*) focused on complaints and criticism in their coverage. The hostile newspaper coverage was mirrored by an even more negative editorial line.[9] The skew against the G.O.P., commented Ellen Hume, shows that reporters are "really out of touch with the resurgent conservative mood in the country."[10]

As these figures illustrate, the national news media continue to embrace their role as a major player in the game of politics, albeit one without governing responsibility or a guiding philosophy, beyond that of challenging all comers. Their aggressive attitude toward political leaders has been reflected in mostly bad press for successive administrations and Congresses controlled by both political parties. In the current media environment, writes *Roll Call* editor Morton Kondracke, "negativism trumps ideology every time."[11]

The media's persistent negativism and superficiality have not gone unnoticed. The public's disapproval has persisted, and in some cases deepened, since the last presidential election. In 1993, barely a quarter of the public (26%) thought that "the press looks out for ordinary people, while 65% thought the press "looks out for mainly powerful people."[12]

A 1994 Times Mirror survey showed that about two-thirds of the public thought television and newspaper coverage of political issues frequently favors one side over another.[13] A 1995 CNN poll found that 60% say the news media are generally "out of touch with average Americans."[14] Nearly three in five Americans (57%) report their belief that "the news media gets in the way of society solving its problems," while only a third (33%) believe the media "helps society."[15]

The *Washington Post's* Howard Kurtz recently wondered why, as the amount of available news grows, citizens are increasingly turning their backs on it. He quoted one focus group participant who complained, "It's more trouble than it's worth to listen to the news and get your hopes up." Another thought news organizations were slanted: "The news is chopped up in bits and pieces. You don't get the whole story." For a variety of reasons, a large percentage of the public in 1995 was ignoring the media. As Kurtz concluded,

> The plain fact is that much of the American public has simply tuned out the news — that is, the kind of traditional news, heavily laden with politicians and official proceedings, routinely covered by the mainstream press. These people see journalists as messengers from a world that doesn't much interest them....
>
> Some of this lack of interest may stem from the way that media organizations define and package the news, news that many people find irrelevant to their daily lives. Some of it may involve a new generation of well-educated, well-compensated journalists who identify more with society's elite than with working-class Americans.[16]

Everyone loses if political leaders must communicate with citizens via information media that much of the public doesn't trust. For better or for worse, the news media are still our eyes and ears on public life. When people doubt the essential fairness and accuracy of the information they receive, they are rendered deaf and blind, hence unable to make informed judgments.

The doubt stems from concerns that the media's own institutional values and interests — not the public's concerns — drive much of the coverage. The public has repeatedly told pollsters that the media are too cynical, too adversarial, and too focused on the misdeeds and personal failings of public officials.[17] Instead of diminishing longstanding public concern over media negativism and intrusiveness, recent trends in journalism have increased the concern over sensationalism and partisanship. As a result, trust in the media is being replaced by skepticism about its understanding of everyday life.[18]

Yet many journalists are still reluctant to acknowledge these problems. When Times Mirror recently asked national media journalists why they think the public is angry with the press, most pointed their fingers elsewhere: 27% replied that tabloids have given the mainstream media a bad name, 22% said the public was blaming the messenger, and 13% said the public was just angry with all institutions. When asked whether the public's disaffection was justified, more national journalists gave an unequivocal no (29%) than an unqualified yes (22%).[19]

Journalists cannot expect to redeem the political process when their own reputations are so frayed. Large segments of the public believe the media are incapable of serving society in a neutral role, let alone a constructive one. Each time reporters adopt a more aggressive posture, their stock drops among the public. As crusading news organizations overreach in their posture of principled negativism, their ability to provide the public with trustworthy information is diminished.

As the reformers proved, media coverage can be changed by rational persuasion and exhortation. Three suggestions that might help journalism rebuild its public standing:

Step One: Lose the Attitude   News organizations need to stop confusing a sharp tongue with serious oversight. The natural instinct of journalists is to question and challenge authority. This is to the good: politicians need to be questioned and challenged. But at the end of the day, when the stories are written, the focus should be more on hard news, and less on soft-core commentary.

The media's skepticism about a second Bush term didn't just ensure that reporters asked the president and his staff tougher questions; it seeped into the tone of their finished stories. They invited the public to share their skepticism and unfairly prejudiced the political environment. They were so skeptical of Bush that they *weren't skeptical* about the Democrats' claims of a failing economy. Hewing more closely to the facts, and reducing the role of speculation and commentary (which is often mislabeled as "analysis") would protect journalists against making these sort of errors in the future.

One consequence of such reportage is that the public increasingly sees the press as just another political player. Ordinary citizens think that journalists get up each morning hoping to add to their scalp collection. The profession would generally benefit from a reduction in the negative posturing that dominates so much of journalism's political writing.

This is not to suggest that reporters should abandon their watchdog role or stop asking tough questions of politicians. But the watchdog role is undermined by overuse — a steady diet of adversarial coverage can leave voters too numb to respond to serious vices or genuine virtue in public life. It also leaves them aggrieved at the messengers as well as the miscreants.

For example, "Ad Watches" put journalists in the position of acting as truth-tellers. But their version of the truth proved as open to debate as anyone else's interpretation. A better policy might be to establish a forum — either within the media or outside it — where candidates could be assured of a public hearing if they have a charge to make against an opponent. The opponent would have a right to respond with supporting evidence — and a public debate would begin.

The notion behind "Ad Watches" was that, in such shouting matches, voters wouldn't be able to recognize the truth unless reporters added their own voices to the melee. A better starting point would be to assume that voters are able to analyze the facts and the arguments, and to separate truth from fiction — as long as they have all the facts in front of them. A full debate, like *MacNeil-Lehrer*'s "Fact or Fiction," works far better than the bottom-line "Ad Watches." And a debate spares reporters the need to risk their impartiality by directly criticizing the candidates.

We are not advocating a policy of witless "good news" reporting. Rampant "positivism" offers as many dangers as unchecked negativism, including flackery and favoritism. Journalists need to rediscover the virtue of neutrality in their reports and to edge back out of their own spotlight. Viewers and readers suspect that the media are becoming advocates of their own agenda. Shifting the attention back onto the politicians would not only put the focus where it belongs — it would also give journalism a sorely needed chance to repair its own credibility.

Step Two: Adopt the Voters' Agenda The best thing about the 1992 campaign was that we saw, via the talk shows, how voters would conduct the campaign. The reformers were right about one thing — the voters' agenda has been ignored by traditional media coverage, and this is a source of conflict between the people and the press. But the problem isn't only that candidates talk about flags and furloughs; it's also that reporters talk ceaselessly about the polls and the process. They view the campaign from the inside, while voters are left without guidance or information about the issues that matter to them.

Instead of just assuming that they speak for the public, reporters need to adopt the voters' agenda, *as the voters themselves define it*. When voters had their chance on the talks shows, they asked about substantive matters, trying to fathom what the next four years would be like under each candidate. They kept coming back to the basics — What is your health care plan? What would you do about the economy? How would you help fight crime? Voters didn't betray a fascination with the process; those who had a chance to question the candidates were absorbed by the stakes and substance of the campaign.

Voters wanted to know about the candidates' stances on the issues, their priorities, and what they would do as president. Reporters asked questions about the candidates' strategies, tactics, and the latest flare-up on the campaign trail. Those are the questions that inform their daily judgment about whether anything "newsworthy" happened on the trail. Reporters want to know *who* will win and *how* they do it. Voters want to know *why* each candidate should win — preferably, in the candidate's own words.

We learned in 1992 that voters didn't seem interested in the technical details — they wanted the basics. The basics bore reporters because they've heard them over and over again. But a candidate's record and platform shouldn't be considered old news until voters have stopped asking about them, which probably wouldn't be until Election Day.

The media's policy stories need to begin with the candidates themselves. Their speeches, we found, were three times as likely as traditional news to stress the substance of the campaign. Reporters would serve the public better if their ears pricked up at each policy proposal a candidate made at speeches or rallies, rather than each negative sound bite uttered. It is hardly fair for journalists to criticize the candidates for shirking substance when most of their coverage does the same. And, it is arrogant for news organizations to offer their own issue agenda until they cover the issues the candidates are running on.

Step Three: Cover the Campaign   Nowhere has the coverage of presidential campaigns lapsed more than during the nominating conventions. In 1992 CBS skipped the second night of the Democratic National Convention entirely, in order to broadcast the All-Star Game. That same night, ABC and NBC offered one-hour specials filled with their own commentary and interviews, and showing almost none of the floor action. Only CNN and C-SPAN offered full coverage of the 1992 conventions.

The networks justified this news blackout on the grounds that conventions fail to generate "news." True, the nominees are known well in advance; even vice presidential selections are now often named in advance. The platform votes are also controlled by the nominees, and the floor presentations are heavily scripted — even the spontaneous demonstrations are carefully choreographed.

The networks argue further that C-SPAN and CNN coverage relieves them of the responsibility to broadcast the conventions. But that argument was rebutted in 1992 by former CBS anchor Walter Cronkite, who declared that "when you're a network and still have 62 percent of the audience, that's no answer. The fact is, there's just no will to do it."[20] Cronkite's successor agrees: "Isn't it right," asked Dan Rather in 1988, "to allow the parties a chance once every four years to do it their way?"[21]

Nothing better illustrates the disconnect between the voters and the media. While exposure to daily doses of television campaign news does not correlate with increases in voter information, voters do learn about the candidates and their platforms from the conventions. They similarly learn from the debates and other live events.[22] The responsibility of the networks is not merely to assess and criticize the campaign — it is also to show it to voters, letting them witness its main events and draw their own conclusions.

The networks' retreat from the conventions is coincident with their increased reluctance to cover day-to-day campaign events. Disdaining "staged" events, the coverage now subordinates the candidates' daily activities and focuses on journalists' own judgment of what is (or is not) important.

But journalists' analyses cannot be properly evaluated by voters unless they share some of the external context of the campaign. Coverage that merely analyzes campaign events, without first offering an impartial recounting of the event, offers voters a take-it-or-leave-it proposition that diminishes their ability to evaluate the candidates.

There is another good reason for journalists to get back on the campaign trail — to protect their own role. Ross Perot showed how, the campaign trail can be bypassed as a primary means of communicating with citizens. The principal value of rallies and speeches lies in the media's coverage of them, which greatly multiplies the audience for each event. If news organizations continue to reject this role, the candidates will continue to seek out new ways to bypass the middleman and take their messages directly to the people.

This would also encourage the candidates not to let the campaign trail languish as a forum for conducting the ongoing campaign debate. Routinely offering lengthier excerpts of their speeches would give the candidates more incentive to use their speeches as a forum for debating major issues. By dismissing campaign trail events as "staged," journalists simply encourage candidates to spend more time off the trail, talking directly to citizens, through interactive media formats.

Clearly, reporters have a crucial job to do every four years. They are the watchdogs who most carefully scrutinize each of the candidates. They challenge them with tough questions, and they issue daily reports. But their role is but one part of a much larger electoral process, and citizens need more views of the campaign than those of journalists. Voters need to witness the campaign more directly, so that they can make up their own minds, based on their own values and priorities.

When news organizations become blind to voters' information needs, they only add to public grievances with the media. Reporters can't get so swept up in their adversarial relationship with the candidates that they lose sight of the voters' need to experience the campaign without commentary, to hear the candidates' words without constant reporter rebuttal, and to begin accumulating the basic information that journalists already possess.

A Job for the Pols: Disentangle the Campaign and the Media

In *Out of Order*, Thomas Patterson argued that "the United States cannot have a sensible campaign as long as it is built around the news media."[23] He concluded that the press is fundamentally ill-suited to fulfilling its inherited role of electoral mediator:

> After every presidential election, scholars and pundits, along with many journalists, say that campaigns would be better if only the press would report them differently. The assumption underlying this conclusion is that the press has the ability to organize the choices facing the voters....
>
> It is an impossible task. The press is far less effective as a linking mechanism than is commonly believed. The problem is that the press is not a political institution. Its business is news, and the values of news are not those of politics.[24]

The challenge for politicians is to disentangle the media's coverage of the campaign from the substance of the campaign itself. Candidates must rise or fall as a consequence of their own actions and ideas. Voters must have an opportunity for straightforward information — not necessarily news — about the choices they face before they are asked to make a decision.

Journalists can take steps to improve their coverage, but the media's incentive structure will invariably lead them in directions poorly suited to rational elections. The reason is not that journalists don't care about the health of the electoral system (their post-1988 efforts prove that they care a great deal), but rather that "news" — the unplanned, eventful, conflictual stuff of campaigns — differs fundamentally from the "information" that citizens need to make organized, rational voting decisions. During campaigns, journalists are expected to provide both news and information, only to have critics complain when one or the other is deficient.

Journalists can tinker with their norms in order to match voter interests, but they can't serve as full-service campaign intermediaries, and they probably shouldn't try. The burden to inform voters falls mostly on the politicians. They need to take back control of the election process and assert the primacy of their relationship with the American people. Their own efforts need to be the centerpiece of the election dialogue, not a mere sideshow to the journalistic chatter.

Several attempts in this direction have been made in the past several years, but all have proven futile so far. The Democratic Party changed its rules to include several hundred "superdelegates" to the convention — elected officials whose presidential preferences would supposedly be immune to the currents of media and public opinion. However, since superdelegates were introduced in 1984, each Democratic field has been rapidly winnowed during the primaries in a process dominated by the media. The superdelegates, unless they pledge early, usually face a choice of only one candidate — a nominee preordained by the media-dominated primary process.

Similarly, efforts to shorten the campaign have enhanced, not diminished, the media's influence. Shortening the lag between the Iowa and New Hampshire primaries only magnified the effect of the Iowa "bounce." Consolidating the number of primaries held on a single date (many of the southern states have grouped on Super Tuesday — the second Tuesday in March — every year since 1984) swells the size of the prize for a candidate riding New Hampshire's momentum.

In 1996, the compression of primaries will be greater than ever. In March, close on the heels of the New Hampshire primary (tentatively scheduled for February 20), the most populous states — New York (March 7), Florida and Texas (March 12), Ohio, Illinois, and Michigan (March 19) and California (March 26) — will choose their convention delegations in swift order. In such an environment, the candidate with media momentum could easily sweep to the nomination before reporters either lose interest or begin their inevitable scrutiny.

Politicians need to remember that they, not the press, determine how long a campaign will last. The official campaign calender is irrelevant; the "shadow campaign" begins as soon as prospective candidates begin seeking donations and courting consultants. If it takes two years of effort to unseat an incumbent, an ambitious pol will start the campaign two years early.

The media increasingly treat these early maneuvers as newsworthy. As a result, for both politicians and reporters, a presidential campaign begins months or even years before the first votes are cast. Preparing for the 1996 race, eight Republicans had officially announced their presidential candidacies by May 1995 — a full 18 months before the election.

Individual politicians will always have a stake in using the media as a means of advancing their prospects. But politicians in general — and the two parties in particular — have a stake in re-asserting the primacy of their conversation with the American public. If the politicians rise to the occasion, the public's skepticism of them may abate. If they live down to their current media-driven reputations, they will have only themselves to blame.

The ability of a political party to police its own nomination process deteriorated rapidly after the 1968 reforms. Candidates are now self-starters who use the media to bypass their party's leadership. As the parties' control of the nomination process has deteriorated, so too has their ability to link the public with the politicians, to police their own candidates, and to establish a meaningful context for elections.

Parties can take several steps to reinstitute control, but they won't be easy to implement. One way might be to resurrect an old rule that the Democrats once used at their conventions — require a two-thirds vote for nomination. The immediate effect would be to delay the inevitability of a nominee, which would encourage trailing candidates to remain in the race. A two-thirds rule might also revive the practice of favorite-son (or -daughter) candidacies — the single-state candidates would show up with delegates and a place at the table.

Delaying the nomination would certainly inflate the clout of superdelegates, finally giving teeth to that old reform. While it probably wouldn't bring back brokered conventions, the nomination would likely be determined by post-primary negotiations. In such circumstances, the supermajority rule would shift some control over the nomination back to party leaders.

Second, changes in campaign finance laws could make it easier for political parties to spend money on behalf of national candidates. Federal contributions to the general election campaigns could be shifted from the nominees to the national committees, ensuring cooperation among the candidate's staff and the party professionals. It might also mean that responsibility for general election advertising would rest in the national committees.

Party control would not, by itself, improve either the media coverage or the quality of citizens' information. But it would give the parties the means to begin exercising control over the process, and parties could institute their own oversight mechanisms.

Currently, the media are in charge of the vetting process — checking the character and background of potential nominees, policing their campaign practices, exposing inconsistencies, etc. The problem is that this sort of personal investigation has supplanted more traditional explanations of where candidates stand on the issues, what they have accomplished in past offices, etc. If reporters are going to get back to basics, the parties need to find a credible way to establish their own oversight of the process.

Parties would have considerable incentive to ensure that their nominees are "clean" — the consequences of failure would be defeat. The media, by contrast, face few consequences for failure, apart from essentially toothless criticism from politicians. Parties would bear institutional responsibility for the conduct of campaigns, for the quality and fairness of ads, and for the integrity of the nominees. If general election campaigns were run by the permanent party organization, they would have more incentive to stay "clean" than an ad hoc campaign group assembled for a single mission.

Further, party control would end the petty debate over the debates that occurs each fall. After the 1988 campaign, the parties did form a bi-partisan Commission on Presidential Debates, which devised a format and schedule for the 1992 general election. But the Commission lacked any leverage over the candidates, and the effort collapsed. Give the parties teeth, and they could agree on a format and schedule that are binding on the nominees.

Giving the party organization more of a say is only the first step. Parties and candidates must then deliver on better campaigns. Our study found that the candidates' speeches offered a coherent and substantive campaign message, but one that voters rarely had a chance to hear. If journalists lost their reluctance to give voters an unfiltered view of the campaign, the public would benefit. But the candidates cannot wait for the media to do the job for them.

In 1992, millions watched Ross Perot lecture about the deficit with his homemade charts and his "voodoo stick." The fact that Clinton and Bush didn't offer similar presentations may have left many voters with the impression that Perot had the most detailed platform. It wouldn't hurt for the candidates to offer a series of speeches to the public, offering their assessment of major problems and solutions.

If candidates aren't eager to do this on their own, the system could be changed to offer incentives. For example, the current general election financing system offers each nominee a flat amount of money — about $55 million each in 1992. The FEC could instead present candidates with a package deal — say, $40 million and ten hours of prime time apiece. The candidates could, if they wished, pool their time and arrange their own joint appearances. Such arrangements could be encouraged by offering additional air time. By alternating the Republican and Democratic nominees' time-slots, voters would be offered an ongoing campaign debate.

At this stage, particular proposals are less important than the general principle of strengthening political responsibility. When the parties ceded control of election campaigns to the media and individual candidates, they abdicated their own responsibility for policing the campaign to a profession whose interests and values are often different from theirs. The results have pleased no one — neither the politicians, nor the public, nor journalists themselves.

Under the current system, candidates answer to no one, and their campaigns are all-or-nothing wagers brokered by the media. In contrast, the parties will continue to exist whether or not their candidate wins or loses the election. Their reputations, and their long-term strength, depend on managing their messages properly and responsibly. And, to those who wonder whether it is democratic or progressive to cede power back to the parties, ask yourself: could it be any worse than the current system?

INCENTIVES TO CHANGE

Chronic voter dissatisfaction with the campaign process is a symptom of a serious and systemic political disorder. We have witnessed increasing public disapproval of presidential candidates, which corresponds closely to increased media influence over elections, and increasingly sensationalized negative images of them. By fixating on the flaws and failings of candidates, political journalism undermines public support for candidates of all parties and ideological persuasions. By exaggerating conflict, the media vastly complicate the processes of coalition-building and governance that are vital to a healthy political structure.

In 1992, journalism professor Jay Rosen argued that the role of the press in public life was compromised by journalists' lack of vision. While their influence was considerable, it was not grounded in a disciplined view of their role in politics.

> "All we own is our credibility," say many in the profession, and they interpret this to mean that the press cannot afford to be caught with an agenda. At the same time, however, they agree that it is the journalists' mission to be "tough" on politicians and a persistent check on government power. The consequences of holding these two beliefs — no to an explicit agenda, yes to a tough, critical stance — have been severe. The journalist's critical method is degenerating into madness as "gotcha" becomes the battle cry of a hardened and increasingly purposeless press.[25]

After 1988, the media tried to develop a new sense of purpose by developing an aggressive agenda to repair campaigns. The consequence was to drive the candidates and voters away from the mainstream media, and to further erode the public's faith in journalism's impartiality. In 1992, the media continued to structure their campaign coverage in a way that left citizens informationally malnourished. The coverage focused on the inside story of campaigns for an audience of political insiders. But ordinary citizens follow politics more sporadically and from a very different perspective. As a result, citizens increasingly felt abandoned by journalists, and they walked away in increasing numbers.

In 1992, Jonathan Alter speculated that if the public's flight continues apace, the national media may cease to be a popular force:

> In the future, the national media may increasingly become an elite media shaping elite opinion — with the *Washington Post*, the *CBS Evening News*, and *Newsweek* all going for the same few million people who run the country. A lot of journalists will make perfectly fine livings doing this (and certain elite advertisers will love it), but the big guns will have ceded the mass market altogether. And they will thus have ceded their connection, however tenuous, to the majority of people who live — and vote — in America.[26]

The experience of 1992 shows that the public, when given a chance, will seek out alternatives to the current brand of campaign coverage. The warm reception voters gave the talk shows and other forms of political communication shows that they are prepared to replace the "incumbent" news media with one more to their liking. Unless traditional journalism responds to voter displeasure, it risks becoming an increasingly marginal feature of a diverse media landscape.

Change is coming. The dominant media of the next century will give voters more control over the information they receive, and thus more autonomy over the decisions they make. The question for 1996 and beyond is whether or not traditional news can adapt to this new media environment.

This is not a trivial concern, for failure will have consequences that reverberate far beyond the news industry. While the media's recent track record is dismal in many respects, the health of American democracy requires an institution with many of the traits embodied by traditional journalism — valuable qualities that would be at risk in the transition to a new order.

Notes

Opening quote: Walter Lippmann, *Public Opinion* (New York: Macmillan, 1922).

1.   CNN's *Larry King Live*, October 28, 1992.

2.   Ellen Hume, *Restoring the Bond: Connecting Campaign Coverage to Voters* (Cambridge, MA: Harvard University, 1991), p. 19.

3.   David Broder, "It's time to replace Sloganeering With Simple Shoe-leather Reporting," *The Quill,* March 1992.

4.   James P. Gannon, "The Loser This Campaign? The Media," Gannett News Service, June 12, 1992.

5.   "The Honeymoon That Wasn't," *Media Monitor* 7, no. 7 (September/October 1993).

6.   "They're No Friends of Bill," *Media Monitor* 8, no. 4 (July/August 1994).

7.   "The November Surprise," *Media Monitor* 8, no. 6 (November/December 1994).

8.   Ibid.

9.   "Media Won't Sign on to G.O.P. Contract," Center for Media and Public Affairs, April 20, 1995.

10.   Quoted by Rod Dreher, "Study Finds Media Critical of GOP Congress," *Washington Times*, April 21, 1995.

11.   Morton Kondracke, "Is Newt Paranoid About Media Bias? New Study Says No," *Roll Call*, April 20, 1995.

12.   David Shaw, "Distrustful Public Views Media as 'Them' — Not 'Us,'" *Los Angeles Times*, April 1, 1993.

13.   Times Mirror Center for The People & The Press, March 16, 1994.

14.   Quoted in the *White House Bulletin*, April 17, 1995.

15.   *The People, The Press & Their Leaders: 1995*, published by the Times Mirror Center for the People & The Press, 1995. Surveys conducted March 22-26, 1992.

16.   Howard Kurtz, "Tuning Out Traditional News," *Washington Post*, May 15, 1995.

17.   *The People, The Press & Their Leaders: 1995*, published by the Times Mirror Center for the People & The Press, 1995. Journalist surveys conducted March 8-30, 1995.

18.   Ibid.

19.   Ibid.

20. Quoted by Peter Ross Range, "Walter Cronkite Is Mad As Hell," *TV Guide*, July 11, 1992.

21. Dan Rather, "A Window on Democracy," *Newsweek*, August 22, 1988.

22. See Dan Drew and David Weaver, "Voter Learning in the 1988 Election: Did the Debates and the Media Matter?" *Journalism Quarterly* 68 (Spring/Summer 1991): 27-37; Bruce Buchanan, *Electing a President: the Markle Commission Research on Campaign '88* (Austin, TX: University of Texas Press, 1991); and Thomas E. Patterson, *The Mass Media Election: How Americans Choose Their President* (New York: Praeger Publishers, 1980).

23. Thomas Patterson, *Out of Order*, p. 25.

24. Ibid., p. 207.

25. Jay Rosen, "Politics, Vision, and the Press: Toward a Public Agenda for Journalism," in *The New News vs. The Old News: The Press and Politics in the 1990s*, a Twentieth Century Fund Paper, 1992, pp. 6-7.

26. Jonathan Alter, "How Phil Donahue Came to Manage the '92 Campaign," *The Washington Monthly*, June 1992.

- SELECTED BIBLIOGRAPHY -

Abramson, Paul R., et al. "'Sophisticated' Voting in the 1988 Presidential Primaries." *American Political Science Review* 86, no. 1 (March 1992): 55-69.

Adams, William C. "As New Hampshire Goes..." In *Media and Momentum: The New Hampshire Primary and Nomination Politics*, edited by Gary R. Orren and Nelson W. Polsby. Chatham, N.J.: Chatham House Publishers, 1987.

———. "Media Coverage of Campaign '84: A Preliminary Report." *Public Opinion* 7, no 2 (April/May 1984): 9-13.

———. "Recent Fables About Ronald Reagan." *Public Opinion* 7, no. 5 (October/November 1984).

Adatto, Kiku. "The Incredible Shrinking Sound Bite." *The New Republic*, May 28, 1990.

———. "Sound Bite Democracy: Network Evening News Presidential Campaign Coverage, 1968 and 1988." Research Paper R-2, The Joan Shorenstein Barone Center, June 1990.

Alger, Dean. "The Media, the Public and the Development of Candidates' Images in the 1992 Presidential Election." Research Paper R-14, The Joan Shorenstein Barone Center, October 1994.

Alter, Jonathan. "Go Ahead, Blame the Media." *Newsweek*, November 2, 1992.

———. "How Phil Donahue Came to Manage the '92 Campaign." *The Washington Monthly*, June 1992.

———. "How the Media Blew It." *Newsweek*, November 28, 1988.

———. "Why the Old Media's Losing Control." *Newsweek*, June 8, 1992.

Barber, James David. "Candidate Reagan and 'the Sucker Generation.'" *Columbia Journalism Review*, November/December 1987.

———. *The Pulse of Politics: Electing Presidents in the Media Age.* New York: W. W. Norton and Company, 1980.

Barnes, Fred. "Why Liberals Hate Politics." *American Spectator*, August 1991.

Bartels, Larry M. "Expectations and Preferences in Presidential Nominating Campaigns." *American Political Science Review* 79 (September 1985): 804-815.

Bennett, W. Lance. *The Governing Crisis: Media, Money, and Marketing in American Elections*. New York: St. Martin's Press, 1992.

Bloom, Howard S., and H. Douglas Price. "Voter Response to Short-Run Economic Conditions: the Asymmetric Effect of Prosperity and Recession." *American Political Science Review* 69 (December 1975): 1240-1254.

Bode, Ken. "Pull the Plug: We Have the Power to Just Say No, to Abandon Our Photo-Op Addiction." *The Quill*, March 1992.

Boot, William. "Campaign '88: TV Overdoses on the Inside Dope." *Columbia Journalism Review*, January/February 1989.

Brady, Henry E., and Richard Johnson. "What's the Primary Message: Horse Race or Issue Journalism." In *Media and Momentum: The New Hampshire Primary and Nomination Politics*, edited by Gary R. Orren and Nelson W. Polsby. Chatham, N.J.: Chatham House Publishers, 1987.

Braestrup, Peter. *Big Story: How the American Press and Television Reported and Interpreted the Crisis of Tet 1968 in Vietnam and Washington*. New Haven: Yale University Press, 1983.

Broder, David. "Five Ways to Put Some Sanity Back in Elections." *Washington Post*, January 14, 1990.

————. "It's Time to Replace Sloganeering with Simple Shoe-leather Reporting." *The Quill*, March 1992.

Broh, C. Anthony. *The Horse of a Different Color: Television's Treatment of Jesse Jackson's 1984 Presidential Campaign*. Washington, D.C.: Joint Center for Political Studies, 1987.

————. "Horse Race Journalism: Reporting the Polls in the 1976 Presidential Election." *Public Opinion Quarterly* 44 (1980): 514-529.

Buchanan, Bruce. *Electing a President: The Markle Commission Research on Campaign '88*. Austin: University of Texas Press, 1991.

Cannon, Lou. *President Reagan: The Role of a Lifetime*. New York: Simon and Schuster, 1991.

Cappella, Joseph N., and Kathleen Hall Jamieson. "Public Cynicism and News Coverage in Campaigns and Policy Debates: Three Field Experiments." Paper presented to American Political Science Association Conference, New York, N.Y., September 4, 1994.

Ceaser, James W. *Presidential Selection: Theory and Development*. Princeton, N.J.: Princeton University Press, 1979.

Clancey, Maura, and Michael J. Robinson. "General Election Coverage: Part 1." *Public Opinion* 7, no. 6 (December/January 1985).

Clinton, Bill, and Al Gore. *Putting People First: How We Can All Change America*. New York: Times Books, 1992.

Crigler, Ann N., Marion R. Just, and Timothy E. Cook. "Local News, Network News, and the 1992 Presidential Campaign." Prepared for delivery at the annual meeting of the American Political Science Association, September 3-6, 1992, Chicago, Ill.

Crigler, Ann N., Marion Just, and W. Russell Neuman. "Interpreting Visual Versus Audio Messages in Television News." *Journal of Communication* 44, no. 4 (Autumn 1994): 132-148.

Cronin, Thomas E. "Looking for Leadership, 1980." *Public Opinion,* February/March 1980.

Crotty, William, and John S. Jackson III. *Presidential Primaries and Nominations*. Washington, D.C.: Congressional Quarterly Press, 1985.

Deakin, James. *Straight Stuff: The Reporters, the White House and the Truth*. New York: William Morrow and Company, 1984.

Denton, Robert E., Jr. *The Primetime Presidency of Ronald Reagan: The Era of the Television Presidency*. New York: Praeger, 1988.

Diamond, Edwin. "Getting it Right." *New York,* November 2, 1992.

Donaldson, Sam. *Hold On, Mr. President!* New York: Random House, 1987.

Drew, Dan, and David Weaver. "Voter Learning in the 1988 Presidential Election: Did the Debates and the Media Matter?" *Journalism Quarterly* 68 (Spring/Summer 1991): 27-37.

Efron, Edith. *The News Twisters*. Los Angeles: Nash Publishing, 1971.

Epstein, Edward Jay. *News from Nowhere: Television and the News*. New York: Vintage Books, 1974.

Erbring, Lutz, Edie N. Goldenberg, and Arthur H. Miller. "Front-Page News and Real-World Cues: A New Look at Agenda-Setting by the Media." *American Journal of Political Science* 24, no. 1 (February 1980): 16-49.

Fair, Ray. "The Effect of Economic Events on Votes for President." *Review of Economics and Statistics* 60 (1978): 159-173.

Flander, Judy. "NBC's Tim Russert: The Insider." *Columbia Journalism Review,* September/October 1992.

The Freedom Forum Media Studies Center. "An Uncertain Season: Reporting in the Post-Primary Period." In *The Media and Campaign '92: A Series of Special Election Reports*. New York: The Freedom Forum Media Studies Center, 1992.

―――. "Covering the Presidential Primaries." In *The Media and Campaign '92: A Series of Special Election Reports*. New York: The Freedom Forum Media Studies Center, 1992.

_____. "The Finish Line: Covering the Campaign's Final Days." In *The Media and Campaign '92: A Series of Special Election Reports.* New York: The Freedom Forum Media Studies Center, 1993.

_____. "The Homestretch: New Politics. New Media. New Voters?" In *The Media and Campaign '92: A Series of Special Election Reports.* New York: The Freedom Forum Media Studies Center, 1992.

Gannett Center for Media Studies (now the Freedom Forum). "The New Elector." *Gannett Center Journal* 2, no. 4 (Fall 1988): vii-x.

Geer, John G. "Effects of Presidential Debates on the Electorates Preference for Candidates." *American Politics Quarterly* 16, no. 4 (October 1988): 486-501.

Germond, Jack W., and Jules Witcover. *Whose Broad Stripes and Bright Stars?: The Trivial Pursuit of the Presidency 1988.* New York: Warner Books, 1989.

Goldman, Peter, and Tom Mathews. *The Quest for the Presidency, 1988.* New York: Simon and Schuster, 1989.

Goldman, Peter, et al. *Quest for the Presidency, 1992.* College Station, Tex: Texas A & M University Press, 1992.

Golson, Barry, and Peter Ross Range. "Clinton on TV." *TV Guide*, November 21-27, 1992.

Gopnik, Adam. "Read All About It." *The New Yorker*, December 12, 1994.

Graber, Doris A. "Kind Pictures and Harsh Words." In *Elections in America*, edited by Kay Lehman-Schlozman. Boston: Allen and Unwin, 1987.

_____. "Political Communication." In *Political Science: The State of the Discipline II*, edited by Ada Finifter. Washington, D.C.: American Political Science Association, 1993.

_____. *Processing the News: How People Tame the Information Tide.* New York: Longman, 1984.

Greene, Jay. "Forewarned Before Forecast." *P.S.: Political Science and Politics* (March 1993): 17-21.

Greenfield, Jeff. "Presidential Politics and Myths of Media Power." In *Campaign '88: The Politics of Character and the Character of Politics.* New York: Gannett Center for Media Studies, 1988.

_____. *The Real Campaign.* New York: Summitt Books, 1982.

Guttenplan, D. D. "Out of It: While Perot Gets Through to the Voters, the Press Gets Lost on the Campaign Trail." *Columbia Journalism Review*, July/August 1992.

_____. "Covering a Runaway Campaign." *Columbia Journalism Review*, November/December 1992.

Hadley, Arthur T. *The Invisible Primary.* Englewood Cliffs, N.J.: Prentice Hall, 1976.

Hallin, Daniel C. "Whose Campaign is it, Anyway?" *Columbia Journalism Review*, January/ February 1991.

Hanson, Christopher. "How to Satisfy a Spin-ster Every Time." *Columbia Journalism Review*, July/August 1993.

———. "Media Bashing." *Columbia Journalism Review*, November/ December 1992.

Hays, Charlotte, and Jonathan Rowe. "Reporters: The New Washington Elite." *The Washington Monthly*, July/August 1985.

Henry, William A., III "Are the Media Too Liberal?" *Time*, October 19, 1992.

———. "Why Journalists Can't Wear White." *Media Studies Journal* 6, no. 4 (Fall 1992).

Hertsgaard, Mark. *On Bended Knee*. New York: Pantheon, 1988.

Hoffman, David. "The Candidate, Packaged and Protected." *Washington Journalism Review*, September 1984.

Hume, Brit. "The Bush Crack-Up." *American Spectator*, January 1993.

Hume, Ellen. *Restoring the Bond: Connecting Campaign Coverage to Voters — A Report of the Campaign Lessons for '92 Project*. Cambridge, Mass: Harvard University, 1991.

Iyengar, Shanto. "Television News and Citizens' Explanations of National Affairs." *American Political Science Review* 81, no. 3 (September 1987): 815-831.

Iyengar, Shanto, and Donald R. Kinder. *News That Matters*. Chicago: University of Chicago Press, 1987.

Jamieson, Kathleen Hall. *Dirty Politics: Deception, Distraction, and Democracy*. New York: Oxford University Press, 1992.

Joslyn, Mark R., and Steve Ceccoli. "Media Messages and Voter Judgments, Is There a Link? Estimating the Impact of News Consumption and Content on Voters' Judgments During the Final Months of the 1992 Campaign." Prepared for delivery at the Midwest Political Science Association 52nd Annual Meeting held in Chicago, Ill., April 14-16, 1994.

Kalb, Marvin. " Too Much Talk and Not Enough Action." *Washington Journalism Review*, September 1992.

———. "TV, Election Spoiler." *The New York Times*, November 28, 1988.

Katz, Jeffrey L. "Tilt?" *Washington Journalism Review*, January/February 1993.

Kennamer, J. David. "Political Discussion and Cognition: a 1988 Look." *Journalism Quarterly* 67, no. 2 (Summer 1990): 348-352.

Kiewiet, D. Roderick, and Douglas Rivers. "A Retrospective on Retrospective Voting." *Political Behavior* 6, no. 4 (1984): 369-370.

Kohut, Andrew, and Donald S. Kellerman. *The People, Press & Politics: October Pre-Election Typology Survey*. Washington, D.C.: Times Mirror Center for the People & the Press, 1988.

Kraft, Joseph. "The Imperial Media." *Commentary*, May 1981.

Kurtz, Howard. *Media Circus: The Trouble with America's Newspapers.* New York: Times Books, 1993.

Ladd, Everett Carll, with Charles D. Hadley. *Transformations of the American Party System: Political Coalitions from the New Deal to the 1970s,* 2nd ed. New York: W. W. Norton and Company, 1978.

Lau, Richard R., and David O. Sears. "Cognitive Links Between Economic Grievances and Political Responses." *Political Behavior* 3, no. 4 (1981): 279-301.

Lewis-Beck, Michael, and Tom Rice. *Forecasting Elections.* Washington, D.C.: Congressional Quarterly Press, 1992.

Lichter, S. Robert. "Misreading Momentum." *Public Opinion* 11, no. 1 (May/June 1988): 15-17.

Lichter, S. Robert, and Linda S. Lichter. "Covering the Convention Coverage." *Public Opinion*, September/October 1988.

Lichter, S. Robert, and Richard E. Noyes. "In the Media Spotlight." *American Enterprise* 2, no. 1 (January/February 1991).

Lichter, S. Robert, Daniel Amundson, and Richard Noyes. *The Video Campaign: Network Coverage of the 1988 Primaries.* Washington, D.C.: American Enterprise Institute, 1988.

———. "Election '88: Media Coverage." *Public Opinion* 11, no. 5 (January/February 1989): 18-19, 52.

Lichter, S. Robert, Stanley Rothman, and Linda S. Lichter. *The Media Elite.* New York: Hastings House, 1986.

Lydon, Christopher. "Sex, War, and Death." *Columbia Journalism Review*, May/June 1992.

Markus, Gregory B. "The Impact of Personal and National Economic Conditions on the Presidential Vote: A Pooled Cross-Sectional Analysis." *American Journal of Political Science* 32, no. 1 (February 1988): 137-154.

Matusow, Barbara. "Fear and Loathing '88." *Washingtonian*, April 1988.

McCann, James A. "Changing Electoral Contexts and Changing Candidate Images During the 1984 Presidential Campaign." *American Politics Quarterly* 18, no. 2 (April 1990): 123-140.

McCombs, Maxwell J., and Donald L. Shaw. "The Agenda-Setting Function of the Press." *Public Opinion Quarterly* (1972): 63-72.

Means, Howard. "Next, Kill All the Journalists." *The Washingtonian*, May 1991.

Meyer, Philip. "The Media Reformation: Giving the Agenda Back to the People." In *The Elections of 1992*, edited by Michael Nelson. Washington, D.C.: Congressional Quarterly Press, 1993.

Miller, Arthur H., Edie N. Goldenberg, and Lutz Erbring. "Type-Set Politics: Impact of Newspapers on Public Confidence." *American Political Science Review* 73 (March 1979): 67-83.

Miller, Arthur H., Martin P. Wattenberg, and Oksana Malanchuk. "Schematic Assessments of Presidential Candidates." *American Political Science Review* 80, no. 2 (June 1986): 521-540.

Mondack, Jeffrey J. "Source Cues and Policy Approval: The Cognitive Dynamics of Public Support for the Reagan Agenda." *American Journal of Political Science* 37, no. 1 (February 1993): 186-212.

Meyrowitz, Joshua "Visible and Invisible Candidates." *Political Communication* 11, (1992): 145-164.

Noyes, Richard E., S. Robert Lichter, and Daniel R. Amundson. "Was TV Election News Better This Time?" *Journal of Political Science* 21 (1993): 3-25.

Orren, Gary R., and Nelson W. Polsby, eds. "New Hampshire: Springboard of Nomination Politics." In *Media and Momentum: The New Hampshire Primary and Nomination Politics.* Chatham, N.J.: Chatham House Publishers, 1987.

Ostrom, Charles W. Jr., and Dennis M. Simon. "The Man in the Teflon Suit? The Environmental Connection, Political Drama, and Popular Support for the Reagan Presidency." *Public Opinion Quarterly* 53 (1989): 353-387.

Page, Benjamin I., Robert Y. Shapiro, and Glenn R. Dempsey. "What Moves Public Opinion." *American Political Science Review* 81, no. 1 (March 1987): pp. 23-43.

Patterson, Thomas E. *The Mass Media Election: How Americans Choose Their President.* New York: Praeger Publishers, 1980.

————. *Out of Order.* New York: Alfred A. Knopf, 1993.

Patterson, Thomas E., and Robert B. McClure. *The Unseeing Eye: The Myth of Television Power in National Politics.* Toronto: Longman Canada Limited, 1976.

Perot, Ross. *United We Stand: How We Can Take Back Our Country.* New York: Hyperion, 1992.

Phillips, Kevin. *Arrogant Capital: Washington, Wall Street, and the Frustration of American Politics.* Boston: Little, Brown and Company, 1994.

Polsby, Nelson W. *Consequences of Party Reform.* New York: Oxford University Press, 1983.

Postman, Neil. *Amusing Ourselves to Death: Public Discourse in the Age of Show Business.* New York: Penguin Books, 1985.

Ranney, Austin. *Channels of Power: The Impact of Television on American Politics.* New York: Basic Books, 1983.

Regan, Donald T. *For the Record: From Wall Street to Washington.* San Diego: Harcourt Brace Jovanovich, 1988.

Roberts, James C. "The Power of Talk Radio." *The American Enterprise*, May/June 1991.

Robinson, Michael J. "Jesse Helms, Take Stock." *Washington Journalism Review*, April 1985.

———. "The Media in Campaign '84, Part II: Wingless, Toothless, and Hopeless." *Public Opinion* 8, no. 1(1985): 43-48.

———. "Television and American Politics: 1956-1976." *The Public Interest* (Summer 1977): 3-39.

———. "Where's the Beef? Media and Media Elites in 1984." In *The American Elections of 1984*, edited by Austin Ranney. Washington, D.C.: American Enterprise Institute, 1985.

Robinson, Michael J., and Maura Clancey. "Teflon Politics." *Public Opinion* (April/May 1984).

Robinson, Michael J., and Andrew Kohut. "Believability and the Press." *Public Opinion Quarterly* 52 (1988): 174-189.

Robinson, Michael J., and S. Robert Lichter. "'The More Things Change...': Network Coverage of the 1988 Presidential Nomination Races." In *Nominating the President*, edited by Emmett H. Buell, Jr. and Lee Sigelman. Knoxville, Tenn: University of Tennessee Press, 1991.

Robinson, Michael J., and Margaret A. Sheehan. *Over the Wire and On TV: CBS and UPI in Campaign '80.* New York: Russell Sage Foundation, 1983.

Rosen, Jay. "Politics, Vision, and the Press: Toward a Public Agenda for Journalism." In *The New News v. The Old News: The Press and Politics in the 1990s*, edited by Suzanne Charlé. New York: A Twentieth Century Fund Paper, 1992.

———. "TV as Alibi: A Response to Michael Schudson." *Tikkun* 6, no. 2 (February 1991): 52-54, 87.

Rosenstiel, Tom. *Strange Bedfellows: How Television and the Presidential Candidates Changed American Politics, 1992.* New York: Hyperion, 1993.

Rosten, Leo C. *The Washington Correspondents.* New York: Harcourt Brace, 1937.

Russert, Timothy J. "For '92, the Networks Have to Do Better." *New York Times*, March 4, 1990.

Sabato, Larry J. *Feeding Frenzy: How Attack Journalism Has Transformed American Politics.* New York: The Free Press, 1993.

Sabato, Larry J., and S. Robert Lichter. *When Should the Watchdogs Bark? Media Coverage of the Clinton Scandals.* Washington, D.C.: Center for Media and Public Affairs, 1994.

Schram, Martin. *Running for President, 1976: The Carter Campaign.* New York: Stein and Day, 1977.

Schudson, Michael. "Trout or Hamburger: Politics and Telemythology." *Tikkun* 6, no. 2 (February 1991): 47-51, 86-87.

Shaw, Donald L. "News Bias and the Telegraph: A Study of Historical Change." *Journalism Quarterly* 44 , no. 1 (Spring 1967): 3-12, 31.

Sigelman, Lee, and David Bullock. "Candidates, Issues, Horse Races, and Hoopla: Presidential Campaign Coverage, 1888-1988." *American Politics Quarterly* 19, no. 1 (January 1991): 5-32.

Smith Ted J., III "The Watchdog's Bite." *The American Enterprise*, January/ February 1990.

Smoller, Fred. "The Six O'Clock Presidency: Patterns of Network News Coverage of the President." *Presidential Studies Quarterly* 16, no. 1 (Winter 1986): 31-49.

Speakes, Larry, with Robert Pack. *Speaking Out: The Reagan Presidency from Inside the White House.* New York: Avon Books, 1989.

Stanley, Harold W., and Richard G. Niemi. *Vital Statistics on American Politics,* 4th ed. Washington, D.C.: Congressional Quarterly Press, 1994.

Stein, M. L. "Politics from the Voters' Point of View." *Editor and Publisher*, March 2, 1991.

Stovall, James Glen. "Coverage of 1984 Presidential Campaign." *Journalism Quarterly* 65, no. 2 (Summer 1988): 443-449, 484.

Stroud, Kandy. *How Jimmy Carter Won: The Victory Campaign from Plains to the White House.* New York: William Morrow and Company, 1977.

Taylor, Paul. "Political Coverage in the 1990s: Teaching the Old News New Tricks." In *The New News v. The Old News: The Press and Politics in the 1990s*, edited by Suzanne Charlé. New York: A Twentieth Century Fund Paper, 1992.

Taylor, Paul. *See How They Run: Electing the President in an Age of Mediaocracy.* New York: Alfred A. Knopf, 1990.

Tocqueville, Alexis de. *Democracy in America*, the Henry Reeve text, as revised by Francis Bowen, now further corrected and edited with a historical essay, editorial notes, and bibliographies by Phillips Bradley, vol. 2. New York: Vintage Books, 1945.

Wattenberg, Martin P. *The Decline of American Political Parties, 1952-1984.* Cambridge, Mass.: Harvard University Press, 1986.

———. "From Parties to Candidates: Examing the Role of the Media." *Public Opinion Quarterly* 46 (1982): 216-227.

Weaver, David H. "Setting Political Priorities: What Role for the Press?" *Political Communication and Persuasion* 7 (1990): 201-211.

Weaver, David H., and G. Cleveland Wilhoit. "Journalists — Who Are They, Really?" *Media Studies Journal* 6, no. 4 (Fall 1992).

Weisman, Steven R. "The President and the Press." *New York Times Magazine*, October 14, 1984.

White, Theodore H. *The Making of the President, 1960.* New York: Atheneum Publishers, 1961.

————. *The Making of the President, 1972.* New York: Bantam, 1973.

Witt, Evans. "Here, There and Everywhere: Where Americans Get Their News." *Public Opinion*, August/September 1983.

Wooten, James. *Dasher: The Roots and the Rising of Jimmy Carter.* New York: Summitt Books, 1978.

Index

The Center for Media and Public Affairs

The Center for Media and Public Affairs (CMPA) is a non-partisan and non-profit research and educational organization, which conducts scientific studies of news and entertainment media.

During the decade since its formation in 1985, the CMPA has emerged as a unique institution that bridges the gap between academic research and the broader domains of media and public policy. Our goal is to provide an empirical basis for ongoing debates over media fairness and impact through well-documented, timely, and readable studies of media content. Our scientific approach sets us apart from media "watchdog" groups, while our timeliness and outreach sets us apart from traditional academic researchers.

CMPA's primary research tool is content analysis, which is applied to both news coverage and the information content of entertainment messages. We also conduct surveys and focus groups to illuminate the media's role in structuring the public agenda. CMPA studies are frequently featured in news accounts and journalism reviews, as well as in scholarly publications and college textbooks.

The results of CMPA studies are published in *Media Monitor*, the Center's bi-monthly newsletter. To obtain a subscription, or to receive more information about the Center for Media and Public Affairs, please call (202) 223-2942 or write:

Center for Media and Public Affairs
2100 L Street, NW Suite 300
Washington, DC 20037

CMPA Staff

Dr. S. Robert Lichter
Co-Director

Dr. Linda S. Lichter
Co-Director

John Thomas Sheehan
Executive Director

Daniel Amundson
Research Director

Richard E. Noyes
Political Studies Director

Mary Carroll Gunning
Project Director/Production & Graphics

Michelle Fernandez
Director of Administration

Jeanne Maynard
Staff Assistant

Tara Hartnett
Administrative Assistant

ALSO OF INTEREST FROM THE CENTER FOR MEDIA AND PUBLIC AFFAIRS

When Should the Watchdogs Bark?, a new study from the **Center for Media and Public Affairs,** by political scientists Larry J. Sabato and S. Robert Lichter, examines how the national media deal with "scandal stories" involving President Clinton.

In on-the-record interviews, dozens of major media journalists reveal their personal feelings about Whitewater, "Troopergate," and Paula Jones's accusations. Their candid comments are contrasted with the actual media coverage of these stories. The book also traces the "story behind the story" of how the *Washington Post, Los Angeles Times,* and other news organizations grappled with the explosive changes of sexual indiscretions against the president.

WHEN SHOULD THE WATCHDOGS BARK?
ISBN: 9643877-0-0
$12.95 paper

PRIME TIME: How TV Portrays American Culture, by noted media critics Robert and Linda Lichter and Stanley Rothman, reveals how prime time television is shaping American values.

PRIME TIME shows how television's images of American life have changed drastically in recent years to include more graphic sex and violence, political commentary, and new images of women and racial minorities.

The authors charge that prime time fantasies reshape our lives before our eyes, as television tries to moralize while pandering to the public's baser instincts. And they warn that TV entertainment has become a leading indicator of a popular culture spinning out of control.

PRIME TIME
HOW TV PORTRAYS AMERICAN CULTURE
Publication date: October 1994
ISBN: 0-89526-491-9
$22.95 cloth

To obtain additional copies of **Good Intentions Make Bad News** or other CMPA books, call **1-800-462-6420.**